JOHN MARTIN'S BOOK OF
THE DANCE

JOHN MARTIN'S BOOK OF
THE DANCE

TUDOR PUBLISHING COMPANY
New York

Designed by Bernard Lipsky

Library of Congress Catalog Card Number: 63-20408
Printed in the United States of America

Contents

American Indian ceremonial, the Tablita Dance, performed in the pueblo of Acoma, New Mexico

6

PART ONE

Basic Dance

DANCING is a very broad term, since it includes a multiplicity of activities ranging all the way from certain natural and instinctive practices of animals, birds and fish to the most elaborate and carefully planned artistic creations of especially gifted men and women. It is all dancing, however, and in spite of many variations in outward appearance and inward motivation, it is all basically the same thing.

This essential unity makes what might seem to be a complex subject actually a very simple one. Once we have grasped the key to its structure we can open at will all of its doors and follow any of its numerous corridors as far as our interest dictates. Sometimes one or another of us without the master key may stumble into a particular corridor by a back entrance, and lacking any awareness of the edifice as a whole, take for granted that this single corridor is all there is to the building. Thus we may find the anthropologist so completely concerned with ceremonial dances of savage tribes that he ignores the ballet as mere idle amusement; or the ballet enthusiast, perhaps, looking down on the folk dance as crude and obsolete; or both of them frowning on the jazz enthusiast as an undisciplined vulgarian.

But as a matter of fact, the most sacred ritual dance of a primitive people, the French court ballet and "rock-'n'-roll" are all simply different aspects, different stages of development, of exactly the same thing; at their roots, if we trace them back, we will find them to be quite indistinguishable from each other. They are all outgrowths of what might be called basic dance, which is the same in all parts of the world, in all times and cultures. It is, indeed, a fundamental element of man's behavior. When we have understood what basic dance is, therefore, we shall have got hold of the master key.

To understand it is simplicity itself. Nature has so constituted us that movement is the medium in which we live our lives, not only in our internal physiological mechanisms but in our outward conduct as well. It is by means of movement that we dress ourselves, prepare and eat our breakfast, board the bus for work and carry on our business, whether it happens to be digging ditches or adding columns of figures. Much of this movement is so habitual that we are scarcely aware of it. The rest of it is generally rational and orderly; that is, we see something to be done and take the logical steps to do it. To this end we are equipped with an elaborate nervous system whose sole business it is to carry the reports of our senses about the objects and conditions around us to the proper set of muscles so that suitable action can be taken with regard to those objects and conditions.

Sometimes, however, these processes do not seem to operate in so orderly a manner. For example, when a terrific noise occurs unexpectedly close behind us, we "jump out of our skins," as the saying goes; that is, we make a combination of violent and totally irrelevant movements, probably grabbing our heads or throwing our arms into the air. Or at another time we hear enormously good news, and "jump for joy," hugging ourselves and skipping about the room in movements that, once again, have no bearing whatever on the news we have received. Or still another time we are deeply agitated with worry and, with hands clutching each other, heads bent and faces scowling, we "walk the floor" — which really gets us nowhere in a practical sense.

Why do we do these things? Because we are in a stirred-up emotional state; our nervous systems are charging our muscles with impulses to move and we cannot rationalize about what movements to make. Like a flood breaking through a dam, these motor impulses break through without waiting for planned direction. But it is important to note that the movements we make under these circumstances have a certain consistency about them in spite of being irrational, and they are by no means unrelated

Yanvalou-Jenou, ritual dance of Haiti, as performed unpretentiously in the countryside as folk material

Native dance as staged for Les Ballets Africaines by Keita Fodeba, Guinea's first Minister of Interior

to the emotional states that prompt them. For example, when we are worried we do not skip about the room hugging ourselves, and when we are startled by a sudden noise we do not walk the floor. The movements themselves actually have in them the essential nature of the emotional experience, even though we have not rationally directed them and they do not specifically "mean" **anything.**

It follows, then, that any emotional state tends to express itself in movements which may not be practically useful or in any way representational, but nevertheless reflect the specific character and quality of that emotional state. Working on this principle, consciously or unconsciously, dancers have evolved all kinds of emotional dances. Religious dancers, carried away with the mystery of the unknown, dance themselves into a frenzy after the manner of the "holy rollers," the "holy jumpers," the Shakers, the whirling dervishes; high-spirited young men and women, excitedly aware of the attraction between the sexes, move gaily together in the measures of the ballroom dance; a sensitive artist, becoming emotionally aware of the splendor of the sunset, or of the nobility of a hero, or of the tragedy of the underprivileged, allows each of these impulses to express itself in movements which he deliberately remembers and develops in order to be able to convey to others something of his own intuitive reaction which is too deep for words.

Thus, at the root of all these varied manifestations of dancing (and of countless other manifestations, as well) lies the common impulse to resort to movement to externalize states which we cannot externalize by rational means. This is **basic dance.**

Quetzales of Pueblo, by Ballet Folklorico of Mexico

Jean Léon Destiné and a partner in a Haitian dance

Variations in Form

But though it is a universal urge, there is no such thing as a universal form in which it manifests itself, for the occasions that inspire it and the traditions that limit it vary over the face of the earth and throughout the course of history. This is not at all extraordinary, as becomes apparent if we compare it with another biological drive such as hunger. Eating is assuredly a universal practice, yet its forms differ immeasurably. Certain climates and soils produce only certain foods; dwellers along the sea are likely to make fish their major item of diet while those in the wilderness eat game; various religions pronounce certain animals sacred or unclean and not to be eaten in either case; the growth of civilization substitutes cooked foods for raw ones, develops scientific methods of producing new foods, and leads in general to refinements of taste and even elaborately complicated recipes to tempt the epicure.

Exactly the same kinds of controlling influence color the styles of movement by which the universal biological motor drives are satisfied. Geography, climate, race, religion, social environment, physique, dress, cultural tradition, historical background, and the very passage of time itself, all affect the ways men move and, more particularly, the ways they translate movement into dance. Through a combination of all these causes we find the dances of the Orient confined in the main to small, slow movements, chiefly of the hands and upper body, with supple fingers bending backwards, toes turned upwards, and lateral movements of the head and neck that are virtually impossible to the western body; we find the African dancer centering his motion largely in the pelvic region, while the European ballet dancer maintains a rigid spine and departs from his Oriental brothers by extending his toes sharply downwards; we find the Spanish dancer stamping vigorously on the ground while the ballet dancer touches it so lightly as to deny gravity.

La Argentina

D'Ora

La Argentinita

Vicente Escudero

Edward Weston

Carmen Amaya

Radford Bascome

Manolo Vargas

Radford Bascome

Roberto Ximenez

Roberto Iglesias, Rosario Galan, Pepe Segundo

José Greco in solo role of his "El Cortijo"

Etienne

Traditional dance by Ballets Basques de Biarritz

Herbert Matter, Studio Associates, Inc.

Shanta Rao, mistress of dance styles of India

All these systems have undergone extensive changes within themselves as history has developed around them. Primitive ceremonials, originally vital and inspired, have been perpetuated from generation to generation until the vitality and inspiration have passed completely out of them and not even the chieftains and high priests can remember their links to experience, understand the words that accompany them or supply any significance to the empty shell of movements that has survived. In the early period of the European court ballet the dancers impersonated gods of the Greek and Roman mythology, for in the Renaissance society of the time there

was a strong desire to pattern behavior upon the graciousness and dignity that classic antiquity seemed to them to contain and contemporary custom to lack. Later when the revival of Gothic mysticism swept over European culture in the early nineteenth century and the Middle Ages seemed to hold the secret of a much desired spiritual re-awakening, the ballet turned to supernatural matters and all the dancers assumed characterizations of haunted maidens risen from the tomb, or became mythical creatures who inhabited the air and spurned what was earthly and mortal.

It is impossible to say that any of these

12

approaches is exclusively right or wrong, better or worse than any other; they all arose out of an inner need and completely satisfied that need — just as we "jump out of our skins" when we are suddenly frightened or hug ourselves when we are overjoyed. They are all absolutely right, therefore, for the specific circumstances under which they have been created.

For us to enjoy them fully as spectators it is incumbent upon us to approach them in this way, not finding fault with the ballet because it does not beat its heels into the ground, or with the Hindu dance because it does not leap and whirl, or with the so-called modern dance because it does not rise upon the points of the toes. When we relate any form of dance to the inward motivations that are responsible for its form, we open the door to its full enjoyment. Naturally, the dance that has grown out of motivations common to our own time and society will have the greatest appeal for us, since its motivations belong specifically to us. If other forms are inevitably exotic and consequently inspire a more objective response in us, they are by no means dull or incomprehensible on that account.

Uday Shankar and the first company of Hindu dancers and musicians he brought from India in 1932

Alfredo Valente

Raden Mas Kodrat and Raden Mas Wiradat, two Javanese brothers, long heads of official dance associations

Ni Gusti Raka, traditional Balinese child dance, in "Legong" which is always danced by very young girls

Basic Music

Thus far movement has been the sole subject under consideration, for movement is the fundamental stuff of dancing. Nevertheless, only in a comparatively small section of the world and in comparatively modern times are dance and music separable arts. In Europe and America, while we rarely find dancing without music, we have a large musical art quite independent of dancing. In by far the greater part of the world, however, such a concept is altogether alien; music without dancing and dancing without music are equally unlikely.

As a matter of fact, the relation between movement and music is not merely a matter of custom but is a basic relationship. To revert once again to our earlier illustrations, when we are frightened by a sudden noise we do not react silently; in addition to our startled movements we almost invariably emit some kind of cry. Similarly, when we skip jubilantly about, in all probability we make some sort of "joyful noise." When all the body is activated by some strong emotion, there is no reason to expect the voice to remain silent.

In his beginnings the dancer inevitably sings as he dances. When, however, his move-

"Singkil" by Philippine dance company, Bayanihan

Tokuho Azuma IV, of Tokyo's Azuma Kabuki Dancers

Kikugoro VI, a master actor and dancer of Japan

15

ments become too strenuous and demand too much breath for him to continue his song, the bystanders take up the singing for him. In time the melodic line of the voice is transferred to an instrument, and since it can play higher and lower than he could possibly sing, it serves even to increase his range of expression. Similarly, the rhythmic beating of his feet on the ground is accentuated, and intensified beyond what he could do by himself, by the clapping of hands, the shaking of rattles and the beating of drums. Eventually the accompanying song may be extended until it is played by a whole symphony orchestra, but if it is really dance music it still retains the rhythmic pulse of his body and the melodic line of his voice; it is still, indeed, potentially the dancer's own song.

Both in movement and in music, from time to time, certain practices which were originally spontaneous and alive become stereotyped and mechanical through mere surface repetition. The dancers look backward at tradition instead of inward at creation; the musicians forget their function of voicing the dancer's song and merely put together sounds for their own sakes. Then the history of dancing, and of music, records a low period. But since dancing is at bottom a biological function, it must necessarily renew itself. In every barren period, accordingly, rebels arise who break through the intrenched traditionalism and set up fresh currents to replace it.

No form is permanent, definitive, ultimate; only the basic principle of dance is enduring, and out of it, like the cycle of nature itself, rises an endless succession of new springs out of old winters.

Japanese Imperial Household Dancers in the ancient form of court dancing known as Gagaku

Members of Inbal, dance theatre of Israel, in "Desert," choreographed by its director, Sara Levi-Tanai

Moiseyev Dance Company in Igor Moiseyev's theatrical re-creation of "Yurochka," Byelorussian folk dance

PART TWO

Dance for the Sake of the Dancer

DANCING falls naturally into two major categories: that which is done for the emotional release of the individual dancers, without regard to the possible interest of a spectator; and that, on the other hand, which is done for the enjoyment of the spectator either as an exhibition of skill, the telling of a story, the presentation of pleasurable designs, or the communication of emotional experience. The second category is largely an outgrowth of the first, but both play important parts in the picture as a whole.

In primitive societies, in which there is no knowledge of natural laws by which seeds grow and crops ripen, animals and humans bear young, or sickness is healed, every manifestation of these commonplaces of life becomes a separate hazard, the outcome of which is unpredictable. Fears easily arise that perhaps this time the seed will refuse to sprout and there will be no grain to harvest, that the sun will not shine or the rain consent to fall. With no awareness of the orderly principles of nature, such an overwrought state of emotion is not to be assuaged by reason, but only by venting itself in movement. When, as a matter of fact, the grain does ripen, the sun does shine and the rain fall, these dances assume in the primitive mind the position of causative forces and are established as ritual.

Every important event of tribal life is accompanied by suitable dances, for they are all mystical experiences; birth, the arrival of the youth at manhood, marriage, the stalking of game, the conquest of enemies, death, and the assurance that the dead man will remain in the grave instead of returning to make trouble, the appeasing of evil spirits who in time past have brought specific disaster, and the honoring (or perhaps more accurately the bribing) of beneficent spirits who have bestowed blessings, all inspire emotional uncertainties which must be somehow resolved.

In some cases, these dances of high emotional tension consist of rather hysterical random movements and lead to frenzy, catalepsy and trance; but in the vast majority of instances, their magic is of a more consistent and, indeed, a more demonstrable character. If, for example, one wishes the corn to grow tall, one suggests it and practically demands it by leaping high, over and over, in the presence of the corn. If the deer is to be hunted, one dons antlers and bits of fur and performs in advance with meticulous accuracy the conduct expected of the quarry from the earliest moment of the chase to the death struggle. By similar processes of pre-enactment, beneficial results are produced upon friends and destructive results upon enemies; and the more exact the mimicry the more certain the efficaciousness of the ritual.

Such magic is not only characterized by appropriateness in every case, but is also based on a logical premise which we in our sophisticated societies are far too prone to ignore. This premise is the inherent contagion that exists in bodily movement. We are so constituted that we yawn when others yawn, laugh when they laugh, weep when they weep, feel sympathetic muscular strains when we watch others struggling under heavy loads, and are stimulated to dance when they dance. When we see a body undergoing muscular exertion, we are naturally inclined to feel it reflected in our own musculatures.

In primitive societies spectators watching a dancer are frequently drawn first into beating a drum for him and then into actually dancing in the ring with him, executing the same steps that he is executing. If this kind of persuasiveness has been experienced in one's own self, why

New York Times

Men of the Ukrainian State Dance Company, directed by Pavel Virsky, in characteristic aerial turns

should one not expect it to be experienced as a matter of course by the deer that is to be hunted, the enemy that is to be destroyed, the corn in the ground? To simple peoples this power of dance to persuade others to imitate it seems supernatural and is employed accordingly; to us it is a scientifically established psychological process, and it constitutes the basis on which we enjoy watching the dance and on which we understand the emotional experience that the dancer is trying to communicate to us.

These primitive imitative dances are not originally planned to be watched by spectators, but only to control the actions of animals, spirits, gods and enemies, who are most probably not even present. Inevitably, however, the particular excellence of some dancer as a mimic must win the especial admiration of the bystanders, and sooner or later we find the development of mimetic dancing for its own sake with only secondary accent upon magic and religion. Out of this root there emerges eventually the quite separate art of the drama, with the music of the dancer's song replaced by the spoken words that are suitable to the character he is imitating. Ultimately not only magic and religion, but also dance movement itself, have passed out of the picture and the purely literary drama has come into being.

Folk Dancing

The "magic" powers of dancing have at least one other important manifestation that must be noted. When the men of a tribe perform a war dance, it is not exclusively for its mimetic influence over the enemy; it is also for the establishment of solidarity in the tribe itself. It is a fact that when an individual dances in unison with a great number of other individuals, he has a sense of participation in a mass movement far greater than anything he could possibly do alone. The group becomes one in conscious strength and purpose, and each individual experiences a heightened power as part of it. Such a principle underlies the military parade, in which the object is to establish the individual marcher (and the onlooker, as well, who participates in a sense through the contagion of movement) as part of a unity infinitely more powerful than himself. When a mile of marching men steps forward on its collective right foot, it is a tremendous step for all to participate in!

The feeling of oneness with one's fellows which is established by collective dancing is one of the principal reasons for the growth and persistence of folk dancing, whether in the olden days or at this very moment. Most of the ritual dances

19

that we have been dealing with are really dancing by the folk, but it is customary to group them in a class of their own, and to consider folk dancing as chiefly recreational in intent. To be sure, harvest celebrations and other common occasions for folk celebration still retain something of their original ritual significance, such as thanksgiving to divine powers, offerings to assure good crops, symbolic rites to bless a marriage with many sons, and the like; but these aspects have a way of fading into the remote background and leaving the elements of simple and hearty play in the ascendancy.

Man is a gregarious animal, and by his very nature has to assemble with his kind every so often and rejoice in the kinship. In the days when travel was difficult and distances were long, it was a matter almost of survival for the people of the countryside to hitch up their teams and meet at some fairly central spot for a long and energetic session of dancing once in a while. In no other way could they remind themselves that they were members of a single community, with common interests and tastes and habits; and having contributed something of physical and emotional vigor to the common activity, each one returned to his isolated home with a larger share of the community strength than he had given.

If people wonder why folk dancing has grown nowadays to even larger dimensions than it en-

Georgi Shengelaya of Georgian State Dance Company in the typical Georgian style of "toe-dancing" for men

Polish State Folk Ballet (Slask)—one of several such companies—in "Trojak" with a chorus of folk singers

joyed in those simpler and less congested days and has been embraced by city dwellers, the reason is exactly the same. The city dweller though he lives so close to his neighbors in a physical sense that there is scarcely elbow room, has just as little genuine contact with them as the isolated peasant. There must accordingly be frequent occasions arranged when he can quit battling with his anonymous fellows for a seat on the subway and buffeting them about in the frantic processes of business, in order to assemble with them on purely social grounds and re-establish their common interests and fundamental fellowship as human beings. Community dancing does not deal in personal differences, bargaining or argument; it is on a far more universal and elementary level than that. It simply affirms the underlying emotional oneness of all men, and sends each of them home re-invigorated with the strength of the common heritage of the race. This is the truly social basis of the dance.

The Cycle of Ballroom Dancing

The folk dancing that is so popular with us today has undergone many refinements, to be sure, since the Middle Ages when, roughly speaking, its present forms began to take shape. In its beginnings it was the lusty and uninhibited expression of crude and unpolished peoples. Its attitude toward sex was likely to be altogether frank, and many varieties of couple dances were openly designed for purposes of courtship. Why else, indeed, should a man and woman dance together? But if these were honest and healthy dances, they were not notable for reticence or refinement.

This was the general status and character of the simple people of Europe at the dawn of the Renaissance, and it constituted something of a problem. Obviously, rude and unmannerly peasant practices, however true to nature and to the needs of emotional release, could not be allowed in the ballrooms of the new aristocracy, yet the new aristocracy could not be expected to forego dancing, for it had exactly the same impulses as the peasants.

Panegyris the Royal Festival Company of Greece

"Berance" by the Yugoslav National Ballet (Tanec)

Before we can fully understand the important effects of this situation upon the future of both the social and the art dance, it is necessary to consider briefly who this new aristocracy was. The princes of the Italian Renaissance were neither nobly born nor nobly bred. As a class they were men without background, culture or scruples. Many of them were condottieri; that is, mercenary soldiers or in many instances virtually gangsters, who sold their allegiance to the highest bidder. Their titles were sometimes bought, sometimes stolen and sometimes taken by the sword. They were unfitted for leadership in every respect except material power and a curious ambition which was partly personal and partly (if only subconsciously) concerned with

Scottish Sword Dance by member of Scots Guards

Out of the same emotional causes grew that bitter and terrible art form, the Dance of Death. This was a kind of dramatic ceremonial whose scene was the graveyard. In it Death called upon each stratum of society — a king, a pope, a soldier, a peasant, a mother, a child, and so forth — and led them all at last in a grim procession into the tomb. This was in effect a desperate statement of the common man's disillusionment with the entire social, political and religious scheme under which he lived; Death leveled all ranks and stations and proved them all ultimately vain.

It is obvious from our present perspective on the scene that these outbursts were indications of the crumbling of the basis of medieval thought. A great emotional rebellion was expressing itself; not rationally, because it did not know where to turn, but in that inevitable first medium for venting pent-up emotional states, movement and its more formal manifestation, dance.

If such phenomena as these were chiefly negative, indicating the collapse of the medieval system rather than the erection of any new systems, they led directly into the more positive aspect of the situation which we have come to call the Renaissance. This was literally a rebirth. Men threw off the old concept of themselves as wretched slaves to mysticism and declared themselves to be emancipated, self-acting individuals. They probably had very little idea what to do with this newly discovered freedom of thought and conduct, but at this revolutionary juncture an unrelated event in a distant part of the world served to shape their direction and progress. In the middle of the fifteenth century the Ottoman Turks captured Constantinople. Here for centuries in this eastern capital of the Roman Empire had been preserved the classic culture of Greece and Rome, which had been undermined and largely destroyed in Rome itself when the barbarians from the north had invaded that western capital of the empire. Now, with the fall of Constantinople, the scholars fled once more to the west, and brought back with them the carefully nurtured scholarship, the artistic lore

the amelioration of the race of men.

This ambition is perhaps the salient aspect of the Renaissance. Throughout the Middle Ages men had been taught to think of themselves as poor wretches without individual worth, as sinners who, unless they made fantastic atonement throughout their earthly lives, could look forward only to an eternity in the fires of hell. Life was physically hard, mentally fearful, dominated by superstition, and without hope. It is not difficult to understand why at length in the fourteenth century after a succession of world catastrophes, wars, plagues, fires, the general state of the human mind was so disturbed that it had to seek outlet for its pent-up emotional conditions in such irrational mass manifestations as the dance manias. Whole communities of people then were stricken with a kind of madness that sent them dancing and gyrating through the streets and from village to village for days at a time until they died in agonized exhaustion.

and the tradition of the ancient culture. It was rich, elegant, and pagan, and it offered to the searching minds of the time exactly the kind of model they needed in order to build a new system of life for themselves entirely contrary to the old one against which they were rebelling.

To be sure, this classic revival affected chiefly the wealthy courtiers, for the common man — still poor, still illiterate, still ill-used — had little contact with the refinements of culture. What got to him seeped down from the top; but it was something. Festivals in honor of the Christian saints were rededicated to the gods of Olympus, and all the practices of medieval life were re-oriented to follow the pagan precedent of the ancient practices, or rather to follow the current ideas — sometimes rather fantastic and generally quite inaccurate, in spite of the scholars from Constantinople — of what those practices had been.

What was of paramount importance, however, was that man had emerged in his own eyes as a creature of dignity, with the capacity to make his life what he wanted it to be. But the contrast between this ideal and what he actually saw of himself was rather marked; he was still a crude,

mannerless lout, who ate like an animal, walked like a clodhopper, and generally comported himself like a peasant. For the princes of the day with their regal palaces, their silk and satin raiment, their pretensions to leadership, this was an impossible situation. Scholars and tutors were attached to the individual courts to remedy intellectual shortcomings, but of equal importance were the dancing masters who were brought in to remedy the gross defects of carriage and deportment. It was the duty of these gentlemen to teach their masters and mistresses how to manipulate their heavy and voluminous costumes — the men, their long shoes stretching out so far in front that the tips had to be fastened to the knees in order to make walking possible, their swords which bade fair to trip them at every step; the ladies, their ruffs and headdresses and yards of train. Clearly the old dances of the countryside were now both impracticable and utterly unsuitable in manner and style; it was up to the dancing masters to create new and more suitable ones.

And here ballroom dancing was born.

By all this the common people were blissfully unaffected; they continued to dance as they had always done. What is more, the dancing

"Cheats and Swings," an American "square set"

Gjon Mili

Swedish folk dance figure in traditional costumes

Gjon Mili

masters took as the basis for the elegant routines they evolved for the courtiers these very dances of the common people, refined them, toned them down and made them intricate and complicated. In fact, so void of spontaneity and spirit did they ultimately become — so lacking in the elements of basic dance — that courtiers frequently slipped away quietly and joined the dances of the much-despised common people, where they could really find some outlet for their emotional exuberance. This practice became so general, indeed, that Castiglione, who was more or less the Emily Post of the early sixteenth century, wrote in effect that it was quite all right socially to join these vulgar rebels so long as a mask was born to indicate that the courtier was aware that he was "slumming."

Yet manifestly the formal dances of the dancing masters would not have survived and developed if they had been totally barren of emotional satisfaction. It was a special emotion, a new one born of the new direction of life, that they were created to satisfy, and obviously did satisfy — the passionate desire for personal elegance and social authority.

Throughout all the five hundred years of its history to date, the ballroom dance has continued to be torn between these two extremes. On the one hand, polite society requires that it be well-mannered, strictly ordered in form, gracious — and unemotional; on the other hand, human nature demands that it serve as a free and unhampered release for emotions, and, in couple dances, that it make no false pretenses about sex. It is nature, of course, that produces the creative dances, and no matter how much polite society frowns upon them, it inevitably has to admit them into its sedate ballrooms sooner or later, making what modifications it can force upon them, but always having to swallow a good deal of its own prudishness.

From the days of the Renaissance right down to today, every dance that has won popularity in conservative circles has had its origins among the "vulgar." The minuet, probably the most mincing and refined of all court dances at its height, began life as a bouncing couple dance of the peasants. The waltz, which was a rambunctious whirling dance centuries ago in Germany, shocked the better people of the nineteenth century ballroom to the core by daring to allow dancers to stand face to face in each other's arms. Now it is held up as a prime example of old-fashioned modesty by that older generation which finds jazz dancing revoltingly coarse.

It is a cycle that must inevitably continue, for recreational dancing, done solely for the sake of providing the dancer with a release for his inner compulsions, no longer serves its purpose when that release is denied. No matter how pretty a dance may be to watch, unless it gives something to the dancer, it is doomed. The couple dance is forever and exclusively a courtship dance; for the satisfaction of other social emotions, the square and circle and longways dances of folk origin have once again found themselves in demand, and by the urban sophisticates. Between them they present a broad and healthy program for the contemporary ballroom, and in spite of adaptations and compromises, still maintain identifiable relationships to basic **dance.**

PART THREE

Dance as Spectacle

IT is easy to understand how the tendencies of the Renaissance courts made the outward appearance of the dance of more importance than its inward satisfactions, or rather, to be more precise, how the inward satisfactions now came to depend largely on the perfection of the outward appearance. Some of the instructions of the most famous masters of the time which still survive lay emphasis upon the necessity of pleasing the eye of the bystander. And this transformation of the essential character of the dance from a mere type of play to a vehicle for the display of personal skills and graces is one of the major sources of the development of that form of dance art that came to be known as the ballet.

Needless to say, it was not the only source; nor was this the earliest manifestation, by any means, of dancing designed primarily to please the spectator. In primitive cultures, as well as in the highly developed cultures of Greece and Rome, it was a common practice for slaves to perform for the entertainment of their masters. There is no evidence that this was dancing of a very high order, though in the days of the later Roman emperors, it is true, there grew up a type of performer known as the *pantomimus* who, in spite of his characteristic decadence, may well have been an artist of considerable attainments in many instances. It is inaccurate, of course, to class the great choric theatre of ancient Greece as spectacle, for the thousands of spectators who attended the annual performances did so as participants in a religious rite and not as pleasure-seekers.

After the fall of Rome, jugglers, tumblers, mountebanks wandered widely over the land, now attaching themselves to the household of some wealthy lord, now playing at fairs and in city streets. Among them dancing was definitely practiced, though again not on a very high level. Such roving dancers and acrobats existed all through the Middle Ages; and later in the Renaissance, still attached to the households of the various lords, they made signal contributions as professionals to the advancement of the spectacular dance as it grew up in the courts.

Out of the teeming life of the Middle Ages came many other influences to contribute ultimately to the ballet's form: processions, maskings and mummings, all of religious origin and many of them pre-Christian; tournaments which had grown into elaborately costumed spectacles of almost theatrical character; banquets in the great houses of the nobles during which floats representing castles or ships, and often great pastries, were borne into the hall carrying companies of singers and dancers to entertain the diners and sometimes to induce them by dramatic presentations of battles between Christians and Saracens to participate in one of the crusades.

Here, indeed, was a rich and gorgeous mass of material to draw upon, but it was so conglomerate and diffuse that it might never have achieved any semblance of conscious artistry without the particular guidance of Renaissance thinking and the fundamental emotional drive that controlled that thinking. The revival of classical scholarship had brought to light the existence of the theatre of the ancient Greeks with its unity of music, poetry and dance, and such a vision served to inspire the musicians and the poets and the dancers to work toward a similar unity in the arts of their own time. Their specific knowledge of the Greek theatre was meager and largely inaccurate, but a mere glimpse of its underlying principles was enough to arouse their enthusiasm. In France shortly after the middle of the sixteenth century, musicians and poets banded together for this purpose in an Academy of Music and Poesy with a charter from the king; in Italy shortly afterwards a similar group was formed under the name of the

Salome dancing before Herod, according to the medieval concept. (From an early 14th-century manuscript)

Camerata. The former actually accomplished nothing, but out of the latter's efforts emerged the early form of opera.

The Court Ballet

Exactly this same impulse toward reviving the unity of the Greek theatre gave the world what was really its first ballet. It came about in the French court at the instigation of the queen-mother, Catherine de' Medici. She was the daughter of one of the greatest houses in Italy, where progress in the dance, music and all the other arts was far ahead of anything the French had accomplished. When she had come to France (ultimately to be the queen of Henri II) therefore, she had brought with her a company of musicians and dancers from her native city of Florence to supervise her artistic presentations, and highly impressive these were.

But the "Ballet Comique de la Reine," produced in 1581, outdid them all. Catherine herself was not primarily interested in its artistry, but for political reasons she wanted to offer something of unprecedented splendor, and took as a suitable occasion the wedding of the sister of the then queen, her daughter-in-law. The important commission of producing such a work fell to her valet de chambre, chief violinist and dancing master, Balthasar de Beaujoyeux, who, in spite of the French form he had given his name, was an Italian. Beaujoyeaux, stirred by the same ambitions as his colleagues to restore the concept of the ancient Greeks, embraced this as his great opportunity. The poetry he commissioned to be written by one of the court poets, the instrumental music by one of the court musicians and the vocal music by another (for at that time the same composer rarely wrote for both voice and instruments). He himself devised the dances and supervised the spectacle, which was, of course, sumptuous and mechanically elaborate. Its story, which seems dull and inconsequential to us, dealt with a Greek hero who was enchanted by Circe and at last freed by the intervention of the gods; but what was important about it was that for the first time a court spectacle of this sort confined itself to a consistent dramatic subject throughout, and all its verses, music and dancing were appropriate to the development of the theme.

26

Pierre Rameau's engraving of a court ball, from his manual of dancing, "Le Maître de Danser," 1725

"Le Ballet Comique de la Reine," the "first" ballet, created by Beaujoyeux for Catherine de' Medici, 1581

The success of the experiment was complete. Thousands of common people attempted to obtain admission to the palace to see it, many of them having come from long distances. Copies of the work were printed and sent to all the courts of Europe, and Catherine's political ambitions were achieved as well as Beaujoyeux's artistic ones. The court was virtually bankrupted by the production, however, as it had cost some 400,000 crowns. The artistic principles it introduced were practiced thereafter on a far more modest scale, if at all, but it had succeeded in establishing them as principles, and the seed it thus sowed was destined to bear fruit for many generations.

From this time on, the French court was the center of the ballet's development. Italy, its original home, had turned with greater interest to opera, a similar attempt at reviving the Greek unity of the arts but with its chief emphasis on music. Both this development and Italy's continued interest in elaborate scenic investiture and mechanical innovation were to exert strong influences on the ballet, but the form itself, in which the dance occupied the chief place in the artistic unity, was to continue for three hundred years as a predominantly French enterprise.

The court ballets that followed the "Ballet Comique" fell just as short of it in artistry as they did in costliness. Their actual forms varied in detail according to the individual tastes of the monarchs or the courtiers directly in charge, but in the main they consisted of a succession of dances (sometimes as many as thirty, rarely less than ten or twelve) by different groups of dancers representing related phases of some common subject. For example, a ballet (if it were a very small one) might consist of entrées representing Europe, Asia, Africa and America, with the participants in each entrée sumptuously clad in a style which, with its plumed headdresses, jewels, panniers and deeply skirted coats, only remotely suggested the natives of these quarters of the globe. The whole was brought to a conclusion by general dancing in which the entire court, duly masked, participated along with the dancers from the spectacle. The emphasis remained social, and the performers, except for a few extremely necessary professionals attached to the court, were amateurs.

Even the "Ballet Comique" itself with all its artistic innovations had not altered the essential pattern of the Renaissance ballroom in any great degree, either socially or physically. As at any court ball, the king and his household sat at the head of the room on a dais; along the sides of the hall, seated in the long galleries or standing along the edges of the floor itself, were the other spectators. At the far end of the hall was a shallow platform which served merely to house the representation of Circe's palace and was not a stage in any sense. The action all took place on the floor with the audience on three sides of it. Such an overall plan, in spite of many internal changes of more or less importance, was to prevail for still the greater part of another century, until, indeed, the ballet itself declined as a court function and took other forms.

The intervening decades before this decline, however, saw an ever increasing delight in its practice by the court. When Louis XIII was king, a single performance in an evening was frequently not enough, and His Majesty and fellow dancers trooped from the royal palace to lesser houses giving a repetition in each, and bringing the night to a close with still another repetition on a great platform erected for the purpose in front of the City Hall for the benefit of the townspeople. True to the formal court pattern, at the end of the spectacle king and courtiers descended to the street and danced with the wives and daughters of the bourgeois. The king's company, of course, was all male, for at this time ladies did not appear with the gentlemen in the court ballets. They staged, from time to time, ballets of their own, but these were of comparatively minor importance.

It was Louis XIV, however, who was the greatest of all royal patrons of the dance, and during his reign the ballet reached new heights. The king was an excellent dancer and delighted in exhibiting his gifts. However outstanding they may have been, they led him to engage and to encourage the most brilliant of musicians, painters and poets to collaborate on his ballets. This was a fortunate thing for the future of the art, for it was Louis' sudden indifference in middle age (when his vanity would no longer allow him to display his once shapely physique grown fat and puffy) that finally ended the long reign of the ballet as a court function. When he ceased to dance, the ballet lost its fashionable pre-eminence. But the very artists he had assembled about him to give it life were happily still at hand to see that it did not die.

The standard male ballet costume of the Renaissance, allegedly modeled after the Greek and Roman warrior

Late 17th-century Florentine stage with dancers. The scene is from Moniglia's drama, "L'Ercole in Tebe"

Marie-Anne de Cupis de Camargo, early 18th-century
virtuoso who shortened her skirts to free her skill

The Ballet Becomes Professional

Chief among these able collaborators was Jean-Baptiste Lully, an Italian-born musician and dancer, who was not only a fine artist but also an able and not too scrupulous politician. By the combination of his gifts and guile he was able to use the ballet's crisis both to his personal advantage and to the enormous benefit of the art itself. By devious means he obtained the charter of the Academy of Music, and into that organization he absorbed the Academy of Dance which, though chartered a decade earlier, in 1661, had never functioned. His next stroke of policy was to persuade the king to turn over to him the magnificent theatre in the Palais Royal, built more than a generation before by Cardinal Richelieu, recently occupied by Molière and his company of actors and now made available by Molière's death. Here he started the ballet on its way as a professional art, alongside its musical twin from Italy, the opera, with a renewal of artistic principles such as it had not enjoyed

since the days of the "Ballet Comique," and an ordering of technical method such as it had never had before.

Lully's major interest was musical, and his greatest contribution to the ballet at this period was his correlation of the two elements in a kind of theatrical unity. The specific dance department of the Academy was in the hands of his colleague, Pierre Beauchamps, likewise a musician and dancer of the court and also something of a genius. For many years the ideal of the classical culture of Greece and Rome had provided an example for the establishment of academies in the various arts and sciences, in which under royal decree could be set up rules and standards for practice. To Beauchamps now fell the opportunity to set up just such authoritative rules for the ballet. Here for the first time we find the five fundamental positions of the feet listed as such, as well as many other systematic developments, including a method of dance notation.

There could, indeed, have been no better time for such a first codification, for the ballet was undergoing changes which were destined to affect it in every conceivable way. The very theatre in which it was hereafter to be housed necessitated fundamental revisions in technical approach. Heretofore, in the court ballets, the dancers had entered at the end of the great hall and had had spectators on three sides of them; now that was no longer to be so. When Richelieu had built his theatre some thirty years before, he had followed the most modern pattern of the Italian theatre, which had long enjoyed leadership over the French in architectural innovations and machinery for the production of scenic spectacle. His theatre, accordingly, was built with an elevated stage on which all the action took place, framed by a proscenium arch, and the spectators all sat directly in front of it, just as in our theatres of the present time. As a result, the dancer now would have nobody behind him or on either side of him, and had only to consider how he would look from one direction. It was incumbent upon him, then, to accept this established front as his focus. It was simple enough to keep his face toward

his audience when he was moving forwards or backwards, but if he moved across the stage from side to side, it necessitated crossing one foot in front of the other, and with his feet in normal position, this proved awkward. In order to do it expeditiously he found it advisable to rotate his hip joint so that the knee and toes pointed outward instead of straight ahead. In this position the legs could be made to cross each other without interference. Similarly, if a dancer facing forward chose to raise his leg directly to the front, it would appear foreshortened to the spectator and the movement would have no design and only limited visibility. If, however, he rotated his hips outward and raised his leg to the side, the movement could be seen in profile while he himself remained facing forward.

It would be erroneous to imply from all this that the turned-out hip was "invented" at this time, for it had certainly been in use to some extent, consciously or unconsciously, from time immemorial, both in and out of the dance. The very structure of the hip joint on the ball-and-socket pattern indicates the inherent serviceability of such a movement in everyday experience. Also, it must be remembered that the ballet itself had frequently played an incidental role on this very stage in the plays of Molière and the earlier productions of Cardinal Richelieu, not to speak of the theatres in Italy of similar type which had housed ballets to greater or less extent. The important aspect of the situation at this time is that now the ballet was on the road to being standardized on a professional basis, and that the practices dictated by the necessities of this particular theatre were shaping that official standardization. Thus it was that the turned-out hip now became for the first time a fundamental technical practice.

At this period the rotation was not very extensive; the feet, when the heels were together, made scarcely more than a right angle. As the technical scope of the ballet increased over the years this angle was steadily widened until by the early nineteenth century it had become a full hundred and eighty degrees; that is, when the

heels were together, the feet made a straight line with the toes pointing in opposite directions. This is one of the distinctive technical principles of the ballet, and a thoroughly logical one. It allows the legs to move freely in every direction with a maximum of visibility from the spectator's angle of vision.

But if totally new forces had been brought to bear on the ballet, their influence was gradual. The tradition of courtliness on which it had been nurtured was not to be instantaneously overturned, and usages which had long since lost their original functions and whose meanings had been forgotten were carried over unquestioningly into the new era by sheer inertia. Not until 1681 were women admitted to Lully's company. As in the days of the court ballet, feminine roles had continued to be danced by men. Masks, an ancient heritage from the ceremonial origins of dancing, were still worn by all dancers, both male

Marie Taglioni in "La Sylphide," whose costuming set further changes in motion in the early 19th century

and female. A kind of standard costume had also been adopted by the court, patterned after Renaissance ideas of the classic Greeks and Romans. The men were dressed according to what was believed to be the model of the Roman warrior, but what they actually wore consisted of high feathered headdress, ornate coat spreading at the waist into a *tonnelet,* or stiff, hooped skirt virtually to the knees, knee breeches, stockings, gloves and heeled shoes. The women's dresses differed mainly in the fact that their skirts were heavily panniered and reached the floor. The movement of the dance was fairly limited in scope and virtuosity as was natural in an amateur art whose aim had been primarily toward elegance and display and whose costumes had accordingly hampered the body's activity considerably.

With the decline of these courtly aims and the growth of professionalism through the passing years, further changes were bound to occur, and a generation after the ballet had ceased to be an amateur art, we find an increased interest in virtuosity and the technical side of movement. This inevitably means that instead of concerning themselves with floor patterns, the dancers began to extend their movements upwards into the air, jumping, beating their feet together while off the ground, and generally giving the dance a concern with verticality where it had formerly been largely bound to horizontal design.

When there finally appears on the scene a feminine dancer who delights in these new technical matters, has a talent for elevation and can make a particularly effective use of crossing and recrossing her feet in the air (basically an old peasant trick, which in its ballet usage has come to be known as *entrechat*), it is clear that something will be done to alter the ladies' costume. Why waste all these skilful manoeuvrings of the feet behind a long skirt which completely covers them? It is Marie-Anne de Cupis de Camargo, then, who takes the revolutionary step of shortening the dancer's skirt to the ankle. There is considerable scandal, to be sure, but the reform endures — a reform destined to be carried on in increasing measure over the centuries.

Noverre and the "Ballet of Action"

Many reforms, indeed, of a more basic nature are due in the momentous eighteenth century, when the Renaissance had worn thin, when the culture of the ancients seemed far less important than the rational thinking of contemporary men, when theories of political democracy, freedom of conscience, and the general rights and potentialities of the individual, superseded the old reverence for self-constituted aristocracies and the authority of tradition. In every walk of life a new and revolutionary attitude toward human affairs was in the making, and as its natural accompaniment in the arts — those mediums through which are voiced the emotional experiences and aspiration of the times — there was a shift of emphasis away from formalism and toward the expression of human emotion and a reflection of life. The democratic revolution and the romantic revolution went hand in hand as manifestations of the same basic drive.

The Royal Academy of Music and Dance, supported by the crown and patronized by the nobility, was not likely by its background and character to be the most open field for such new and iconoclastic tendencies; but since, as we have already noted, movement is a medium highly sensitive to underlying and irrational emotional drives, the same issues that were growing in the life of the times at large found their expressions also in the dance, in spite of academic opposition.

A significant early figure in this new movement was Marie Sallé, a contemporary and arch-rival of Camargo. Her concern, unlike that of the brilliant virtuoso, was with dramatic realism and expressiveness. She, too, urged costume changes, but instead of being merely reforms as Camargo's changes were, hers were revolutionary. She wanted to abandon altogether the set uniform of the ballet and to dress each character in something that approached its own true style. Her ideas were vehemently opposed by the directors of the academy, and in order to give them expression she was forced to go to London. There she presented a ballet, "Pygmalion," in which as

Galatea she put aside the conventional panniers and jeweled headdress and donned Greek draperies patterned after classic sculpture. To be sure, she wore them over her conventional corset and petticoats in a manner that to us is far from realistic, but for her own time it was a striking step forward toward representationalism. The experiment was a tremendous success and London flocked to see her, but her next venture (Handel's "Alcina," in which she attempted to dance the role of a boy) was unsuccessful, and she returned to Paris. Here her efforts were as unwelcome as before, and after a few unhappy seasons she retired from the ballet in disappointment.

But her ideas were not to die. A young man named Jean Georges Noverre was fired with the same enthusiasm, much of it no doubt lit directly by her, for though he was very young when she quit dancing, he often visited her in retirement. His theory was much broader than hers and extended beyond costume to all aspects of the ballet, making it an independent theatre art instead of a mere decorative adjunct to opera. But though a generation had passed since Paris had rejected Sallé, the ballet was still completely hostile to Noverre. He perforce accepted positions as ballet master in other cities, and carried on, mainly in Stuttgart, the evolution of what he called the "ballet d'action," that is, the ballet in which the dance actually carries forward the dramatic action instead of simply interrupting it with pretty interludes as in the stereotyped practice then current.

He wanted dancing not only to arouse his admiration for its technical brilliance, but to move him emotionally by its expressiveness just as drama and tragedy did. He demanded that the ballet become within its own medium an imitation of life. Like Sallé's notion of realism, Noverre's ideas seem to us far from realistic or expressive, but they constituted a revolutionary doctrine in their day. Though they were officially rejected at the Paris Opéra (now the home of the Royal Academy of Music and Dance), their influence crept into that sacrosanct institution any-

how, for many of its dancers were loyal admirers of Noverre. The use of the mask was abandoned, costuming was reformed to a certain extent, and the new concept of verisimilitude made itself felt. Eventually Noverre himself was accepted as ballet master at the Opéra, but by then his ideas were no longer novel. His tenure was brief and unhappily riddled by intrigues, of which he himself was by no means innocent, and he resigned.

The publication of his book, "Letters on the Dance and the Ballet," in 1761 was of paramount importance, for here he outlined his principles in a manner that made them available far beyond his sphere of personal influence and, indeed, beyond his own time. His ardent disciple, Dauberval, carried on his teachings with vigor in the south of France, and Dauberval's pupil, Salvatore Viganó, developed them even further in Milan in the early nineteenth century. His critics, indeed, found that Viganó's "choreo-drama" had taken dancing altogether out of the ballet and left it pure dramatic pantomime. With him the direct line of Noverre came to an end, but the principle of the "ballet d'action" had come to stay, and still largely prevails among us.

Meanwhile in Paris the French Revolution had wrought other changes in the ballet. Echoes of the contemporary world had found their way into the repertoire, and though the Greek gods and goddesses continued to dance in many ballets, and still wore garb that was closer to the courtly uniform of Louis XIV's day than to the attire of the ancient Greeks, there were new ballets dealing with the sans-culottes of revolutionary Paris, others celebrating the American Revolution, and even such characters as priests and nuns were pictured in ballets protesting against religion and the church. The ancient tradition of dancing about lesser Greek classic personages, such as nymphs and shepherds in poetic pastorals, now found itself reflecting the new democratic tone in works with contemporary peasants as their subjects.

As the nineteenth century dawned, there came still further reforms. The painter, David, deeply interested, as many of his colleagues had recently become, in archeological accuracy, had persuaded his friend, Talma, the great tragic actor, to discard the old traditional style of reputedly Greek and Roman costuming which had persisted in the dramatic theatre as stubbornly as in the ballet. This astounding new "realism" was so successful that the ballet of necessity adopted it as well, and for a generation the ballet's still persistent Greeks disported themselves in tunics and chitons with some regard for authenticity.

The Romantic Revolution

These were all merely transitional steps leading to the truly revolutionary change that impended for the ballet. This was the birth of the romantic ballet. It was simply the culmination in the field of the dance of that total re-orientation of thinking known as the Romantic Revolution. Like the parallel growth all through the eighteenth century of the social revolution which came to a head in the American war for independence and in the French Revolution, it was concerned with the inherent rights and potentialities of the "natural man" which the great thinkers of the Reformation had celebrated, and was opposed to social, political and religious hierarchies of all sorts.

So large was its scope and so radical its nature that it rivaled in importance even such a historical overturning as the Renaissance. The latter had touched mainly the courtiers and the ruling classes, but the Romantic Revolution was a movement of the common people in both its political and its artistic manifestations. In effect it was a kind of counter-Renaissance. It repudiated the classical Graeco-Roman model which had been arbitrarily adopted by the Renaissance, and determined to pick up the direct road of progress from which it had deviated at the end of the Middle Ages. It renounced paganism for a return to Christian values; it demanded an end to the artist's slavery to the abstract and impersonal unities of classical culture and his freedom to treat instead of the moral conflicts of life.

Victor Hugo became the spokesman for the entire movement when it had reached its peak of artistic rebellion in the early nineteenth century, and his preface to his play, "Cromwell," was a declaration of its principles. Here he demanded emancipation from "the despotism of systems, codes and rules," and insisted that the true presentation of life consisted of both the beautiful and ugly, the good and evil, elements in conflict.

The days of the classic Greeks were now over in the ballet; it was the picturesque Middle Ages that intrigued its fancy as a model for the past. Indeed, a revival of that medieval mystic dualism which pictured man as a creature always torn between the spirit and the flesh largely dominated the scene. Supernatural creatures of the air fell in love with mortal men and came to tragic ends; dead maidens rose from the grave to haunt unfaithful lovers; and in general there were moral victories of the aerial and spiritual creatures over the earthly and sensual. If much of this seems mawkish and sentimental to us (and, indeed, actually was so as the original impulse of the revolution faded), it was nevertheless based on a vital emotional urge and had both inherent validity and power.

In the interest of theatrical illusion in the ballet, it became customary to attach the dancers of aerial roles to wires by which they could literally fly above the level of the stage. (This device was already waiting to be used, for Didelot had created a sensation by introducing it purely as an ingenious production novelty in his ballet, "Flore et Zéphire," in London in 1796.) But because movement itself is automatically expressive of compelling emotional drives, this mechanical device was not sufficient to satisfy it. The dancers, already able to leap into the air for brief moments of suspension without artificial aids, now actually sought to sustain this quality of suspension in terms, not of wires, but of their own movements. It is perhaps quite natural that in response to this desire to inhabit the air they should have risen onto the points of their toes, even though at first they were unable to remain there for any extended length of

Scene from Philippe Taglioni's "La Sylphide," which is virtually the archetype of the "romantic" ballet

time. Thus out of a strong inner emotional compulsion this great technical innovation of dancing on the tips of the toes — the *pointes,* as they are technically called — came about. Because it was so obviously right for its purpose, it was naturally developed, until with the aid of a reinforced shoe it could be transformed into a veritable new way of moving, suggestive of floating rather than walking, and to all intents and purposes ignoring the pull of gravity.

This new aerial style of moving came about so gradually that there is no record of who the first dancer was who danced on her "pointes," but it was probably introduced some time in the 1820s. Not until 1832 was the ballet presented that really crystallized the romantic style in general. This was "La Sylphide" — not to be confused with "Les Sylphides" created by Michel

Fokine more than seventy years later. It was composed by Phillippe Taglioni for his daughter, Marie, and it told the story of a woodland creature of supernatural character who fell tragically in love with a Scotsman. For the costume of the nymph, the artist, Eugène Lamy, devised the full and filmy white skirt reaching halfway to the ankles which was destined to become almost as standard a costume for the ballerina as the old panniered dress of the court had been.

These ethereal ballets—sometimes referred to as "ballets blancs," or white ballets, because of the stageful of filmy white-clad dancers they employed — were produced in profusion, and one of the most successful ones of the period survives after a fashion in today's repertoire. This is "Giselle," created by Jean Coralli in 1841 for Carlotta Grisi. It has been copiously altered with

35

Fanny Elssler in "El Sapateo de Cadiz," from a music cover printed in New York during her American tour

Carlotta Grisi in "Giselle," created for her in 1841 by Coralli (and, unofficially, her husband, Perrot)

the passage of time, especially in Russia in the late nineteenth century, and it is that version that forms the basis of the ballet as we know it now. Nevertheless, in spite of all the remaking, it retains much of the flavor of its period when it is staged with sensitiveness and danced by a ballerina with a sense of style.

Besides the mystic and supernatural qualities of ballets such as "Giselle" and "La Sylphide," the romantic ballet also contained elements of a very different sort. Since it was influenced by the ideology of democracy on the one hand and was emotionally devoted to the Middle Ages, it could scarcely fail to find a fresh interest in both folk ways and the romantic problems of the lowly born. Peasant dances abounded in the supernatural ballets and, in addition, ballets of straight dramatic import about people of various exotic nationalities enjoyed a popularity of their own.

If Taglioni was the symbol of the mystical side of romanticism, the earthy side was equally symbolized by her rival and complete opposite,

Fanny Elssler, who specialized in these more full-blooded romances. She was a Viennese woman of considerable beauty, as contrasted with Taglioni's marked lack of physical allure, and she danced with dramatic fire and personal charm altogether removed from her colleague's spiritual detachment. It was part of her practice to utilize in her ballets adaptations of folk dances such as the Italian tarantella, the Spanish cachuca, and dances from Russia and Poland. Elssler was the only one of the great galaxy of ballerinas of that day who ever came to America, and her two seasons in this country in the early 40s were phenomenally successful.

It is not surprising that a period which sentimentalized womanhood as the romantic period did should have raised the ballerina to an unprecedented height of esteem. This she was able to sustain in terms of technical accomplishment by her newly acquired ability to dance on her *pointes,* which gave her a distinct advantage over her male colleague. Why he, too, was not ex-

M. and Mme. Achille, "from the Italian Opera House, Paris," very early 19th-century visitors to America

Fanny Cerito in the Shadow Dance from "Ondine," the famous ballet created and danced by her and Perrot

pected to rise to the tips of his toes is explained only by the mental attitude of the time, which considered the woman as the spiritual type whose native element was the air and the man as her comparatively base and unaspiring consort. At any rate, the male dancer, poor soul, after having dominated the dance for centuries both by right of his superior social position in other days and by his greater athletic ability to leap and turn, found himself downright unpopular. He was apparently endured at all only because he was needed to support the ballerina in some of her more effective moments.

Quite naturally, with all these new emphases and opportunities, the matter of technique became of increasing importance. But if Paris was still the artistic center of the ballet, it was indebted to Italy, as it had always been, for improvements of a technical sort. The summation of the new technical basis for this much broadened period of the ballet was to be found in the work of Carlo Blasis, Italian-born dancer

who had danced in France and England and eventually returned to Milan as the greatest ballet master of his day. He re-codified the entire method and practice of the art, and established a system of training and education which to a large extent still provides a background for today's teaching methods.

The combination of artistic revitalization and technical organization made the 1830s and '40s a "golden age" of the ballet. So complete was its conquest over all traditions and accomplishments that had gone before it that it has come to be regarded as the virtual source and criterion of ballet practice. When we refer to the "classic ballet," it is this period and the styles and methods it established that we are thinking of, using the word "classic" not in its sense of referring to the ancient Greek culture but rather in the sense in which we apply it to the works of Shakespeare, Milton, Bach and Beethoven, as examples of an academically authoritative standard of excellence.

37

Nineteenth Century Decline

But as with every period of unusual inspiration, its finest impulses were eventually spent, and the innovations it had made were perpetuated only as empty surfaces with their original emotional motivations quite forgotten. The great inner urge had been satisfied. The new technical range that was opened up was now increased and elaborated solely for its acrobatic potentialities. Dancing on the *pointes* lost all its spiritual significance and was treated simply as a means for providing an irreducibly small base for the ballerina to stand on while she performed miracles of balance and executed sequences of otherwise impossibly rapid turns.

The long, fluffy skirt which had been conceived as the poetic apparel of a creature of the air was now an unquestioned uniform. To be sure, it progressively shortened as time went on in order to facilitate the more and more involved technique, and ultimately it was reduced to little more than a puff of tulle around the hips. But certainly it did not indicate a supernatural creature any longer; it implied no characterization at all. If the ballerina was supposed to be a peasant, she wore a little apron over it in front; if she was an ancient Greek, she had a key pattern on its edges; if she was a queen she added jewels and a crown. Jewels she wore in any case, if she owned any, and her hair was dressed in the latest fashion of the day whether she was an Egyptian princess or an American Indian. She also wore pink tights and slippers, irrespective of race or period, and danced on *pointes,* employing the same basic vocabulary for all roles.

The pattern of the late nineteenth century became fairly set. The story was most likely a romance of the olden days, or frequently, as an inheritance from the mystical ways of the romantic ballet, a fairy tale. It was usually in three or four acts and lasted for a whole evening — including intermissions sometimes as long as forty-five minutes each, in order to allow the aristocrats in the audience to visit. Its plot was unfolded in terms of pantomime which consisted in the main of a sign language of the hands, devoid of expressiveness and often unintelligible without the aid of program notes. The action was interrupted periodically by dance numbers, either by the soloists or by the corps de ballet in mass manoeuvres, without relation to the drama itself.

The climax of the evening was the *grand*

Four figures from Luigi Manzotti's "Amor" (1866), a grandiose spectacle, using horses and elephants, and depicting Man's history from Creation to Milan's deliverance from Barbarossa, all under Love's guidance

pas de deux by the ballerina and her cavalier. It assumed a four-part form. The first part, called "adagio," consisted of slow and sustained movements in which the ballerina, supported by her partner throughout, was exhibited to her best advantage; the second was a solo, or "variation," by the man; the third, a solo, or "variation," by the ballerina; and the fourth, a "coda," in which the two danced together again, this time in rapid and brilliant movements.

The final act usually contained a long succession of *divertissements,* or specialty dances, by the various soloists of the cast in their roles as guests at a ball, villagers at a fête, entertainers before a king, or something of the sort.

Music was ordinarily turned out to order by staff musicians, who were merely instructed to provide so many measures in 3/4 time, so many in 4/4, so many fast and so many slow passages. The scenery was similarly designed by staff artists along regulation lines, frequently with a grand transformation scene or other spectacular feature. By and large, everything was subordinated to the technical virtuosity (and, of course, the feminine appeal) of the ballerinas.

For perhaps obvious reasons, not many ballets from this period survive in the popular repertoire today, except in the Russian theatres where many of them have been kept alive continuously as a traditional policy. (Of that there will be more to say later on.) The few exceptions are those which somehow escaped having scores by the usual hack musicians and have lived accordingly on the strength of their music. These include "Coppélia," for which Delibes wrote one of the most charming of ballet scores; and the three Tchaikovsky ballets: "Swan Lake," "The Nutcracker," and "The Sleeping Beauty." Most of these are generally given in shortened versions, and "Swan Lake" is commonly reduced to its second act alone.

Of these four, only the earliest, "Coppélia" (1870), stems originally from Paris, though its choreography in that first production has long since been lost. The form in which we know it best is a made-over version from Russia in the '90s, though the Royal Danish ballet has a lively version entirely its own. The other three were all direct products of Russia in the '90s, when the ballet in its time-honored homes in Italy and France was all but literally dead. It was sterile and vapid in Russia, as well, but it was from there that the next great impulse of life was to spring.

From left to right they are: Antonietta Bella as Amor; Giuseppina Cecchetti as one of Caesar's warriors; Amelia Lombardi (?) as the primal woman, a non-Biblical version of Eve; and Enrico Cecchetti as a satyr

Fokine Reawakens the Ballet

The ballet came to Russia first as part of that mass importation of western culture begun by Peter the Great. In 1735 the Empress Anna established an academy of sorts and it has existed ever since under all the tsars and on into the Soviet regime under the patronage of the state. Though this was fairly late in the history of the art, the finest masters were imported from France and Italy and enormous sums of money were lavished upon it by one of the world's wealthiest courts. There were years of particular growth under Catherine the Great; then Catherine's son, Paul I, summoned Charles Louis Didelot to take charge in 1801, and it was well on the way to being the best ballet anywhere in the world, and probably the most splendid.

But it remained an importation. All through the nineteenth century, though it produced ever finer dancers out of its own ranks, it continued to be directed by French and Italian masters and to bestow most of the stellar roles upon celebrated foreign artists — until, indeed, the decline of the art in western Europe left no celebrated artists to bestow them upon. Possibly because of the continued subsidy and direction of the imperial house during these lean artistic years, the ballet in Russia maintained a far higher standard than existed in other countries where royal patronage had long since ceased. But from the standpoint of artistic vitality and that inward urgency that produces progress, it was as lean in Russia as elsewhere.

Under the surface, however, there were important stirrings among the artists, but in so strictly regulated an organization, murmurings of discontent from below had a hard time reaching the surface, and even when they succeeded in doing so, they received short shrift. It was in 1904 that there came the first artistic expression of rebellion. This was in the form of a letter to the directors from a gifted young Russian of 24, who had been graduated from the academy with distinction six years previously, had stepped immediately into important roles, was a teacher of some of the junior classes now, himself, and

Michel Fokine as Amoun in his ballet, "Cléopatre"

Michel Fokine, Ivan Tsarevitch in "L'Oiseau de Feu," with Alexis Bulgakov as Köstschei, the "Immortal"
Dance Collection, New York Public Library

had a desire to become a creator of ballets. His name was Michel Fokine (to use the form in which it has become famous in the western world), and the letter, which was in the main a request to be allowed to create a specific ballet, denounced the sterility of contemporary practices and outlined a definite program for reforming them. It is one of the most important documents in the history of the art, but its receipt by the directors was never even acknowledged. The only result it produced was a bulletin instructing singers in the opera no longer to interrupt the action by taking bows after their arias. Ten years later, Fokine developed his ideas and restated them in a letter to the Times of London where they had public circulation for the first time.

These ideas, of course, went deeper than the business of operatic bowing. They were essentially a restatement of the same principles that Noverre had preached nearly a hundred and fifty years earlier, now enriched by the knowledge and cultural evolution of the intervening generations, and the personal urgency of an artist of genius. Like Noverre, Fokine wanted to make the ballet an expressive art, a mirror of life comparable to the drama. The five major planks of his platform for reforming the current stereotyped methods, were: first, that the use of ready-made movements, right out of the academic classroom, should be abandoned on the stage, and every ballet should have a style of movement suitable to the country and period in which its

Michel Fokine and Vera Fokina in the title roles of his "Daphnis et Chloë"

Thamar Karsavina in "L'Oiseau de Feu"

Adolph Bolm in Fokine's "Prince Igor"

action was laid; second, that the entire dramatic action should unfold continuously in terms of movement instead of consisting of scenes of pantomime to relate the plot, interrupted by meaningless dance numbers of entirely unrelated character; third, that the conventional sign-language, which was known as pantomime and was totally unintelligible even to dancers playing a scene together, should be discarded, and that the entire body of the dancer should be expressive at all times; fourth, that not just the soloist but the whole company should be used to forward the dramatic theme and to be expressive, instead of keeping the corps de ballet for purely decorative interludes that served only to allow the principals to get their breath and change their costumes; fifth, that the music should be no longer a mere succession of little dance numbers, but should be a unity carrying forward the dramatic action just as the dancing did, that the scenery should similarly be creative in style just as the movement was, and that the costumes should no longer be held to the tradi-

tion of ballet skirt, pink tights and toe slippers, but should accurately reflect the style of the country and period in which the action was set. The whole work, in short, should involve the active collaboration of choreographer, musician and designer.

He considered the academic technique indispensable for teaching but not an adequate vocabulary for artistic expression; he found it foolish for ancient Greeks to be pictured dancing on *pointes* instead of barefooted in conformity with historical accuracy; *pointes* he returned to the supernatural or purely imaginary characters for whom they were originally designed.

It has frequently been said that Fokine's reforms were inspired by Isadora Duncan, who at that period had begun to startle the artistic world with her radical approach to the dance, but this theory is untenable. Fokine's ideas had begun to take shape before he had ever seen Isadora dance (she did not appear in Russia until 1905), and were fundamentally quite different. They are far closer to Noverre's, of which, indeed, they are a virtual fulfilment. He unquestionably admired Isadora, was influenced by her in a measure and encouraged by her insurgency, but the goals toward which the two of them were driving had little in common. To the end of his life, Fokine, with his deeply rooted ethnological conviction of style, persisted in considering Isadora to be a mistress of the classic Greek style and nothing more, completely overlooking the quite opposite emphasis of her art on purely subjective expression. Whatever similarity existed between the two artists was due to the fact that they were both sensitive creators animated by the same emotional drive that was at work in the world at large. These years marked the beginning of what has become known as the modern movement, and Fokine and Isadora felt its urgency in their own terms, just as the musician Debussy, the painter Cézanne, the architect Frank Lloyd Wright, felt it in theirs.

The Russian Ballet in the Western World

That modern impulses should find their way into so traditional an institution as the imperial theatres of Russia was unthinkable. Many of Fokine's colleagues, especially the younger ones, were enthusiastic about his ideas, but the only opportunities he had to put them into operation were on private and semi-private occasions such as benefits and students' performances. Even here, when he attempted to put his Greeks into bare feet, he was forced to accept the ridiculous compromise of dressing them in pink tights with toes painted on them.

But the force of the revolt continued to grow within the company, and the directors of the institution no doubt greeted with relief an opportunity that now presented itself to allow the excited rebels to work off their enthusiasm at a safe distance from the home organization.

Raoul Barba

Scene from "Pétrouchka" in a revival by the Ballet Russe de Monte Carlo. (Tamara Toumanova, center)

Thamar Karsavina in the original "Pétrouchka"   Vaslav Nijinsky in the original "Pétrouchka"

Serge Diaghileff, formerly attached to the direction in an administrative capacity, asked leave to borrow the insurgents during their long summer vacation for a season in Paris. It was a fine solution all the way round, and in 1909 Paris saw "Russian Ballet" for the first time. Probably no other artistic event of modern times has made so deep and so instantaneous an impression. The news was published around the world and a new era began for the art of the ballet.

Because of the outbreak of World War I in 1914, these annual Paris seasons during the summer vacations of the dancers from St. Petersburg and Moscow were few in number, but they served to revivify a moribund art. Fokine's ideas had free rein at last; he had the full collaboration of such painters as Benois and Bakst, and such a musician as Stravinsky, plus the use of music by Chopin, Schumann, Rimsky-Korsakoff and other composers whose work had never been

turned to dance purposes before Isadora's time; his company of dancers included Karsavina, Bolm, Nijinsky, and for one season, Pavlova. Fokine, himself, though his fame as a choreographer has overshadowed his career as a performer, was also a dancer of exceptional ability.

Half a dozen of what might be called his standard masterpieces were introduced to Paris during these years—"Les Sylphides," "Carnaval," "Pétrouchka," "Schéhérazade," "Prince Igor" and "Le Spectre de la Rose;" not to mention "L'Oiseau de Feu," "Thamar," "Daphnis et Chloe," "Le Coq d'Or," "Cléopatre," "Le Pavillon d'Armide" and others which for one reason or another did not live as long.

It is practically impossible for us today to judge of the true importance of these works, for as they exist in the repertoires of the various companies, they are mere shadows of their original incarnations. Not only are the companies,

44

Maurice Goldberg

Anthony

Tatiana Riabouchinska in title role of "Coq d'Or"   Irina Baronova as Queen of Shemakhan in "Coq d'Or"

"Les Sylphides" as revived by the Ballet Russe de Monte Carlo. (Tatiana Riabouchinska, center)

Raoul Barba

45

especially as regards the ensembles, inferior to the magnificent group from the Imperial Ballet which first performed them, but the ballets themselves have been largely forgotten and handed around by memory from one ballet master to another. This is perhaps most unfortunate where "Pétrouchka" is concerned for it was an epoch-making work which introduced a stylization of psychologically expressive movement into the ballet for the first time. The ballet which fares best is "Les Sylphides," mainly because it utilizes the standard academic vocabulary of movement which all ballet companies know. It was created as a sentimental memory of the period of Taglioni, and was accordingly well within the range of Fokine's insistence on observing the styles of other periods.

The mere passing of time has dimmed their revolutionary aspect; what was once a completely new approach has long since been accepted as the basis of general practice. A new generation of reformers has arisen, indeed, to rebel against it as already old-fashioned, and to lead the art ahead in further advances. We cannot, therefore, expect to share the impact upon their time that was produced by Fokine's early ballets; we must inevitably look upon them as masterpieces of another era, milestones of progress which only yesterday were passed on the road to ever increasing achievement.

After the great days of his triumphs, which were not entirely happy ones for him because of his antagonism toward Diaghileff's domination and political manipulations within the company, Fokine continued to create for other companies in other parts of the world (including many years in America) with the same skill and the same artistic convictions until his death in 1942.

Scene from the Gluck "Don Juan" as created by Michel Fokine for René Blum's Ballets de Monte Carlo

Group from "Paganini," created by Michel Fokine for the Original Ballet Russe. (Dimitri Rostov, right)

Fokine's "Cinderella" with Tatiana Riabouchinska in title role, created for the Original Ballet Russe

Maurice Seymour

Fokine's "Bluebeard," created for the Ballet Theatre. (Alicia Markova, Anton Dolin, Lucia Chase, center)

Anton Dolin as "Bluebeard" and Irina Baronova as his seventh wife in the Fokine-Offenbach comedy ballet

Alfredo Valente

"Russian Soldier," Fokine's tribute to simple heroes of the war. (With Yurek Lazovsky, Galina Razoumova)

Alfredo Valente

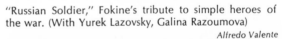

Pavlova and Nijinsky

The two outstanding personalities among the dancers who emerged from the period when the Russian ballet made itself known outside its own country for the first time were, of course, Anna Pavlova and Vaslav Nijinsky.

Pavlova was one of the earliest supporters of Fokine in his agitations for reform. For her he composed "The Swan" to be danced at a benefit way back in 1905, and she appeared in "Les Sylphides," "Le Pavillon d'Armide" and "Cléopatre" in the first Paris season. But she was not sympathetic to Diaghileff's ideas in general, and early disassociated herself from his group to tour with a company of her own with Moscow's Mikhail Mordkin as her leading male dancer. She had already made one or two tours outside Russia, chiefly in Scandinavia, under Bolm's direction, before the Diaghileff project had been launched. It was with Mordkin that she made her American debut in 1910 at the Metropolitan Opera House, and gave this country its first flush of excitement over the Russian ballet.

Anna Pavlova as Ta-hor in "Cléopatre"

Her art was unsympathetic to Diaghileff's constant emphasis on novelty and experiment; its kinship was rather with the spirit of Taglioni, broadened and enriched, but unaltered in substance. A dramatic actress of wonderful eloquence in movement, and an exquisite stylist, she carried forward the essential tradition of the romantic ballet into new dimensions.

She was not a choreographer herself, having composed only one ballet, "Autumn Leaves," but she made many personal alterations in the versions she used of the standard works. Of necessity she could not always surround herself with a company worthy of her, and many of the works she appeared in were below the level of her genius. But the perfection of her personal art was such that in her touring of the world persistently over many years she made undoubtedly more converts to the art of the ballet than any other artist has ever done.

Nijinsky, except for his status as an artist, belongs at the opposite end of the scale. A protégé, both personal and professional, of Diaghi-

Vaslav Nijinsky as the slave in "Schéhérazade"

leff from almost the beginning of his career, he was deeply concerned with modern directions and created some highly revolutionary choreography. His "Le Sacre du Printemps," for example, found not even his patron, the radical Diaghileff, in sympathy. Here, nevertheless, though the evidence seems to indicate that musically and in almost every other way he was out of his depth, Nijinsky opened the way for a use of movement which the ballet had never seen before, and which was nearer to the attitude of the modern dance than of the ballet. The movement he employed was purely invented, out of his personal reaction to the savage music of Stravinsky and the prehistoric subject of the ballet. Actually it was necessary to call in a teacher of Dalcroze Eurythmics to enable him to cope with the score (a teacher, by the way, who was later to make history in England under the name of Marie Rambert). To it he set choreography in defiance of the academic tradition — heavy movements, short phrases, angular and broken lines, the toes violently turned in. Certainly the ballet world was not ready for any such modernism in 1913, and Nijinsky's career ended before he could prove whether or not he might have developed it further.

As a performer he was perhaps one of the finest male dancers the ballet has ever known (if such things can be measured over the passing centuries), not only for his technical accomplishments, which included especially spectacular elevation, but also for his powers as an actor. In this latter capacity he was declared by Sarah Bernhardt, after she had seen his performance of "Pétrouchka," to be the greatest actor in the world. This phase of his art is frequently overshadowed by his more startling ability to leap, which is certainly of less consequence in the final analysis. His dancing, however, must obviously remain in the field of legend.

Of the four ballets he created as choreographer, only "L'Après-midi d'un Faun" survived, and that in a form that bore the faintest possible relationship to the original, which was a stylishly courageous work. "Le Sacre du Printemps," the cause of a riot in the theatre at its première, re-

Abbe

Anna Pavlova in "Snowflakes"

Nijinsky and a nymph in "L'Après-midi d'un Faune"

Dance Collection, New York Public Library

ceived only six performances; "Jeux" fared scarcely better; and "Tyl Eulenspiegel," produced in New York, was abandoned at once and never seen at all in Europe.

In spite of his worldwide fame and subsequent more or less romantic immortalization, Nijinsky's career lasted slightly less than ten years from the time of his debut with the Imperial Ballet in St. Petersburg in the spring of 1908. Even a very considerable part of this brief period found him inactive, for his relations with Diaghi-leff were broken off summarily upon his marriage in the autumn of 1913, he danced hardly at all between that time and the outbreak of the war, and he was then interned as an enemy alien in Austria. He was not released from this detention until 1916, when he joined the Diaghileff company (or what was left of it) in its first North American tour, and after one more season in the Americas, he returned to Europe where he was committed to an insane asylum shortly afterwards.

Anna Pavlova, with Alexander Volinine and Laurent Novikoff, in "Les Coquetteries de Columbine"

Abbe

Diaghileff and the International Period

The first World War brought to a definite end the short epoch of the Russian ballet in western Europe. Not only were many of the leading artists cut off from each other in various countries, but Diaghileff's access to the great state schools and companies was forever ended by the Russian Revolution. It was up to him to proceed henceforth on an entirely different basis. The company was now not even informally an offshoot of the Imperial Ballet, but his own enterprise to do with as he pleased.

Little by little its character was transformed into something that reflected his own tastes ever more clearly. Its dancing personnel remained predominantly Russian but no longer exclusively so. The list of composers and painters now included, besides Stravinsky and Larionov, who were as international in taste as Diaghileff himself, such names as Poulenc, Auric, Milhaud, Satie, de Falla, Laurencin, Picasso, Dérain, Pruna, Rouault. The general flavor, no longer Russian, became that of the international art movement that centered in Paris. Experimentation, in which Diaghileff delighted for its own sake, flourished, particularly in the areas of music and décor. Since money was always scarce in spite of Diaghileff's skill at raising it, great ingenuity had to be practiced to reconcile artistic necessity with limited means, and this only added to the experimentation. The company's home was no longer St. Petersburg but Monte Carlo, where it played an annual season, gave many of its premières, and spent much of its rehearsal time and its leisure. The male dancer assumed pre-eminence, usurping the place held so long by the ballerina, since Diaghileff was innately indifferent to feminine charms. For the first time in its long history, the ballet, heretofore always stultified by the stuffiness of royal patronage, was officially encouraged to be daring, unconventional and novel. As long as Diaghileff lived, his company, for better or worse, was in the very forefront of the *avant garde.*

Maurice Goldberg

Tamara Toumanova and Leonide Massine in a revival of his "Le Tricorne" for the Monte Carlo Ballet Russe

Leonide Massine

During the years between the war and Diaghileff's death in 1929, three choreographers shared the responsibility of creating the repertoire, namely, Leonide Massine, Bronislava Nijinska and George Balanchine.

Much the greater part of it fell to Massine, whose expert craftsmanship was in large measure responsible for carrying the company forward during the first years after the war. He had been discovered by Diaghileff as a young student at the drama school in Moscow, and had been brought into the company at the age of seventeen to be developed as a successor to Nijinsky when the latter was dismissed by Diaghileff for having married. He danced his first leading role in 1914 in "La Légende de Joseph," created for him by Fokine, and he choreographed his first ballet, "Soleil de Minuit," in 1915.

Both his style as a dancer and his approach to choreography showed his early leaning toward the dramatic stage. Throughout his dancing career, he exhibited, for example, one of the rarest gifts of a dancer, which, is paradoxically enough, the ability to stand still on the stage, and he had a genuine flair for characterization, particularly in comedy roles. Most of his ballets, especially those created during the years with Diaghileff, were devoted to storytelling, usually on comedy themes and dealing with farcical characters, such as "Boutique Fantasque," "Tricorne" and "The Good-Humored Ladies." Works of the same general type that date from after Diaghileff's death include "Le Beau Danube" and "Gaîté Parisienne."

A more serious and abstract trend was early indicated in his restaging, along different lines from Nijinsky's, of "Le Sacre du Printemps." This trend really began to become important to him toward the end of Diaghileff's regime in such works as "Le Pas d'Acier" and "Ode," in both of which, however, he was also concerned to a large extent with the use of stage mechanics along with movement for the creation of his effects.

His full tendency toward the abstract ballet came about after Diaghileff's time in his turning to visualizations of symphonic music, generally with symbolic dramatic programs for the action — "Les Présages," set to the Fifth Symphony of Tchaikovsky; "Choreartium," set to the Fourth Symphony of Brahms; "Seventh Symphony" to Beethoven's music; "Symphonie Fantasque" to Berlioz's; "Rouge et Noir" to the First Symphony of Shostakovich. Some twenty years later when asked how he felt about the idea of such ballets, he was quoted as saying that he still thought the idea was sound, though at the time he was creating in that idiom he was far less capable of doing so than he would have been at this later period, when he had concentrated his attention on mastering the fundamental principles and practices of choreography as

Museum of Modern Art

The young Leonide Massine in "Soleil de Minuit," his first ballet creation, with Pflanz and Klementovich

Massine with Alexandra Danilova in a revival of "La Boutique Fantasque" by the Monte Carlo Ballet Russe

Sasha

his major interest.

Perhaps his most distinguished work, though one that did not prove to be a box-office favorite, falls into none of these categories; it is "Nobilissima Visione" (renamed "St. Francis" in America), a biography in medieval terms with music by Paul Hindemith and décor by Pavel Tchelitchev. Here again Massine's feeling for the dramatic theatre stood him in good stead as both choreographer and dancer.

In recent years he has continued to choreograph for various companies and in various styles. Perhaps his most notable work has been a large medieval ritual, "Laudes Evangelii," actually staged in the Basilica di San Dominico in Perugia.

Raoul Barba

Massine, Leon Woizikowski and David Lichine in "Les Matelots," in revival by Monte Carlo Ballet Russe

Danilova and Massine in "Le Beau Danube"

Maurice Goldberg

Massine's "Scuola di Ballo," based on Goldoni's play in a production by the Ballet Russe de Monte Carlo

Raoul Barba

Massine's "Le Beau Danube," set to a Strauss medley in décor after Constantin Guys. (David Lichine, center)

Raoul Barba

Baron

Massine as a Peruvian tourist in Second Empire Paris in "Gaîté Parisienne" set to Offenbach's best tunes

"Les Présages," set to Tchaikovsky's Fifth Symphony, first of a series of "symphonic ballets" by Massine

David Lichine and Irina Baronova in "Beach," created for Ballet Russe de Monte Carlo with accent on chic

Iris

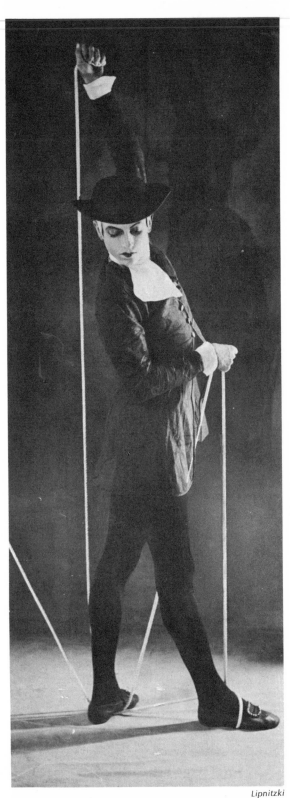

Lipnitzki

Serge Lifar in Massine's "Ode," highly experimental visually in its use of fabrics, lighting and cinema

Alicia Markova (Woman) and Frederic Franklin (Leader of Red Forces) in "Rouge et Noir," created in color-symbolism by Massine in collaboration with Henri Matisse, its designer, to Shostakovich's First Symphony

The final movement in Massine's "symphonic ballet," "Choreartium," set to the Fourth Symphony of Brahms

Massine's "St. Francis" ("Nobilissima Visione") with music by Paul Hindemith, décor by Pavel Tchelitchev

"Labyrinth" by Massine and Dali (Schubert's Seventh Symphony) with Tamara Toumanova and André Eglevsky

Alicia Markova and George Skibine in "Aleko," ballet by Massine on the Pushkin poem; designed by Chagall

Tamara Toumanova as the elusive Beloved in Massine's visualization of Berlioz's "Symphonie Fantastique"

Bronislava Nijinska

Bronislava Nijinska, separated from the Diaghileff company by the war in 1914, returned seven years later to prove herself not only the excellent dancer she had formerly been but also for the first time an equally excellent choreographer.

During her several years as chief creator of ballets for the company, she produced, among other things, two works of major importance. The first was "Les Noces," which was treated in a manner that, in spite of its success, the composer, Stravinsky, never quite approved of. When it came to performance it caused almost as much public excitement as her brother's "Sacre" had done. Set to Stravinsky's revolutionary music scored for pianos, percussions and voices, it was a primitive Russian wedding ceremonial, with starkly simple scenery by Natalia Gontcharova, and an unornamented, architectural use of movement, mostly by solid groups of dancers. There was a marked kinship here to her brother's use of purely invented movement for expressive purposes, though in a more ordered and less violent form. Of particular interest was her employment of *pointes*, not for aerial illusion or for conventional acrobatic effect, but as an instrumentality for expression in a highly stylized idiom. Her peasant maidens did not so much rise onto the tips of their toes as dig them into the earth with a kind of inarticulate, archaic passion. The work was seen in the United States in 1936 in a revival by the DeBasil Ballet Russe, but its special musical requirements make it an impractical "repertory work." It remains, nevertheless, one of the outstanding modern masterpieces.

The second ballet of outstanding importance which she contributed to the Diaghileff repertoire was "Les Biches," a sophisticated and satirical picture of the decadent social life of its time (1924), without any specific plot. Its value lay once again in its original comment. As in her use of *pointes* in "Les Noces," Nijinska here employed the elements of the academic ballet to deny its own traditional style and to achieve a piquant contemporary expressiveness. She her-

Daily Mail

"Les Noces," revolutionary ballet made by Bronislava Nijinska on the score by Stravinsky, with designs by Gontcharova. Above, the Departure of the Bridegroom; below, Felia Doubrovska in the role of the Bride

Abbe

self considered this ballet as establishing a new essential approach to a vocabulary of movement for the modern ballet just as "La Sylphide" had established an essential approach for the lush romantic period.

Since the Diaghileff days she has headed companies of her own and created for companies of other directors, and her range has continued to be wide and exploratory. Here was the first choreographic version of Ravel's "Bolero" (for Ida Rubenstein); and for her own companies she has done both "Hamlet" and a Bach "Etude," with a "Chopin Concerto" for the Polish Ballet and a "Pictures at an Exhibition" for the Marquis de Cuevas' Ballet International, and countless other equally contrasted pieces all exhibiting her grasp of form, her distinctive style of movement and her rich inventiveness.

Numa Blanc; Dance Collection, New York Public Library

Bronislava Nijinska as the hostess in "Les Biches," her satirical ballet on contemporary social themes

Nijinska's ballet on Moussorgsky's "Pictures at an Exhibition," for the de Cuevas Ballet International

Fred Fehl

"The Snow Maiden," Russian legend set to Glazounov's "The Seasons." (Nathalie Krassovska in title role)

Fred Fehl

Deteille; Dance Collection, New York Public Library

Leon Woizikowski, Nicholas Zverev in "Les Biches"

58

David Lichine and Irina Baronova in "Les Cent Baisers," created by Nijinska for Original Ballet Russe

Two works in comparable styles but different approaches created by Nijinska for the Opéra Russe de Paris: "Les Comédiens Jaloux," basically a story ballet, and "Beethoven Variations," essentially a musical one

Bach "Etude," created for the Opéra Russe de Paris, later presented by the Ballet Russe de Monte Carlo

Lipnitzki

Halsman

"Légende de Cracovie," produced by the Polish Ballet   "Brahms Variations" (Viola Essen, André Eglevsky)

"Schumann Concerto," another musical work, created for Ballet Theatre. (Alonso and Youskevitch, center)

Sedge LeBlang

George Balanchine

The third member of Diaghileff's choreographic triumvirate and the youngest was George Balanchine, who did not join the company until late in its life. His education had begun in the old imperial Russian academy in St. Petersburg and had continued there after the Revolution. But his new and radical ideas about choreography found no encouragement whatever in official circles, in spite of the Revolution. Because of his burning desire to work in his own direction, Balanchine managed after some effort to get permission to go to western Europe for a little tournée, taking with him several of his colleagues who agreed with his artistic ideas, among them Alexandra Danilova and Tamara Geva. It was the end of his Russian career, for Diaghileff found his approach congenial, took him and his companions into the company, and when Nijinska vacated the post of choreographer in 1925, put him into it, though he was only twenty-one.

Of the ten ballets he created for the company before its dissolution at Diaghileff's death,

one was a landmark in the development of the ballet. This was "Apollon Musagète," created in 1928 to Stravinsky's classically minded score. The music had been commissioned by Elizabeth Sprague Coolidge for the music festival at the Library of Congress in Washington, where its world première had occurred only a few months earlier in a choreographic version by Adolph Sprague Coolidge for the music festival at the Bolm, under its original Greek title of "Apollo Musagetes."

This was the beginning for both Balanchine and Stravinsky of a neo-classic approach, and initiated a long and close artistic collaboration between them. Certainly for Balanchine it amounted to the declaration of a new faith, which he has never recanted. He has called the work the turning point in his life. The ballet, now known simply as "Apollo," is one of the principal pieces in the repertoire of the New York City Ballet, where in a newly simplified production, it finds Jacques d'Amboise as a notable interpreter of its title role.

Lipnitzki

Serge Lifar in George Balanchine's original production of "Le Fils Prodigue" for the Diaghileff ballet

61

New Soil — New Roots

Balanchine occupies a strategic position in this country as a link between the old world and the new, for in 1933 he was brought to New York by Lincoln Kirstein as the key figure in a long-term plan to establish the ballet as part of the artistic life of America.

Looking at history, Kirstein saw that the Italian roots of the art had been transplanted to France and supported there in such a manner that they eventually blossomed into a specifically French art; that these Italian-French roots in turn, transplanted to Russia and nurtured there, had flowered into still another brilliant manifestation, colored by the Russians' particular gifts as a people. If these Italian-French-Russian roots could be transplanted to America and once more encouraged to acclimate themselves to a new environment, there seemed no reason to believe that a specifically American form of ballet should not emerge in due time. To that end he set up not only a producing company, but what was more basic, a school, properly organized and oriented along lines congenial to Balanchine, to serve as the nearest equivalent to an official academy that was practicable in a strongly competitive field.

The major difference, however, between this new transplantation and those that had so successfully preceded it lay in the fact that in this country there were no such funds to draw upon as those of the French and Russian courts. Almost from the first, financial stringencies threatened repeatedly to terminate the experiment. As a result there were re-organizations, changes of name and continual adaptations to insure survival. The company was originally called the American Ballet, and under that title sought temporary refuge for several seasons in the Metropolitan Opera as its official ballet, though quite unsuccessfully from both opera's and ballet's standpoints. A small subsidiary troupe, in which Balanchine did not participate, was organized under the name of Ballet Caravan to devote itself exclusively to the work of American choreographers. Later this was combined with the parent

Dorothy Wilding

Anton Dolin in Balanchine's "Le Bal" created for the Diaghileff company in its final season; and a second ballet about a party, "Cotillon," made by Balanchine for the Ballet Russe de Monte Carlo's first season

Raoul Barba

William Dollar, Gisela Caccialanza in the Balanchine "Baiser de la Fée," created for the American Ballet

Richard Tucker

organization, with Balanchine again at its head, rechristened the American Ballet Caravan, and sent on a South American "good-will tour" under the auspices of the United States State Department.

Meanwhile, the lean and uncertain years forced Balanchine much against his inclinations into the Broadway theatre from time to time. But whatever his personal objections may have been, he ushered in a new era in musical comedy dancing in the '30s when he choreographed four shows with characteristic taste and elegance for Dwight Deere Wiman — "On Your Toes" (containing the ballet, "Slaughter on Tenth Avenue," with Ray Bolger and Tamara Geva, which has endured, at least in reputation, as a classic), "Babes in Arms," "I Married an Angel" (containing an enchanting "Honeymoon Ballet" with Vera Zorina), and "Stars in Your Eyes" (with a corps de ballet that included Nora Kaye, Alicia Alonso, Jerome Robbins and a dozen other young dancers on the verge of making distinguished careers for themselves in the ballet).

During World War II, with Kirstein in the Army, all activities of the parent company were necessarily suspended, and Balanchine along with certain of his dancers again took refuge in another organization, this time, the Ballet Russe de Monte Carlo. After the war, independent activities were resumed, but now as a private subscription organization under the title of Ballet Society. In 1948 it joined forces with the newly set up New York City Center of Music and Drama, and took the title of the New York City Ballet.

Here began its first experience as an institutionalized company, though without the financial support that the city's auspices would seem to imply. Even under these conditions, however, and with no subsidy, the company has achieved the stature of one of the great ballets of our time. The theatre which has cradled it is a poor one, and lack of funds has kept its productions far from sumptuous (except as private donors have provided means for occasional ventures into more spectacular dimensions), but

"Ballet Imperial," homage to the art of pre-soviet Russia, with Tchaikovsky music and Dobujinsky décor

Frederic Franklin, Alexandra Danilova in "The Night Shadow," retitled "Sonnambula" in many repertoires
Maurice Seymour

Balanchine's artistic ingenuity has managed to turn even these limitations to account by evolving a style that focuses concentratedly on the musical-choreographic elements of his art. Another left-handed blessing, so to speak, and a very great one, has resulted from the city's insistence that admission prices at the City Center be kept low. This has conduced to the building of a wide new public that has come to the ballet unspoiled, has grown up aesthetically in the uncompromisingly creative atmosphere established by Balanchine and Kirstein, and has accepted it as a matter of course. The elevation of public taste that has been thus produced is enormous. Everything, indeed, has conspired toward the eventual move into a more auspicious home in the Lincoln Center for the Performing Arts.

It has not been the idea of the institution to restrict the repertoire in any sense to Balanchine, and other choreographers have contributed from time to time. Jerome Robbins has even occupied, at least nominally, the post of associate artistic director and has made a number of ballets. Among others are Frederick Ashton, Antony Tudor, Birgit Cullberg, John Taras and Todd Bolender. But it is inevitably a Balanchine company, for his personal style and the technique of his dancers are so characteristic in their line, their simplicity of bearing, their strongly piquant flavor, that other choreographers work at something of a disadvantage from the start.

Balanchine's own ballets in the repertoire concern themselves rarely with story, and are nearer in substance to musical compositions than to dramatic ones. Invariably they are inspired by, and actually built on the forms of, specific musical works, though certainly with no "interpretative" intent. He approaches the ballet not as an expressive medium but rather as an absolute aesthetic one, and it is interesting to see how he has steadily transformed it from an imitative art to a creative one.

All ten of the works he created for Diaghileff had aspects of plot and impersonation, and it was only in his own short-lived company, "Les Ballets 1933," that he moved in the direction of musical abstraction—most conspicuously in "Mozartiana." The first ballet he made in America

"Theme and Variations," created by Balanchine to music from Tchaikovsky's Third Suite, on commission from Ballet Theatre for Alicia Alonso and Igor Youskevitch. Scenery and costumes designed by Woodman Thompson

was "Serenade," completely innocent of either narrative or impersonation. Both these works, however, carried over an element of dramatic implication, so to speak, in which in certain sections the dancers were under the spell of some unspecific emotional situation which colored their movement. What was important to the choreographer was not the hypothetical situation but only this choreographic resultant, which paralleled what he read in the texture of the music, perhaps.

"Cotillon," which preceded "Mozartiana," hinted at this same process, for during the course of a debutante ball, things (never mind what) happened without tangible reference, producing quite tangible choreographic atmosphere. Later in "Ballet Imperial," a strictly abstract classic ballet, there was a "mimed" scene, in effect straight out of an old "imperial" ballet, in which there was no meaning to the gestures and no actual situation beneath them. Even more striking, however, is "Scotch Symphony," in which he has created virtually an entire story-ballet of the romantic period but with the story removed and only the beauty of design and flavor remaining. The result is certainly one of his loveliest creations.

In such ballets as "Symphony in C," however, he has moved all the way into musical abstraction, creating simply great classical divertissements, in a sense glorifications of the ballabile of the old ballet, in which soloists and corps used to perform quite irrelevantly to give the principals a chance to catch their breath. Some of his finest works fall into this category in a variety of textures and depths, from the brilliant Mozart "Divertimento No. 15" to the evocative "Concerto Barocco" (Bach).

When he carries the same approach into modern music, he achieves some extraordinary results. Chief among them, perhaps, are Stravinsky's "Agon" (created by both composer and choreographer under the suggestion of a medieval dance manual and its illustrations, and provided by both of them with excruciating difficulties — and wit!); "Ivesiana" (set to music of that adventurous American composer who was a full generation ahead of the European modern

Lew Christensen and Annabelle Lyon in Balanchine's "Orpheus" (Gluck-Tchelitchev) for the American Ballet; Nicholas Magallanes and Francisco Moncion in his "Orpheus" (Stravinsky-Noguchi) for New York City Ballet

George Platt Lynes   *George Platt Lynes*

Diana Adams, Allegra Kent, Jillana and Jacques d'Amboise in "Apollo," a revival by Balanchine for the New York City Ballet of his early and epoch-making neo-classic work in collaboration with Stravinsky

Balanchine's "Concerto Barocco," to Bach's double violin concerto. (Diana Adams and Tanaquil LeClercq)

musical movement); and "Episodes" (employing all the orchestral works of Anton von Webern, and by way of additional challenge, bringing in Martha Graham as a guest artist to choreograph the first half of the work).

In this field, though his basic idiom is still strictly that of the classic school, he observes its law frequently by violating its specific ordinances. The automatic reaction he produces, without emotional means or emotional intent, is a sharp one; and if audiences often laugh in the wrong places, they nevertheless stay with him all the way. He is outspoken in his opposition to the use of the dance as a means of "expression" — that is, merely as the channel for conveying something outside itself — but he is manifestly not against its being communicative and evocative in its own right.

He is innately experimental and generally surprising, though his early passion for novelty for its own sake has faded along with the Diaghileff influence of his youth. When he is praised for his inventiveness, he is likely to protest that he has never invented anything but has taken everything bodily from Petipa. In this semi-facetious half-truth there is a certain validity, for his line of descent from the elegant tradition of old St. Petersburg is straight and strong (as the first American visit of the Kirov Ballet from Leningrad in 1961 made perfectly. clear), but this does not in the least explain his individual talent.

He is a rapid and a fecund creator; his list is a long one, and, within the markedly personal limitations he has set for himself, a wide one. His inquisitiveness of mind and his alertness to the world around him have led to experiments with electronic music and so-called modern jazz, but almost bolder, perhaps, is his experiment with such an old warhorse as the Brahms "Liebes-lieder Walzer," on which he has made a lovely and nostalgic work. In the same conservative area he has done full-length productions of Tchaikovsky's "The Nutcracker" and Mendelssohn's "Midsummer Night's Dream," with both their casts overflowing with children — and attracting an equal flow of them to the theatre for extended annual seasons.

Similarly contrasting items from his extensive catalogue of masterpieces are the Stravinsky "Orpheus" and "Monumentum ad Gesualdo," the Brecht-Weill "Seven Deadly Sins" (first produced by his "Ballets 1933"), Prokofieff's "Prodigal Son" (first produced for Diaghileff), "Gounod Symphony," "Bourrée Fantasque" (Chabrier), "Four Temperaments" (Hindemith) and "La Valse" (Ravel).

He has also developed a galaxy of ballerinas that is hard to match. They include (in the alphabetical order which his programs wisely observe) Diana Adams, Melissa Hayden, Jillana, Allegra Kent, Patricia McBride, Violette Verdy and Patricia Wilde; and from earlier seasons, Maria Tallchief and Tanaquil LeClercq. There are also a dozen youngsters only waiting for an opportunity to step into that listing. His attitude to the dancer is an all-important one, for this is the instrument upon which he plays his particularized performance of the composer's music. He knows his dancers, indeed, as well as his scores, and in much the same way.

Whether he is doing with the future of the ballet in America what Kirstein had in mind when he inaugurated the project of school and company will not be known, of course, for another fifty years. What is already well established, however, is his outstanding mastery of the art and his individual re-orientation of it.

Roger Wood

Two Mozart ballets: "Symphonie Concertante" with Tanaquil LeClercq, Todd Bolender, Maria Tallchief and a large ensemble; and "Divertimento No. 15" with virtuoso roles for nine soloists — Barbara Walczak, Nicholas Magallanes, Diana Adams, Melissa Hayden, Jonathan Watts, Yvonne Mounsey, Roy Tobias and Barbara Milberg   *Fred Fehl*

Tanaquil LeClercq, Francisco Moncion in Balanchine's choreographic setting of Maurice Ravel's "La Valse"

Tanaquil LeClercq and Jerome Robbins in the lively "Bourrée Fantasque," to music of Emmanuel Chabrier

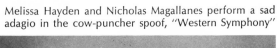

Melissa Hayden and Nicholas Magallanes perform a sad adagio in the cow-puncher spoof, "Western Symphony"

Tanaquil LeClercq in "Western Symphony," a leader of café society in Balanchine's blithe frontier epic

Maria Tallchief and André Eglevsky in Balanchine's somewhat unorthodox one-act version of "Swan Lake"

Other "Swan Lake" twosomes: Melissa Hayden and Jacques d'Amboise; Allegra Kent and Nicholas Magallanes

Balanchine's restaging of his "Seven Deadly Sins" with Kurt Weill's music, Bertolt Brecht's words, and designs by Rouben Ter-Arutunian. Allegra Kent, Lotte Lenya are the two Annas — one dancing, one singing

70

Fred Fehl

The first act of Balanchine's full-length revival of "The Nutcracker" for an annual Christmas season. Roy Tobias in the foreground, and, in this case, Balanchine himself at the right as the hearty old Drosselmayer

Francisco Moncion and Maria Tallchief in "Firebird"
George Platt Lynes

"Native Dancers" — Jacques d'Amboise, Patricia Wilde

"Gounod Symphony," created by Balanchine and dressed by Karinska to evoke the style of Gounod's own time

Edward Villella in "Prodigal Son," a late Balanchine work for Diaghileff, which remains fresh and vital

Balanchine's exquisite "Liebeslieder Walzer," set to the Brahms song cycles with far more than nostalgia

Arthur Mitchell and Diana Adams in "Agon," a witty, complex antique suite by Balanchine and Stravinsky

"Electronics," an experimental work to electronic music by Remi Gassmann, with Balanchine's choreographic style and David Hays' décor deriving from the quality of the score. (Diana Adams and Jacques d'Amboise)

Balanchine's full-length "A Midsummer Night's Dream" set to various music of Mendelssohn: Arthur Mitchell as Puck with the little fairies; Melissa Hayden as Titania and Roland Vazquez as the transformed Bottom

Fred Fehl   *Fred Fehl*

73

George Platt Lynes

Eugene Loring's imaginative "Billy the Kid," with score by Aaron Copland, produced by Lincoln Kirstein's little touring company, Ballet Caravan. (Loring himself shown here in the title role, kneeling center)

Walter E. Owen

Francisco Moncion and Melissa Hayden in the William Dollar ballet, "The Duel," for New York City Ballet

Martha Swope

Edward Villella, Violet Verdy in Lew Christensen's "Con Amore," in the New York City Ballet production

74

Lew Christensen's "Filling Station," with a score by Virgil Thomson, another topical American production by Ballet Caravan, afterwards revived for the New York City Ballet. (Christensen himself at the right)

Patricia Wilde, Frank Hobi in "Cakewalk," a minstrel ballet by Ruthanna Boris for New York City Ballet

Among Todd Bolender's hilarious "Souvenirs" are John Mandia and Irene Larssen making like silent movies

75

George Platt Lynes

Frederick Ashton's "Illuminations" (Rimbaud) set to Britten's song cycle. (Nicholas Magallanes, center)

Nicholas Magallanes and Nora Kaye in Jerome Robbins' "The Cage," shocker about mating habits of insects

George Platt Lynes

George Platt Lynes

Diana Adams and Jacques d'Amboise in Ashton's unusual fantasy on Tristram and Yseult, "Picnic at Tintagel"

Violet Verdy, Jacques d'Amboise and Melissa Hayden in Birgit Cullberg's "Medea" set to music of Bartók

Ballet Theatre

The founding of Ballet Theatre in 1940 was another important step in the development of the ballet in America, though the basic approach of its founder, Richard Pleasant, was altogether different from Kirstein's. Instead of wishing to transplant seed for the ultimate emergence of a ballet that should be American in character, it was his purpose to set up a producing organization which in its own field should be the equivalent of a museum of art. In it he wanted to give a place to already existing works representative of all periods and national origins, while simultaneously sponsoring the creation of new works from all contemporary sources. His initial scheme of activities included a classical wing, a Fokine-Diaghileff-Russian wing, and contemporary American, British, Negro and Spanish wings. Sooner or later he expected to extend his definition of ballet to include also productions by the American modern dancers. The preparations for the inaugural season were long and financially as expensive as such an enterprise must necessarily be if it is to be worthy of its ideals. The project was not taken too seriously by the cynics in advance, but to their surprise it established itself as a success, both artistically and popularly, overnight.

Unfortunately, as soon as its success had been demonstrated, it was besieged from both within and without by intriguers and self-seekers, and its foundations were seriously undermined. Pleasant's policy, which was the project's *raison d'être*, was repudiated by some of its financial sponsors, and he was forced to resign. The company was refashioned to conform to the prevailing pattern of the Ballet Russe, and its repertoire was even announced as "Russian Ballet" to cash in on the then profitable trend. Only the persistence of some of the personnel and the solid foundations laid in its beginnings kept it from disappearing as a major organization. Eventually, Lucia Chase, who had been the principal figure in its original financing, took over its direction, with the scenic designer, Oliver Smith, as co-director, and kept it alive by her indefatigable

Alfredo Valente

Antony Tudor's "Pillar of Fire": Nora Kaye with Hugh Laing; below, with Annabelle Lyon and Lucia Chase

Alfredo Valente

efforts at money-raising, though without any definite artistic policy. After several alterations of its name, it finally became the American Ballet Theatre.

In its memorable opening season it introduced the English Antony Tudor to American audiences, presented the first ballet by Agnes de Mille (a work for Negro dancers called "Black Ritual" to music of Milhaud), and made a notable experiment, though an unsuccessful one at the box-office, in combining speech with ballet. This was "The Great American Goof," for which William Saroyan wrote what he termed the "balletplay" and Eugene Loring designed the choreography. The music was by Henry Brant.

With one notable exception, de Mille has done virtually her entire repertoire in the ballet medium for this company over the years, including "Tally-Ho!," "Fall River Legend" and the finished version of "Three Virgins and a Devil," first done in a simpler form in London. The major exception is her most popular work, "Rodeo," which, though it has long been in the Ballet Theatre repertoire, was created for the Ballet Russe de Monte Carlo.

As a result of the success of "Rodeo," de Mille was engaged by the Theatre Guild to choreograph the Rodgers and Hammerstein musical comedy, "Oklahoma!," and in it she brought about a revolution in the Broadway musical. Not only were all her dances integrated into the action of the exceptionally good book, but besides this her ballet scene called "Laurie Makes up Her Mind" actually advanced the de-

Baron

The murder of Tybalt (Antony Tudor) by Romeo (Hugh Laing) in Tudor's "Romeo and Juliet," set to music of Frederick Delius with scenery and costumes designed by Eugene Berman in the production by Ballet Theatre

78

velopment of the play itself. This was virtually without precedent, and for years the so-called "psychological" ballet became an inevitable part of all musicals, no matter how far it may have fallen below the "Oklahoma!" standard. Naturally her success in the theatre took de Mille away from the ballet, except as an incidental creative indulgence.

There was not another step so radical in the Broadway musical until Jerome Robbins came along with "West Side Story," of which the entire production, including its story, was his own conception. He directed it, also, leaving the choreographic detail to an assistant. It was accordingly perhaps the most completely choreographic musical yet to be seen on Broadway. No matter what one's personal reaction may have

been to it as glibly social-conscious and shallow, it was theatrically fresh and potent. Robbins has continued to do his best work in the theatrical field, including non-musicals as well as musicals.

For many seasons, however, he has been Associate Artistic Director of the New York City Ballet, chosen by Balanchine because of the leanness and directness of his ballet style. He has also had a small company of his own, designed for European showings and very successful there, under the title of Ballets U.S.A. But it was with the Ballet Theatre that he made his choreographic debut with the lively and original "Fancy Free," and his first success as a performer was in a small role in de Mille's "Three Virgins."

Other native choreographic debutantes with the company were Michael Kidd, whose only

Alfredo Valente

Alicia Markova and Hugh Laing, for whom Tudor made his version of Shakespeare's "star-crossed lovers"

Larry Colwell

A group from Tudor's "Dark Elegies," a choreographic setting of the "Kindertotenlieder" of Gustav Mahler

79

Foto-Semo

Antony Tudor, Alicia Markova, Hugh Laing and Karen Conrad in "Jardin aux Lilas" for the Ballet Theatre

George Platt Lynes

Hugh Laing and Nora Kaye in the New York City Ballet production of "Jardin aux Lilas," freshly remounted

ballet was "On Stage," and Herbert Ross, who came into the fold with his "Caprichos" and followed with several others of shorter life. Both of them, however, have concentrated chiefly on Broadway and the "commercial" field.

The distinguished Swedish choreographer, Birgit Cullberg, presented both her "Lady from the Sea" and her "Eden — Pas de Deux" in their world premières for this company, and her staging of her already well-known "Miss Julie," for it was her first work in America. Other European artists have likewise restaged portions of their repertoires for the Ballet Theatre. Among the great names from the Diaghileff era, Fokine, Bolm, Massine, Nijinska and Balanchine all either created new works or revived old ones or both over the years, and the roster of contributors is a long one, of wide range in both time and quality.

In the department of performing, the story is a comparable one. It is of interest that both Nora Kaye and Alicia Alonso rose to stardom out of the corps de ballet, and two European artists also found here a place for notable growth: the British Alicia Markova, who spent the richest years of her career in this company, and the young Dane, Erik Bruhn, who here, on loan from the Royal Danish Ballet, attained by virtually unanimous consent the rank of the greatest male dancer of his time.

Maurice Seymour

Erik Bruhn and Addy Addor in a later casting of the original Ballet Theatre production of the same work

Alfredo Valente

Two glimpses of Tudor's witty fantasy, "Dim Lustre": Tudor himself with Nora Kaye; and Rosella Hightower

Antony Tudor and Neo-Romanticism

The most significant single artistic accomplishment to the company's credit, however, may well be the introduction to this country of Tudor, who became under its auspices one of the truly imposing figures in the contemporary ballet. More than any other choreographer, he has taken up the tradition of expressiveness in the ballet where Fokine left it and carried it forward into new dimensions. Where Fokine, following in the footsteps of Noverre, wanted to make the ballet an imitation of life, Tudor has turned it rather into an interpretation of life, probing below the surface of action into the psychological workings which lie at the bottom of it. In this he has much in common with the purposes, if not with the methods, of the modern dancers.

It was at the instigation of Agnes de Mille, who had worked with him in London, that he was invited by Pleasant to come to this country to participate as both dancer and choreographer in the Ballet Theatre project. To the repertory he brought four works originally created for various London companies: "Jardin aux Lilas," "Gala Performance," "Judgment of Paris," and "Dark Elegies." In 1942 he presented for the first time "Pillar of Fire," set to Schoenberg's "Verklaerte Nacht," which is generally considered to be his greatest work and which won immediate acclaim. It dealt, probably for the first time in the ballet's history, with sex as a psychological instead of a purely romantic subject, and may properly be considered as inaugurating a new era for the ballet as a medium for the expres-sion of penetrating insight into human experience.

It served also to reveal Nora Kaye, for whom the central role was created, as an outstanding actress-dancer. Though she has exhibited her notable gifts in the works of other choreographers, it was under Tudor's guidance that she assumed her place among the first artists of the contemporary ballet. She was by no means limited to the grim realism of "Pillar of Fire," for in his "Jardin aux Lilas" she was the thwarted romantic heroine, in his "Gala Performance" she was a broadly comic Russian ballerina, in his "Dim Lustre" she captured the very essence of his wit, and in his "Romeo and Juliet" she was able to follow Markova, for whom the role was created, with her own superb authority.

In Juliet, Markova found one of her finest roles. It gave her an opportunity to prove herself not only the mistress of the classic style which

Nana Gollner, Hugh Laing in Tudor's grim "Undertow," with a score especially composed by William Schuman
Alfredo Valente

Diana Adams, Hugh Laing and (in the background) Nora Kaye in Tudor's "Nimbus," music by Louis Gruenberg
Eileen Darby, Graphic House

Eugene Loring and Agnes de Mille in the latter's medieval lark, "Three Virgins and a Devil," set to the Respighi arrangements of antiques dances, first staged in London and later adapted for the Ballet Theatre

so many of her other roles, from her magnificent "Giselle" to her delicately travestied portrait of Taglioni in "Pas de Quatre," had proclaimed her, but also an actress of top rank. In all his ballets Tudor has been extraordinarily successful in bringing out qualities in individual dancers which perhaps they themselves have not been aware of, and which the conventional casting and the conventional repertoire would be unlikely to discover.

In "Undertow" he carried his delving into the recesses of the human mentality to even further depths; so much so, indeed, that he required a kind of psychoanalytical symbolism for his full expression. If this is a grim, somewhat obscure and unpleasant work, it is also a courageous and disturbing one. Here for the first time, incidentally, he employed music especially composed for his purpose instead of relying on already existing compositions. It was written on commission by William Schuman.

Of all his dancers, Hugh Laing proved the most indispensable. Having worked with him in

England and collaborated with him in founding the London Ballet Company in 1938, he also came to New York with him and danced the leading male roles in all his ballets here. Laing's dramatic powers were broad, intensely keyed and sensitive; among the male dancers of the ballet he was in a class apart. His quitting of the field for that of photography, was a distinct loss.

Tudor requires the strictest of academic techniques as the dancer's foundation, but in his compositions he distorts it at every turn to produce the total result he is after. He has used to the full the psychological effect, as well as the theatrical effect, of curious and involved acrobatic lifts, and his invention is rich and intuitive throughout the range of movement. He works slowly, is an out-and-out perfectionist, and makes the most stringent demands upon his dancers, both technically and emotionally.

Toward music he is unusually sensitive, not only to the outward form (against which he habitually composes phrases of movement in counterpoint rather than in rhythmic unison), but also to the inward spirit, which he never violates to the smallest degree. It is characteristic of his selection of music for his ballets that he manages to find works whose musical entity will not be strong enough to overbalance a choreographic setting. If it is not always music of the top rank as a result, it is nevertheless of suitable quality to make for unity in a total theatre work.

He makes no compromises with audiences and their possible likes and dislikes. He can be exceedingly cruel in mood, as in the tortured "Undertow," and he is not gentle in his caricature, as in the relentlessly sordid humors of "Judgment of Paris" and the pointed laughter at temperamental ballerinas in "Gala Performance." The sombreness of "Dark Elegies," set to the "Kindertotenlieder" of Mahler, is unrelieved, and he spares nothing of the emotional ordeal of the introverted heroine of "Pillar of Fire." There is naturally a section of the public that finds him too strong for pleasure, and the arch-classicists are, logically enough, not among his admirers.

Of recent seasons he has been unproductive, devoting his energies to teaching. It may well be that with the rise to favor of the classic, as opposed to the dramatic, ballet, his characteristic style is in eclipse, at least temporarily, but there is no denying his creative powers.

John E. Reed

Anton Dolin and Janet Reed in de Mille's "Tally-Ho!" which takes a look at the sex chase in old Versailles

A scene from the same work, perhaps less demure in substance than its Watteau-like milieu might suggest. (John Kriza, second from left; Muriel Bentley, center on floor; Lucia Chase, Dimitri Romanoff, right)

Baron

Maurice Seymour

Agnes de Mille in "Rodeo" to music of Aaron Copland, her first great success, presented by Ballet Russe

Hugelmeyer

Scene in de Mille's "Fall River Legend" with Alicia Alonso as Lizzie Borden, center, with Michael Maule

One of the ensemble dances created by Agnes de Mille for "Oklahoma!," the musical comedy by Rodgers and Hammerstein in which she instituted a revolution in the style and function of stage dancing on Broadway

Vandamm

Jerome Robbins' "Interplay," with Zachary Solov (seated left), Melissa Hayden and John Kriza (center)

William Dollar's "Jeux," set to the score of Debussy, with Nora Kaye, Igor Youskevitch and Norma Vance

Birgit Cullberg's "Lady from the Sea," on Ibsen's play. (Glen Tetley and Lupe Serrano, supported left)

André Kertész

Viola Essen, Eugene Loring in "Peter and the Wolf" by Adolph Bolm in the Ballet Theatre's first season

Hurrel

Jerome Robbins in "Fancy Free" with Donald Saddler, Muriel Bentley, John Kriza, Janet Reed, Harold Lang

John Kriza and Lupe Serrano in Dollar's "The Combat," presented by Ballet Theatre in décor by Wakhevitch

The servants' midsummer celebration in Birgit Cullberg's "Miss Julie," based on the Strindberg play. (Glen Tetley is the butler and Toni Lander Miss Julie in the production staged by Cullberg for Ballet Theatre)

Toni Lander and Scott Douglas in "Swan Lake"

Erik Bruhn and Lupe Serrano in "Don Quixote"

Alicia Alonso in the first act of "Giselle," in the Ballet Theatre production designed by Eugene Berman

Igor Youskevitch as Albrecht in "Giselle," in which, as Alonso's vis-à-vis, he achieved notable results

Alicia Markova in "Giselle," a role with which she is closely identified as one of its greatest exponents

Ruth Ann Koesun and John Kriza in "Caprichos," a set of Goya vignettes in theatre terms by Herbert Ross

Other American Developments

It is clear that, whatever the particular philosophy and the particular sources may be, a distinctly American approach to the ballet has begun to emerge over the years, not only on the creative side of the footlights but in the audience as well. No doubt some of this can be attributed to the fact that during the war years Europe's activities were sharply curtailed and many of its artists who were not actively involved in helping to prosecute the conflict found a field for their professional practices in this country. But besides this, a substantial background had been in the process of preparation for many years and by many individuals.

A hundred years before, there had been a great ballet flurry here, but it had failed to perpetuate itself, and it was not until after the first World War that new signs of life became evident. Russian artists who had been part of the group that had invaded western Europe with Diaghileff, settled in America from time to time and opened schools and companies, and others who had not been associated with that particular invasion did likewise. Among those who actually formed companies in one section of the country or another were Fokine, Bolm, Mikhail Mordkin, Alexander Gavrilov, Andreas Pavley and

Maurice Goldberg

Adolph Bolm in his own "Apollo Musagetes," première of Stravinsky's ballet, at the Library of Congress

"Minni" Photo

"Guns and Castanets," Ruth Page's choreographic adaptation of "Carmen," presented by the Federal Theatre

Maurice Seymour

"Frankie and Johnny," choreographed by Ruth Page and Bentley Stone to the old song, both words and music, with the choreographers themselves in leading roles

Serge Oukrainsky, and the Kosloff brothers. Not all their efforts prospered, but some of them did for longer or shorter times, and the larger number of schools that blossomed and flourished more or less dislodged the Italian tradition that had previously prevailed.

In the course of time there developed significant movements under the direction of native-born artists, among them notably Ruth Page in Chicago, Catherine Littlefield in Philadelphia and Willam Christensen in San Francisco.

Page has made Chicago the center but not the circumference of her activities. As a teenager she made a tour of South America with Pavlova and later joined the Diaghileff Ballet for a season. Off and on, indeed, she has danced virtually everywhere, including the Far East and the Soviet Union; with various partners, including Adolph Bolm and Harald Kreutzberg; in concert and on Broadway as well as in ballet companies.

Bolm was an important shaping force in her career. She was his pupil as a youngster and his leading dancer in all his Chicago activities, including the Chicago Opera, and in many of his touring projects, including his Ballet Intime.

"Minni" Photo

Larry Colwell

Frederic Franklin and Nikita Talinn in Ruth Page's "The Bells," a fantasia on themes from Poe's poem

Since she became a choreographer in her own right, which was in the middle '20s with the Chicago Allied Arts, she has been in and out of the Chicago Opera (what with its many re-organizations over the years), was long the choreographer for the Ravinia Opera in its annual summer season on Chicago's "North Shore," teamed up for several years with Bentley Stone to form the Page-Stone Ballet, choreographed for the Federal Theatre and for the Ballet Russe de Monte Carlo, and still finds time to produce in Paris occasionally. Her present company, called Ruth Page's Chicago Opera Ballet, was started in the middle '50s, and makes annual tours, with celebrated guest stars borrowed from various companies both here and abroad — Alicia Markova, Melissa Hayden, Marjorie Tallchief and George Skibine, Kirsten Simone and Henning Kronstam — and with equally celebrated designers to provide the scenery and costumes.

At one period she was intrigued with Americana and made ballets on "Frankie and Johnny," "Billy Sunday" and Poe's "The Bells." With her present company she occupies herself chiefly, but not exclusively, with adapting the scores and stories of well-known operas and operettas — "Il Trovatore," "Carmen," "La Traviata," "The Barber of Seville," "Die Fledermaus," "The Merry Widow." Her first venture into this field was a version of "Carmen" produced for the Federal Theatre in Chicago under the title of "Guns and Castanets."

She has always been open to fresh ideas and methods, whether as a concert dancer or the director of her own company, and her eager and unflagging enthusiasm has made a definite contribution to the ballet in this country.

Littlefield, beginning in the middle '30s, did admirable and outstanding spade work with both her school and her own ballet company in Philadelphia. The latter was known first as the Littlefield, and later as the Philadelphia Ballet. She was also director for several seasons of the Chicago Opera Ballet during one of its re-organ-

Kenneth Johnson and Sonia Arova in Ruth Page's "The Merry Widow," created for her Chicago Opera Ballet

Maurice Seymour

Sonia Arova as the young Azucena in Page's "Revenge" based on "Il Trovatore," with its story made clear

Maurice Seymour

izations, and made a marked impression there.

Her background, her tastes and her talents were perhaps equally catholic. She had studied in Paris with Egorova and danced in the Ziegfeld Follies, and she recognized the broad values of popular performing as well as the meticulous ones of classic tradition. The repertoire she produced contained, against a background of European tradition and insurgency, a number of works with American subjects and American music, covering a wide area — from "Café Society," set to Ferde Grofé's music, to "Barn Dance" of rural milieu, folk tunes and an innocent age. There were also "Ladies' Better Dresses," dealing with the contemporary garment industry, and "Terminal," set in a metropolitan railway station, both with scores by Herbert Kingsley. In other departments she made settings of Ravel's "Daphnis and Chloë" in lovely romantic style, and of Carlos Chavez's "HP," in modern Mexican mechanistic terms, with décor by Diego Rivera. There were "Prince Igor," too, and "The

Fairy Doll," and new works ranging through the music of Lully, Bach, Chopin, Johann Strauss, Franck, Saint-Saëns, Debussy, Satie and Poulenc. Perhaps her most ambitious undertaking was a full-scale production of the "Sleeping Beauty," which was the first such in America.

Out of her organization came many young dancers to provide strength for other burgeoning companies, notably the Ballet Theatre in its beginnings and the American Ballet of Kirstein and Balanchine. That she would have been an increasingly vital figure in the later growth of the ballet if she had not died at the height of her powers seems obvious, for she had a fine foundation, a fine performing sense, admirable teaching ability and a keen sense of the direction in which the art should move.

One of the most important figures to emerge from her school and company is Zachary Solov. Besides making a career for himself as a dancer with both the American Ballet and Ballet Theatre, as well as on Broadway and in televi-

Ruth Page's "Mephistophela," adapted from a ballet scenario by Heinrich Heine and with music from "Faust" scores by Berlioz, Boïto and Gounod. (Dolores Lipinski, Patricia Klekovic, Kenneth Johnson, Larry Long)

Catherine Littlefield's comic "Barn Dance" by her Philadelphia Ballet. (Dorothy Littlefield, center)

Catherine Littlefield and Alexis Dolinoff in a first American revival of Petipa's "The Sleeping Beauty"

sion, he helped to make history by a seven-year incumbency as choreographer at the Metropolitan Opera during which he managed to revivify the long moribund ballet there. The company he inherited consisted only of a corps de ballet without soloists, since its requirements during the opera season were minimal and the traditional opera public, which went solely to hear singers, sat through the incidental ballets with grim indifference. Solov immediately introduced distinguished soloists, sometimes on a seasonal basis and sometimes as guest artists — among them Alicia Markova, Melissa Hayden, Mia Slavenska, Janet Collins, Maria Karnilova, Mary Ellen Moylan, Carmen de Lavallade, Violette Verdy; and on several occasions he danced himself. In spite of the system of tenure that prevailed, he was able also at least to improve the quality of the corps.

Because of his excellent musicality, his inventiveness and his ability to work quickly, he replaced the old and moth-eaten ballets in the standard repertoire with smart and sometimes controversial new ones, keeping always in mind (as even Balanchine had not done during his seasons there with the American Ballet) that he must

Jerome Robbins' ballet on contemporary themes, "Events," created for his own company, Ballets: U.S.A.

not make them so alien in style as to embarrass the stodginess that characterized the presentations of many of the operas themselves.

Perhaps his greatest artistic triumph was his treatment of Gluck's "Orfeo," in which he had Markova as the Happy Spirit. Here he achieved a notable atmosphere of classic serenity which captured intuitively Gluck's half Greek and half eighteenth-century style. In sharp contrast was his "Aida" which he treated, especially in the Triumphal Scene, as a lusty, Verdian circus. With those other warhorses, the Dance of the Hours in "La Gioconda" and the Bacchanale in "Samson and Delilah," he made highly original innovations, especially in the former which he transformed into a characteristic Renaissance court ballet centered about a duel between the Queen of Night and the Sun King. His "Manon" was equally a gem of period style; his handling of the first act of "Rigoletto" provided an unprecedented texture of dancing against which all the action was played; and he came up with a charming little Scottish dance in "Lucia," in which few people ever realized there was any ballet at all. His Walpurgisnacht scene in "Faust," even

Robbins' "N. Y. Export, Opus Jazz," also made for his own company. (Bob Bakanic, Tom Abbott, Jay Norman)

95

Shilkret

Zachary Solov and Irina Borowska in his "Orpheus"

Alexandra Danilova, Roland Vazquez in "Mlle. Fifi," which Solov shaped deftly to the ballerina's gifts

John Lindquist

though the customary ballet music had been excised (wisely enough) by the director, emerged as a superbly fantastic overtone to the action; in "Eugene Onegin" he evoked the rich tapestry of Pushkin's poem with sensitive brilliance, from the peasant dances, through the lively and busy family party, to the courtly polonaise; and so on through the entire repertoire, thanks to a lively gift for theatrical invention and an innate sense of style.

He also produced two independent ballets, "Vittorio" and "Soirée," which were less successful and overtaxed the company at his disposal. But his tenure as choreographer set an eye-opening precedent for the Met. Unfortunately after his departure the opera ballet slumped to an unprecedentedly low level, but at least he had demonstrated the potentialities of the field.

The built-in frustrations, artistic and political, of opera-house ballet, however, led him eventually to withdraw for other activities, including the formation of a small company of his own, the Zachary Solov Ballet Ensemble, which makes occasional tours. The most distinguished work he has created for it thus far is his "Orpheus," based on his choreographic setting of the opera, in which he dances the title role. He also occupies himself with musical comedy choreography from time to time.

Another successful touring company, older and somewhat larger, is the Robert Joffrey Ballet, which employs a repertoire of both old and new ballets by various choreographers. Joffrey's approach to the project is quite different from that of most touring companies, for the heart and soul of the enterprise are to be found in the allied school, called the American Ballet Center, also under his direction. This has made a name for itself as one of the best institutions in the field, and from it the company is largely drawn.

Since most of the truly great companies of the world have proven this to be the only sound method for creating a company of style and substance, Joffrey has precedent all on his side. It is a slow method, to be sure, but an excellent start has been made; the performances even at this

Solov's ballet in the Metropolitan Opera Company's production of Massenet's opera, "Manon"

Solov's ballet, "Vittorio," created for the opera ballet to music of Verdi, designed by Estéban Francés

Robert Joffrey's "Pas des Déesses," an evocation of a divertissement by Taglioni, Grahn, Grisi, St. Léon

Jonathan Watts and Beatrice Tompkins in the Joffrey ballet, "Bal Masqué," to music of Francis Poulenc

stage of progress meet a standard that requires no apologies, and since Joffrey is held in high respect, the future looks definitely hopeful. He has already made a successful tour of Southern Europe and Southeast Asia under the auspices of the United States State Department.

The San Francisco Ballet, now under the direction of Lew Christensen, has Kirstein as its artistic director, and thus enjoys at least an informal affiliation with the New York City Ballet, with which it frequently exchanges dancers and repertoire. Christensen was an early member of the American Ballet, of which he became leading male dancer. He was also both a dancer and one of the choreographers in Kirstein's little touring Ballet Caravan, which confined itself to presenting new works by young native choreographers. For this he created the cartoon ballet, "Filling Station," which was later revived by the New York City Ballet with Janet Reed (herself a prod-

uct of the San Francisco company) in its chief role. From the same source the New York company has transplanted one of its leading classic dancers, Conrad Ludlow, and another highly amusing Christensen ballet, "Con Amore."

In its earlier years, the company was something of a pioneer in the modern production of full-length ballets, including "Swan Lake," and it still presents a full-length "Nutcracker" as an annual Christmas feature. It has also toured South America under the auspices of the State Department.

Other companies continue to be formed with headquarters in various cities from which they make tours as occasion offers. In Washington, besides the long-established Washington Ballet of which Mary Day is director, a new National Ballet Company made its debut under the direction of Frederic Franklin in January 1963.

Canada has made admirable progress of recent years with companies of its own. It now has three representative organizations functioning both at home and on tour. They are the National Ballet of Canada, directed by Celia Franca, with headquarters in Toronto; the Royal Winnipeg Ballet, founded some years ago by Gweneth Lloyd and Betty Farrally, and now directed by Arnold Spohr, located in Winnipeg; and Les Grands Ballets Canadiens in Montreal under the direction of Ludmilla Chiriaeff.

Significantly enough, none of these organizations limits itself in any degree to native subjects for its repertoire, though all of them employ such subjects from time to time as inspiration dictates. It is a mistake to assume, as has so often been done in the American field, that the mere making of ballets on American themes constitutes the basis of an American ballet. Massine once made a ballet called "Union Pacific," but it

was far less American in quality than, for example, Agnes de Mille's "Three Virgins and a Devil," which has a medieval theme, Italian music and English scenario, scenery and costumes. It is the American mind and the American body (which is quite different from the European body) that constitutes the native element, and this manifests itself less in its choice of subject than in its attitude to movement and its method of composition.

Naturally the so-called modern dance has had considerable influence in these latter departments. It is a native American development to begin with, and its persuasiveness, especially in the use of the body, has been potent in the local ballet field.

Somewhere to be classified in this field where American influences have colored the academic ballet is the lone and virtually unclassifi-

Rehearsal shot of Lisa Bradley and Nels Jorgensen in Joffrey's "Gamelan," built on Lou Harrison's music
Martha Swope

Roderick Drew, Sally Bailey and Michael Smuin in Lew Christensen's "Original Sin" (San Francisco Ballet)

99

Leslee Gearhart and Robert Davis, leading dancers of the Washington Ballet, under direction of Mary Day

able figure of Paul Draper. He is actually a tap dancer, but a tap dancer with a difference, for like some early Renaissance dancing master, he has subjected this age-old peasant form to the refinements of courtliness. In his case it is the academic ballet that has colored the American manifestation, rather than the other way round. Upon the fundamental rhythmic tapping of the feet on the floor he has superimposed the carriage of the body, the "turn-out," the *port de bras,* of the classic ballet technique, together with adaptations of many of its standard steps and combinations.

In effect he has transformed the body into an additional musical instrument (possessed also with related visual values) upon which to play variations and counterpoints to the compositions of both classic and popular musicians. The nearest precedent to be seen is the Spanish dance, in which the beating of the heels on the floor, the snapping of the fingers and the playing of the castanets provide similar musical additions. In the beating of the floor, however, Draper's emphasis contradicts that of the Spanish dancer. The latter's accent is down, chiefly with the heels, underlining the force of gravity and earth; Draper, following rather the precedent of the ballet, brushes the floor as lightly as possible,

National Ballet, Washington — Andrea Vohdenal, Eugene Collins in Frederic Franklin's "Hommage à Ballet"

Jim Mahan

chiefly with the toes, with the emphasis upward and aerial, denying gravity.

The musical territory he covers is a vast one. Though at first he shocked the conservatives by tapping to Bach, his musicality and his creative artistry soon banished any suggestion of sacrilege, and there is no area of "serious" music that he has not laid under successful aesthetic siege. At the other extreme, he is a superbly objective revealer of the form and substance of many jazz and "popular" pieces that have generally not been suspected of possessing any. Folk tunes, show tunes (including of course that *sine qua non* of tap dancing, "Tea for Two"), submit with equal grace to his elegant *claquerie*. In concert hall or night club he is equally an artist.

One of his finest (and most musical) compositions is an unaccompanied sonata. A regular feature of his program is a grand finale in which he and his pianist (necessarily a top-notch one) improvise a medley to titles called out by the audience, and ranging mercilessly from the "Liebestod" to "Yes, We Have No Bananas."

If there is nobody else who can begin to approach his art, he has nevertheless had a wide effect on the field and has certainly elevated tap dancing to a level it has never even aspired to before.

Margaret Mercier and girls in classic ballet by Eric Hyrst for Les Grands Ballets Canadiens of Montreal

Brian Macdonald's "The Darkling" (music by Benjamin Butler) performed by Canada's Royal Winnipeg Ballet

Campbell and Chipman

Lois Smith and David Adams and corps de ballet in the second act of "Swan Lake," as staged by Celia Franca for the National Ballet of Canada, which has its headquarters and a full-time training school in Toronto

Paul Draper, who has elevated tap dancing into a fine art as much at home with Bach as with boogie

Europe after Diaghileff

In Europe, after the death of Diaghileff, no figure arose to dominate the field as he had done. The personnel and the ideas that survived him were dispersed among several rapidly shifting organizations, differing chiefly in business and financial arrangements and not at all in artistic principles. They employed the same dancers and choreographers as far as possible, claimed Monte Carlo as their headquarters at one time or another, sued each other in the courts over rights to works which belonged equally well in any of their repertoires, and in general were indistinguishable from each other in creative aims. There is no point, then, in considering the organizational differences that divided the post-Diaghileff Ballet Russe into such separate bodies as the Ballets de Monte Carlo, Ballet Russe de Monte Carlo, Col. W. de Basil's Ballets Russes de Monte Carlo, Original Ballet Russe, and so forth. The only survivor was the Ballet Russe de Monte Carlo, directed by Sergei J. Denham, which took refuge in America during World War II, made its legal and official home in New York, in spite of its title, and dominated the American field during the war years.

It is evident, however, that the Ballet Russe, as such — that European adaptation and watering down *à la Riviera* of the great Russian tradition, which began with Diaghileff after World War I — ceased to function as an influence with World War II.

Almost immediately following Diaghileff's death, Serge Lifar, his last *protégé*, was invited to become director of the ballet of the Paris Opéra. There he introduced an *avant-garde* attitude which he had acquired as a matter of course from Diaghileff into a company that had become lethargic and dull, and during his incumbency of roughly thirty years, he succeeded in enlivening the repertoire and keeping the activities of the organization spirited and controversial, whatever the result may have been in artistic progress. This he was able to do without being himself in any way an outstanding choreographer, since it is the tradition of the French public to value spectacle,

Maurice Seymour

David Lichine, Tatiana Riabouchinska in "Graduation Ball," created by Lichine for Original Ballet Russe

103

Mia Slavenska in "Swan Lake": As Odile in the "Black Swan" pas de deux, presented separately by the Ballet Russe de Monte Carlo; as Odette (with Michel Panaieff) in its earlier production of the second act alone

scenery and costumes more highly than choreography. From time to time other choreographers have made additions to the repertoire, including both national and international figures. There have been frequent changes in the company's top directorship, largely as the result of the politics, both internal and external, to which any government-operated institution of the sort is subject, and Lifar has been in and out on several occasions. Nobody else, apparently, has thus far been able to rival him in the handling of the extremely devious assignment.

A younger generation of choreographers has grown up of recent years in Paris, full of new and individual ideas. They are the product of revolt partly against Lifar and partly against the ponderous workings of the Opéra itself. Talented young dancers have rebelled and disappeared from the picture, small companies have come and gone; but perhaps the three most influential figures who have emerged are Roland Petit, Janine Charrat and Maurice Béjart.

Petit's greatest success was his choreograph-

ic version of "Carmen" with the engaging and gifted Renée Jeanmaire in the title role. He has also created ballets for both the British and the Danish Royal Ballets, but his style is nearer to that of the revue and the music hall than of the classic ballet. Perhaps for that reason his "Croqueuse de Diamants," which includes songs, is his most consistently satisfactory work.

Charrat is a genuinely fine creator, with imagination, style and emotional conviction. Her originality has worked against her in a measure with the Paris public, though she has built up a substantial following notwithstanding. Perhaps her most ambitious work was the full-length "Abraxas," created for the Städtische Oper in West Berlin to music of Werner Egk, but she has produced many shorter works of distinction for her own and other companies. Until she suffered an almost fatal accident by fire in 1960, she was also a dancer of notable artistry, able to bring to her own ballets an authenticity of style and conviction that no other dancer could match. Only in 1963 did she begin to dance again.

Serge Lifar in "Icare," presented at the Paris Opéra in 1935, embodying aesthetic principles enunciated in his "Manifeste du Chorégraphe," issued simultaneously, advocating use of percussion accompaniment alone

Serge Lifar in "Giselle" at the Paris Opéra

Yvette Chuviré in "La Dame aux Camélias"

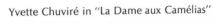

Béjart is out-and-out *avant-garde*. In music he employs novelties up to and including *musique concrète;* in scenery he explores space and design with unlimited daring; in movement he utilizes not only the academic technique but also modern dance ingredients and all sorts of acrobatic and unorthodox inventions. He has toured widely with a company of his own, and in 1962 was invited to Brussels, along with his newly organized Ballet of the Twentieth Century, to become director of a large and permanent ballet project at the nationally subsidized Theâtre Royale de la Monnaie.

Bernand; French Cultural Services

Scene from the Tatiana Gsovsky production of "La Dame aux Camélias" at the Paris Opéra, to the music of Henri Sauguet, with décors by Jacques Dupont. Yvette Chauviré in title role and George Skibine as Armand

"Romeo and Juliet" at the Paris Opéra, employing the score of Sergei Prokofiev and the scenario of Leonid Lavrovsky, with choreography and staging by Serge Lifar, and scenery and costumes by George Wakhevitch

Bernand; French Cultural Services

Bernand; French Cultural Services

Tamara Toumanova and Serge Lifar in "L'Inconnu," telling of two soldiers and their respective fates — love and death

Lycette Darsonval, Michel Renaud in Albert Aveline's "La Grande Jatte" (Music, Fred Barlou) at the Opéra

Bernand; French Cultural Services

Christine Vaussard and Roger Ritz in the Balanchine "Palais de Cristal," first draft of his "Symphony in C"

Bernand; French Cultural Services

The death of Marguerite, a scene from "Abraxas," full-length dramatic ballet on the Faust story created musically by Werner Egk and staged and choreographed by Janine Charrat for the Städtische Oper, Berlin

Janine Charrat and Peter Van Dijk in "Les Algues"

Dick Sanders and Claire Sombert in "L'Emprise"

Renée Jeanmaire in Roland Petit's ballet, "Carmen"   Janine Charrat (top figure) in "Légende de Licorne"

Entrance of Escamilo, here treated as a foppish matinée idol, in final scene of Roland Petit's "Carmen," created for Les Ballets de Paris to excerpts from Bizet's opera; scenery and costumes by Antoni Clavé

"Contrepointe," Roland Petit's jazz abstraction set to Marius Constant's music for the Ballets de Paris

Elsa Marianne von Rosen, the original "Miss Julie" in Birgit Cullberg's work for Royal Swedish Ballet

"The Prisoner of the Caucasus," the Soviet ballet based on Pushkin's poem with music by Boris Asafiev, in new version created by George Skibine for the Grand Ballet du Marquis de Cuevas. (Skibine himself, right)

Gisela Deege, Gert Reinholm in Stravinsky's "Apollo" staged by Tatiana Gsovsky, Städtische Oper, Berlin

Kaj Selling and Mariane Orlando, top ranking artists in the casts of the Royal Swedish Ballet, Stockholm

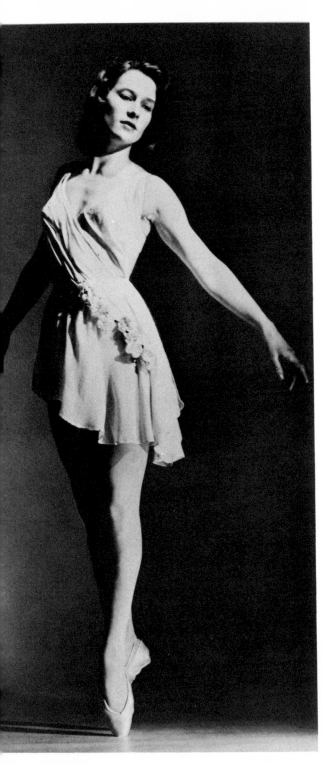

Doris Laine of the National Ballet Theatre, Finland

Kari Karnakovski, Viola Essen and Francisco Moncion in Edward Caton's "Sebastian" for de Cuevas Ballet

Scenes from two ballets by Ana Ricarda for the Grand Ballet du Marquis de Cuevas: "Dona Ines de Castro," with Rosella Hightower and George Skibine; and "Del Amor y de la Muerte" (Ricarda herself and Skibine)

Toni Lander, Danish ballerina, also of Paris Opéra, London Festival Ballet and American Ballet Theatre

The Berlioz opera, "Roméo et Juliette," produced by the Grand Ballet du Marquis de Cuevas in courtyard of the Louvre with complete ballet company and a different choreographer for each act in addition to singers

Bernand

Marjorie Tallchief and George Skibine in title roles of
the de Cuevas "Roméo et Juliette" at the Louvre

Georgette Bavoillot

Rosella Hightower in the title role of her ballet on
"Salomé," created for the Grand Ballet of de Cuevas

British Royal Ballet

The dissolution of the Diaghileff ballet left London adrift, as it were. Britain had never had an official ballet of its own, but had always provided an enthusiastic public for visiting companies, and for twenty years had depended largely upon Diaghileff. Immediately after his death it determined to change this situation, and accordingly established the Camargo Society to arrange an annual series, making use of what native material there was at hand together with guest artists invited from elsewhere. In practice the project disclosed that the native material — or at least the resident material — was stronger than had been anticipated, and could serve as the foundation of a more permanent organization.

This resident material was drawn chiefly from two specific sources: the somewhat tentative producing activities of Marie Rambert and Ninette Valois, centering around their respective schools. Both of them had been associated with Diaghileff for varying periods.

Rambert had been engaged as a teacher of Dalcroze Eurythmics to help Nijinsky with the difficult music of "Le Sacre du Printemps" in 1912, and under this influence had herself turned to the classic ballet. Later in her London studio she had set up the Ballet Club, where she presented ballets with her pupils.

Eventually this was to grow into the Ballet Rambert, which continues to make extensive tours of Britain and elsewhere. It was from the first Rambert's especial genius to discover and develop new talents in both the performing and the choreographic fields. Out of the Rambert ranks have come some of the most distinguished figures in the British ballet, including both Frederick Ashton and Antony Tudor in their choreographic debuts, and scores of dancers. She has continued to foster young talent, and in Norman Morrice has found her latest choreographer of parts.

De Valois had been a dancer with Diaghileff for two seasons only, when she decided to establish a school of her own in London with the idea

"Les Patineurs," Frederick Ashton's popular ballet, set to various music of Meyerbeer, shown here in the décor and costumes designed by William Chappell for original production by Vic-Wells Ballet in 1937

J. W. Debenham

"Horoscope," distinguished Ashton ballet (music, Constant Lambert; designs, Sophie Fedorovitch), no longer producible because of wartime destruction of only score. (Michael Somes and Margot Fonteyn, center)

of creating a performing company ultimately. How well she succeeded is one of the remarkable achievements of ballet history, for just thirty years later, in 1956, that hypothetical company had become the Royal Ballet, chartered by Queen Elizabeth II, the first such institution in the country's annals.

The first step in this unforeseen direction was taken when Lilian Baylis, director of the Old Vic and Sadler's Wells Theatres, invited de Valois to install some incidental ballet features in both these virtually (but not quite) national homes of drama and opera. From this small group of occasional dancers grew a company known as the Vic-Wells Ballet; but soon the Old Vic was dropped from the schedule and the company became the Sadler's Wells Ballet, with the latter theatre as its center. Here it made a great name for itself, producing not only new and small ballets, but eventually a full-length "Swan Lake" (or "Lac des Cygnes," as London calls it). Heading the company were Alicia Markova and Anton

Dolin, both English in spite of the Russian names given them when they joined the Diaghileff company as youngsters. In 1935 they departed to form their own Markova-Dolin Ballet, and their places were taken by the young Margot Fonteyn and Robert Helpmann. Fonteyn has remained with the company ever since to become one of the greatest ballerinas of modern times.

During World War II, the Sadler's Wells Theatre was bombed out, but the company moved into central London and gave nightly performances with fine courage (and incidentally to packed houses) throughout the city's siege. De Valois has said that it was this that gave them the prestige and the affection that led to their later establishment at the Royal Opera House, Covent Garden, and ultimately the royal charter.

But things besides prestige and affection were involved in the rise of the organization. One was de Valois' genius for organization, another was the high calibre of the dancers she was able to produce, and still another was the presence, almost from the start, of Ashton as choreographer-in-chief. Eventually he was to succeed to the directorship of the company upon de Valois' retirement at the end of 1963.

Ashton has proved himself to be one of the few great choreographers of our time. He is a meticulous craftsman, with a sensitive musical approach, a fine eye for stage design, a keen sense of comedy, both high and low, and superb feeling for the theatre. He composes admirably for the individual dancer, and has played a large part in the development of both of Britain's leading ballerinas, Markova and Fonteyn, as well as many other leading artists, past and present, of the Royal Ballet.

His scope is exceptionally broad. He has produced with equal authority musical abstractions ranging from "Symphonic Variations" (Franck) to "Scènes de Ballet" (Stravinsky), and including the brilliant coronation ballet, "Homage to the Queen" and the even more brilliant "Birthday Offering," created in celebration of the ballet company's twenty-fifth anniversary; witty trifles such as the Gertrude Stein "Wedding Bouquet" and the apparently immortal "Façade;" and tragic story-ballets such as the full-length "Romeo and Juliet" (Prokofieff) for the Royal Danish Ballet, the daring "Tiresias" for his own company, and for the New York City Ballet one of his most adventurous works, "Illuminations." He has also re-created in his own terms some "lost" ballets of other days; for example, the Delibes "Sylvia" in a ravishing production, and the much older "La Fille Mal Gardée," in a hilarious one, with even its long forgotten original score reassembled and adapted to contemporary usage. His original treatment of another ballet with at least an old theme, "Ondine," supplied with a strikingly modern score, and startlingly set and costumed in the epoch of Lady Hamilton, must rank among his masterpieces, though the conservative British public found it difficult to accept, apart from the magnificent performance it made possible by Fonteyn.

But acceptance or no acceptance, of the choreographers now creatively active, there is only Balanchine to be named in the same breath with him for sheer artistry and accomplishment.

Margot Fonteyn and Michael Somes in Ashton's "Dante Sonata," to Liszt music, "after a reading of Dante"

Moira Shearer and Ashton in "Façade," set to William Walton music first meant for Edith Sitwell readings

Margot Fonteyn as "Ondine" in the Shadow Dance in Ashton's original ballet on de la Motte Fouqué poem

Pamela May, Michael Somes, Margot Fonteyn and Moira Shearer in Ashton's "Symphonic Variations" (Franck)

Ashton's re-creation, necessarily in his own terms, of that ancient, long-abused classic, "La Fille Mal Gardée," with even its original score exhumed for present-day use. (David Blair, Nadia Nerina, center)

"Prince of the Pagodas," first all-British full-length ballet, produced by Royal Ballet with choreography by John Cranko, special score by Benjamin Britten; scenery by John Piper and costumes by Desmond Heeley

Svetlana Beriosova and Donald Macleary in Stravinsky cantata, "Persephone," produced by Frederick Ashton

Ashton's "Birthday Offering" (Nadia Nerina, Phillip Chatfield) on twenty-fifth Royal Ballet anniversary

Michael Somes, June Brae, Richard Ellis in Ninette de Valois' "Checkmate," in décor by McKnight Kauffer

De Valois' "The Rake's Progress" with designs by Rex Whistler, and Alicia Markova in her original role

Margot Fonteyn in the second act of "Giselle"

120

Margot Fonteyn and Michael Somes in grand pas de deux from "The Sleeping Beauty," in the new production with which the Sadler's Wells Ballet began its tenure at the Royal Opera House, Covent Garden, in 1946

"Bluebird" pas de deux — Rowena Jackson, Brian Shaw   Frederick Ashton as the malevolent fairy, Carabosse

The New Russian Era

The heightened international awareness that has arisen since World War II has led many countries on all the continents to participate in a general cultural exchange, including the sending of dance companies of every sort—classic, modern, ethnological, theatrical, ritual — on extended foreign tours, generally under government auspices. In the ballet field this has given the Western World an opportunity to see what was going on with the great Russian ballet tradition during the years when it operated behind the Soviet Union's "iron curtain." It has also allowed the Soviet Union to see the work of the Western World in the field of dancing.

When, after the death of Stalin, the country opened its doors to tourism, it became evident to the visitor from the West that that great tradition had not only survived but also grown in certain respects. During the forty years when the Soviet arts had all been cut off from outside contacts, they had perforce stewed in their own juices, as it were. The creative aspect and the entire theatrical department of the ballet — scenery, costumes, plots, music — had failed signally to progress.

This was inevitable, for the established formula is a sterile one, and because of strict official restrictions no new and rebellious choreographers (if, indeed, any such exist) have been allowed to violate its essential pattern, which is primarily a literary one. A ballet that has no specific objective theme (though not necessarily political in nature) is considered to be no ballet at all. "Abstraction" is the term of scornful derogation applied to any work of art that is not at least capable of being a vehicle of "socialist realism."

Thus the prevailing form is to all intents and purposes an exact carry-over from the late nineteenth century. In the Bolshoi Theatre in Moscow and the Kirov in Leningrad, as well as in the many companies throughout the country as a whole, the repertory is made up of long, scenically spectacular, full-evening ballets on dramatic subjects, danced by huge casts, and con-

122

Galina Ulanova in a light-hearted mood in "Giselle" (Act 1), which is one of her most celebrated roles

Galina Ulanova, with Yuri Kondratov, her partner in concert appearances at the Florence Festival, 1951

Foto Levi

sisting predominantly of miming (though not of the pre-Fokine sign-language type), with the actual dancing confined to two sorts of interruptions, so to speak. One is extensive folk-dance interludes justified somehow by the background of the story, and the other is periodic bursts of virtuosity by the principals — solos, pas de deux, small and large ensembles, couched in the academic idiom, but with the accent on acrobatics rather than choreographic composition. For these, also, justification is furnished by the plot, to be sure, and more particularly by the dramatic powers of the individual dancers, which are usually very great.

During the long period of isolation from the rest of the world, however, if no progress was made in the artistry of the ballet form, the dancing itself enjoyed a development equaled nowhere else. This is a purely technical field which involves nothing politically controversial, and accordingly it seems to have been the area of the art in which the urge to progress found its greatest concentration. If the taste of the accomplish-

Galina Ulanova and Yuri Zhdanov, "Romeo and Juliet," staged by Leonid Lavrovsky to the Prokofiev score

The court dances which open the ballroom scene in the Bolshoi Ballet's production of the Prokofiev "Romeo and Juliet," with scenery and costumes designed by Peter Williams. (Alexander Radunsky, Capulet, center)

Maya Plisetskaya as Odile and Nicolai Fadeyechev in the grand pas de deux ("Black Swan") in "Swan Lake"

Maya Plisetskaya as the gentle Odette, the enchanted princess-into-swan of the first act of "Swan Lake"

ment in this area may not always seem compatible with western ideas, its strength, its virtuosity, its range, its resourcefulness, its sheer performing possibilities constitute something of a revelation of what the human body can be made to accomplish. And since the Slavic dancers may well be the most exciting performers, as such, in the world, they have been well suited to just such a development as this. By contrast, the technical practices of the western ballet, by and large, seem weak and anaemic and perhaps constitutionally incapable of supporting anything more exacting than the one-act ballets of which the repertoire has consisted so predominantly since the day of Diaghileff.

Until very recently, such short works in the Soviet Union have been reserved exclusively for "benefit performances," banquets, and so forth. Since the reopening of contact with the West, however, the short ballet has begun to find its way into use, chiefly, it is maintained, as a medium for developing the young choreographer who is not yet strong enough to create in the formidable dimensions of the established form.

This reopening of contact must inevitably produce other and more fundamental changes on both sides of the "iron curtain." On the western side there has already been a notable increase in technical scope, since the first visit of the Bolshoi Ballet to Europe and America in 1957.

On the eastern side of the curtain, the most revolutionary event was the tour of the Soviet Union by the New York City Ballet in 1962. Its largely storyless and sceneryless ballets, its concentrated elegance of technique, its musicality, its emphasis on form and ensemble composition, and even its "abstractness" made a deep impression, not only on the public but also on members and directors of the state-controlled companies and schools themselves. It was a revelation of new dimensions for their art, which the highly intelligent artists were quick to react to.

Other western companies have visited the country, to be sure, but none of them has had any comparable effect, since none of them has brought in any striking departure from conventional ballet practice. Actually, though the Soviet public is naturally not aware of it, Balanchine's art with its passion for stripping everything down to essentials is considered radical and "precious" by much of the western world. The Soviet Union, however, is more vulnerable than the West is to its unorthodox approach, for there is throughout the country a strong suspicion among the people that they have been cut off from world progress during their long years of isolation and they are accordingly eager to catch up with the most forward-looking thinking. The ideological face-saving that will be necessary to bring about any changes of approach along these new artistic lines is considerable, but the pressure from the freshly awakened convictions of the artists can scarcely fail to produce major adjustments, unless a stern official hand is laid upon them.

The divergence in characteristic style by the two chief Soviet companies still exists, as it has long done, with the elegance and tradition of classic dancing carried down in the direct international line in Leningrad, while the Moscow company's stress is laid rather on native vigor and dramatic forcefulness.

Actually Moscow was already an old city and had long been the capital when Peter the Great built St. Petersburg from the ground up after the model of the culture of the West, and transferred the court there. Naturally the ballet developed there according to the courtly tradition in which it had been born.

Moscow, however, as the local Soviet writers now proudly proclaim, started its ballet beyond the reach of court interference, and directed it accordingly to the tastes of a more democratic audience. Its beginnings date from 1773, when Filippo Beccari, formerly a dancer in St. Peters-

Maya Plisetskaya in "Laurencia," ballet by Vakhtang Chabukiani based on Lope de Vega's "Fuente Ovejuna"

Raissa Struchkova in the title role of "Zapushka" (or "Cinderella," as we know it) to Prokofiev's music

Raissa Struchkova and Alexander Lapauri in "Valse"

burg, undertook to train the students in the Moscow Orphanage into a ballet company. So well did he progress that three years later performances began to be given regularly at the Orphanage, and when the Petrovsky Theatre was later established (on the site of the present Bolshoi), the Orphanage still supplied most of the personnel. The style of the Bolshoi company, therefore, is perhaps inherently more Russian, more popular. In the early twentieth century it came strongly under the influence of the dramatic teachings of Konstantin Stanislavsky, director of the famous Moscow Art Theatre, and became also more basically dramatic.

The paths of the two companies were nevertheless parallel however far apart. When Fokine was proposing his great reforms in the Maryinsky Theatre in St. Petersburg, Alexander Gorsky was transforming the Bolshoi company in Moscow along the realistic lines derived from Stanislavsky. After the "October" Revolution of 1917, both companies experienced something of the same *avant-garde* struggles, in St. Petersburg (or rather Leningrad as it was at this time) under the leadership of Feodor Lopukhov, and in Moscow under that of Kasyan Goleizovsky. Experimentation was the byword, academic precedents were

Olga Lepeshinskaya as Kitri, the stellar role in the Petipa-Minkus "Don Quixote," in spite of its title

Marina Kondratieva in the Bolshoi Ballet's "Gayane"

cast aside, in what was a bright new world. All the new art movements then prevalent in the West were tried out, bare feet and general nudity replaced the traditional dresses, and there was an upsurge of aesthetic radicalism. It was short-lived, however, and soon the classic tradition was re-instated, though now with a difference, since it was viewed through fresh eyes. The new direction was crystallized on the tenth anniversary of the Revolution with the production of "The Red Poppy," which is generally considered to be the first "Soviet" ballet. It dealt for the first time with a contemporary subject and with communist doctrine. In spite of its now recognized naïveté, it still remains in the repertoire and is performed occasionally, more as a historical landmark than as a valid work of art.

Other politically oriented ballets followed in profusion, until the practice became an accepted one, no doubt because of its giving justification to the existence of the ballet as an instrument of "socialist realism," at a time when such justification might well have determined the continuation or abolition of the medium on grounds of relevance to the new society. The doctrinaire element still persists in large measure, though with diminishing emphasis and life-or-

127

Antagonists in Bolshoi's "The Stone Flower": Nina Timofeyeva, the mountain witch, pursues unwilling hero, Vladimir Vasiliev, and a wicked bailiff, Vladimir Levashev, molests innocent heroine, Ekaterina Maximova

death importance. At the same time, the old repertoire has been kept admirably alive, with the steady restoration, restaging, polishing up, of numerous ballets from the last century, including many of Petipa's, which exist nowhere else in the world, even though Gorsky "improved" many of them to their ultimate detriment, not to mention Petipa's personal fury.

With the restoration of Moscow as the capital, it became necessary to increase the stature of the Bolshoi Ballet to meet the new situation, and leading artists from Leningrad's Maryinsky Theatre (now renamed the Kirov in honor of a revolutionary hero) were transferred liberally to Moscow in spite of protests from the former city. Even the great teacher, Agrippina Vaganova, was thus transferred, but after a brief period was returned at her own vigorous demand to the Kirov school. Here she had ordered and oriented the traditional ballet technique after its period

of anarchy, and in doing so produced what is considered by some to be the finest teaching method of modern times. Under her tutelage emerged the new generation of ballerinas, including Marina Semenova, Galina Ulanova, Olga Lepeshinskaya, Natalia Dudinskaya, and Tatiana Vecheslova, many of whom were sent down to Moscow early in their careers. To be sure, Moscow has produced its own brilliant figures, also, chief among them being the superb Maya Plisetskaya and Raissa Struchkova, together with a number of outstanding male dancers and actor-dancers.

Out of the Bolshoi has come, also, perhaps the most significant new movement in the dance world. Here Igor Moiseyev, long a dancer and choreographer, first concentrated his attention upon the folk dance, and transformed it into a highly creative theatrical medium all its own, with eventually its own touring company quite apart from the Bolshoi.

Though he demands a strictly classic technical training for his dancers, he takes both his themes and his actual choreographic materials from folk sources. These he develops into short compositions of marked form and originality, covering an enormous range both of geography and of style. They are variously dramatic, humorous, satirical; romantic, legendary, fantastic, occupational; solos, small ensembles and tremendously energetic large ones, and their source material comes from virtually every one of the individual republics of the USSR, and includes one riotously devasting glance at a subject so far afield as American rock-'n'-roll. Among the creative choreographers of our time, indeed, the name of Moiseyev ranks high.

It is still, nevertheless, in the Kirov company that one finds the pure, classic beauty, the traditional validity and the inherent elegance of the archetypal ballet. Out of it have come Fokine, Pavlova, Nijinsky and the generation of artists whom Diaghileff took to western Europe in 1909 to rejuvenate an already senile art. Out of it, also, a whole generation and several revolutions later, came Balanchine, whose highly personal contemporary style stems unmistakably from this same source.

No doubt, the very downgrading of the city of Leningrad from the status of capital has made it possible for these virtues to survive and continue to grow in comparative obscurity, now in turn beyond the reach of "courtly interference," or its Soviet Socialist equivalent. But if Leningrad is now politically a provincial city, its ballet is the exact reverse of a provincial ballet. It may well be, indeed, the fountainhead of **the art.**

Irina Kolpakova and Vladilen Semenov in vision scene of "The Sleeping Beauty," as produced by Leningrad's Kirov Ballet, the former Maryinski Ballet of glamorous memory, still glamorous under its new Soviet name

Alla Sizova and Yuri Soloviev of the Kirov Ballet in the bravura pas de deux from "The Corsair"

Two of the most distinguished artists of the Kirov Ballet's older generation in the second act of their company's production of "Giselle": Natalia Dudinskaya in title role, and Konstantin Sergeyev as Albrecht

Scene from the ballet, "Dilbar," with music by A. Lensky, produced by the typical State Opera and Ballet Theatre of Tadjikistan, one of the republics in Central Asia, on the southern border of the Soviet Union

Asaf Messerer in "The Red Poppy," the epoch-marking ballet in which he appeared at its première in 1926

"Gayane" presented by the Erivan (Armenia) Opera and Ballet Theatre with A. Araratova and V. Khanamaryan

Dudinskaya and Sergeyev in "The Bronze Horseman," on Pushkin's poem extolling St. Petersburg (Leningrad)

L. Sakhanova, Buryat-Mongol Opera and Ballet Theatre in Ulan Ude in a dance from the opera "Madagmasha"

The Royal Danish Ballet

Happily, the pattern of international culture exchange that now prevails has by no means been confined to this opening up of hitherto politically tabu territory. One of its most conspicuous results has been the bringing forth into the orbit of the world at large the Royal Danish Ballet, thus rescuing it from a long and unwarranted international neglect, largely of its own making.

This company vies with the Kirov for the title of the oldest of all existing companies, except, of course, that of the Paris Opéra, which is the mother of them all. Though the Royal Danish Ballet may not have established a formal academy as early as that of the Empress Anna in St. Petersburg, it imported its first great ballet master, Vincenzo Galleotti, in 1775, twenty-six years before Didelot was installed in St. Petersburg in a similar historic role.

Galleotti was the first of three notable leaders who have shaped the course of the Royal Danish Ballet. He was at its helm for forty years, and one of his works has remained in the repertoire since its creation in 1786. Unfortunately, this is only a short, gay piece which he himself did not consider important, though even today, after the many unavoidable erosions of time, it is full of charm. It is "The Whims of Cupid and the Ballet Master" and is the oldest ballet extant. To be sure, that same year Dauberval created his more famous "La Fille Mal Gardée" at Bordeaux, but nothing remains of the original work except the outline of the story. It was choreographed anew and its musical score replaced in a Russian production in the late nineteenth century. This is the version which we have known exclusively until Ashton made his delightful new one for the British Royal Ballet.

The second and greatest of the triumvirate of masters of the Danish ballet was August Bournonville, who dominated it for nearly half a century beginning in 1830. His technical method, indeed, is still the basis of the company's practice, and it is this method that makes the company unique, for it exists nowhere else in the world.

It is not its age, to be sure, that gives it importance, but the fact that it is actually the method of the great "Romantic" ballet of the time of Taglioni and Elssler, and not even the Paris Opéra, once its center, has preserved its practice. Bournonville, himself a fine dancer and the son of a pupil of Noverre, had been himself the pupil of the celebrated French dancer and teacher, August Vestris, and an active participant in the French field before he returned home to Copenhagen to take charge there.

During his long incumbency he created many ballets and tried many styles. His main interest, however, was in story-ballets of the romantic school, full of that eloquent miming which the Danes do so excellently, and richly

Henning Kronstam, Margrethe Schanne in Royal Danish Ballet's "La Sylphide," August Bournonville version

Mogens von Havn

Ballroom scene in Frederick Ashton's "Romeo and Juliet" (Prokofiev) for the Royal Danish Ballet

adorned with folk-derived dances. The best known of his surviving works are his own version of "La Sylphide" (which follows only in story the original version created by Fillippo Taglioni for his daughter), "Napoli," "Fjernt fra Danmark," a one-act version of "Konservatoriet," and a few outstanding pas de deux from other ballets.

His "La Sylphide" was created for Lucille Grahn, the most celebrated dancer to emerge from his tutelage. At the height of her career, she quarreled with him and departed for Paris, where she became one of that constellation of "Romantic" ballerinas that included also Taglioni, Elssler and Grisi among others.

The third leader of the Danish company was Harald Lander who was elevated to the position of ballet master (a title which in Copenhagen signifies director-in-chief) in 1932, and removed from it because of internal politics in the company in 1951. One of the most brilliant figures in his field, he was even as a student eager to introduce other styles into the Danish company, and studied more or less all over the world to acquire them. As this would indicate, he was hostile to the Bournonville tradition on the ground that it was old-fashioned. But as he ma-

The marriage ceremony in Ashton's "Romeo and Juliet"
— Arne Meldert, Kirsten Petersen and Flemming Flindt

134

A divertissement from the still popular last act of the Bournonville "Napoli" by the Royal Danish Ballet

tured and became more cosmopolitan, he came to see it in a different light and was actually instrumental in restoring many Bournonville ballets to the repertory. In this he had the valuable assistance of former dancers who had been active in the Bournonville repertory. Chief among them was Valborg Borschenius, who had been the ballerina of the company during the regime of Hans Beck, a faithful disciple of Bournonville and himself a successful ballet master.

Lander never lost his "progressive" views, however, and was largely responsible for the movement to export the company to other countries. It was on his initiative, also, that a teacher of contemporary Russian technique was imported as the chief figure in the school. This was Vera Volkova, herself a pupil of the Soviet's finest teacher, Vaganova. It was not Lander's purpose, however, to destroy the Bournonville method by this move, but rather to open up another field in addition to it in which the company could show its powers in terms of the repertoire prevailing in the rest of the ballet world. His dismissal from the post of ballet master inevitably has tended to unsettle this balance of viewpoint, and a strong movement has developed to substi-

Henning Kronstam, Mona Vangsaa in "Moon Reindeer," made for the Danes by the Swedish Birgit Cullberg

tute the Russian technique exclusively, or virtually so, in order to put the company on a more even competitive footing with other companies in the international field.

As a choreographer Lander is thought to have reached his creative maturity with two works produced in the early '40s. These are "Qarrtsiluni," on an Eskimo ritual theme, and "Etude," set to an arrangement of the famous musical exercises and compositions of Czerny, and following their theme of development from elementary technical training to the final consummation in a grand and spectacular ballet. This latter work has been restaged by Lander for other companies, including the Paris Opéra, London's Festival Ballet, and the American Ballet Theatre.

So far no strong figure has emerged out of the political embroilments of the Danish company to take over with authority. On the eventual

Scene from the "The Whims of Cupid and the Ballet Master," created in 1786, the only surviving example of the work of Vincenzo Galleotti, who was the first great ballet master in the history of the Royal Danish Ballet

Inge Sand and Fredbjørn Bjørnsson in Danish version of "Coppelia," created as such by Hans Beck (1896)

"Konservatoriet," a one-act restoration by Hans Beck and Valborg Borschenius of the Bournonville ballet

appearance of such a figure depend the preservation of the Bournonville tradition and the enrichment of the contemporary repertoire by means other than the importing of foreign guest choreographers.

The company has perhaps one other aspect that tends to make it unique, and that is the predominance of its male dancers over its female ones. This is due in part, no doubt, to the Bournonville tradition, which, in accordance with the technical methods of Bournonville's own day, provides more brilliance for the male style. In order to compensate for this in a measure, re-

vivals of the Bournonville ballets frequently put the ballerinas on *pointes* where originally they danced only on half-toe.

Chief among the male dancers of the present period is Erik Bruhn, who, like Lander, has made a point of learning the styles and techniques of other companies, from the United States to the Soviet Union. Like Lander, also, perhaps because of this internationalism, he has come to an ever higher respect for the Bournonville tradition. It would surprise no one if sooner or later he became the much needed strong man to take over the ballet master's responsibilities.

PART FOUR

Dance as a Means of Communication

INDUBITABLY no other art form has been so inaptly named as the "modern dance." Not only is the phrase non-descriptive, but it is markedly inaccurate, since there is absolutely nothing modern about modern dance. It is, as a matter of fact, virtually basic dance, the oldest of all dance manifestations. The modern dancer, instead of employing the cumulative resources of academic tradition, cuts through directly to the source of all dancing. He utilizes the principle that every emotional stage tends to express itself in movement, and that the movements thus created spontaneously, though they are not representational, reflect accurately in each case the character of the particular emotional state. Because of the inherent contagion of bodily movement, which makes the onlooker feel sympathetically in his own musculature the exertions he sees in somebody else's musculature, the dancer is able to convey through movement the most intangible emotional experience. This is the prime purpose of the modern dance; it is not interested in spectacle, but in the communication of emotional experiences — intuitive perceptions, elusive truths — which cannot be communicated in reasoned terms or reduced to mere statement of fact.

The principle is at least as old as man himself; primitive societies, as we have seen, have found it so potent that they have called it magic and based religious and social practices on it. But it had never been consciously utilized as the basis of art, so far as any record exists, until the turn of the present century when Isadora Duncan

made it the very center and source of her practices and the so-called modern dance was born.

Isadora Duncan

Isadora discovered it for herself through experence and not by studying any other systems, past or present. She has recorded her theories and her struggles toward the achievement of them in her autobiography and especially in the posthumous collection of her writings called "The Art of the Dance," which is one of the master works of dance literature. She tells with wonderful clarity of her conviction that all expressive movement sprang from the "soul," by which she means the seat of the emotions; of how she stood for hours before the mirror trying to locate the place in the body where these impulses centered; of how she evolved, under certain emotional stimulation, key movements which were so true and so fundamental that they gave rise automatically to other related movements growing out of them and developing the same theme. It was her deepest desire to discard all artifices, all invention, all traditional methods and established vocabularies such as the ballet employed, and to get to the source of man's expressiveness, using only the natural movements of the body without exaggeration or surface ornamentation, and allowing them to produce themselves only under inner compulsion.

There was nothing at all of the theatre in her dancing. It was a purely lyric art; that is, one of personal expression rather than of characterization, storytelling or the exhibition of skills. Her performances were therefore not theatrical presentations but dance recitals, an altogether new form of art.

Her chief inspiration came from music; in Chopin, Schubert, Tchaikovsky, Wagner, Gluck, she found, in a sense, a model for her practice. Here was an expression of inner feeling such as she sought, and though it was considered heresy to dance to such music, she could not help herself. Contrary to popular opinion, both of her own time and later, she made no effort whatever to "interpret" the music or to "visualize" it; it served simply as the "motor" which she placed in her "soul" to make it function. She acknowledged that this was not an ideal practice, and she inferred that some day when she had fully mastered the art of producing movement she would dispense with it, but that day never came.

Quite in keeping with her whole desire to affirm nature and deny artifice, she turned her back completely on the conventional methods of dance costuming with their restrictive corsets and shoes and their general fanciness and ostentation. To the horror of the world, she took off not only her corsets but also her shoes and stockings and danced barefooted and barelegged in the simplest of Greek tunics. Here the body was free to move, free to reveal itself in the full beauty of what it actually was without pretense or convention.

For one long period she turned to ancient Greece as her guide, studied the dancing figures in the museums, and at last actually went to Greece. But in the end she concluded that she was not a Greek, even at heart, but primarily a Scotch-Irish American. There was more than just fantasy, however, in her feeling of kinship with ancient Greece, for though nobody today can say authoritatively how the Greeks danced, it seems likely that their great choric dramas were built on principles of movement very similar to Isadora's rediscovery of basic dance.

It is not surprising that the America of President McKinley's day rejected Isadora's art, for all that no other country and no other time could possibly have mothered it. New forces were at work in the world's thinking, and painters, musicians, architects, psychologists, folklorists, actors, physiologists, philosophers, everywhere were turning with fresh interest to the relations between the inner, emotional man and his outward means of expression. In Russia, as has already been noted, Fokine was reacting with marked sensitiveness in his own field of the dance, reforming a tradition so old and so deep-seated that it could never be wholly denied. In America no such tradition existed; when the dawning new world mentality touched the dance here there were no such resistances to be met within the art

Arnold Genthe

Isadora Duncan in the Marseillaise

itself. Isadora went directly to the roots of the subject, where Fokine inevitably only pruned out the dead wood and allowed new growth to function on the old plant.

It is significant, also, that though Isadora

Action sketches of Isadora Duncan from the many hundreds made by A. Walkowitz in black-and-white or color from life or immediate memory, which constitute the only true and substantial visual record of her art

was received with acclaim (as well as with an admixture of shocked dismay) all over Europe, it was in Germany, where the French-Italian classic tradition had never taken firm root, that she was most fully understood. That she was persecuted there, too, goes without saying, for she was flying in the face of worldwide traditions other than those of the dance, in her daring costume, her use of music, her theories of education and of personal morality. Nevertheless, it was there that her ideas took hold most firmly and, a full generation after she had left the country, had much to do basically with the emergence of the vital modern dance movement of the German Republic after World War I.

Meanwhile in her native land other influences were at work. That she was responsible for them in a measure cannot be gainsaid, for even a world that rejected her art with self-righteous indignation could not resist the effects of its general upheaval. "Barefoot" dancers were all about, "natural" dancers abounded, practically everybody "interpreted" the musical classics, and more "Greeks" flitted about the dance world than had ever done so before, even in the peak days of the Renaissance. It is ironic, however, that in America where the modern dance has developed to its fullest expression, it can trace no direct line of descent from Isadora.

Denishawn

The actual line of descent of the American modern dance goes back rather to a dancer who was in most respects the very opposite of Isadora. This was Ruth St. Denis, whose fundamental theory of the dance was less important than the inspiration of her personal genius and her unflagging courage and persistence in the face of opposition. As an artist she was actuated by two contradictory forces; one was an instinctive threatricalism that loved not only impersonation and representation but also and especially the eye-filling use of color and light, of elaborate costuming and scenery; the other element was an ascetic sense of religious mysticism, at the opposite extreme from Isadora's essential paganism. Her career as a dancer did not begin until she stumbled onto Oriental art and found in the exotic ritual dance of India, which she knew only from books, exactly the field in which to combine her religious feeling with her spectacular sense of the theatre.

Her first production in this medium was "Radha, a Hindu Temple Dance," which aroused laughter (mixed with applause for its unconventional display of the body) at its initial presentation in a "smoking concert" on the New York Theatre Roof. It was later to win a sensational success both in this country and in Europe, and was the beginning of an upsurge of imitative "Oriental" dancing. Her own dancing made no pretense to being authentic in style; it was frankly a pictorial approximation of Eastern styles, used for its spectacular qualities together with its aspects of religious ritual.

St. Denis was never concerned with technical method, but relied on a native gift for beautiful movement, a facility for improvisation, and an instinct for theatrical effect. When, however, she married her young dancing partner, Ted Shawn, and their Denishawn school and company came into being, other elements were added. Shawn, formerly a divinity student, shared St. Denis's approach to religious values in the dance. He was also as predominantly theatrical in taste as she was. But his interests were much broader, his outlook more eclectic and his respect for technical training considerably more marked.

Though the Denishawn method still contained much Oriental material, it also dealt in Spanish and American Indian material, and employed a basic technique adapted to barefoot use from the academic ballet. In its later years it embraced many other methods, including Dalcroze Eurythmics and even modern German dance.

As an advocate of nudity, Shawn surpassed Isadora herself. He was also a militant worker for the return of men to dancing, and for the destruction of the stigma of effeminacy which had clung to the male dancer ever since his decline as an institution in the nineteenth-century ballet.

In such an atmosphere St. Denis could not well have remained exclusively in her Oriental pattern, even if she had been so inclined. Perhaps her most important innovation during these years was her idea of "music visualization." This

Ruth St. Denis in "White Jade"

Ted Shawn in "Ramadan"

was frankly influenced by Isadora's use of music, but it added a practice instituted by Emile Jaques-Dalcroze in his system of musical education whereby the form of a symphonic work was mirrored by having each dancer follow a specific instrument in an orchestral score note for note, under the overall direction of a choreographer. In her remarkable autobiography, "Ruth St. Denis — An Unfinished Life," St. Denis has denied any knowledge of the Dalcroze precedent, however. In her new orchestral approach to dancing she had the assistance of one of her young dancers, Doris Humphrey, who was largely responsible for freeing the form from its implicit rigidity and developing it into a mature and legitimate practice. St. Denis has claimed in her autobiography that this was the beginning of what grew later into the American modern dance,

and it is a claim that would be hard to deny.

The modern dance was nevertheless not so much an outgrowth of Denishawn as a rebellion against it. New ideas among its dancers, inspired by progress in outside fields, were frowned upon officially, and important defections occurred accordingly in the ranks. First Martha Graham left, then Doris Humphrey and Charles Weidman, to build independently upon their own artistic convictions. Ultimately Denishawn itself was dissolved, with St. Denis devoting herself to religious dance and Shawn first organizing a men's group and later establishing a "university of the dance" at Jacob's Pillow, near Lee, Massachusetts. The old organization had served its purpose nobly. A new era in the dance was coming into being.

Ruth St. Denis and Ted Shawn in "Quest"

Ruth St. Denis and Ted Shawn in Spanish duet

White

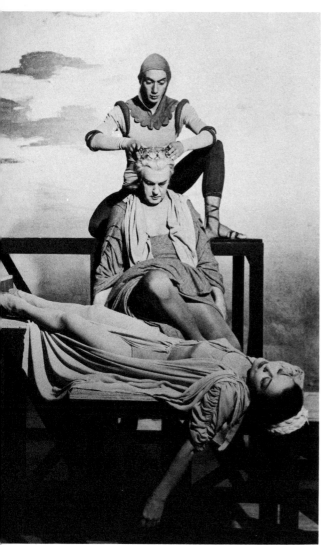

A group of Denishawn dancers, with Doris Humphrey in front, on their return from an Oriental tour, 1925

Ruth St. Denis in "Radha" revived after forty years

Jack Mitchell

Ted Shawn, with William Milié and Myra Kinch, in the latter's "Sundered Majesty," on "King Lear" themes

Dwight Godwin

Ted Shawn's group of male dancers in "Threshing Floor," a section of his "Labor Symphony"

Mary Wigman in "Traumgestalt"

Ch. Rudolph

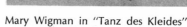

Mary Wigman in "Tanz des Kleides"

Mary Wigman

But meanwhile there were important activities in Europe. The seed planted by Isadora was bearing fruit. Immediately in her wake there had been a wealth of fresh accomplishment, especially in Germany and Austria. It was not so much an imitation of her as it was a freeing of native impulses under the stimulation of her example. It ranged all the way from the educational systems of Bode and Dalcroze to the performances of such widely popular lyric artists as the Wiesenthal sisters, Clothilde von Derp and Ronny Johansson.

At the close of the war, however, there were new and more profound manifestations of the same fundamental impulses. Not only were the German people as a whole encouraged to use the dance as a means to rehabilitate themselves physically after their years of wartime undernourishment, but a phenomenal interest arose in the dance as an expressive art.

Among the many artists of greater or lesser achievement was one who towered above the scene like a giant. Except for Isadora herself, no figure in the history of the modern dance occupies a higher position than Mary Wigman, in part for her specific artistic creations, but mainly for her widening of the range of the art and the advancement of its underlying theory. She had studied with Dalcroze at Hellerau, and had spent the war years as a pupil of Rudolf von Laban in Switzerland. The Dalcroze school had been not only an extremely advanced institution for musical education, in which music was related directly to movement, but had also expanded naturally into modern theatre experimentation along the lines of Adolphe Appia and Gordon Craig and their colleagues, and was one of the most stimulating artistic centers in Europe. Laban was virtually the father of the theory of the German modern dance, having experimented in the psychology of movement, the analysis of space, and

144

many other problems, and eventually he was to work out the most impersonal, scholarly and practical of all systems for the notation of movement on a written score. From both these sources she was undoubtedly enriched, but when she broke away at last to work independently, it was along lines absolutely her own.

Her dance, like Isadora's, grew out of "ecstasy," but where Isadora allowed her ecstasy to flow along the course of the music that inspired it, Wigman demanded that her ecstasy create its own forms. Form, indeed, was to her as indispensable a part of the creative process as emotional impulse.

In many of her early dances, in order to free herself from the domination of musical form, from which Isadora had never been able to escape, she composed works entirely without music, and great portions of her repertoire continued to be entirely musicless or to employ musicless passages. Once this pressing problem of absolute choreographic form was solved, she made free use of music, and in this lay one of her most valuable contributions, for it marked a return to the practice of basic dance. Her characteristic method was to use a simple melodic line, frequently played on a primitive flute or something of the sort, with rhythmic support from percussion instruments of many kinds. Thus, like primitive dancers, she projected her own song and her own pulse into the music that accompanied her. Tendencies in this direction were general, it is true, throughout the German field, but Wigman achieved by far the most impressive, the most musical and the most choreographic results with them. It is possible to believe, indeed, that in her application of the first principles of basic dance, she showed the way to the perfect solution of the problem of music's relation to dance. That a special type of musician, highly sensitive to movement and willing to sacrifice traditional musical theories, is required, goes without saying, but the difficulties involved in practice do not in any degree invalidate the soundness of the principle.

Another contribution of Wigman was her awareness of space. Isadora moved as a sculptural figure, as it were, self-contained and complete, regardless of physical surroundings; Wigman, on the other hand, placed her dance consciously in a three-dimensional area, relating the moving figure always to its surroundings in what might be called the architectural sense. Laban's experiments with space had been predominantly intellectual; he had seen the human body as standing theoretically in the center of a many-sided geometrical figure (an icosahedron), and had formulated the directions and the extent and the paths of travel in which its various members could move. Wigman's attitude to the subject was emotional; she felt space as the medium through which she moved in much the same way that the swimmer feels water. Where Isadora's dance was merely the outpouring of personal emotion, to all

Mary Wigman and members of her original dance group in "Totentanz," using masks dramatically

August Scherl

intents and purposes, in a vacuum, Wigman's became inherently dramatic because of the constant awareness of space as an element presenting limitations to the range of movement or resistance to actual motor effort, and in general as a symbolic representation of the universe in which the single individual finds himself, and to which he must reconcile himself and adjust if he is to survive.

If Isadora freed the dance from the exclusive use of an established vocabulary of specific movements and sought to achieve a definite link between inner feeling and outward gesture, her results were of a somewhat general nature. A child of her own period, she was strongly influenced by its standards. For her a work of art must be "beautiful," and the aesthetics of the pre-Raphaelite Brotherhood came perhaps nearest to conditioning her concept of beauty. She had also her generation's attitude toward Greek art as the epitome of simple, always harmonious line and form, even though the subject might be inharmonious and tragic. In her writings, and necessarily in her thinking, as well, she spelled Love, Truth, Beauty, Life, and all such generic terms, with capital letters. It was entirely logical, then, that the movements she evolved should be limited in range, natural in quality (so long as the more realistic and inharmonious aspects of nature were excluded), and should consist chiefly of such fundamental and elementary ingredients as running and skipping. Since her power of projecting emotion was incredibly great, this was all the means she required. It was not, however, all that those who followed in her name required, and explains in large measure why her art as a concrete thing, died with her.

Wigman, also a child of her age, was for that reason less bound to such abstract standards of beauty. Her movement was conceived in the inner recesses of her individual psychology, and she had trained her body to serve as a transparency through which she could express the subtlest of emotional shadings. No movement, however odd or superficially ugly, was rejected so long as it was evocative. Her entire body was a sensitive instrument, and the movement it produced was never invented but always intuitively realized, whether noble in style or grotesque.

Thus, if Isadora discovered the "soul" of the dance, Wigman gave it its body. There has always been much about her work that is alien to American taste; her costuming, her philosophical bent, her preoccupation with death, her general introspectiveness, are all essentially German and demand to be seen as such before they can be accepted. But this is merely a process of translation such as any foreign art must undergo. Her greatness can never be denied, and her three American tours in the early '30s had a broadening and salutary influence on the American dance.

Mary Wigman and her dance group in "Der Feier." (Hanya Holm is the fourth figure from the right)

S. Enkelmann

Mary Wigman in a suite of Polish folk songs

Second Generation

The great period of the modern dance in America can be said to have started in the mid-1920's. Martha Graham gave her first independent New York recital in 1926; 1927 saw the debut of Helen Tamiris; early in 1928 Doris Humphrey and Charles Weidman set out on their own, assisted by a group from Denishawn, with which institution they were still connected.

Dance recitals of one sort or another had already become numerous, but they were in the main either evidences of artistic tendencies already on the decline or else merely performances by individuals with certain personal gifts but no particular direction. What was shaping itself as the modern dance had no definable qualities that separated it from these other activities, yet there was from the beginning a sense of latent vitality in it that set it somehow apart.

In retrospect it is now possible to see the trend of the whole period; the dance was transforming itself from an imitative art into a creative one. The dancer, having been touched by Isadora's revelation of the expression of inner personal experience, was rebelling against merely pretending theatrically to be somebody else,

whether a Hindu goddess, an Aztec warrior, a butterfly or a swan, and mimicking that somebody's behavior. The first problem was to throw off all these "false whiskers," so to speak, and get to the heart of one's own emotional self according to Isadora's example.

But Isadora's dance was not of the theatre, as she had freely admitted. The second problem, accordingly, was to develop this great discovery of "self-expression" (falsely so called) back into an art of the theatre. Music was the instrument for solving the first problem; one simply let the music stir the emotions into actions as Isadora had done. The next step was to get rid of this self-inflicted tyranny of music, as Wigman had done, so that expressive movement could be free to create its own forms. When movement had thus been isolated so that it could function without leaning on either musical form or theatrical impersonation, the actual substance of the dance had been found. From that point on the dancer was really in the position of an artist who knew his materials. Little by little he was able to add music where he needed it, costumes and scenery, characterization and dramatic situation, even spoken words, and still keep movement as the stuff of his art with his own emotional convictions as its animator.

Doris Humphrey

Of all the dancers of this notable second generation, Doris Humphrey best exemplified this line of development. In her early work with St. Denis on "music visualizations" she had begun to approach the subject of non-representational movement. At this stage it was still formally the slave of music, but by 1924 she had created a choreographic "visualization" of Edward MacDowell's "Sonata Tragica" which had so much independent form that the music was finally discarded and it was performed in silence. But no firm basis for creating in terms of absolute dance had been laid by this procedure, for music had been its shaping force whether it was audibly played or not. Two other works carried these experiments

147

to fulfilment. One was "Water Study," which Humphrey knew was a transitional step, for it was merely substituting external nature rhythms for the rhythms of music as a formal guide. (Actually its value lay not in its recourse to an outward model but rather in its technical employment of the rhythms of breath and blood pulse as a conscious basis for group movement.) The second work was "Drama of Motion," a three-part group composition without music, which depended on no auxiliary devices whatever and was a work of pure dance as absolute as any symphony.

In the six years that had elapsed between the "Tragica" and "Drama of Motion," Humphrey had evolved an extraordinarily original theory. She was not at the moment concerned with the relation of emotional impulse to movement; that was a creative matter with which she knew how to deal. What she was seeking was rather the nature of motion in space, irrespective of how it was inspired, so that she might find principles on which to build in terms of independent form. Like Isadora, she stood for hours before the mirror, but unlike Isadora, she was not seeking any mystic enlightenment; she was watching the actual mass of her body in its relation to gravity and the behavior patterns that emerged from this relationship. Her findings, based not only on observation but also on knowledge of the body and the principles of physics involved, constituted one of the most important contributions that anybody has made to dance theory. It actually comprises what might be called the kinetic laws of the dance.

The matter of equilibrium was the crux of her experimentation. She knew that the body tends to be thrown off balance by any movement, however slight, and that it is constantly making automatic compensatory movements to maintain equilibrium. In her experiments before the mirror she studied the effects of a sideward swaying that increased in range until it actually involved falling to the ground. The wider the sway and the greater the loss of equilibrium, the more vigorous the compensatory movements that were automatically made to restore balance. Also, the

Thomas Bouchard

Doris Humphrey in her trilogy known as "New Dance," after the title of its closing section, in which she is seen above. Below, as the Matriarch in the second section, entitled (after Blake) "With My Red Fires"

Thomas Bouchard

speed with which the body fell increased as the fall progressed. All motion, then, she concluded, was "an arc between two deaths;" there was the "death" of complete inactivity in which there was no contest with gravity, and at the other extreme was the "death" of destruction in which gravity defeated all efforts at resistance.

Obviously, the movements that were most interesting to watch were those in the sphere of danger, where destruction was being defied and at the crucial moment avoided. As Wigman had made space her spontaneously existent dramatic antagonist, Humphrey thus made gravity hers, and gave her dance immediately a color of drama in its very essence. The fundamental rhythm of moving now appeared clearly to be the alternation of balance and unbalance, of fall and recovery; the natural increase in speed as the body approaches the bottom of the potential fall added a dynamic element by invoking a corresponding increase in muscular tension to resist it. Other natural principles of design were involved in the fact that compensatory movements are inevitably opposite in direction and at least equal in strength to the forces that are tending to produce the unbalance. Such rich creative possibilities were unfolded in this absolute field that Humphrey continued to compose in its terms throughout her career, even after she had moved on to other developments and no longer concentrated on it.

Having freed her basic movement from all outside dependencies, however, she began at once to build toward large theatre forms. There were many compositions of high quality during this transition, containing experiments with various kinds of music outside the orthodox orchestral range, and with settings, costumes, speech. "Life of the Bee," with sound accompaniment but no music; "La Valse" to Ravel's score; "Orestes" to Milhaud's music for orchestra and chorus; "Dionysaques" to music of Florent Schmitt; "The Shakers," using voice, accordion, and bursts of hysterical speech, were notable examples. But the full fruition of her genius as a choreographer and master of large forms came with the "New Dance" trilogy. This consists of "Theatre Piece," "With

H. Hewett

Doris Humphrey and Charles Weidman in their romantic duet, "Rudepoema," to music by Dane Rudhyar; below, in a passage from the dramatic ensemble work called "Inquest," with a trenchant spoken text from Ruskin

Gerda Peterich

The Humphrey-Weidman company in its greatest period in one of Doris Humphrey's compositions for ensemble. (William Bales and Catherine Litz, center, in first picture; Sybil Shearer, far right in second picture)

My Red Fires" and "New Dance," a heroic work on the subject of man's relation to man, which, though it was never performed in its entirety on a single program, would have filled an entire evening. Its first section is a protest against competition in terms of pungent satire; its second section is a tragedy of universal dimensions based on human possessiveness, with the principal figures personally characterized; its third section (which, incidentally, was created first) is a resolution of the preceding themes of conflict in terms of absolute dance. Unfortunately all that remains of this outstanding masterpiece is its middle section and the "Variations and Conclusion" of its final section.

There were, of course, other works of moment, though of smaller dimensions in these same general terms. Two of them, "Passacaglia" and "Song of the West" are, like "New Dance," compositions of deep emotional significance and dramatic content though without literary program. "New Dance" had a special and remarkably creative score composed by Wallingford Riegger along with the choreographic creation of the work. In "Passacaglia" however, she dared (and at this period it was breath-takingly daring) to match her choreographic concept against the formal mastery of Bach's C minor "Passacaglia and Fugue," without fear of its being overshadowed. As, indeed, it was not. "Song of the West," though never quite finished to her satis-

faction, was nevertheless a triumph of what might perhaps be called emotional landscape painting, capturing topography, history and the emanations of prehistoric peoples in a penetrating and communicative poetry.

Another great work (the last one in which she herself appeared) was "Inquest," departing altogether in approach from everything that had gone before. It was a burning tragedy of social protest, using a spoken text out of Ruskin's "Sesame and Lilies" and set in the atmosphere of that era, with an eloquent score by Norman Lloyd to reinforce it. Here a sordid story was translated by means of both pantomime and high abstraction into universal terms of exalted beauty.

But she could also be funny — at least in a satirical vein. She was the first choreographer to see the possibilities in James Thurber's drawings, and her choreographic version of his "The Race of Life" was as hilarious and as full of comment as his.

Because of arthritis, Humphrey was forced to retire as a dancer in 1945, and from then on until her death in 1958 she devoted herself exclusively and intensively to the practice and the teaching of choreography, with some of her finest pieces appearing in this period, most of them for the company of José Limón, of which she was artistic director.

Scene from "With My Red Fires," dealing with destructive maternal love, in Doris Humphrey's "New Dance" trilogy with music by Wallingford Riegger, the only section of the work on a personalized dramatic theme

Charles Weidman

Charles Weidman was closely associated with Humphrey from the Denishawn days, to their mutual advantage. Not only his personal presence in the company, but also his interest in developing male dancers in the so largely female-dominated modern dance made it possible for the Humphrey-Weidman company to have both men and women in its casts from the very beginning, thus carrying on the Denishawn practice without interruption. This was obviously a better balanced arrangement than that which generally prevailed as an inheritance from Isadora's exclusively feminine ensembles.

Weidman's dance arose out of a different basic from that of any of his colleagues. Though he developed skills in absolute dance, he has always worked best and most significantly, both as dancer and as choreographer, in terms of movement that derives from pantomime. It is by no means realistic pantomime when he gets through with it, for he takes actual gesture and reduces it to its very essence as movement.

Sometimes it is dramatic, as in his group composition, "Lynch Town," and in the lurid melodrama of "This Passion," based on a sensational murder case of the day; sometimes it is poignant, as in his biographical solo cycle, "On My Mother's Side," in which he achieves eloquent and affecting portraits in abstraction of female

H. Hewett

Charles Weidman in a characteristic lyric movement

151

as well as male ancestors, and more deeply in his "A House Divided —" in which he makes an intuitive dancing portrait of Abraham Lincoln noble and moving.

Generally, however, he has preferred to be either gaily comic or devastatingly satirical, for he has a wonderful gift for observing and visualizing the vagaries of men and manners. (Nor, to be truthful, are his personal caricatures invariably models of sweetness and good nature.) His most celebrated work is his adaptation of Thurber's "Fables for Our Time," in which he uses both Thurber's own words and a musical score by Freda Miller. He has also tried his hand with other famous satirists; rather charmingly with Max Beerbohm's "The Happy Hypocrite," and with more daring than wisdom, with Voltaire's "Candide." The latter, however, for all its shortcomings, may well have been the first full-evening composition in the American field of modern dance.

With his little solo, "Kinetic Pantomime," he achieved a genuine novelty in that it was a study in pure nonsense, in comedy pantomime that actually means nothing literal in spite of seeming to; and this same intriguing genre was developed in an excellent group work called "Opus 51." In the main, though, he has stayed closer to recognizable comment, ranging all the way from his amused and nostalgic biography of his father, called "And Daddy Was a Fireman," to the hilarious kidding of silent movies called "Flickers." His second go at a Thurber original, "The War Between Men and Women," fell far below his first.

During their long association, he and Humphrey danced as a matter of course in each other's works. After her enforced retirement, he formed a small company of his own which functioned for a time, and was eventually dissolved, though he continued to assemble casts for semi-occasional performances here and there. Of recent years, however, he has devoted himself largely to teaching, both in New York and on widely extended and very successful teaching tours. He has also established, in collaboration with Mikhail Santaro, the Expression of Two Arts Theatre, which gives periodic performances of small dimensions. The two arts involved are the graphic and choreographic ones.

Charles Weidman in two of his varied characterizations: as Abraham Lincoln in "A House Divided-"; and in "The Unicorn in the Garden," from the "Fables for Our Time" (Thurber) with Jack Ferris and Felisa Conde

Gerda Peterich *New York Times*

Flatow

Joyce Trisler, John Barker in Doris Humphrey's "Dawn in New York" (Garcia Lorca), for Juilliard company

Charles Weidman and the Humphrey-Weidman company in "Flickers," a typical Weidman laugh at silent films

Martha Graham in "Frontier," a notable early solo to Louis Horst's music and with Isamu Noguchi's décor

Paul Hansen

Martha Graham

The artist who has come to be most generally the symbol of modern dance in the popular mind is that other rebel from Denishawn, Martha Graham. This is easy to understand, for though the casual public might not immediately recognize the true quality of her art, it could not fail to note that her independent approach to the dance resulted in the same startling surface quality as had already been found in modern painting and modern music. It was inevitable, then, that her dancing should be called "ugly," "angular," "obscure" and "modern."

Because of her challenging personality, she created a sharp division of opinion from the start, some of it violently antagonistic and some almost idolatrously rapturous, and all of it transforming her into a one-woman *cause célèbre*. With the passage of the years, the sharpness of this cleavage has been tempered and she has won a wide and, at the very least, respectful audience more or less all over the world. This is not only because of her maturity as an artist but also because with increasing familiarity her art has ceased to appear perverse, which, as a matter of fact, it never was. It has remained, nevertheless, consistently provocative throughout its virtually continuous

changing of form and surface.

Graham is the only one of her artistic generation who has continued to dance, even though well into her sixties. What she has inevitably lost in technical strength, she has more than compensated for in artistic substance. Her creative impulse, indeed, has continued to increase its range, depth and adventurousness, and her mastery of form has attained a miraculous authority. Not without reason is her name frequently linked with those of the considerably older masters in other fields, Stravinsky and Picasso, for the similarly perpetual freshness and challenge of her creative genius.

Interestingly enough, in view of the once common accusation that she was too "abstract," in her Denishawn days Graham was considered too theatrical to be admitted to the concert company. Instead she appeared chiefly in the vaudeville branch of the organization's activities, including especially the Aztec dance-drama, "Xochitl," with Ted Shawn. (One of the classic anecdotes of this time tells of the young Charles Weidman, who was put into the cast of this piece opposite her at the beginning of his career and was so intimidated by her passion and physical violence in performance that he wrote home to his father for advice on how to defend himself.) When Graham left Denishawn in 1923, it was to appear in "The Greenwich Village Fol-

lies," but even after she had turned independently to the recital field, she still danced Hindu and Greek and exotic dances with many typical Denishawn trappings, and was described as "graceful," "pictorial" and without much technique.

This, however, was exactly the approach against which she was in the process of rebelling, and when she ultimately found her own direction it was in every respect the direct opposite. The adjectives that were now applied to her were "stark," "gymnastic" and "intellectual," for she stripped away everything but the essentials both of stage production and of movement itself. In revolt against the arbitrary softness of the old and sentimental style of legato movements, she developed what she called percussive movement; that is, movement initiated by a sharp attack like that of a drum beat. Instead of producing diffuse gestures that seemed to float off indefinitely into space, she sought to center the body and to integrate its movement within its own sphere of action. Her entire approach to the dance, indeed, had become one of integration, as if she were trying to focus the world about her — or at least those aspects of it that immediately inspired her — within herself in order to communicate it in its highly concentrated essence. Her purpose was, and still is, to evoke a heightened awareness of life, and not merely to present its surface.

Martha Graham and her company in a revival of one of her first great group works, "Primitive Mysteries," three dances on American Indian ceremonial themes with a score by Louis Horst drawn from native sources   *Barbara Morgan*

Martha Graham and her company in "Appalachian Spring," with a score by Aaron Copland and décor by Isamu Noguchi, premièred at Library of Congress. (Erick Hawkins, center; Martha Graham, May O'Donnell, right)

To this end she has always been stimulated by external objects, multifarious and unpredictable. Her environment, both mental and physical, is a continual source of creative inspiration and her artistic life is shaped and reshaped, colored and recolored, by her sensitivity to her surroundings. Most frequently it is large, heroic influences that touch her into creation — the vast American landscape, the culture of the American Indian, the ritual practices of antiquity, the great drama of the ancient Greeks; sometimes it is individual and specific, and even personal phenomena — maps, the flower paintings of Georgia O'Keefe, the poems of Emily Dickinson, the warped world of the Brontës, the sanctification of Joan of Arc, the heroism of Judith. If she treads fearlessly in the path of tragedy, she can also be the quintessence of lyricism or a hilarious figure of comedy.

The forms and surfaces of the works thus variously inspired are necessarily vastly different, but there remains beneath them a constant element which is the personal style of the artist herself — a passionate intensity that is so controlled as to achieve an incandescent quietness, with an immersion in the emotional elements of a situation that brings movement of curious character and eloquence virtually out of the subconscious.

With the broadening perspective of maturity, this has been ordered into an increasingly systematic discipline — in a sense, a personal classicism — but it is useless to look for an objective theory in a style so completely outside the realm of the intellectual in its origins, if not, of course, in its development. It has little continuity with the past, little projection into the future; it exists solely in the perfection of its own being here and now.

In her greatest period, which began in 1958 with the presentation of the full-length "Clytemnestra," it has become clear that from the beginning she has been working, however subconsciously, toward the discovery of a new heroic theatre, rather than merely the development of the dance within its own particular limitations. With the contributory elements of it she has been almost as creative as in the field of movement and choreography itself. In costuming she was early a radical in both design and choice of materials, and no matter whose name may be programmed as her designer, it is Graham herself who has been responsible for the structure of the costumes and has put at least the final touches to their designs. Often with a new work, she has changed the costume at every performance until she has found what is right. Her approach to stage setting has been controlled in a measure by the financial

155

Clytemnestra's murder by Orestes; Martha Graham and Bertram Ross in her heroic drama of "Clytemnestra"

Martha Graham with Jane Dudley and Sophie Maslow in her fantasia on the Brontës, "Deaths and Entrances"

stringencies of the dance world, but it is doubtful if it would have been widely different if the problem of cost had not existed. She has worked with a number of gifted and original stage designers, especially the sculptor Isamu Noguchi, and her settings consist in the main of isolated units of related décor and properties, sculptural "objects," and great attention to lighting. The result is almost invariably a vivid and evocative stage. Her occasional employment of words as background began with "Sarabande" and "Pantomime" in a suite called "Transitions" back in 1934, and has been consistently creative in its motivations and its functions in the particular frame of the work at issue. She herself, incidentally, has never done the speaking.

In the field of music she was fortunate in having in the beginning of her independent career and for many years afterwards the collaboration of Louis Horst as musical director and composer-in-chief. His influence throughout the whole area of modern dance has been a rich one, but for the crucial years of her career he devoted

himself primarily to her repertoire, whether helping in the selection of music or actually composing it according to her needs. Beginning in 1934 she has worked exclusively with especially commissioned scores, with the lone exception of "Episodes," in which she worked jointly with Balanchine on the setting of all the orchestral compositions of Anton von Webern, each choreographer supplying half of a single program. Many of the important modern composers have worked with her from time to time.

For this great theatrical period, which has been financially underwritten by the B. de Rothschild Foundation, she has developed a company of superb quality and a standard of physical beauty to match it. Among them are Bertram Ross, an artist with an inner strength that equips him to stand up even to Graham herself; Helen McGehee, Ethel Winter, Matt Turney, Linda Hodes, Yuriko, Mary Hinkson, Robert Cohan, David Wood, and a contingent of upcoming youngsters such as Richard Kuch, Richard Gain and Robert Powell. Among her gifts is that of perceiving the individual capacities of young dancers and shaping them for the time when they will be called into service to fill the gaps in the company that inevitably occur as the seasons progress.

The repertoire of this period, dominated by the fairly overwhelming "Clytemnestra," includes also "Alcestis" and "Phaedra" deriving with characteristic Graham penetration from the antique Greek theatre with its natural and supernatural laws. From biblical sources she has evolved "Samson Agonistes," the witty "Embattled Garden," and one of her most powerful dramas, "Judith," which had its première in Israel in 1962. "Seraphic Dialogue" is an exquisite treatment of the Joan of Arc theme, a triumph of lyric form and beauty; and out of her own comic genius has come the hilarious (and visually beautiful) "Acrobats of God," based on the trials of the dance studio itself.

Also of theatrical character were those fine works of an earlier period: "Letter to the World" (Emily Dickinson), "Deaths and Entrances" (the Brontës), "Dark Meadow," "Appalachian Spring," and the devastating travesty of a foolish woman in love, "Every Soul Is a Circus." But the still earlier years teem with works of equal artistic significance if generally of smaller dimensions. "Adolescence," "Heretic," "Primitive Mysteries," "Dithyrambic," "Lamentation," "Primitive Canticles," "Ekstasis," "Frenetic Rhythms," "Sarabande," "Act of Piety," "Frontier," "El Penitente," are all of more than passing moment, though most of them are now forgotten even by Graham herself. Actually they are deserving of perpetuation, and in a more rational world than that of the dance, their choreographic scores would be readily available with the equivalent of Koechel numbers.

A group passage from "Dark Meadow," a mystic ritual to the music of Carlos Chavez with décor by Noguchi
Arnold Eagle

Martha Graham as Jocasta in "Night Journey," one of her cycle of works on themes from Greek mythology

Jack Mitchell

Scene from "Alcestis" — Linda Hodes, Martha Graham, Dan Wagoner and Helen McGehee are in the foreground

Martha Graham in her irresistibly funny "Acrobats of God" with David Wood, Ethel Winter and Bertram Ross

Arnold Eagle

Jack Mitchell

Helen McGehee and Robert Powell in the Martha Graham frolic called "Secular Games," made for her company

Martha Graham and Bertram Ross in "Episodes," joint project with Balanchine, using the music of Webern

Martha Swope

158

Helen Tamiris

Helen Tamiris, one of the most important pioneers of this important second generation, hails from a background quite apart from that of her three colleagues who came from Denishawn. Her first training was in the classes of Irene Lewisohn, who was later to make a major contribution to the American dance as director of the Neighborhood Playhouse with its school and producing center. The Metropolitan Opera ballet school, a touring Italian opera company in South America, the class of Michel Fokine, a brief sampling of the Duncan school (all of which she heartily disliked), led her to the conviction that the kind of dancing she wanted to do would have to be of her own making. Night clubs, revues and moviehouse presentations supported her while she worked it out.

She had come from an artistic family, with two painters for brothers, and she was very much in touch with the creative movements of the day in all the arts. It is not surprising, then, to find her early recitals, when she got around to the point in 1927 when she was ready to give them, sponsored by J. B. Neumann and the New Art Circle. It is not surprising, either, that the music she danced to was by Poulenc, Satie and Florent Schmitt; John Powell, Louis Gruenberg and George Gershwin. This seems commonplace enough, perhaps, until we remember that the most popular dance composers of the day were still Brahms and Schubert and Chopin and Mendelssohn, with a touch of Scriabin and Debussy for spice.

These first programs were listed as "Dance Moods" and were divided into "Moods Diverse" and "American Moods." They were extremely experimental dances in many ways; one of them was danced without accompaniment, another used as music the patterned beating of piano strings, still another used a siren, the Gershwin jazz was treated seriously, two of them were Negro Spirituals, several of them made conscious use of movements adapted from athletics, one of them experimented briefly with nudity. All of them were characterized by direct and vigorous move-

Thomas Bouchard

Helen Tamiris in "Joshua Fit de Battle of Jericho"

Solo by Helen Tamiris on a Federal Theatre program
Federal Theatre

ment of great inherent beauty, backed by a lively and completely contemporaneous mind.

Since Tamiris has always been a clear thinker and superbly articulate, it is characteristic that her basic theory was printed as a "Manifest" in one of her early programs. This is not only an interesting historical document, indicative of the insurgency of the dance world in that stimulating day, but a key to Tamiris's individual practice, which, though it has been enriched as she has progressed, is substantially outlined here. It reads as follows:

Art is international, but the artist is a product of nationality and his principal duty to himself is to express the spirit of his race.

A new civilization always creates new forms of art.

We must not forget the age we live in.

There are no general rules. Each work of art creates its own code.

The aim of the dance is not to narrate (anecdotes, stories, fables, legends, etc.), by means of mimic tricks and other established choreographic forms. Dancing is simply movement with a personal concept of rhythm.

Costumes and music are complements of the dance. A dancer's creation should stand the test in the nude and the experience of motion without music.

Sincerity is based on simplicity. A sincere approach to art is always done through simple forms.

Authenticity tries to convince with the exact reproduction of details: costumes, postures, regional music and photographic make-up. A dancer must create his own reality, independent of the reality we live in. Reality has no interest for what it actually is but for what the artist sees in it.

Toe dancing . . . Why not dance on the palms of the hands?

To give primary importance to facial expression is just as bad as to give primary importance to the feet. Both are elements of the ensemble, spokes of the same wheel — neither is the center.

It is false to create atmosphere or mood with exact reproduction of costumes belonging to a period or contemporary with a character. It makes one think of children who, to appear as men, paste moustaches on their faces.

The word pattern has become a standard term for choreography, decorative poses and external attitudes. Pattern is really what style is in any other art: an individual form of expression.

The dance of today is plagued with exotic gestures, mannerisms and ideas borrowed from literature, philosophy, sculpture and painting. Will people never rebel against artificialities, pseudo-romanticism and affected sophistication? The dance of today must have a dynamic tempo and be valid, precise, spontaneous, free, normal, natural and human.

This is a document written in 1927, but though its author might wish to add to it today,

"How Long, Brethren?," a suite based on Negro songs of protest by Helen Tamiris for the Federal Theatre

Federal Theatre

Alfredo Valente

Helen Tamiris in "Liberty Song," solo from her suite of dances based on songs of the American Revolution

Gerda Peterich

Another group of American songs inspired the "Bayou Ballads," danced by Helen Tamiris and Daniel Nagrin

it contains truths that are timeless, and a spirit of rebellious dedication, indeed, that has become so dulled in contemporary modern dance practice that the field at large could read and study this "Manifest" with profit.

Before she gave over her experimentation in what might be called the periphery of dancing, she worked on the idea of self-accompaniment, using cymbals, triangles, wood-blocks, gourd rattles and the like.

Outside of strictly artistic matters, she was equally adventurous. She was the first of the modern dancers to make a European tour, including the Salzburg Festival. This was in 1928. It was she who organized the Dance Repertory Theatre, in which for the first time all four of the modern dancers of this lively generation pooled their interests in seasons of joint performances in 1930 and 1931. Through the bickerings and battling that inevitably beset co-operative projects of this sort by artists, especially such dedicated ones as these, without a neutral overlord as the ultimate authority, the project quickly perished, but the lack of just such an organization as this one was designed to be has

caused the modern dance to languish and all but give up the ghost. Actually Tamiris has never lost her faith in it, and has continued to work for its establishment on a sound basis.

In the days of the Federal Theatre Project, Tamiris was the most active spirit in its department of dance production in New York. For it she produced, among other things, a large dramatic work dealing with the Spanish civil war, "Adelante;" and one of her most interesting group works, "How Long, Brethren?" set to Negro songs of protest, as perhaps a disturbing companion piece to her earlier and quite admirable suite of Negro Spirituals. Later she made excellent use of other groups of songs as background material. "Liberty Song" employed songs of the American Revolution, and a charming suite of "Bayou Ballads" was set to songs from Louisiana.

But it is doubtful that the mere use of songs as such interested her in any experimental sense, for she was finding herself drawn less and less to the mere seeking of fresh methods and new tools and more and more to the exploration and publishing of human values. This did not

161

make her in the least sober-sided or didactic, for her verve and lively sense of proportion were unquenchable; on the other hand, it made evident a gift for lightness and gaiety that grew out of honest feeling instead of being superimposed as a form of theatrical coquetry.

This was in large part responsible for her pronounced success with Broadway musicals. Without sacrificing anything of her artistic integrity or a single principle of the modern dance, she devised movement that was both winning and communicative, and in every way supported the action of the piece.

Among her most celebrated musicals were "Up in Central Park," with an enchanting Currier-and-Ives skating ballet; "Inside U.S.A.," which introduced Valerie Battis to Broadway and success; "Annie Get Your Gun;" a revival of "Show Boat," with Pearl Primus and a brilliant Negro group; and "Plain and Fancy." In this last and also in "Annie" her longtime concert partner who became also her husband, Daniel Nagrin, was a featured dancer.

Nagrin himself developed as a major artist under her guidance and inspiration, though he was already a dancer before he joined her in concerts and night clubs. When she put aside her personal dancing for a new career as a choreographer for Broadway, he worked along with her as both performer and assistant choreographer.

For himself he has worked out a strikingly vigorous and pointed style and artistic purpose. This is epitomized in a series of solos that first established him as an important figure in the field. They are essentially portraits, reducing to succinct terms of movement the essence of various characters who have emerged as types in the contemporary scene. One is "Strange Hero," a frank facing of the glorified gangster of a certain level of popular fiction; another is "Man of Action," a humorous study of the young man on the make in the hectic business world; and most devastating of them all is the long, merciless unveiling of a man who refuses to come to terms with the world he lives in, under the title of "Indeterminate Figure." Nagrin's technique is strong and extraordinarily controlled, and he is eminently direct in saying what he has to say.

With him as co-director, Tamiris has returned of recent seasons to the concert field, which has always been her major interest, though she no longer dances herself. After a long and thorough preparatory period, during which they established a school for the purpose, they presented the first performance of the newly-organized Tamiris-Nagrin Dance Company in 1960, and opened another creative chapter in their annals.

Two hard-hitting portraits in a series of distinctive vignettes by Daniel Nagrin: "Indeterminate Figure," the man who is aware of little about anything; and "Strange Hero," the inexplicably glorified hoodlum

Peter Basch

Hanya Holm and her company in the section called "The Lament," from "Trend," her first major work in this country, in its original presentation at the Bennington (College) Festival with setting by Arch Lauterer

Barbara Morgan

Hanya Holm

From still another background, and a more remote one, came the fifth important leader of the American modern dance. This was Hanya Holm, who was a member of the original group with which Wigman made history in Europe immediately after World War I, later headed the faculty of the central Wigman school in Dresden, and finally came to America during Wigman's tours of this country to open a branch school in New York.

Holm had not been in this country for many months before she had fallen completely in love with its vigorous rhythm of living, the fresh vitality of its young dancers, its speed and dash; and she realized that here lay the future for her and her ideas of dance. Its rhythms, too, must be more vigorous, and she began a process of quite intuitive adaptation to the new land and its pulse.

Over the intervening years she has evolved a personal art and a personal method, which, though rooted in Wigman's theories, which she helped to evolve, are as far removed from them in development as Humphrey, Weidman and Graham are from Denishawn. They are, indeed, so clearly of American influence and American growth as to be essentially a native product.

Because of her gifts as an educator and the notably sound educational system she has created, she has necessarily spent much of her energy in teaching, not only in her own school in New York, but also in a New York theatre school devoted to the musical stage, and in the annual summer session of Colorado College in Colorado Springs. But this activity has in no sense interfered with her major interest, which is in choreography; it has, indeed, fed and enriched it. As a choreographer she has created in many fields — concert, theatre, opera — and always with a lively and individual approach.

Shortly before she came to this country she collaborated with Wigman on the production of a massive anti-war work called "Totenmal," presented in Munich in 1930. This highly experimental theatre piece involved a huge company of dancers, a speech-chorus, a large percussion orchestra and elaborate lighting schemes.

She was in this country for six full years, not only teaching but also learning, before she felt she was ready to present a composition that had grown out of her new environment, and could make use of dancers of her own training. When she did, it was a significant one, created in its original form for the Bennington Festival in 1937. It was called "Trend," and employed a large group with soloists (of whom she was one, though by no means in any stellar sense). Its music was extremely radical, both as music and as a precedent-setting technological event. It consisted of an especially commissioned score by Wallingford Riegger for small orchestra, together with the "Ionization" of Edgar Varèse, scored exclusively

163

Hanya Holm in "Trend"

Thomas Bouchard

An action shot of Hanya Holm and her company, caught at a climactic instant of rehearsing in the studio

Thomas Bouchard

for percussions and demanding instruments altogether outside the orthodox orchestra, and Varèse's "Octandre" for woodwinds. This was specially recorded for the production, and required for its presentation equipment devised for the purpose by Mirko Paneyko. The result was an extraordinary and a revolutionary use of mechanical means for the creation of a virtually new type of music. It anticipated all the present-day *musique concrète* and electronic experimentations. The work also employed the first modern stage setting the American dance had seen, designed by Arch Lauterer; and when it was later presented in New York at the then Mecca Temple (now the New York City Center), its action extended out over the entire main floor of the hall, and the audience was seated in the two balconies. The production proved too costly to be practical, but it assuredly was the occasion of a distinguished debut for Holm.

Though her style, in smaller studio recitals, had seemed essentially lyric, this was an intensely dramatic work and one that made use of all the elements of the theatre, which was patently the medium she liked to work in.

Of recent years, indeed, she has devoted herself chiefly to Broadway musicals, to which she has brought the same meticulous artistry as to her concert works. With no condescension to a "popular" medium, she has treated this field simply as a lighter form of art, but just as good art, for all that. To be sure, she has not consented to choreograph uncritically for everything that has been offered her, but has accepted assignments only where she has seen qualities of interest. Her very first venture into the field was the enormously successful "Kiss Me, Kate," and she was also the brilliantly collaborative choreographer in that long-run record-holder, "My Fair Lady."

But though she has embraced the Broadway musical eagerly for its purely theatrical extension of the dimensions of modern dancing, she has kept alive her interest and her activity in other fields at the same time. New concert works are created every summer for the festival at Colorado Springs, and she has also staged, among other things, Gluck's "Orfeo" for the Vancouver Festival, and various new operas for the summer series at Central City, Colorado.

Her compositions, whether dramatic, humorous or lyric, for theatre or concert hall, are characterized by a natural sense of form, a fine musicianship (she was also a graduate of the Dalcroze Institute at Hellerau), a lively pleasure in experimentation, and an instinct for style.

A sponsor of the Dance Notation Bureau from the start, she is the first choreographer in the Broadway milieu to have all the dances for her productions written down in Labanotation, the scores reduced to microfilm, and copyrighted.

José Limón

Out of the companies of all these leading artists have come other figures who have either broken away in protest to carry out artistic ideas of their own in the perpetual revolution of art, or else have carried the established line forward gradually in new personal directions.

In this latter division is José Limón, the most important figure in the group, who has taken his place in the top rank of modern dancers. As an idealistic, musical-minded, discontented young student painter, Mexican born and California reared, he found the answer to his aesthetic searching, much to his own surprise, in the classes of Humphrey and Weidman. Here his enthusiasm, his energy and his quite apparent gift for movement urged him on over difficult technical and emotional hurdles until at the end of the struggle he found himself the company's chief male dancer except for Weidman himself.

Since he was of creative mind, choreography was inevitably in his blood, and upon his release from military service after World War II in 1945, he formed a company of his own. Humphrey, who had just retired from active dancing, became his artistic director and together they enjoyed many fruitful seasons until her death. These included a steady building of the company, the production of many new works, tours of this country and, under State Department auspices, tours of South America and Europe. Since Humphrey's death, he has continued his

José Limón in "Danza"

Alfred A. Cohn

José Limón, with Beatrice Seckler and Dorothy Bird, nucleus of his first company, in Vivaldi "Concerto"

Gerda Peterich

José Limón, with Pauline Koner, Lucas Hoving, Betty Jones in "The Moor's Pavane," an Othello in essence

José Limón and Pauline Koner in the "Ritmo Jondo" of Doris Humphrey, set to the music of Carlos Surinach

company with perhaps the most active schedule of any of the contemporary modern organizations.

His compositions have extended over many areas, from his Vivaldi "Concerto" to "The Emperor Jones," with music by Villa-Lobos; from biblical dramas about the banishment from Eden, the Annunciation and Judas, to a wholly hilarious piece called "Performance (Over the Footlights and Back)" set to a series of variations composed by all the members of the musical faculty of the Juilliard School. Outstanding, however, are three unquestionable masterpieces, also of markedly different character from each other. One is the simple retelling of a Mexican legend, "Malinche;" another is a brilliant choreographic version of Othello, set to music of Purcell, under the title of "The Moor's Pavane," in which the dramatic line itself never loses the pattern of a formal dance; and the third is the noble and profoundly moving "Missa Brevis," set to Kodály's "Missa Brevis in Tempore Belli," and inspired by the first visit of the company to war-wracked Poland.

For the company Humphrey also created a number of admirable works including "Day on Earth" to Aaron Copland's music, definitely one of her greatest achievements, for all its simplicity; "Lament for Ignacio Sanchez Mejías," to the poem by Garcia Lorca and a score by Norman Lloyd; "Night Spell," to Priaulx Rainier's string quartet; "Ruins and Visions," after poems of Stephen Spender, with music from the first and second quartets of Benjamin Britten; and another very funny and very pithy cartoon-inspired satire, "The Story of Mankind."

The company started as a trio, of which the other members were the richly talented Dorothy Bird and Beatrice Seckler. In its later and larger form it continued on a high level, if with the usual transiency. Its leading figures, have been Lucas Hoving, originally from the Kurt Jooss company; Betty Jones and Ruth Currier, the latter with gifts as a choreographer to match those as a dancer. But its chief ornament was a guest artist who dropped in like the famous man who came to dinner and stayed for a decade or more. This was Pauline Koner.

Pauline Koner

Miss Koner had already had a distinguished career of her own in many departments of the dance — a pupil of Fokine in the classic ballet, a partner of Yeichi Nimura in the Oriental dance, a modern recitalist in her own style, and even one of the earliest choreographers to experiment with television.

Feeling the need for guidance in the matter of choreography — somebody to discuss her problem with on a professional level — she sought Humphrey and persuaded her to become her artistic director. Since Humphrey was already serving in the same capacity for Limón and his company, it was only natural that sooner or later there should be some alliance between the two, however informal.

It was a fine move for everybody concerned. Koner brought a weight of artistry and authority into the group that met Limón on something of his own level, and in return she received the benefits of working with a first-rate ensemble under first-rate direction. It was a precedent-making thing for an artist of her standing to make such an alliance, but in this enlivening association she reached the peak of her achievement up to that point, as both dancer and choreographer.

One of Koner's most important gifts is that of sheer performing, which is an art in itself and one not generally given the rank it is entitled to. She is always "somebody" on stage, whether in her own choreography or that of somebody else; every gesture takes on value, every emotional color is clean and sharp, and design emerges with full awareness though without underscoring. Some of her performances with Limón have been memorable; it is difficult to imagine the title role in "La Malinche," Emilia in "The Moor's Pavane," or the mother in "Ruins and Visions" in anybody else's hands.

Breaking away after Humphrey's death to resume her individual career, she created a beautiful and impressive work to express her appreciation to her late mentor. Entitled "The Farewell," it is set to the final movement of Mahler's "Das Lied von der Erde," and is notable not only for its intrinsic beauty but also for the subtle manner in which it echoes and evokes the creative spirit of Humphrey herself. A more fitting honor could scarcely have been paid by one artist to another.

Pauline Koner and José Limón, as Mary and Joseph, in an exalted passage from his work, "The Visitation"
Peter Basch

Pauline Koner in her vivid portrait of the prophetic "Cassandra," using Aaron Copland's Piano Variations
Peter Basch

José Limón (left) rehearsing "The Traitor" (Judas), with all-male cast including Lucas Hoving (right)

Pauline Koner in the title role of Limón's legend of Mexico, "La Malinche," to the music of Norman Lloyd

José Limón in "Missa Brevis," built on the music of Zoltán Kodály and deeply inspired by war's tragedy

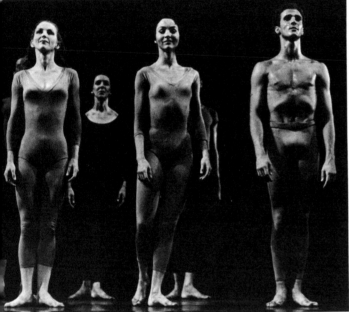

The Limón company in two numbers: his "I, Odysseus" with Ruth Currier, Lola Huth, Louis Falco; and Doris Humphrey's last work, "Brandenburg Concerto," with Lola Huth, Louis Falco and Ann Vachon in foreground

Sybil Shearer et al

Also out of the Humphrey-Weidman background came Sybil Shearer, stimulating and remarkably creative maverick. Determined to find for herself what movement meant and how to use it for communicative purposes, she withdrew from the competitive field of New York, the great market place of the arts, to work quietly and concentratedly in a small community on Chicago's North Shore.

The signs of such a trend were already in evidence to those with wits enough to recognize them, when just after her graduation from Skidmore College, she turned up at the first session of the Bennington School of the Dance, at Bennington College in 1934. Her curiosity was boundless—about all the arts, about nature, about human experience — and she was too unselfconscious to disguise it. Her early morning walks through the woods, while most of her student colleagues were still sleeping off their muscle fatigue, found her tapping every tree she passed,

like another Dr. Johnson tapping London lampposts with his cane. For reasons (or instincts) that could not have been more sound, she chose to join the Humphrey-Weidman group, where she learned the fundamentals of the art at an irreproachably high level. But she was always singularly her own creature.

On the Illinois plains over a period of years she has found herself, with the support and collaboration of Helen Balfour Morrison, photographer, specialist in light, and maverick herself. There she established a studio, began to teach widely in the public schools of the area, built up a company and became in no time at all something of a tradition. Occasionally she has made a foray into New York for a single recital, to which she has drawn every important figure in the dance world, shocked them, stirred them up, and departed — only to return a year or so later with a completely new set of principles, arrived at quite inevitably and wholeheartedly through her innocent yielding to the concepts of basic

Katherine Litz

Norman Solomon

Sybil Shearer

Helen Balfour Morrison

Midi Garth John Wulp

dance.

In her own territory, where her audiences are quite unattuned to the reputation of the modern dance as something esoteric and *outré,* she has acquired a large following which has found her unquestioningly persuasive. And that, one might say, is exactly what she went there to do. The sophisticates in the field, however, have regularly made pilgrimages from New York and elsewhere to her performances, and though she still might find the going rough if she tried to set up shop in the market place, she is accepted and admired as a courageous prophet who has proved the theory of the better mouse-trap. The path has been beaten to her own little theatre in the community center at Winnetka, where she has given programs, nominally once a month, but actually whenever she has had something she felt ready to show. More recently she has been appointed artist-in-residence at the handsome Arnold Theatre of the National College of Education in Evanston, though she is in no sense a member of the faculty and still maintains her independent studio.

Her approach to movement continues to be supremely personal, and her turn of mind incurably inquisitive, so that she is forever evolving fresh and evocative material. But however fully she may create by sheer intuition, her technical practices are rigorously disciplined and evince a keen sense of the body and its functioning. If her art seems at times altogether fey, it depends largely on where you stand; certainly it is honest and uncompromising and in a perpetual state of growth.

The company she has gathered about her comes from various sources — modern dancers, ballet dancers, and simple workmen in whom she has espied unsuspected qualifications for movement. That it is inclined to be a shifting personnel, does not mean that it is less than a devoted one.

Two other dancers of importance have developed their own art in directions inspired by contact with her at an earlier period. One is her erstwhile colleague in the Humphrey-Weidman company, Katherine Litz, who while dancing in Chicago in "Oklahoma!," fell under the spell of her new magic. To be sure, what Litz was so strongly affected by has long since passed out of Shearer's practice, and she has developed it on lines of her own to impressive stature. Her bent is much more sharply directed to the theatre than Shearer's, is less volatile and more introspective. Perhaps it can be epitomized as a dramatization of the ludicrousness of the tragic.

If we titter, we are also moved by her frustrated creatures, her emotional tatterdemalions, in "Fall of the Leaf," "Fire in the Snow," "And No Birds Sing." But her finest work to date is her brilliant dramatization of Bram Stoker's Victorian novel, "Dracula." She has by no means burlesqued it or tried to recapture the gaudy nonsense of the silent movies; the work has been treated with respect and with a sensitive awareness of the style that underlies it as a product of its own era. Having been directed in the old days many times by Charles Weidman, she in turn now directed him in the title role. With Ray Harrison as the "hero" and herself as the heroine, it was a triumphant performance. Whatever debt she may owe to Shearer, there was no trace of Shearer here.

She, too, has been active as artist-in-residence at various universities, dancing, directing and being generally creative.

Midi Garth touched the Shearer influence at an even more susceptible period, and bore away at the beginning obvious marks of the contact which have since been removed by assimilation and maturity. She has given a minimum of public performances, her first full evening's program, indeed, having taken place only in 1958.

Very few others have followed, but enough to make clear the authenticity of her talent. She has the gift of beautiful and eloquent movement, together with the simplest and most unpretentious approach to choreography. Whatever she does is pure, direct and concentrated; its line is never confused, nor its phrase vague, and through an intuitive motor sense is conveyed a genuine lyric experience.

It is perhaps unwarranted to group these artists together as representing anything like a "school," but the three of them (together with Paul Taylor in his most creative aspects, and perhaps also Murray Louis) have enough in common to justify the belief that in this direction lies the brightest hope for the creative trend of the modern dance.

Eleanor King

To this group — except for the physical distance and lack of any continuing contact between them — might also be added the name of Eleanor King, another Humphrey-Weidman alumna of the same period as Shearer and Litz. From the very start she grasped with singular firmness that basic relation between inner feeling and actual movement which is the essence of modern dance. Like Shearer, she too took herself early out of the competitive arena to work out her own art. Though her headquarters were first in Seattle and of more recent years at the Fine Art Center of the University of Arkansas, she has danced over wide areas, from Amsterdam to Tokyo, but not for many seasons in New York.

Her concept of the dance has taken her over an even wider area, for with her intuitive sense of the universal substance of the dance, she has seen it as virtually without limitations in subject matter, style or ethnological background. She has been equally inclusive in her use of music, and has danced also to spoken words (in several languages) and in silence.

Among the early solos that manifested the quality of her particular gift were two suites in medieval (but markedly different) key, one called "Roads to Hell," dealing with the seven deadly sins, and the other, "Characters of the Annunciation," set to music of Hindemith; and two other works of vastly different color, one called "Moon Dances" and set to three sections of Schoenberg's "Pierrot Lunaire" in a style as curiously otherworldly as the music, and the other, "Who Walk Alone," to music of Alban Berg. In these latter pieces she deals in substrata of the mind that are rarely touched in the dance but are haunting and strangely disturbing.

Eleanor King   *Robert McAfee*

Her first ambitious effort in the ensemble field was not an unqualified success by any means at its première in (of all untheatrical places) the Sculpture Court of the Brooklyn Museum. This was "Icaro," based on the poetic play by Lauro de Bosis, and spoken in Italian, with a special score by David Diamond. It was later developed in Seattle, where she was able to come to grips with ensemble composition, as with other elements of her diversified art, and generally to come of age as an artist.

Her dramatic background is strong and has deeply influenced the character of her art, which is primarily that of the theatre in its broad and creative meaning — dance theatre, in short.

Paul Taylor

Paul Taylor is an enormously challenging figure, with a rich and original talent which he has subjected from time to time to unwarranted peril by teetering on the brink of *avant-gardisme*. He has a fine body, capable of strong and sustained movement, but especially eloquent in terms of a curious idiom of its own, in which it appears to defy the presence of normal joints and bone structure. His hands and feet are especially vivid and unorthodox in action, and if it all may seem essentially neurotic, it is nevertheless undeniably striking and persuasive. Certainly it contains that element of contagion that makes dancing communicative.

Unhappily, as a choreographer he is frequently the reverse of communicative, and seems at times deliberately and almost belligerently unintelligible. How much of this is due to "beatnik" influences from which he has not completely fought himself free, and how much to the natural experimentalism of a creative mind in search of new dimensions, cannot be ascertained. Certainly, however, he is potentially a major figure in the art.

The height of his power thus far was achieved during the five years when he was a leading member of Martha Graham's company during her present great theatre period. His performance as the evil Aegisthus in her "Clytemnestra" is second only to her own in that work, and in her "Alcestis" his genial and drunken Hercules captures the full flavor of the satyr play and is another superb job.

Paul Taylor in his "Insects and Heroes," with Elizabeth Walton, Maggie Newman, Linda Hodes, Dan Wagoner

During these same years he was invited by Balanchine to dance one solo section of the Webern "Episodes" with the New York City Ballet, and this was likewise something of a triumph. Balanchine had choreographed it for him entirely in terms of the curious Taylor style of movement, carrying it, perhaps, even farther for the sake of its significance in this fairly frightening work. There is not another dancer either in the ballet company or even in the modern field at large who can follow Taylor in this role, and when he is not available, that section of the ballet is simply omitted (to the detriment of the whole, let it be said).

With as much talent as he possesses, it is understandable that he cannot remain exclusively a member of anybody else's company, but must create for himself. In this he has been only partly successful thus far, though he has made some excellent pieces. Among them are "Meridian," set to *musique concrète* by Boulez; "Epitaphs," a comedy fantasy utilizing a recording of the Laneville-Johnson Union Brass Band; "Tablet," "Images and Reflections," "Rebus," an amusing bird solo about "The Least Flycatcher," and a lovely ensemble piece called "Aureole."

His most experimental program consisted of seven numbers in which he wore street clothes and all but stood still to the sound of metronomes and what-not. This was an early essay, however, which as an adventurous-minded young artist he had to get off his chest; he has not come so near the brink of the cliff since. But however cryptic he may still elect to be with his choreography and his secretive titles, his manner is simple, open and engaging, his compositions are actually simpler than they seem in many instances, and he has a delightful humor which he frequently chooses to employ.

Pearl Lang

With the Graham company, as with every other company, over the years many dancers have defected, either through rebellion or simply in order to pursue more individual paths. Among them are Anna Sokolow, Sophie Maslow, May O'Donnell, Jean Erdmann, John Butler, Merce

Walter Strate

Pearl Lang

Cunningham, Erick Hawkins — all of whom have made careers of their own in different areas. Some have worked into educational fields, some have turned to the theatre and television; some have traveled "far out" among the "beatniks," and some have progressed in a more balanced manner toward goals of their own.

In this last category, the most recent rebel to succeed in finding herself in her own terms is Pearl Lang, whose departure from the fold occurred in the early '50s after an outstanding performance as Death in Graham's "Canticle for Innocent Comedians" (a lovely work, unfortunately no longer in the repertoire). Many of her roles, indeed, were unforgettable, and in some cases have not been so well done by anybody else.

Her battle for independence was a valiant one, for the mark of Graham lay heavily upon her art, but she gradually emerged as her own

Merce Cunningham

Gerda Peterich

creature with a degree of triumph.

With personal beauty, high temperament, a superb technique, fine musical sensibility and a strong dramatic sense, she has earned in every way the position she occupies in the art. She has also built a fine company about her, in which with excellent imagination she has selected artists whose particular styles she requires even though they have not come out of her own training. It was in her company that Taylor first made an impression.

As a choreographer she has ventured into a wide territory, and since she is a genuinely creative artist her work never invites less than respect.

Alwin Nikolais

Light years removed from Shearer's projection of the body itself into a state of communication, and also from all these concepts of theatre dance, is the artistic practice of Alwin Nikolais, who is not a dancer himself but directs a company of his own that is completely the outgrowth of his individual aesthetics.

He has described the milieu he has created as a new theatre of motion, which seems very apt, for the word "motion" indicates simply the opposite of the state of rest whether for animate or inanimate objects. The word "movement," on the other hand, as it is applied to dancing, is characterized by the implication of volition. Nikolais' dancers in performance are almost totally depersonalized, and share his compositions so completely with the imaginative scenic appurtenances and properties that are an integral part of his invention, as to become almost inseparable from them. This is not because they are incapable of moving, for they are trained admirably and concentratedly, and their bodies are superbly at their command. Indeed, in their classes there is to be seen far more of what is generally thought of as dancing than is to be found in his stage conceptions. The nearest precedent, perhaps, for this use of dancers was the Triadische Ballett established under Bauhaus influence in Germany between the two World Wars, in which the dancer served mainly as a motor inside a mechanical figure to transport it about the stage in the required design.

For music Nikolais employs recorded soundtracks of his own composing or assembling,

Alwin Nikolais Dance Company in his suite called "Kaleidoscope." (Murray Louis third figure from right)

David S. Berlin

chiefly for percussion instruments played by his dancers, plus excerpts from Indonesian gamelan music, contemporary electronic compositions, *musique concrète* and works by *avant-garde* musicians who compose along these general lines. His lighting is ingenious, creative and brilliant, and comprises a significant element in his creations, and he achieves extraordinary effects with ropes, fabrics, masks, poles and platforms.

His programs usually consist of a single work, made up of a series of somehow related compositions. At first their titles were descriptive, as "Masks, Props and Mobiles," which consisted of études built around specific appurteances; later they had a master title indicative of a more unified theme, such as "Allegory," "Totem," "Nimbus." If these are elusive, they are fitted to works without literary theme and are themselves vague in content. They are, nevertheless, invariably eye-filling, attention-gripping and sometimes a trifle ear-splitting. For all their deviation from established procedures, the pattern tends to become a rigid one. Its relation to dancing is little more than incidental, but within its self-created genre it is original and absorbing as a manipulation of theatrical elements, including bodies, to artistic ends.

Nikolais started as a pianist, and was drawn into his present activity by the fascination he found in Wigman's use of music. Accordingly, in order to learn how to play such unorthodox instruments and to absorb their essential aesthetic qualities, he enrolled with Holm, who was Wigman's representative in this country at the time. From her he acquired also, however, so thorough a knowledge of movement that he became one of her principal teachers. It is still possible to see, even in his present work, the seeds of both Wigman's and Holm's teachings on the production of movement, choreography and musical relationships.

With a small but excellently equipped theatre home in the Henry Street Playhouse, and a large school to go with it — both under the auspices of the Henry Street Settlement — he has established one of the most provocative institutions in New York, which draws devoted audi-

Sam Falk, New York Times

From the highly personal workshop of Alwin Nikolais: One movement from the suite candidly entitled "Masks, Props and Mobiles"; and below, two "vehicles" (Coral Martindale, Murray Louis) in the suite, "Allegory"

David S. Berlin

Murray Louis

Sam Falk, New York Times

ences in spite of its remoteness from the center of theatrical activities. Out of it, however, he has toured fairly extensively, both at home and abroad.

Oddly enough, from out of his training has come a dancer who is anything but inexpressive and depersonalized. This is Murray Louis, who has become not only his chief dancer but also his co-director. But for all his devoted discipleship, Louis has followed his own personal directions in his creative work, and has done so with the complete approval and co-operation of Nikolais.

Though he is naturally influenced by Nikolais' approach to the creation of movement and choreography and makes free use of similar musical and visual ingenuities, his compositions are centered in human experience and easily dominate their surroundings. He has made many admirable solos — funny, fantastic, moving, improvisatory; and he works well also with a partner or a small group. Of particularly evocative power is his tender bit of introspection called "Journal," which is not only full of substance but also original and beautiful in form. He has a remarkably eloquent body, improvises with unusual authority, and is altogether a sensitive and communicative artist — one of the best, indeed, and not too remote in kind from Shearer and her milieu.

176

Lester Horton

By all means the most influential modern dancer to make his headquarters on the Pacific Coast, far from his origins in the Middle West and even farther from the general clearing house which is New York, was Lester Horton. His career developed contemporaneously with the development of the modern dance in the East, and paralleled it with remarkable closeness. As a matter of fact, during the middle and late '30s his themes and his titles in more than one instance proved to be so similar to those of Graham and Humphrey, though there had been no contact of any sort between them, that he abandoned work well along in progress when he discovered the situation.

Primarily a theatre man, his tastes were eclectic, and his activities astonishingly varied and energetic, not only in style but also in dimen-

Bella Lewitzki in "Soldadera," from Lester Horton's suite, "Estila de Tu," on his "Choreo-'50" program

sions. They ranged from tribal dances of the American Indians (perhaps his earliest dance interest) to Ravel's "Bolero," from Stravinsky's "Le Sacre du Printemps" in the huge Hollywood Bowl to solos and duets in his own small dance theatre in Los Angeles.

Beneath this variety of surface, and perhaps in large measure because of it, he developed a strong technical method and his teaching produced many fine dancers, chief among them being Bella Lewitski. Since his death in 1953, and even before that, a number of other dancers have spread his name and his methods across the Great Divide and have presented some of his compositions in New York and elsewhere. Now active from their own various headquarters in New York are, among others, Carmen de Lavallade, Joyce Trisler, James Mitchell, Alvin Ailey and James Truitte.

Asadata Dafora in "Kykunkor"

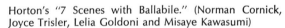

Horton's "7 Scenes with Ballabile." (Norman Cornick, Joyce Trisler, Lelia Goldoni and Misaye Kawasumi)

The Negro Dance

One of the most significant aspects of the American modern dance revolution was its opening of the way for the Negro dancer to find himself as a creative artist. For the first time it put at his disposal a means for dance expression that was not only of his own time and place but also belonged as much to him, in spite of any racial discriminations that might surround him, as to anybody else. Its entire basis was the relationship between inner emotional awareness and outward muscular activity, and in the possession of these elements he was demonstrably the peer of any man alive.

Naturally the movement he produced thus, without the superimposition of any arbitrary limitations, would differ from that produced by Caucasians, Mongolians or Malayans, and would accordingly release in communicative essence the uninhibited qualities of the racial heritage, no matter what the immediate subject of any specific dance might be. At last, in other words, he would not have to try to pretend to be somebody

177

else, or deny that he was who he was. Perhaps no greater area of equality had ever been opened to him.

It would be quite erroneous to consider the emergence of so large a body of gifted American Negro dancers as merely a by-product of the intensified civil rights movement of recent years, most specifically since World War II. Though it has certainly been cross-fertilized by such political and social forces, this is a cultural emancipation, springing from the same root but at a more subjective level.

It first began to manifest itself significantly along with the general blossoming of the modern dance in the late '20s and early '30s, and it has pursued a parallel course all the way, though with a notable independence. It, too, after all, is a cutting through of tradition to basic dance, for all that its handicaps and resistances have been almost entirely different.

As for dance tradition, the American Negro as such has virtually none. His ancestral African tradition is so remote that instead of having to overcome it, he has found himself eagerly undertaking to investigate it, both for its hitherto unrealized formal beauties and for his own self-knowledge. From Caribbean and South American sources, closer in both time and geography, he has become aware of still further enrichment. His North American tradition, however, is extremely meager, for here he was never master of his background and lived in cultural isolation, as it were. Even so, the spirituals, the work songs, the play songs, the songs of protest, were the seeds of a native art; and on the other hand, bits of folk frolic, the cake-walks and struttings, the exuberant cavortings designed to be shown by slaves to their "white folks," led straight into the minstrel show, through which eventually the Negro dancer was channeled into the commercial entertainment field. There he has completely changed the music of the world and much of its popular dancing with what we now call jazz. And though clog dancing is virtually universal among folk practices, his particular development of it has produced that independent department of virtuoso stage dancing known as tap.

Into all these areas of source material the contemporary Negro dancer has delved with creative curiosity and profit; in a sense he has had to acquire a tradition in order to overturn it intelligently. In the field of commercial entertainment in which he has been virtually confined until recently, he has revealed, however, certain qualities that must follow him into any field, for they belong to him intrinsically. One is his uniquely racial rhythm; far more than just a beat, it includes a characteristic phrase, manifested throughout the entire body and originating sometimes so far from its eventual point of outlet as to have won the description of "lazy." It is not ideally adapted to European music in general, and, especially when it is employed in company with non-Negro dancers, it can easily appear to be "out of time," and has frequently been called so by non-Negro choreographers.

Closely allied to this pervasive rhythm is the wide dynamic range of his movement itself, with, at one extreme, vigor and an apparently inexhaustible energy (though, be it noted, a minimum of tension), and at the other extreme, a rich command of relaxation.

Another quality, less physical and more temperamental, is the sense of performing, in which the Negro is rivaled perhaps only by the Slav. This involves not so much any violent method of projection as an easy, outgoing manner, which, at the same time, is open to every overtone of an audience's mood and able accordingly to manipulate that mood more or less at will.

But all this innate equipment is capable of being turned to more substantial and creative ends than mere time-pleasing, and time-pleasing is the tradition that the Negro artist has bent his efforts to overthrow.

While he has been looking into his own traditions, however — whether African, Caribbean or "show business" — he has also taken a glance at the traditions that his American colleagues of other races have been concerned with, especially the academic ballet. By and large, he has been wise enough not to be drawn into it, for its wholly European outlook, history and technical theory are alien to him culturally, temperamentally and anatomically.

It is an anthropological oversimplification, to be sure, to speak of such a thing as the Negro body, especially when one considers in Africa alone the contrast between the Watusi and the Pygmy. Nevertheless, in practice there is a racial constant, so to speak, in the proportions of the limbs and torso and the conformation of the feet, all of which affect body placement; in addition, the deliberately maintained erectness of the European dancer's spine is in marked contrast to the fluidity of the Negro dancer's, and the latter's natural concentration of movement in the pelvic region is similarly at odds with European usage. When the Negro takes on the style of the European, he succeeds only in being affected, just as the European dancer who attempts to dance like the Negro seems only gauche.

The interchange of racial practices of moving is incompatible with subjective artistic processes, and even in large measure with imitative ones, if for no other reason than the differences in body structure. The European ballet has been itself a means of making this clear in its transplantations (for various reasons having nothing to do with art) over the alien world, including Japan, Turkey and the Soviet Union's Mongolian republics on the steppes of Asia. In the last category, moving pictures of the Kirghiz ballet, among others which have been circulated in the United States, provide convincing evidence of basic incongruousness canceling out whatever degree of skill.

Parenthetically, however, be it said to the credit of the Soviet Union that it has offset its own apparent attempt at forced cultural standardization along these lines by establishing also native and racially genuine dance companies in its constituent republics, many of which have made official tours over other parts of the world. The increasingly widespread awareness of the values of the individual racial ethos in every division of the human family, which must inevitably build a new interracial, intercultural awakening and rapprochement, is one of the most hopeful signs of human progress in this period.

To the above generalities, of course, there are exceptions, though they are surprisingly rare in view of history's longtime and steady intermingling of racial strains, and the everpresent possibility of biological sports. In the very short period during which the American Negro dancer has been brought into practical contact with the academic ballet, there has been only one instance of the appearance of a Negro ballerina, beautifully equipped physically, technically and stylistically. This is Janet Collins, for three years leading ballerina with the Metropolitan Opera under the direction of Zachary Solov, who cast her with full regard for her racial difference from the remainder of the company and choreographed for her with sensitive imagination. She, however, was understandably far more interested in other fields of her art in which she could, and did, function more creatively.

In the days around 1930, when the new era was dawning, the most popular aspect of the subject for discussion was "Which direction shall the Negro dance take?" Because it was full of energy and experimentation, it tried them all before a broad general approach worked itself out on the principles of the modern dance under which each creative individual makes art out of his own background, experience and vision.

Those first formative years produced no outstanding figures to compare with Graham, Tamiris, Humphrey and Weidman, but it had its leaders who did vital spade work and set a number of precedents. Hemsley Winfield, Edna Guy, Wilson Williams were fairly indomitable, giving recitals of their own, advocating and even forming such organizations as the Negro Dance Theatre and the New Negro Art Theatre.

Zora Hurston gathered together sixteen Bahama dancers and presented them in folk dances and songs (the two being, of course, inseparable), which opened a startling area of experience to non-Negro audiences.

In 1931, Randolph Sawyer joined the newly formed Dance Center of Gluck Sandor and Felicia Sorel, which may have set a precedent in what has since been more self-consciously underlined as company "integration." Then it seemed, and was, the most natural thing in the world, for Sawyer was appropriately cast and irreplaceable.

In 1933, Winfield became the first Negro ever to dance with the Metropolitan Opera company when he did the Witch Doctor in Louis Gruenberg's operatic version of "The Emperor Jones," and he took his whole company into the production with him. That same year he and Guy and the sixteen Bahamians and others went into the cast of Hall Johnson's "Run Lil Chillun" with Doris Humphrey as choreographer, and shortly afterwards Frederick Ashton came over from London to choreograph for the all-Negro cast of the Gertrude Stein-Virgil Thomson opera, "Four Saints in Three Acts." And in Chicago Ruth Page created the ballet, "La Guiablesse," to the music of William Grant Still, for herself and an otherwise all-Negro company, which included the youthful Katherine Dunham at the beginning of her career.

"Kykunkor"

In 1934, the first really great splash in the field was "Kykunkor," produced in a loft far from the theatre district by Asadata Dafora Horton. He was born in Sierra Leone and was the great-grandson of a Nova Scotia slave who had returned to Africa when he was freed and taken along with him the adopted name of his former owner, which his great-grandson was to drop professionally early in his American career.

Dafora had studied singing in Italy in his youth and he accordingly conceived "Kykunkor" as an opera. It was based on tribal life and consisted fundamentally of tribal dances, built around a fictional plot and interspersed with vaguely Italianesque arias sung by Dafora himself in the title role. Its cast included fellow Africans from various tribes, including prominently a one-time medicine-man, Abdul Assan, in a role recreating his former calling, and American-born Negro dancers and singers, among them Sawyer. It was not merely an assembling of folk material; it was a created work.

Though its production was sketchy in the extreme and its improvised surroundings totally inadequate, it was a stunning success and a revelation of the possibilities of the field it opened up. A distinguished public, including many figures from the world of the arts, jammed the loft, paying excessive scalper's fees for the privilege of standing against the wall or sitting on top of the unused piano. Before it had run its record-breaking course of approximately three months, it had been ejected from its original quarters (wisely) by the public safety department and played four other halls and theatres. But as time went on, the performance lost most of its quality, since its largely unprofessional company was unable to sustain it, and the production had to be closed down temporarily so that Dafora could pull it back into shape. Eventually it reopened for a final five weeks in its last home atop the Chanin Building.

Dafora followed "Kykunkor" over the years with other works of the same character, which he now called dance-dramas, and the form was taken up by others, including the Federal Theatre, which presented "Bassa Moona" in 1937. But the impact of "Kykunkor" was never repeated; there was no need for it to be, for it had performed its function.

Katherine Dunham

It was not until the early '40s that the first two unmistakable masters appeared on the scene to define and clarify the essential American Negro dance and its broad field of operations. They were Katherine Dunham and Pearl Primus, who could scarcely be more different and at the same time have more in common. Both are college women with master's degrees in anthropology, both have been sponsored by foundations in research, and in spite of these perhaps frightening intellectual attainments, both are first-rate artists and courageous trail-blazers. Their differences can be roughly summed up by saying that Dunham is primarily of the theatre and treats her ethnological material simply as subjects for her personal creations in that medium, while Primus employs the practices and devices of the theatre chiefly as a means for publishing the beauties

180

she finds in her ethnological material. Both utilize ritual, folk customs, everyday life in Africa, the Caribbean and North America, but Dunham is suave, sensuous and detached, while Primus is intense, personally involved and direct. Dunham has won wide success in popular fields, including Broadway and Hollywood, and her own productions have taken the general form of the revue; but she has retained her interest in more serious aspects of the subject, and until it became financially impossible, she maintained a New York school of broad scope and potent influence, with an experimental group functioning under its auspices with the talented Syvilla Fort as director. Primus has also danced popularly, in night clubs and Broadway musicals, but her finest work has been in the concert field, where her temperament, imagination and prodigious technique immediately won her a high place as a dancer. Dunham, on the other hand, has always disclaimed any pre-eminence as a dancer, but has prided herself upon her choreographic ability.

Now, roughly two decades after they first commanded attention, they have both all but lost themselves to the field in which they have made history, and in characteristic directions: Dunham in literary activities, in which she has great gifts, though she still comes up occasionally, if perhaps only for financial reasons, with another revue, or even the staging of the ballet in "Aida" for the Metropolitan Opera; and Primus in the pursuit of more and more material in Africa together with a veritable missionary zeal for converting the Africans to the richness of their own dancing.

Dunham burst upon New York from her native Chicago in 1940 with a Sunday evening performance with her group called "Tropics, Le Jazz Hot, Br'er Rabbit," which was such a triumph that she repeated it on nine other Sundays before the season was over, even though to do so involved virtual commuting from Chicago. Nothing since "Kykunkor" six years earlier had compared with this event in its popular success; in true importance it may have surpassed "Kykunkor," for it was actually the first glimpse to be offered of the basis of a genuine American Negro dance art. Several numbers, indeed, proved

to be classics in their field — "Rara Tonga," "Woman with a Cigar," "Bahiana," "Florida Swamp Shimmy," for example. In that first company, also, was the teen-age and frisky Talley Beatty, before whom lay a far more brilliant career than could have been suspected at that point.

To be sure, this was not a debut for Dunham; she had been extremely active in Chicago, dancing for Ruth Page and on her own, and choreographing for the Federal Theatre and other theatrical productions. What was especially notable about her first New York series, however, was the presence of a mind behind it; not the typical intellectual dryness that is the antithesis of art, but a pervasive comment, an objectivity toward the subject matter that conveyed a pointed delight in it. Thus its prevailing eroticism, though it proved a strong box-office feature, lacked all offense and became an instrument of

Katherine Dunham in "L'Ag'Ya," her dramatic story of love and magic and the fighting dance of Martinique

style. Most of the individual numbers were based on keen observation of authentic material, but every one of them was a "composed" work and not a mere lifting of literalism out of life.

Though the program was in form a concert, it nevertheless had the germ of the revue in it, and indicated the direction that Dunham would eventually take. In 1943 she was an important member of the cast of the Broadway musical, "Cabin in the Sky" (for which, incidentally, Balanchine was the choreographer); from there she went to Hollywood, and when she returned to the dance field with a mantle of glamour about her shoulders, it was with the first of a succession of revues. These, in turn, took her to Europe, smart success, more than a little "chichi" and a downward trend in her art. Her company, especially her men, were in large measure seduced by the, for them, spurious elegance of the academic ballet, and her productions took on something of the typically Parisian overemphasis on superficial visual matters and lost in proportion all vital concern with movement and choreography.

In none of her revues, however, has she failed to come up with interesting new pieces, from the suite of "Rites de Passage" (suggested by primitive practices but definitely creative compositions) and the stunning African and Caribbean-based "Shango" and "L'Ag'ya" (the latter originally created for the Federal Theatre), to the enchanting visual trifle from the Caribbean in which Dunham herself reclines in an immense white hammock reading "Mme. Bovary."

If she is not, as she maintains, an outstanding dancer, she is undeniably a superb performer and an illuminating personality, and creatively she has made an immeasurable contribution to the arts in her unfoldment of true premises of the American Negro dance.

Pearl Primus

When Dunham made her New York debut, Primus was scarcely aware there was such a thing as professional dancing; she was working night and day at any odd job she could find to sustain her while she studied toward a medical degree. (She already had a master's in psychology.) In the spring of 1941, one of her jobs (in addition to being a night switchboard operator) was in

Katherine Dunham as a dancehall "hostess" with a "client," Vanoye Aikens, in "Blues"   *Vandamm*

the wardrobe department of the National Youth Administration, which happened to be preparing a group of "Lindy Hoppers" to appear on a big joint program sponsored by the New Dance Group. At the last minute Primus was shanghaied into the group to replace a defector. In the middle of the performance she suddenly awoke to the delight of physical movement, cut loose and stole the show, to nobody's greater surprise than her own.

The immediate result was her pursuit of a working scholarship from the New Dance Group which meant studio house-cleaning in exchange for instruction on an hour-for-hour basis. But the New Dance Group was a lively organization, including among its leaders many first-rate modern dancers — Jane Dudley, Sophie Maslow, William Bales, Nona Schurman, Nadia Chilkovsky, Eve Gentry, Beatrice Seckler and others of comparable standing — and it knew an outstanding talent when it saw one. Under its auspices Primus developed, and with such incredible rapidity that in exactly two years she won a place on a program, shared by four other newcomers, under the auspices of the Dance

Center of the Y.M.H.A. On it she presented five dances of her own composition, and once again walked away with the honors. Four of them still remain among the best dances of her career — "African Ceremonial," "Rock Daniel, a Lesson in Jazz," "Hard Times Blues" and "Strange Fruit."

From then on she was a professional dancer, though it was a difficult thought for her to accept and she went right ahead with her university studies, compromising only by shifting from medicine to anthropology. But the forward-looking Barney Josephson, who had no such difficulty, engaged her straightway for his Café Society Downtown, and for many months she did her concert numbers for night club audiences in a space scarcely large enough to turn around in and too low of ceiling to jump in.

Here, newcomer or not, was obviously the greatest Negro dancer of them all. Her body had superb control and range and she could out-jump any man. (She had been a star athlete throughout her school days.) But besides strength and speed and elevation, her movement had a beautiful quality, a beautiful muscular phrase,

Pearl Primus in one of her earliest successes, "Rock Daniel, A Lesson in Jazz"

Gerda Peterich

and was an open channel for her inward power and her pervasive, outgoing honesty.

It is interesting to note that on that debut program there was only one African dance (her very first composition), and that she had acquired painstakingly out of books. In her other numbers, which had grown out of personal experience and background, her innate gifts as an artist were made plainer. Over her first five years the African numbers came slowly — "Dance of Strength" (Sierra Leone), "Dance of Beauty" (Watusi), "Te Moana" (subtitled African rhythms). From her own family, which was from Trinidad where she spent her early infancy, she drew the necessary data for many Caribbean dances — "Yanvaloo," "Play Dance," "Caribbean Conga," "Shouters of Sobo," "Santo" and others.

An extended tour of the "deep south" in 1944 gave her new insights into the spirituals and the frenzy of revivalist religion that prevailed. But she still produced fine underived pieces, also, on all levels of emotion — "The Negro Looks at Rivers," the curious "Chamber of Tears," and the deliciously lighthearted "Study in Nothing" and "Mischievous Interlude." In 1946, the ever alert and eager Ruth Page invited her to Chicago to dance the Witch Doctor in the opera, "The Emperor Jones," the role created thirteen years earlier by Hemsley Winfield.

The great turn in her life came in 1948 when she was sent by the Rosenwald Foundation to Africa for an extended study of the native dances. From that time on, though she became more and more the skillful and dedicated dancer, the anthropologist took over in increasing measure from the individually creative artist. How deeply she was affected is illustrated by the following paragraphs which she wrote from Nigeria (after government-sponsored performances there with the turning out of entire villages in turn to do their dances for her) just before her departure for the Belgian Congo to study the Pygmies, the Watusi, the Mangbetu and the Baluba peoples:

Pearl Primus with her New York company in a concert version of an African dance; and below, dancing with the help of native drummers and singers in Liberia

What strange adventures lie ahead are as unpredictable as those I have already had. I have passed through all the stages from hysteria to near death, but the people loved me with a fierce, passionate love. They spoiled me in their own strange way, they dropped to their knees before me, they named me into their tribes, and when they saw me dance they swore I was juju woman indeed.

Their dancing is losing the strength and freshness which they claim my dancing has. They compared me to the thunder and lightning and many feared me when I moved. But from them I learned the inner conversation of muscles and the enjoyment of subtle movement. Dance, except in certain societies, is generally looked upon as a good-for-nothing hobby. There are no professional dancers as before, and when people dance in most instances there is no emphasis on perfection.

I am fortunate to be able to salvage the

still existent gems of dance before they, too, fade into general decadence. In many places I started movements to make the dance again important. Ancient costumes were dragged out, old men and women — toothless but beautiful with age — came forth to show me the dances which will die with them. I saw dances which had not been done for twenty-five years; I saw some which will not be seen again for twenty years. I found the people from whom came the "Shouters of Sobo," and when I danced down the streets with them no one knew who was American and who was African.

Since then she has spent much — perhaps most — of her time in Africa, including a long period in Liberia, where she set up, under incredible hardship, a performing arts center in Monrovia; and another long expedition into fifteen African countries, chiefly the new republics, learning and teaching and propagandizing for the dance as an art precious to them all.

With her through all these later adventures has been her protégé, partner and husband, Percival Borde, whom she discovered in Trinidad and who, besides being her strong right arm, is an impressive dancer himself. Together and with assisting groups of various sizes they have given New York performances between African commitments. But with such welcome and absorbing work to do there, there is little temptation to struggle with the sketchy and uncertain rewards of the American concert field.

Talley Beatty

Fortunately, however, the American field continues to be a rich one with new figures emerging continually. Chief among them is Talley Beatty, who though certainly not literally a new figure, has newly proved himself to be perhaps the most original and freely gifted choreographer yet to appear in the Negro dance. The obstreperousness of his adolescence in the early Dunham days has disappeared through the years of his development with its inevitable struggles, and maturity has brought a simplicity of manner, an integrity of approach and a sense of perspective — along with a boldness in creative adventure — that

mark him as one of our substantial artists.

To Dunham he owes much, both in actual experience and in her establishment of the dimensions and directions of the Negro dance. After the general pattern of her revues, he formed a company of his own and toured with a program called "Tropicana" for some five years both in this country and abroad. Together with a handsome physique, an engaging personality, a fine technique and an excellent performing sense, he possessed also a persistent drive toward choreography. Long before he had a company he was choreographing wherever an opportunity offered itself, and in the most informal "workshop" projects some of the very numbers in his company's repertoire had their first tentative presentation.

Naturally his "Tropicana" days were colored by "show business" tendencies, and it was not until 1958, in a pair of solo recitals (as far as the record shows, his first) under depressingly undistinguished auspices that he suddenly showed himself to be an artist to be taken seriously, with passion, imagination and a courageous breaking through of forms. It included, among other things, a suite of primitives, a piece about Toussaint l'Ouverture, an almost surrealistic one called "Nobody Came" performed to sound effects, and another impressive if equally undefinable one in modern dress and involving a ladder and a book. There was also a stunning performance in "Icarus," composed for him by his colleague, Ernest Parham. It was a new aspect of Beatty and an eye-opening one.

The following year came his major breakthrough with a long ensemble work called "The Road of the Phoebe Snow." It was built, far from literally, around his childhood memories of games and fights and romances, with the railroad tracks in outlying Chicago as their milieu. Its music was recordings by Duke Ellington, and its form was absolutely its own. At first glance it seemed to be a suite of quite separate dances, generally related in style, using the same set of more or less individually characterized dancers, and with a sense of locale indicated by the lights of the famous Lackawanna train, the Phoebe

Snow; but at its conclusion it had accumulated tension to the point of a specific dramatic clash — a gang fight, indeed — and its resolution came only with the return of the Phoebe Snow's lights. For all its freedom and passion, it was astonishingly classic in structure.

The following season he followed with another work equally brilliant and even more formal, if that does not imply constraint. Its title is "Come and Get the Beauty of It Hot," and quite apart from its derivation from Joyce, it is a literally descriptive title. The dancing is "hot" to the music of four jazz composers, and it is extraordinarily beautiful in its own terms. It is full of human relations and implications but essentially an abstraction; so much so that the only possible way to end it with a full and convincing stop is by means of a flagrant but inspired bit of irrelevance in which a girl is swung in head-down on a rope.

His next assignment was the staging of the movement, again with distinction, in Jean Genêt's *avant-garde* drama, "The Blacks," in its long and successful off-Broadway run. From this he adapted one macabre number, "Look at All Those Lovely Red Roses," for concert use.

In the haphazard world of the concert dance, and perhaps most markedly in the Negro branch of it, there are ups and downs, barren interludes and enforced departures into alien territory for the purpose of making a living, and Beatty has escaped none of them. Between his own projects he has danced with Ruth Page in both Chicago and Paris, with the Ballet Society (before it became the New York City Ballet) in Lew Christensen's minstrel ballet, "Black Face," in an *avant-garde* film for Maya Deren, at the Spoleto Festival, in musical shows and night clubs, and has popped up with an occasional solo such as his brilliant "Mourner's Bench."

Sometimes he has managed to get his own programs on by the very skin of his teeth, and then only with the help of such colleagues as Syvilla Fort and the gifted Herman Howell to step in and fill out the evening. But in spite of everything — the disorders growing out of the pressures of time and the always overhanging spectre of fundlessness — he has come through with a distinguished and original art.

Alvin Ailey

Another leading figure in the present field is Alvin Ailey, who is something more of a newcomer. A product of the Lester Horton school and company on the West Coast, he came to New York in the early '50s, but has managed to establish himself with remarkable rapidity as an artist to be reckoned with.

Talley Beatty (front) with Ernest Parham (top) and Thomas Johnson in "The Road of the Phoebe Snow," his fantasia on life along the Chicago railroad tracks; and "Region of the Sun," from his revue, "Tropicana"

As a performer he has been impressive from the start, for he is strikingly handsome, with the genuine theatre artist's inborn power of projection. His technique is strong and his quality of movement is notably beautiful, like that of a svelte, nervously alert animal.

In addition, however, he has a vigorous mind capable of the analysis that is essential to good teaching and of the imagination that leads to creativeness as a choreographer. In all three of these fields — performer, teacher, choreographer — he has proved himself, and since he is equipped with an enormous amount of personal drive, the future looks definitely bright for him.

Thus far he has given comparatively few performances of his own in New York, though he has made an extended tour into Indonesia, the Philippines and Australia under government auspices, with Carmen de Lavallade and his company. Matt Turney has also appeared with him as guest artist in, among other things, a setting of Milhaud's "Creation of the World."

Inevitably he has taken fliers into other fields, sometimes simply for a livelihood and sometimes for artistic reasons. He has danced in two Broadway musicals, "House of Flowers" and outstandingly in "Jamaica," and played leading roles in several straight dramatic plays both on and off Broadway.

His choreographic output is still small, but already he has made two works of particularly high distinction. One is a group piece called "Roots of the Blues," which is taut with atmosphere and intuition, and the other is a solo suite of remarkable power which takes its title from its music, the "Hermit Songs" of Samuel Barber.

Donald McKayle

Starting at about the same time as Ailey was the New York-born Donald McKayle, who began his dance study while he was a student at the College of the City of New York. Like Primus he probably owes his beginnings largely to the New Dance Group, in whose school he was also a scholarship pupil.

In spite of his impressive gifts as a dancer, it is possible that his chief interest lies in choreography. He had been dancing for only two years when in 1950 he turned out his first group composition. It was called "Games" and dealt with the play of children in the city streets, based on his first-hand knowledge of the subject. Though it was his initial effort, it proved to be an excellent work and has already become something of a classic. Two other works, highly contrasted in style, are outstanding in his repertoire: "Rainbow Round My Shoulder," set to chain-gang songs; and "District Storyville," a bold and bawdy

Alvin Ailey, shown here both as a striking dancer, and as a choreographer in a dance from "Revelations," a suite built on Negro Spirituals, with Minnie Marshall, Ella Thompson and James Truitte as the dancers

Zachary Freyman   *Jack Mitchell*

Donald McKayle in "Her Name Was Harriet"

Esta McKayle

picture of that period in New Orleans at the turn of the century when the roots of jazz were taking shape.

For the usual financial reasons, he has unfortunately had to devote much of his time and effort to commercial activities — dancing on television and in Broadway musicals as well as assisting in the choreography and staging of them; staging acts for well-known theatrical stars; and teaching in any number of colleges and professional schools. He has found time, however, to dance with many modern dance companies, including Martha Graham's on its tour of the Orient on the State Department's cultural exchange program; to participate in the direction of a highly successful production of "The Tempest" in Central Park's outdoor Shakespeare theatre; and to study with virtually every teacher who had anything to offer him in the broadening of his background.

In 1951 he formed his own company, but, like all such companies, its performing activities, whether in New York or on tour, have inevitably lacked continuity.

The "Integrated" Company

In the quality and the number of its performers, the Negro field is overflowingly supplied. Only a few of them, however, are attached to permanent companies, since so few such companies exist. For the most part it is a matter of short-term engagements — with Beatty or Ailey or McKayle or anybody who may happen to be planning a performance or a series. If one great company were ever organized to bring this floating contingent together, there would be an embarrassment of riches.

Donald McKayle's "Games"

Janet Collins

The few who have regular affiliations have them necessarily with non-Negro companies. Matt Turney and Mary Hinkson have been leading members of Martha Graham's company for a number of years, and Clive Thompson, Mabel Robinson and Dudley Williams also work in that company when there are roles for them. John Jones has been associated with Jerome Robbins' Ballets: U.S.A. since its inception. The New Dance Group from its beginning has employed and encouraged Negro dancers on exactly the same terms as non-Negroes. But these organizations do not give continuous seasons by any means. The only dancer who is steadily occupied is Arthur Mitchell, a soloist with the New York City Ballet. After a long period in which he was not always wisely cast, he has now found a place in the repertoire in which he functions with distinction.

During Solov's regime at the Metropolitan Opera, the Negro dancers he engaged were all used from the start with a full realization of their individual abilities and in such a manner that they were automatically protected from "racialist" criticism. Janet Collins, the first Negro première danseuse in the history of the Metropolitan, danced not only in the Triumphal Ballet in "Aida", but also on "pointes" as the Queen of Night in his version of the Dance of the Hours in "La Gioconda." Later, Carmen de Lavallade

and that Trinidadian jack-of-all-arts, Geoffrey Holder, were used with equal naturalness and success.

Certainly the "integrated" company is a normal artistic development, and the only problem it involves is to keep the Negro dancer from having to pretend to be what he is not and to deny what he is. To cast a Negro as one of a community of Jews in a Sholom Aleichem village in Russia, or as a pioneer woman in the eighteenth-century Appalachians, or as a member of a medieval German prince's hunting party in "Swan Lake," is to make him conspicuously non-integrated. It is like casting a woman as King Lear or a man as Juliet, and expecting nobody to notice it on the grounds of some spurious sort of politeness. With this, art has nothing to do.

The Negro artist, like the artist of any other race, works necessarily and rightly in terms of his own background, experience and tradition. He makes no fetish of it, but on the other hand, like any other artist, he recognizes that there are some roles and categories that do not suit him. Race — exactly like sex, age, height, weight, vocal range, temperament — carries with it its own index of appropriateness. Nevertheless, again like any other artist, he still draws creatively from the whole spring of human experience. Certainly his entrance into the dance art constitutes a major broadening and deepening of its channels.

Geoffrey Holder   *New York Times*   Carmen de Lavallade   *Jack Mitchell*

Index

Harry Moore

15' May 1992

WHAT
Really
WORKS WITH
MEN

WHAT
Really
WORKS WITH
MEN

Solve 95% of your
relationship problems
(and cope with the rest)

A. JUSTIN STERLING

WARNER BOOKS

A Time Warner Company

Warner Books, Inc., 1271 Avenue of the Americas, New York, NY 10020

 A Time Warner Company

Printed in the United States of America
First printing: May 1992
10 9 8 7 6 5 4 3 2 1

Library of Congress Cataloging-in-Publication Data

Sterling, A. Justin.
What really works with men : solve 95 percent of your relationship
problems (and cope with the rest) / A. Justin Sterling.
p.   cm.
ISBN 0-446-51573-6
1. Interpersonal relations. 2. Men—United States—Psychology.
3. Dating (Social customs). 4. Mate selection—United States.
5. Single women—United States. I. Title.
HQ801.S823   1992
305.31—dc20   91-50405   CIP

Book design by Giorgetta Bell McRee

To that voice which speaks to you in a feminine tone.
That voice which you so often ignore,
much too often ridicule and all too often deny.
Let it sing.

This book is dedicated to all of the women who have had a profound influence on my life, each marking a passage for me and an important contribution to making this book a reality. Most of all to my daughter Aislinn and your daughters who I hope will never have the need to read it.

ACKNOWLEDGMENTS

Because this book is the culmination of fifteen years of work, writing this acknowledgment has caused me some deep thought and reflection. Because my work with women and their relationships is more of a personal commitment than a job, I was not sure how far back I should start and where I should stop. Many women should be mentioned as major contributors to this book.

As I traveled back through the development of my career I saw many faces of women who should be mentioned. As their faces appeared I realized there were hundreds of them, thousands of them. Each with unique features, a different past, varied hopes and dreams. Soon, I began to see that what they had in common began to overpower anything that made them different from one another. I soon began to see only one face. The face not of a particular woman but the face of all women. Women of the past, women of the present and women of the future. It was an ageless, timeless, pain-filled, joy-filled, innocent, power-filled, hope-filled and beauty-filled face. It became *one* woman.

It was the woman who believed in what I had to teach women, who put her reputation on the line by producing the Women's

Weekend. It was the woman who said this workshop should be brought to women in other areas. It was the woman who told her friend about the effects this Women's Weekend had on her life. It was the woman who, by reaching out to another woman in a very personal and courageous way, has made this book and most of all its message able to reach all women. It was you, the women who have trusted me throughout the years; and you know who you are and what you have done.

I cannot let this moment pass without also acknowledging the women who have taught me the most about relationships, women and love: my mother, my wife and my daughter.

CONTENTS

WHAT Really WORKS WITH MEN

ONE

Relationship with a Capital R:
What You Can Expect
from This Book

Ariel

The president of her own image consulting firm and a former model, thirty-five-year-old Ariel was tall and slender with startling blue eyes and every blond hair in place. Simultaneously confident and coy, she had an air of seductive sophistication that was captivating and I could easily see why her casual acquaintances and business associates assumed she could get any man she wanted and have him eating out of her hand in no time flat.

"When people look at me, they can't believe I could have relationship problems," Ariel said with a hint of resentment in her voice. "They think I have men falling at my feet, that I must have had dozens of marriage proposals over the years. 'So what's the problem?' they'll ask. 'Why are you still single?' "

Ariel told people that she had not met her "Prince Charming" yet. "And in a way that's true," she commented. For the past fifteen years, she had been having brief affairs with younger men and older ones, fellow models and "average guys next

1

door," extravagant celebrities and staid, stable businessmen. "But no matter who they were, there was always something about them that convinced me they weren't really right for me," she said. "They were *too* something—too demanding, too set in their ways, too unreliable. Or they weren't *enough* of something else—not quick, spontaneous or understanding enough, not adventurous or stable or ambitious enough. Sometimes it wasn't them. I just decided that what I really wanted was to devote more time and attention to my career." Or she concluded that she was wasting too much time and energy driving (or flying) back and forth to be with a man who had interested her precisely because the geographical distance between them would prevent them from getting too close too quickly.

"I've never had a relationship that lasted more than six months," Ariel said with a sigh. "But now I want to settle down. I'm thinking about things that never seemed important to me before, like having kids and growing old with someone. And I'm seeing a man I really care about. The other day, I actually said to myself, 'This one I want to keep.' But then it dawned on me that *I don't know how.* I don't know how to keep a guy or keep a relationship going. I only know what I know: how to be attractive, capture a man's attention and have brief passionate flings."

Over the past decade, I have talked with, listened to and advised thousands of women like Ariel. Smart, talented, capable women. Bright, ambitious, articulate women. Women whose average age was thirty-five, whose average income was $35,000 per year, who had, on the average, completed four years of college. They expected to be as successful in their relationships with men as they were in other areas of their life. But they were not. Because they knew how to run businesses, diagnose or treat illnesses, make sound financial investments, "ace" college courses, cook gourmet meals, climb mountains and keep their wits about them in a crisis, they thought they were supposed to know how to handle relationships. But the truth was that they did not. They didn't know how to get new relationships off the ground. The relationships they had weren't working, but they didn't know how to make them work. They were angry at men or disgusted with themselves or ready to give up on relationships altogether.

Some of those women came to me individually for counseling. Others gathered one or two hundred at a time for the intensive two-day experiences known as Sterling Women's Weekends. They were single or married or had been married or were about to marry for the second or third time. Some, like Ariel, had spent their adult lives spotting fatal flaws and logistical problems just as the passion of new romance was waning and had never gotten around to tackling the real business (or facing the real risks) of being in a serious, lasting, intimate relationship with a man. Others were afraid of repeating the mistakes they had made in the past. All arrived with the same question in mind: "Is it possible to have a truly successful, productive, fulfilling, long-term, committed relationship with a man, and if it is, how can I do it?"

If you have been wondering about that yourself, then you picked up the right book. In this book, I will answer that question.

Times Have Changed

There was a time when women did not have to ask someone like me to tell them how to have a successful, intimate relationship with a man. Thirty or forty or fifty years ago there were no books like this one and no books about women who love too much or women who love men who hate women, either. Your grandmothers and their mothers and grandmothers before them had never heard of "dance away lovers" and "Casanova" complexes, yet many of them knew how to have satisfying, lasting, intimate relationships with their men—and they shared what they knew with one another. As women had done for centuries, they advised one another. Of course, if you asked for their advice today, you would not be thrilled with it. You would call it old-fashioned, demeaning or downright ridiculous. No smart, savvy, self-respecting *modern* woman, you'd think, would do the sort of things women did for their men back then.

"Things are different today," you would tell yourself. And you would be right.

For the past thirty years women have dedicated themselves to proving their equality. They have devoted themselves to gaining access to what were once exclusively male domains and to competing with men (and one another) for equal status, equal pay, equal rights and equal respect. As a result, all the rules for relationships between men and women have changed. Women's expectations for themselves and the men in their lives have changed. Their ideas about who should do what for whom in a relationship have changed and, regrettably, so has the probability of actually establishing and maintaining satisfying relationships.

If the women I have counseled and the women who attend the Sterling Women's Weekends I conduct are any indication—and I believe they are—those changes have brought women more confusion and disappointment than happiness. They have created more self-doubt and low self-esteem than self-confidence and emancipation. This did *not* occur because the pursuit of professional success and personal fulfillment was an unworthy goal. There is no doubt in my mind that women embarked upon their new path with good cause and the best of intentions. Unfortunately, somewhere along the way, they lost touch with the true source of their power as women and lost sight of what had been for millions of years women's number-one priority: Relationship with a capital R.

Relationship with a Capital R

When I refer to Relationship with a capital R, I am speaking generically, using an umbrella term that encompasses friendships, parent/child relationships, business relationships and the relationship among community members as well as long-term, committed relationships with men. I am talking about a series of interactions between individuals: intellectual, emotional and spiritual exchanges that result in growth and ultimately create a sense of well-being and satisfaction for everyone involved. Taking on a life of its own, Relationship has the power to make things happen and to enrich people's lives. I am also referring to the art of Relating, the process of nurturing and managing relationships in a way that leads to success and satisfaction. That has always been a woman's art. It requires the talents, skills and instincts women have been cultivating for centuries.

Throughout history, the importance of Relationship has gone unrecognized. Yet, Relationship—this area in which women are natural leaders—is the most powerful tool known to mankind. It is a bridge or pathway to everything that is truly important to women and indeed to civilization as a whole. The principle behind Relationship, the principle of fostering growth, enabled communities and cultures to develop. Through Relationship, the values and standards of society were maintained. Without it, we would not have survived for all these years. We would not have pulled together during times of crisis or recovered from wars, plagues and famine. In fact, for millennia, women's skill and propensity for Relationship has been the balancing force that kept men's drive to fight and compete from destroying us all.

The Hope of the Women's Movement

The hope of the women's movement was that women would bring their number-one priority and their talent for Relationship into the male domain and once again save the world. But that was not what happened. Just ask Colleen, a fifty-year-old senior executive in a Fortune 500 company. She describes her trip up the corporate ladder this way: "I did everything I could to play down my femininity. I controlled my emotions and dressed conservatively. I didn't have family pictures on my desk. I didn't flirt. I bent over backwards not to draw attention to the fact that I was a woman. I trained myself to act and even think like a man." So did many other women. In order to get into positions of power, they sacrificed their number-one priority and adopted its opposite, man's number-one priority: competition.

To a certain extent, this switch was unavoidable. After all, they were on men's turf. It was his playing field, his ball, his bat. They had little choice but to play by his rules. But once they were in positions of power, women continued to compete rather than Relate. As Colleen put it, "At first there was the business person and the real person, the woman I was at work and the other woman, the one who still planned to fall in love, get married and raise a family. But after a while, the other woman disappeared. Maybe I tried so hard to convince my employers that I wasn't interested in those traditional things that I wound up believing it myself."

The longer Colleen allowed herself to be guided by male priorities, the more distant and unreal her other priorities became. "I was so functional," Colleen continued. "I had gotten so good at functioning, at handling everything on my own and shutting down my emotions, that I couldn't really remember what relationships were good for or why I ever wanted one."

She is not alone. Countless women today have forgotten, chosen to ignore or never known about Relationship. They have carried their newfound competitiveness and thirst for victory into every area of their lives, and many have suffered because of it. The quality of life for women has not improved over the past three decades. More women live below the poverty level than ever before. There are more divorces, more children of divorce. And the failure to live up to the superwoman myth, the realization that they do not and, in all probability, cannot "have it all" has dropped women's self-esteem to an all-time low.

Does that mean women should give up their careers, their interests, their independence? Am I suggesting that anyone with two X chromosomes has only one path in life and must reconcile herself to being someone's "little woman," an obedient stay-at-home wife who cooks, cleans, bears children and maybe organizes a PTA bake sale now and then? Absolutely not. I am simply acknowledging what I have observed and what women have told me about the price they pay for looking at and dealing with life as if they were men.

The Price of Victory

I still remember the women who attended the first Sterling Women's Weekend (which wasn't really a weekend, but rather one very long Saturday). They were among the first wave of female executives. They had been swept away by their struggle to succeed in a man's world; and once they washed up on shore, they realized that their personal lives and peace of mind had been lost at sea. Their sense of themselves as women was missing in action. They had begun to recognize that while competing with men, acting like men and thinking like men helped them get ahead professionally, it was not a comfortable way to live their lives. Nowhere was this more apparent than in their struggle to have lasting, intimate relationships with men.

They had postponed marriage only to discover that they no longer knew how to behave in such a relationship. They had tried to act like men in their relationships and to convince the men in their lives to think and act more like women. Their relationships were projects to work on, problems they spent so much time trying to solve that they had no time to enjoy. As far as I can tell, this situation has not improved in the past ten years. Fifty-two percent of today's female executives are single or divorced (as compared to 4 percent of male executives). And as I mentioned earlier, over the course of the decade I have heard literally thousands of smart, savvy, professionally successful women openly admit that their personal lives are in a shambles.

Heather, a thirty-one-year-old investment banker, put it this way: "In so many areas of my life I'm running marathons. I'm *winning* marathons. But when it comes to my relationship, I barely know how to crawl."

And Sarah, a twenty-eight-year-old nursing supervisor, explained, "I feel like a part of me has died. My emotions have atrophied. I keep saying I'm ready for a relationship, but my battery's dead. There's no juice. No matter how much I want to, I just can't get excited about any man I meet."

"Dating is a nightmare," Melissa, a thirty-six-year-old psychologist and author of a self-help book, claimed. "It seems like everything I say, every move I make intimidates the guys I go out with. When I tell them what I do for a living, they clam up because they think I'm psychoanalyzing them. Or they calculate how much money they think I earn and start making comments like 'Maybe *you* should pay for dinner,' or 'I guess you won't ever need a man to support *you*,' and then I never hear from them again. But what am I supposed to do? Tell them I check groceries at the Acme?"

"I wish men came with an owner's manual," Emily, a forty-five-year-old police dispatcher, said with a sigh. "Because I swear I could live to be 110 and never figure them out. I'm three years into my second marriage and it's already heading the same direction as my first—straight downhill."

Chances are that you picked up this book because you are in a similar predicament. Well, I'm going to tell you how to get out of it. I am going to offer you the same advice I have been giving to women for the last ten years and which they have used to become successful, productive and satisfied in serious, lasting, intimate relationships with men. I am going to explain what works in a long-term, committed-type relationship with a man—and what doesn't.

Ninety-Five Percent of a Woman's Relationship Problems:

- *begin before the relationship does* because women who are determined to get a man lose sight of what they want from their relationships. In this book, I will show you how to make one of the most important decisions any woman will ever face: the selection of a lifetime mate.
- *are by-products of low self-esteem* and women's inability to trust and accept themselves as they are. Throughout this book I will encourage you to get reacquainted with your natural self and to be all the woman you can be.
- *stem from the inherent differences between men and women,* and the conflicts that arise when you expect men to think and act the way a woman would. A great deal of this book is devoted to helping you understand and accept how men behave in relationships, what they are looking for from their relationships and what they have to offer you.
- *are the inevitable outcome of trying to control the direction your relationship is going and trying to compel men to give you what you want when you want it.* This book will teach you how to manage

a relationship without controlling, how to have men make you happy without changing their basic natures and how to nurture your relationship so that it will bring you success and satisfaction.

- *dissolve when quitting is NOT an option,* when you have committed yourself to the discipline that being in a serious, long-term, intimate relationship with a man requires. In this book, I will explain what that discipline entails, how to master it and why you should.

In this book, I am going to show you how to solve 95 percent of your relationship problems (and cope with the rest). That's the good news.

The bad news is that you are going to hate my advice. You are not going to like what I have to say. The things I tell you will challenge some of the attitudes and beliefs you have embraced in recent years; and if you are like most "modern" women, you would rather prove that your beliefs are correct than do what it takes to succeed in a relationship. You want your relationship and you want to have it *without* paying attention to, much less doing, anything that isn't fashionable, that doesn't conform to your ideas about what smart, savvy, sophisticated, liberated women are supposed to do or that might not be acceptable to your peers. That's a problem because at least some of what goes into a successful, lasting relationship with a man isn't fashionable. But it does work.

Just as you dismiss the fact that countless women for countless generations have succeeded where you have not and refuse to admit that your grandmothers and their mothers and grandmothers before them must have been doing *something* right, you will be tempted to reject the advice you find in this book. And if the advice women who have proven that they know how to have satisfying, lifelong relationships with men would give you makes your skin crawl, you're going to find what I have to say even harder to swallow. You'll be offended, appalled, and outraged and will want to fight me every step of the way. You'll think I'm spouting some sort of he-man philosophy or pushing some sort of self-serving psychological theory. I'm not. There is nothing philosophical or theoretical about this book. This book is about what works.

What Works

How do I know what works? Because for the past thirteen years I have been telling women who attend the Sterling Women's Weekends that it works, and women are still coming to these Weekends even though I don't advertise or do the talk show circuit to recruit them. Women are attracted to the Weekends by the success of other women, by friends, sisters, mothers, daughters and coworkers who have participated in the Weekend. They can see with their own eyes that these women are on track. They trust themselves as women. They have strong, supportive relationships with other women and stable, satisfying relationships with men. Because they want what graduates of Sterling Women's Weekends have, women come to one of these Weekends themselves. When women stop coming to the Weekends, I'll stop giving them and know that what I'm saying has stopped working.

Until then, I'll keep asking women to do what this book asks of you: to forget for a moment popular social trends or your own reluctance to disrupt familiar behavior patterns; to step back and take an objective, fearless look into your own heart and psyche where you can discover the truth about yourself and the courage to dismantle the barriers that prevent you from having a successful, productive, fulfilling, long-term, committed relationship with a man.

Yes, that is a tall order and, yes, it asks an awful lot of you. But then, the sort of relationship I'll be talking about in this book is not for every woman. It is only for women who are *serious* about being in an intimate, committed relationship with a man. You may not be. You may think you have to have that sort of relationship to please your mother or impress other people with the fact that you are successful in *all* areas of your life. But you are not obligated to be in a relationship. You can choose a different path.

You may think you are entitled to a successful, satisfying relationship with a man. But a truly intimate and lasting relationship is not your birthright. It is not owed to you.

Being in a relationship has become fashionable again. Fear of AIDS and other sexually transmitted diseases has made commitment and monogamy popular again. But wanting to settle down with one man because it is the latest trend is not the same as committing yourself to be in and do what it takes to stay in a relationship. If the trend changes, you'll lose interest in the relationship. You'll want to try the latest fashion. I call that being a relationship dilettante, a weekend hacker—like the person who hacks around on the tennis court until she pulls a muscle or realizes she'll never be a Chris Evert and then quits, tossing her racket and her designer tennis outfits into the hall closet next to the golf clubs and the running shoes and the weights she also hacked around with for a month or two. The information I give you is going to backfire if you approach relationships that way or if you use it to get a man or experiment with a relationship until something better comes along. If you want to do that, you can do it any way you want. You don't need this book.

On the other hand, if you *are* serious about having a successful, productive, fulfilling, long-term, committed relationship with a man, if that is what you really want, then I can tell you how to go about it.

A Few Points to Keep in Mind While Reading This Book

In this book I will give you the tools and technology you need to be successful and satisfied in a long-term, committed relationship with a man. You don't have to *like* those tools any more than a mechanic has to like the wrench he uses to tune up your car. Rather than questioning the rightness or fairness of what I have to say, ask yourself: "How can I use this to tune up my life and get what I want?"

As you read this book, try to remember that it is not important to agree with what I say. It is even less important to argue with me mentally or find exceptions to the general statements I make. There *are* exceptions and if you are willing to gamble on being one of those exceptions when the odds are against you, I can't stop you. However, I urge you to think twice before taking

that risk when the stakes (your happiness, peace of mind and
the survival of your relationship) are so high.

Time and time again you will interpret what you read based
on what you already believe. Your reaction to my words will
reveal more about you than anything else. However, because I
don't want you to misconstrue or misunderstand the things I
say, in each chapter I will try to address the questions (and
protests) that typically arise when those points are covered during a Sterling Women's Weekend. In addition, I have attempted
to capture some of the spirit and emotion of those weekends
through anecdotes about real women's experiences. In most
instances, I have used women's actual words. However, for con-
fidentiality, I have changed names and other identifying information and occasionally have collapsed several women's
experiences into one composite anecdote.

Because everything in this book is designed to get you somewhere, I also urge you to go the distance, to read the book all
the way through, before you decide that it won't get you where
you want to go. The pieces may not fall into place for you until
the fifth chapter or the eighth or even the last. So please, keep
looking, searching inside yourself for the place where what you
read strikes a truthful chord. Allow yourself to hear the ring of
truth in ideas that may initially outrage or threaten you, hang
in long enough for the entire picture to take shape and try to
figure out how you can make those ideas work in your own life.

Finally, even though it won't always seem that way, *I am on
your side*. I want you to have the relationship you want. I want
you to find and nurture and be successful in a relationship that
satisfies you, that lasts a lifetime and that fits the vision you've
held in your heart and mind since you were a young girl. Of
course, you can't have that relationship with just any man and
you won't have it if you have forgotten or are not sure about
what you are looking for in a relationship. As I'll explain in the
next chapter, knowing what you want is the first prerequisite
for success.

TWO

Do You Know What You Want?: Women Are the Architects of Their Relationships

Kelly

When I first met Kelly, a twenty-seven-year-old social worker, she and Gary, a thirty-five-year-old dentist, had been living together for two years. Two turbulent, trying, tiring years, according to Kelly. "It's like a twenty-four-hour-a-day job," she said. "When I'm not with Gary, I'm thinking about Gary and wondering what's going to go wrong next." Something was always going wrong, Kelly claimed.

"But it wasn't always that way," she assured me, her glum expression briefly brightening. Her weary brown eyes momentarily came to life as she reminisced about the first few months of her relationship. "In the beginning, Gary paid a lot of attention to me. He was very attentive and interested in the things I had to say. He used to call me fascinating and tell me that he wanted to know everything about me because he had never known a woman like me." Gary had known lots of women. In fact, there had been one "little hitch" at the outset of their relationship. When he and Kelly started dating, Gary was in-

13

volved with someone else. However, Gary soon stopped seeing the other woman, and Kelly took that as irrefutable proof that he loved and wanted to be with her—and only her.

"I was thrilled when he asked me to move in with him," Kelly continued. "I knew that was a first for him. He made a point of telling me he had never even considered asking any of his other girlfriends to do that." Gary also made a point of giving Kelly plenty of other information about her predecessors, none of it good. Viewing each "war story" as a cautionary tale, Kelly promised herself never to do the things those other women did. She was determined to make her relationship last.

"But as soon as I moved in with Gary, things started going downhill," Kelly recalled. "Every other word out of his mouth was critical. I was too demanding, he said. But when I backed off, he told me I was too distant. I was too sensitive. I took the things he said too seriously, but I didn't take the pressure he was under at work seriously enough. I could stand losing a few pounds. My clothes took up too much room in the closet. You name it; if I did it, he found something wrong with it."

Gary was extremely possessive as well, insisting that Kelly account for her whereabouts twenty-four hours a day and sulking each time she left the house without him, even if she were only going to see patients in the private psychotherapy practice she was trying to get off the ground. "He was always very jealous, very worried that I'd start cheating on him," she said. "So you can imagine how surprised I was when I found out *he* was cheating on *me!*"

According to Kelly, she and Gary had been living together for six months when she discovered that he was not only involved with someone else, but had been having brief "flings" with other women all along. "I was all ready to leave him," she said. But Gary begged her to stay. "We were up all night talking and crying and finally we both agreed to try harder to adjust and make the relationship work."

Kelly kept her end of the bargain, using every trick in the book to "fascinate" Gary again and guarantee that he would love and want to be with her and only her. She went on a diet, spent a small fortune on enticing lingerie, even rented the X-rated videos Gary liked so much (but which she found pretty dull and disgusting herself). Kelly limited her evening office hours and cut down on the time she spent with family and friends. She bought Gary little presents, planned romantic adventures and arranged surprise seductions. "And what did I get for my trouble?" Kelly said with a sigh. "More criticism than ever. Rejection. Gary acted like he was doing me a favor whenever he spent a couple of hours with me." And he was still seeing other women.

Kelly kept trying, but realizing that bending over backward to please Gary wasn't working, she changed tactics. She begged Gary to go into counseling with her, interrogated him before he went out and again when he returned, went through his pockets looking for telltale signs of his latest infidelity. When he wanted to have sex, she turned him down flat; and for a while, she would "break down" on a weekly basis, crying and pleading with Gary to explain his behavior. "Why?" she would weep. "Why are you doing this to me?"

Clearly in agony, Kelly came to a Sterling Women's Weekend looking for answers, hoping to find something—anything—she could use to turn the relationship she had into the relationship she wanted it to be. "I don't know what else to do," she said. "I've tried everything I can think of. But the relationship still isn't working."

How Hard Should You Work on a Relationship That Isn't Working?

Could Kelly and Gary's relationship work? Was there a way to make it work? That was what Kelly wanted to know. What I wanted to know was why she thought it was worth the effort. With all the work she had put into getting and keeping Gary and all the trouble she had gone through to make Gary show her that he loved and wanted to be with her and only her, had she ever actually enjoyed the relationship? The question took Kelly by surprise. Although she was painfully aware of everything that was wrong with her relationship, she was hard-pressed to come up with a single thing that was right or re-warding about it. "At the moment, we're barely speaking to each other," she said, "except to argue and I'm so tired of arguing. I'm tired period. This relationship has drained me dry. I'm completely exhausted."

Just listening to Kelly describe how hard she worked on her relationship was exhausting, and I wondered where she found the time and energy to function on her job, treat her private practice patients or ever have any fun. It was a safe bet that she wasn't doing those things well or at all.

Like Kelly, some women today work so hard on their relation-ships that they can't do anything else. They'll have to find a cure for cancer or run for president some other time. Right now they have "this relationship problem" and they need to work it out.

Women keep working and working on their relationships because they think work will make the relationship better. They confuse being active with being productive. But all the talk and tears, maneuvers and machinations do not turn the relationship they have into a successful, fulfilling relationship. They only produce more problems.

Working *on* a relationship is not the same as doing what works in a relationship. Instead it is the inevitable outcome of compromising yourself and what you want from a relationship just to get or hang onto a man. I don't want you to work like that on your relationship anymore. I want you to extract some-thing of value from it. I want it to be the relationship you've always dreamed you would have—and that is rarely the case when you spend more time working on your relationship than enjoying it.

Women's Romantic Vision of a Relationship

Was the relationship Kelly had the one she really wanted? Was her current relationship the one she envisioned when she was a young girl and first pictured herself in a relationship with a man? Did she imagine herself living happily ever after with a man who cheated on her? Did she spend hours on end fantasizing about the ways she would worry, manipulate and try to change or control him? Of course not.

The relationship Kelly fantasized about was "very romantic and exciting, but also very solid. The man I was going to be with would be strong and sure of himself and very much in love with me. He would do anything for me, ride through hell and back, slay dragons, you name it. But he would also have a life of his own. He would go off and do whatever he did and I would do whatever I did: take care of our kids, sit in the garden talking with my girlfriends, be a nurse—which is what I thought I wanted to be back then.

"My heart would flutter when I knew he was on the way home. I would do things for him. I would *want* to do things for him. But most of all, my fantasy relationship was full of laughter and surprises. In one version, I'd have dinner ready and be asking him about his day when he'd suddenly get this mischievous look on his face, literally sweep me off my feet and carry me off toward the bedroom . . ."

Now that's a positive, vibrant, heartwarming vision of a relationship with a man: a romantic vision of a relationship that has the potential to be successful, satisfying and to last a lifetime. And somewhere in the recesses of your mind, you harbor a similar vision. Like virtually every woman on the planet, you have dreamed about the relationship with a man you would have one day. In fact, you have known exactly what you wanted from that relationship since you were nine or ten years old. Not only did you envision the kind of relationship you would have, but you also pictured the man with whom you would have it.

He would be exciting, dominant and spontaneous; strong, confident and unpredictable. Although he could show tenderness and compassion, he'd rarely talk about his doubts or fears. In fact, he wouldn't appear to be afraid of anything at all. The man of your romantic vision would always seem to know what he was doing (even if *you* never quite knew what to expect from him). He would be strong-willed and a little rough around the edges, adventurous and hell-bent on doing things his way. He would be Indiana Jones, Sir Lancelot and Rhett Butler rolled into one, the archetypal hero and "man's man," a knight in shining armor with specific qualities that would suit your unique personality and desires.

Even though many years have passed and you have changed in countless ways, your romantic vision of a relationship and the man with whom you'd have it still lingers in your memory. It stays with you even when you try to discount it or deny that you still want it or alter it to fit the man you've been dating. If you have not found that relationship yet, one reason may be that you are not absolutely certain you want it.

To have the relationship of your romantic vision you must open your heart to a man, letting him into the places you treasure and getting to know him in that dimension too—without trying to control him, without doing all the things you may have grown accustomed to doing in your relationships with men. That is dangerous and frightening, and you may not want to take the risks involved. What's more, having a relationship that fits your romantic vision takes commitment. It requires certain sacrifices. It may ask you to look at men and relationships in new, unfamiliar and at times uncomfortable ways. You may not be ready to take those steps just yet. You may prefer to play it safe, at least for now and maybe indefinitely. That's your prerogative.

However, if you do want the relationship of your romantic vision, then you should have that relationship. I believe you deserve it and I know that it is possible to have it, *without* working so hard at it that you have no time to enjoy it.

Why Buy a Handyman Special When You Can Have Your Dream House?

I want to stop talking about relationships for a moment and talk about houses instead. I want to talk about buying your dream house, the house you've always wanted and for years have scrimped and saved to buy. Because you started thinking about that house long before you were in a position to purchase it, when you actually begin looking for your dream house you have a very detailed picture of it in your mind. You know that you want a ranch house or a Cape Cod, a big kitchen or a small one, a skylight, a fireplace in the living room, a sun porch, and with that vision in mind, you look at houses until you find one that resembles your vision. Then you visit that house. You check the roof, the basement, tap the walls, stamp on the floor. You call in a plumber and an electrician and an exterminator to inspect the house. You're making an important decision. You want to make sure that the house not only looks right but also will be standing and keeping you warm and dry ten, twenty, maybe even fifty years from now. You put a lot of work into finding your dream house, but it's worth it because you end up with the house you've always wanted.

Now, let's say that you *don't* go about buying your house that way. Let's say, you find a house that has some of the features you want, but isn't in terrific condition. Of course, it's in a good location and you can get it for a lot less money than you had been prepared to pay. In fact, it's such a good deal that you're sure someone else will snatch it up if you take too long making a decision. Besides, your landlord is about to raise your rent and make you sign a new lease. It's now or never, you tell yourself. Thinking that with the money you save, you can redo that horrendous kitchen, put in the skylight, build a sun porch and fix the plumbing problems (which the real estate agent assures you are very minor), you compromise your vision of the house you've always wanted and buy the house you found. Then you spend a small fortune on remodeling and repairs. As soon as you fix one thing, something else breaks. It seems like every spare moment and every spare dime goes into that darn house. You want to kick yourself for buying it. You end up hating it and maybe even start looking around for a different house to buy.

Exactly the same thing happens when you get involved with a man who doesn't fit into your romantic vision, when you compromise your vision of a relationship to fit a man.

Regrettably, many women today do approach their relationships that way. They settle for someone "in the ball park" (or out in left field) and spend the rest of their lives rationalizing, regretting or paying for their choice.

Why Invest in Short-term Rewards Instead of Long-term Results?

Where relationships were concerned, women used to be visionary: able to know how things could be and to allow them to be that way. But, as I mentioned in the first chapter, women have become more and more like men over the past thirty years.

To succeed in the competitive business world, women have learned to act like men and, unfortunately, have started to think like men too. You have started to look for immediate rewards, instant gratification. Waiting for relationships to unfold, for their potential to be revealed to you, takes too long. You have things to do, places to go, no time to waste. And so you have stopped investing in long-term results or considering long-term consequences.

Nowadays, you see a guy. He has muscles, great hair. He's not too tall or too short, and he dresses the way you like a man to dress. Based on this once-over, you decide he's your "type." So you talk to him and maybe go out on a couple of dates. You find out that he's got a steady job, a house, a car, a finalized divorce or anything else he needs to have for you not to immediately reject him. Something "clicks" and you think, "I'm definitely attracted to this guy. This guy really turns me on." Just looking at him makes your head spin and your heart flutter, and your resolution not to sleep with a man until you know him well and trust him flies out the window.

Sex is terrific. Okay, it's merely good, but that "kaboom" is there: that intoxicating mix of exhilaration and sexual chemistry that makes most new lovers act like a couple of giddy drunks. Now you're thinking, "This feels right. This feels good. This could be 'it.' Boy, do I want this to be 'it' because I'm sick of the singles scene and guys who say they'll call but don't and my mother calling to ask if I've met a nice 'fella' yet."

However, a "click," a "kaboom" and a man who meets your basic requirements do not necessarily mean that you have the makings for a successful relationship. In fact, the "click" and the "kaboom" can be bad news. They divert your attention. You don't notice that you're making the same mistakes you've made dozens of times before or that your new "Mr. Right" is the same old jerk you always end up with, except he's in a slightly different package. You move full speed ahead, oblivious to the fact that the attraction between two people changes over time and that things that matter in the short run not only matter less over the long haul but will also look a whole lot different further down the line.

You get involved with a man because you admire his intellect and appreciate the fact that he is interested in you for more than your body. A year or two passes and you're complaining that he'd rather talk than have sex. You are attracted to a man for his ambition and his commitment and dedication to his work. By your third anniversary, you're calling him a workaholic. That exciting, spontaneous guy with the devil-may-care attitude will look flighty, childish and irresponsible once you've lived together for a while. And you'll get sick of mothering the man who needed you or feel smothered by the man you were drawn to because he wanted to take care of you. But *he* will not have changed. He will be the same man you fell in love with, the same man you married. *You* didn't bother to look at the big picture. You thought that what you wanted and needed at that instant was all there was to the picture.

WHAT WORKS WITH MEN

To solve 95 percent of your relationship problems (and cope with the rest):

Remember that the very thing that most attracted you to a man in the first place will ultimately be what you berate him for when things don't go right, and will be the reason you destroy the relationship.

Buy Now, Pay Later

Instant gratification is not the only reason women rush into relationships and live to regret it. They don't think about long-term results or consider long-range consequences when they are unhappy with themselves or their lives and want to be rescued; or when they are desperate ("I'm not getting any younger, you know. This could be my last best shot. I may never get another chance like this.") or afflicted with a case of "Baby Brain" (a side effect of listening too anxiously to the ticking of their biological clocks). Women with "Baby Brain" want to have children while they still can; and since they'd prefer for their children to have a father, they set out to find a man and get into a relationship as quickly as possible. But most of all, women rush into things and compromise their romantic vision of a relationship because they're not really interested in a relationship. *They just want to get a man.*

When you are more invested in short-term rewards than long-term results, getting a man seems more important than having a relationship. You approach your relationship with the credit card mentality—the "buy now, pay later" attitude—that seems to permeate all areas of our lives these days. First you'll get the man. Then you'll worry about the relationship.

Give me a man with these surface qualities, you think. Just make sure he doesn't have a drinking or drug problem, has a good job, isn't crazy, wants kids. Get me that man and I'll work the rest out later. I'll make the relationship work somehow. That makes about as much sense as going to work for a company because you like its building. But that's what you do. Although you see potential problems, you choose to put up with them because you think you'll be able to fix them once you get that man where you want him. That was precisely what Kelly did.

Kelly knew what she was getting the moment she got involved with Gary. She had an inkling that fidelity did not rank among his top ten virtues. After all, for the first few months they were dating, *she* was the other woman. In addition, his scathing post mortems of his previous relationships should have tipped her off to his critical nature, warning her that he would be exceedingly difficult to please. But Kelly made light of both danger signs. "I knew Gary wasn't perfect," she understated, "but I still thought he was the man I wanted to be with." She also thought that once she was with him and once he saw that she was different from the other women he had been with, he would change. She thought that if she tried hard enough, she could make the relationship fit her romantic vision of a relationship, even though she had initially compromised that vision, indeed completely ignored it, in order to get her man. She was wrong.

If you think you can get a man and work out your relationship afterward, then you'll end up in the same predicament Kelly found herself in. You've got to stop approaching relationships that way. It doesn't work. It won't make you happy. Trying to change a man after you've got him where you want him will not lead to success in a long-term, committed relationship. It only leads to conflict, arguments, frustration. Thinking, "He'll change. When he sees how wonderful I am, he'll change," is a prescription for lowering your self-esteem. When your man doesn't change, you're going to think you weren't wonderful enough. You'll try to make yourself into someone you're not and resent it. When you compromise the relationship of your romantic vision to fit a man with traits you know you can't live with but think you can fix at a later date, I can guarantee that you'll spend so much time and energy working on your relationship that you'll never get around to enjoying it. You won't feel fulfilled. You'll be exhausted.

———— WHAT WORKS WITH MEN ————

To solve 95 percent of your relationship problems (and cope with the rest):

Have a vision for your long-term, committed relationship and trust it. THEN find a man who fits into that vision.

Women Are Relationship Architects

Just as you need a blueprint to build a new house (or remodel the one you have), to have a satisfying, intimate relationship with a man (or be more successful and satisfied in the relationship you have), you need a long-term vision of that relationship. If you don't have that vision, if you don't know what you want beyond the surface qualities that bring instant gratification, then you should not be in a long-term, committed relationship with a man. Your chances of succeeding are minimal.

Adding to the foundation created by your original romantic vision, you need to figure out what you want from your relationship over the long haul. You need to identify your absolute essentials: the basic necessities you must have in order to feel satisfied with your relationship; the vital, fundamental things you want from the relationship; and what behavior or treatment you will not accept because it would require you seriously to compromise your values or pose a threat to your physical safety and emotional well-being. Your list of absolute essentials should include only those things that are truly crucial to the success of your relationship. It should not be a long, long list. If it is, you're nit-picking. You're avoiding intimacy by setting standards no man or relationship can meet.

You must, however, be sure of what you want so that you'll recognize it when you find it. You must also learn to trust your vision. If you don't have confidence in it, you will alter your vision the next time you "click" with a man. You know that doesn't work, so really put some time and thought into creating your vision. Although you'll intuitively know when you have the right one, here are some points to keep in mind:

- A relationship that fits your romantic vision should give you all the things that money *can't* buy.
- A relationship that lasts is not fun and games all of the time. It is not just laughing and doing things together and sharing an intimate moment now and then. That's casual dating.
- A relationship that fits your romantic vision is not a bump and run relationship: one in which two people who are attracted to each other spend time together, run away when

things start to heat up, come back, readjust, begin to resent each other and run away again. You may do that for a while when you are seriously dating, but it will destroy a long-term relationship.

- The relationship of your romantic vision should be more than "a negotiated agreement between two consenting adults usually involving sexual exclusivity." Regrettably, that is precisely what many relationships between men and women are these days. Negotiated agreements are fair. They're equal. Everything is split down the middle. He does this. You do that. You each keep score to make sure the other person is living up to the terms of your agreement. But that is not a committed relationship. Your agreement can be unilaterally renegotiated at any time. When the terms become inconvenient, when the relationship stops feeling good, the agreement is null and void and you start looking around for a better deal.

The relationship of your romantic vision is like a piece of sculpture, a work of art. It does not become what you envisioned overnight. A successful relationship is an artistic creation, a symphony, a painting, a piece of architecture that moves from vision to reality in phases. *You are the architect of that relationship.* It is your job to make sure that the artistic creation you end up with fits your vision, your blueprint. You do that by working smart from the outset, by starting out with the right material, the right medium for your artistic creation. With your vision of the relationship in mind, you look for a man who fits that vision, a man who is close to the object of your romantic fantasy.

Yeah, but . . .

Does that man exist? You may not think so. You may conjure up images of all the jerks you've met lately. You may picture all the men you've dated in recent years who were looking for mother substitutes, were afraid to commit, needed "space" or tried to take over your entire life. Yes, that looks good on paper, you may be thinking, but there aren't any decent men out there.

Well, I'm telling you they are out there. They've been out there. They've been walking up to your front door while you were looking out the back window. Your selection process, not the pool of available men, is the problem here. You have been going about things the wrong way. You think finding the right man should be quick and easy, that you will be able to know him on sight. It doesn't work that way.

You may have to date lots of men in order to find the right material. You may have to keep going out and rejecting men who are the wrong medium for your artistic creation. That won't kill you. It can even help you develop a clearer idea of what you want or don't want.

You must learn to look beyond the superficial. A man's hair style or his bank account may have nothing to do with the relationship of your romantic vision. Stop looking at men in terms of their "potential," thinking of them as raw material that you can transform through the power of your love and thus increase their value. If a man is not valuable enough to you now, assume that he won't be later. Don't take half and think you can make it whole. Either accept half and enjoy what you get or don't take it.

As I will be explaining in more detail later in this book, to find a man who is close to the object of your romantic fantasy, you must "interview" likely candidates. I don't mean hold a conference where you talk about what you want and ask what he wants. You won't get an accurate picture of a man from what he says to you. If he's interested in you he's going to say whatever he thinks will impress you. He's going to say what he thinks you want to hear. Watch him. Observe and read his actions. Familiarize yourself with his personality, his habits and behavior patterns. That's how you will figure out who he is and what he's likely to expect from a relationship. Then decide whether or not you can accept what you see because your chances of changing a man's basic nature and expectations are very slim.

As the architect of your relationship, your job does not end when you find the right medium for your artistic creation. A successful relationship is one that will last a lifetime. And three, six, even twelve months of sharing intimate parts of yourself are only a small portion of that lifetime. Locating a man who is close to the object of your romantic fantasy is merely where the creative process begins. Turning your vision of a relationship into a reality is going to take time, patience, discipline, certain sacrifices and certain changes in your overall life-style. And the question you must ask yourself now is: "Will you do what it takes?" Your answer determines whether or not you will have the relationship you want. As I will explain in the next chapter, you can't have that kind of relationship with just any man, and you can't have it by doing whatever you want whenever and however you want.

THREE

Will You Do What It Takes?:
Making a Life-style Change to
Accommodate a Relationship

Meg

"Last weekend, my grandparents celebrated their *fiftieth* anniversary," said Meg, her violet eyes widening in awe each time she mentioned the number of years her grandparents had been together. "We threw a big party for them and when they waltzed to the same tune they danced to at their wedding, I kept thinking, '*Fifty* years. They've been married for *fifty* years and I couldn't even make my marriage last five.' "

As Meg told the story, when their waltz ended, her grandfather, Lou, whispered something to his wife, Claire. She blushed and fluttered her eyelashes like a flirtatious schoolgirl, then, feigning disapproval, wagged her finger at her naughty mate. "You're a dirty old man," she teased him.

"A sexy senior citizen," he corrected with a laugh and, cupping his wife's face in his hands, planted three gentle kisses on her forehead, nose and lips.

Through a blur of unexpected tears, Meg took all this in and tried to imagine her ex-husband or her current lover, Dan, look-ing at her with the tenderness she saw in her grandfather's eyes. "I couldn't picture it," the thirty-year-old advertising account executive claimed. What was their secret, she wondered. "I'd do *anything* to have a relationship like that with Dan," she said and meant it—until her grandmother began telling her what it had taken to stay happily married to Lou for so many years.

"I let him win at canasta," Claire said. With her eyes twinkling merrily, she added, "Canasta and everything else. Your grand-father's only five-foot-six, but I make sure he feels ten feet tall."

"You mean you feed his ego?" Meg said. That wasn't what she wanted to hear.

"Call it what you want," Claire shrugged. "I call it letting him win at canasta—even when I have a better hand. So he isn't a genius with figures, which I know because I keep his books. I don't tell him that. So he never could remember little things like my birthday or to wipe out the sink after he shaves. I don't make a fuss about it. He wants to think he's the world's best businessman, the world's greatest husband. I make sure he does. Every chance I get, I tell him it's true."

"But that's dishonest," Meg protested.

"Little white lies. To make him happy. When your grandpa's happy, he makes me happy. So what does it hurt?"

Meg acted as if the very idea mortally wounded her. "I would *never* do that," she declared indignantly. "I won't let a man think he's right when he isn't. I'm entitled to my opinion. I don't want to spend all my time boosting *his* ego and bending over backward to make *him* happy."

Of course, Claire had not said anything about *all* of her time. Patiently, she tried to explain that with kids to raise, helping out in the business, socializing and volunteer work, she spent maybe forty-five minutes a day making Meg's grandfather "feel like a king." But Meg didn't believe her. In fact, she didn't really hear her. Claire's words kept getting twisted and turned upside down in Meg's mind. When Claire said, "make him feel like a king," Meg heard, "cater to his every whim, be his servant, his little Geisha girl," and acted as if she were being told to jump in front of a speeding train. "I *won't* be anyone's docile, obedient 'Stepford wife.' No way, not me," she declared.

What You Won't Do

You probably know just how Meg feels. You don't want the man in your life to boss you around or control you. You won't put your needs on the back burner so that he can fulfill his. Every woman has a list of "intolerables," the things she simply won't do for or accept from the man in her life. In fact, I could fill an entire book with the "I won'ts" I've heard from women over the years. They won't clean up after a man, laugh at his jokes when they don't think they're funny or let him get away with making blatantly sexist comments. They won't tolerate cigar smoking or his obnoxious friends or his habit of being twenty minutes late. They absolutely refuse to give up their career, their financial independence, their friends, their sobriety or their standing appointment with the best manicurist in the city. There is no way that they would stay in a relationship with a man who expected them to have sex first thing in the morning, to overlook his infidelities or to pat him on the back when he "tricked" his insurance company into paying $1,000 for $200 worth of damage to his car.

"I don't have to put up with that stuff," they say. And they are right. The good news is that doing what it takes to be in a successful, long-term, committed relationship with a man does *not* mean doing anything "necessary" no matter how vehemently you may be opposed to it. Every woman is entitled to her bottom line: the absolute essentials she will not compromise for the sake of being in an intimate relationship. In fact, no woman should get involved in something as important as a long-term committed relationship with a man without knowing her bottom line. She should not be in a relationship that requires her constantly to cross that line, compromising her values or endangering her physical health and emotional well-being.

The trouble is that some women have so much on their bottom line that they can't get their relationships off the ground. Their absolute essentials run the gamut from the trivial ("I won't watch 'Monday Night Football' with him") to the unrealistic ("I won't *ever* lie about my feelings"), and there are so many of them that no man on earth could go more than a day or two without doing something unacceptable. Worse yet, far too many

women's "won't" lists are jam-packed with the very things that have enabled countless women for countless generations to have successful and satisfying lifelong relationships with men. Meg's certainly was.

"No sensible, well-informed, self-respecting woman today would do the things my grandmother did," Meg said. Approaching men and relationships in the way Claire did just didn't seem right to Meg. Her methods weren't acceptable in this day and age. They went against everything Meg believed; and she was quite certain that, being the smart, self-sufficient, modern woman she considered herself to be, she was not supposed to:

- blatantly flatter a man;
- keep her negative opinions about his behavior to herself;
- encourage him to feel successful when he was not;
- allow him to do what he wanted to do when he wanted to do it;
- let him win an argument when she knew she was right or end one before he admitted that she had a valid point.

If you feel the way Meg did, I have some bad news for you, some news that you won't want to hear and would prefer not to believe: When you are intimately involved with a man, there will be times when those "taboo" behaviors and Claire's unpopular "old-fashioned" approach are precisely what it takes to turn your romantic vision of a relationship into a reality.

If you won't do those things because you don't believe you should do them or because you don't see other "liberated" women doing them or because you just don't feel like doing them, then your relationship is not going to work. It's not going to work because you'll persist in doing what you believe you should do instead of what you know deep down inside could lead to success, productivity and satisfaction in a lasting intimate relationship with a man. You're going to trust the latest fashions, popular trends and the things done by women whose relationships are no more successful than your own, instead of your own intuition. Just to prove that you're free to do what you want to do when you want to do it (and that no one can stop you or tell you how to live your life), you're going to insist on doing things *your* way, even when you have ample evidence that your way isn't working. You'll even sacrifice your relationship to prove your point, because, if you are like most women today, being right is more important to you than being successful in a long-term, committed relationship with a man. That is why you can't find or turn the relationship you have into the relationship of your romantic vision. You are not ready to be in that kind of relationship. You aren't willing to do what it takes. And you can't have a successful relationship with a man *if you won't do what it takes.*

Don't Kid Yourself

"Hold on just a second," Meg commanded, her righteous indignation reverberating throughout the room. "Are you telling me I am *incapable* of having a successful relationship?"

No, I assured her. She *was* capable of having a long-term, committed relationship with a man. She simply wasn't *ready* for one. She wasn't willing to do what it takes to have that kind of relationship.

Naturally, Meg disagreed. "I am ready," she protested. "I love Dan and I'll go the distance with him, *if* he'll just meet me halfway. I definitely want our relationship to last, *but* I'm not going to keep my opinions to myself." She was willing to do whatever it took, she insisted, *as long as* she didn't have to give in to Dan when she knew she was right. She was prepared to make a commitment, she claimed, *if* she knew that she and Dan could work as a team.

Women are always saying things like that to me. "I'm ready for a 'real' relationship," they say,

"BUT there aren't any decent men around."

"BUT I don't want to give up my autonomy (or my apartment)."

"BUT he has to understand that my career comes first."

"I'm ready to make a commitment. I'm prepared to go the distance. I'm willing to do whatever it takes to have a successful relationship," they insist,

"IF he shows me he's willing to do that too."

"IF it doesn't take any time away from my kids (or my job or training for the New York Marathon)."

"IF I know I'll be getting something in return."

Just in case you make statements like those yourself, let me tell you something about those "ifs" and "buts": they tell *me* that you're kidding yourself. You may be sincerely interested in having the relationship of your romantic vision. You may have that vision, a man who fits it and the best of intentions. You may yearn for an intimate relationship and you may think and say and honestly believe you are ready for one. But you are not truly *committed* to having a successful, productive, fulfilling, lifetime relationship with a man. You do not have faith in your relationship nor do you trust the choice you made when you decided to get involved in it. You don't really want to or are afraid to take risks or make sacrifices, compromise or make changes in your life-style for the sake of your relationship. And you knowingly or unknowingly, consciously or unconsciously set things up so that you won't have to do that.

You trot out your "I won't" list. You place too many restrictions on what you will do for or accept from a man. You establish conditions which must be met before you'll do what needs to be done. And that does not constitute being willing to do whatever it takes. That is doing what you want, doing things that are comfortable or convenient, doing it your way. Of course, that's your prerogative, but it's also like trying to replicate your favorite chef's walnut torte without following his recipe: "I really want to bake this," you think. "I can practically taste it. I had to beg for the recipe, but now that I have it, I'm ready to go. I'm going to do it and it's going to be wonderful. But maybe I'll use raisins instead of walnuts. And I should run out to the store and get more eggs, but I don't feel like it, so four eggs will have to do even though the recipe calls for six. And you know I really don't have a whole hour to spare, so I'll just bake this at a higher temperature for forty minutes and hope for the best." You'll get *something* by tinkering with the recipe that way, but it won't be the walnut torte you set out to bake and it won't taste nearly as good.

Relationship Is a Discipline. Will You Master It?

One of the primary ways women kid themselves about being ready to have a long-term, committed relationship with a man is by thinking that having that sort of relationship should come naturally and that they can just "wing it." However, Relationship is not a recreational activity. It is not something that you do just for fun and can do any way you please. It is like that walnut torte. To get the desired result, you must follow the recipe— and if you don't know a sifter from a snifter or how to work your food processor, you'd better figure that out before you tackle something as complicated as baking a walnut torte.

Romantic fantasies don't just come true. You turn them into realities through your own efforts. A long-term, committed-type relationship with a man is an artistic expression, a work of art. It is created thoughtfully with a vision in mind, with attention to detail and with the consummate skill that results from mastering a *discipline:* "a training that corrects, molds or perfects one's mental faculty or moral character." Trying to have such a relationship without mastering the discipline involved is equivalent to saying, "I want to be a concert violinist, but I'm not going to practice. I'm just going to show up at Carnegie Hall, walk out on stage and dazzle them." Of course, that won't be what happens. No one gets to Carnegie Hall that way and you will not have the relationship of your romantic vision that way.

To master a discipline, you must learn the necessary skills. You must practice those skills, incorporating them into your overall life-style. You must begin living your life and operating in your long-term, committed relationship as if quitting were not an option. Eliminating that option changes your perceptions. It forces you to look for other options and to take positive steps that you don't even bother to consider when you are thinking, "Oh well, if things don't improve, I can just walk out."

Relationships Require Sacrifices. Will You Make Them?

As any concert violinist can tell you, mastering a discipline some-times means doing things you don't feel like doing and it always requires you to make certain *sacrifices:* "to forego something of value for the sake of something having a more pressing claim." When I tell women that, they usually act as if I'm asking them to commit suicide; but if you think about it, you'll quickly realize that you have made millions of sacrifices during your lifetime (and none have killed you yet). You make them every day. You forego that second piece of chocolate cake because not gaining weight (or not looking like a glutton) has a more pressing claim. You forego sleeping until noon because getting up and going to work has a more pressing claim. Or you forego a day's pay because your responsibility to stay home and care for your sick child is more important.

For the sake of your long-term, committed relationship with a man, you may have to forego immediate gratification or hav-ing the last word; pass up opportunities to correct, criticize or prove you're right; yield battles or stop trying to change your man. Because your relationship has a more pressing claim, you may have to adjust your expectations, break certain habits or change certain routines. You may have to operate in ways that are neither comfortable nor convenient for you. Clearly, there will be some things you are not willing to sacrifice for the sake of your relationship—your entire career, for instance, or your religious values or moral convictions, your passion for fitness or acting or art. If that's the case, don't get involved in a long-term, committed relationship with a man who expects you to make those sacrifices. However, if something is less important than your relationship and if it is preventing you from being successful and productive in your relationship, you must forego it, sacrifice it—because your alternative is to forego the relation-ship of your romantic vision.

Where Do You Stop on the Way to Your Dreams?

Let's say that you have made a commitment to devote one Saturday each month to pleasing your man. You have promised yourself that you will go along with whatever plans he makes, let him be the boss for the entire day and take every available opportunity to give him what he wants. You are operating on the principle that giving him what he wants is a gesture that shows your *desire* to give. You know that giving is part of relating and relating is part of giving. You understand that he wants to relate also by giving to you in return.

Let's say that you've done that for a couple of months, and sometimes it's been difficult for you; but it's never been horrible, and it *has* had a very positive effect on your relationship. But now his Saturday has rolled around again and he wants to go to the boat show and then see one of those "slasher" movies where a Jason or a Freddy terrorizes one scantily clad, airheaded woman after another. Neither activity falls under the heading of "fun" in your book. Besides, there's work you've brought home from the office and a million chores you'd really like to get to. Considering the circumstances, would you:

- decide that going to a boat show and seeing a slasher movie is a stupid, pointless waste of time and, despite your commitment, simply decide not to do it?
- rebel at the last minute? ("I don't have to do this just because he wants to. I have a mind of my own. I'll decide what I do or don't do—and I'm not doing this," you conclude. Just as your man is heading for the door, you inform him that you aren't happy with his plans and that he can either come up with an acceptable alternative or go alone.)
- try to live up to your commitment with the least amount of effort or discomfort, sending your body along to the boat show but expressing no enthusiasm, putting on your Walkman and taking a snooze during the movie or doing anything else you can think of to just make it through the day—defeating your purpose of making your man feel like a king in the process?
- quit halfway through, thinking "that's good enough," after

the boat show and talking your man out of the movie so you can go home and do what you wanted to do all along?

- initially resist, tense up, argue with yourself and get angry, then remind yourself of your commitment, take a deep breath and plunge in? ("That wasn't so bad," you realize after the fact, but the agony you put yourself through beforehand was horrendous.)

- keep your promise but seethe inside and resent every minute of it and, at the first available opportunity, blast your man for "making" you waste an entire day doing things he should have known you would hate?

- keep your promise without any fuss or bother because you are truly committed to pleasing your man on that day, trust the original commitment you made and have faith that it will work to your benefit and help your relationship in the long run?

Even though the situation I described isn't likely to make or break your relationship, your reaction to doing something distasteful in order to live up to your commitment is quite telling. For one thing, if you are like most women today, that last option is also the last one you'd choose. Secondly, the response you would have had to that situation is apt to be identical to the reaction you will have each time doing what it takes to succeed in a long-term, committed relationship with a man demands more from you than you feel like giving. Finally, it shows you how far you are really willing to go in order to have the relationship of your romantic vision—and if you are like most women today, that isn't far enough to make your vision a reality.

WHAT WORKS WITH MEN

To solve 95 percent of your relationship problems (and cope with the rest):

STOP doing only what you want to do when and how you want to do it.

To Get Where You Want to Go, You Must Commit Yourself. Will You?

To honor a discipline, you must commit yourself to it. You must make a choice and surrender to it, trusting the decision you have made without constantly questioning it, and following the path you have chosen without looking for excuses to turn back. Being committed enables you to find your way when you get lost. When you face choices that could affect your relationship, you base your decisions on what is best for your relationship, what is most likely to bring you success in your relationship and bring your vision of a productive, fulfilling relationship to fruition. That is what Meg's grandmother, Claire, had done, and that was why, after fifty years, her relationship was not only intact but still vital, vibrant and going strong.

Claire never claimed that her marriage was problem-free. No relationship is. There were plenty of times when she felt like quitting, when she got tired of letting Lou "win at canasta" or doing anything else her relationship required. But when Claire felt that way, she reminded herself of her commitment. "Sure, I'd love to pack my bags and leave right this minute," she thought, "but I made a promise. I committed myself to this marriage. I vowed to stay with this man for better or worse, and that is what I'm going to do." Then, having eliminated quitting as an option, she looked for and found ways to get what she wanted and needed from the relationship she had. In other words, divorce, except in the most extreme cases, is just a euphemism for "quitting."

"But, women like Meg's grandmother had no choice," I've been told by countless modern women. "They had to stay in their marriages because there was nowhere else for them to go. We have other options." You certainly do. You have lots of options; and although I am not suggesting that your options should be taken away from you or that women should return to the narrowly defined roles they were assigned in the past, I have seen time and again how having all those alternatives has caused problems for modern women.

You see, ever since they began to enter previously all-male bastions, to succeed in the male-dominated business world and to realize that they did indeed have choices and could make their own choices, countless women have used the fact that they have options available to them as an excuse not to stick with any path they turn onto or commit themselves to any choices they do make. They want to keep their options open. They get out of fulfilling their commitments by deciding that their original commitment is infringing upon their freedom of choice. They want to be free to do what they want to do when they want to do it, but that is the adolescent version of freedom.

Teenagers make decisions without thinking them through or trusting them. But then, they can get away with that behavior because someone—a parent, teacher or some other voice of authority—will step in to protect them from themselves and stop them before things get out of hand. As an adult, you don't have that sort of safety net. When your determination to do whatever you want whenever you want to do it leads to failure, you suffer the consequences. You pay the price, and there is indeed a steep price to be paid. When you go through life without making commitments, when you try to keep your options open and avoid getting tied down, you end up getting wrestled down in other ways.

True freedom is not the same as freedom of choice. In fact, the fewer choices you must make, the freer you are. When you have already made the important decisions, you can go with them, stick with them and conduct your life in accordance with them instead of constantly looking back, second-guessing yourself and agonizing over whether you did or will do the right thing. You are free from the burden of choosing over and over again.

You are guided by your commitments, by your acts of engaging and pledging yourself. That's why you make them. When you get lost or disoriented, you refer to your commitments in order to find your way. It does not matter whether you are committed to a relationship or a career, to raising children or being a concert pianist, to a spiritual path or to making a fortune and retiring by age forty, when you surrender to something, trust something and put your faith in it, you know where you are going and you don't let anything stand in your way. You don't have to fret and stew about every move you make or repeatedly re-evaluate your position or live your life mired in self-doubt because you have your commitments to keep you on track, to navigate for you. Other people's disapproval, the latest fashion, every little temptation that comes down the pike cannot lead you astray. You are in the driver's seat. You have charted your course, and you follow it because you know in your heart that it will take you where you have already decided you want to go.

Of course, truly committing yourself to a relationship or anything else is a risky, frightening step to take. The mere thought of "surrendering," of giving yourself to something, may scare the hell out of you. When you surrender you must be guided by something other than your own will and desires. You are frequently called upon to forego immediate gratification in order to honor your commitment. Your commitment dictates what you can or cannot do in given situations. In essence, it controls you, limiting your options and preventing you from doing whatever you feel like doing at any particular moment. For some of you, that seems like a fate worse than death. But the fact of the matter is that you can't outsmart the system.

Even when you do what you feel like doing, you are committing unconsciously to your feelings, trusting them, surrendering to them and allowing them to guide your decisions. They are in the driver's seat. And because your feelings change from one moment to the next and from one situation to the next, they steer you in circles. You never really get anywhere. You chase your immediate desires all around the globe.

I call that having a faulty navigational system. If many of your daily decisions and especially the choices you make about what you will or will not do in an intimate relationship are based on your feelings, your fears, your problems, other people's opinions, the latest fashions, your immediate needs or a desire for instant gratification, then you have a faulty navigational system. And you simply will not reach your destination, get control of your own life or do what it takes to have the relationship of your romantic vision until you dismantle that navigational system and replace it with one that works. You must get rid of your negative commitments, control the things that have been controlling you and then consciously select the things you *want* to be committed to, incorporating them into your overall life-style.

_____ WHAT WORKS WITH MEN _____

To solve 95 percent of your relationship problems (and cope with the rest):

Decide what things are truly important to you. Put them in a comfortable, natural order for yourself. And simply live in accordance with that order of priorities.

Making Life-style Changes in the Area of Relationships

Like millions of other Americans, Hilary, a forty-year-old legal secretary and single parent, took to heart the preliminary reports she read about diet, exercise and longevity. Making a commitment to become more physically fit, Hilary quit smoking and stopped eating junk food. She learned as much as she could about nutrition and began reading labels more carefully and preparing more healthful meals for herself and her kids. She rearranged her schedule to accommodate a forty-minute workout every other day and even found someone to exercise with her so that each could motivate the other whenever their willpower alone didn't do the trick. Hilary made a life-style change in the area of health and fitness. She figured out what she needed to do, committed herself to doing those things and did them. She chose a path that would take her where she wanted to go and stuck to it. She got what she wanted and was successful in improving her health and fitness because she made life choices and then changed her life-style to accommodate those choices. Success in the area of relationships requires precisely that sort of life-style change.

You must eliminate the attitudes and behaviors that prevent

you from having a successful, productive, fulfilling, long-term committed relationship with a man. In Meg's case, the thing that had to go was her determination to have the last word and prove that her ideas about modern relationships were right. Her beliefs were getting in her way.

Sarah, the twenty-nine-year-old nursing supervisor mentioned in Chapter One, needed to do something about the adverse effect her work was having on her. "My job is very demanding, very draining," she explained. "I work long hours in a stressful environment. People's lives are in my hands. I give and give and give. I give so much that when the work day is over, I have nothing left. No energy to get dressed up and go out. No desire to act interested in what some guy is saying or to come up with something witty to say myself. I'm too exhausted to do anything but curl up on the sofa and be lulled to sleep by the TV." She wasn't going to meet the man who fit her romantic vision of a relationship that way.

Stubbornness . . . worrying about things that could go wrong . . . sexual "hang-ups" . . . fear of being tricked, hurt or betrayed by men . . . guilt . . . shame . . . addictions . . . recovering from addictions . . . financial insecurity . . . perfectionism . . . fear of failure or rejection or criticism . . . being everyone's therapist: these are just a few of the things that may be stopping you dead in your tracks, blocking the path that leads to the relationship you've always wanted. They are your excuses to indulge in confusion and ambivalence instead of doing what it takes to make your dreams come true. You've got places to go, things to do, problems to solve. You have to concentrate on getting that promotion, training for that marathon, helping your sister cope with her divorce, working on yourself. You'll just have to skimp on what you do in the area of relationships—virtually guaranteeing that you will not have the sort of relationship you say you really want.

To have that relationship, you must be at least as committed to it as you are to other aspects of your life. You must be willing to change your life-style so that the relationship you want will fit into it. You must figure out what isn't working for you and stop doing those things. Get the rubble out of the way. Start learning from your mistakes instead of suffering from them and stop making matters more complicated than they are.

Yeah, but . . .

At this point in a Sterling Women's Weekend, someone invariably says, "But I *can't* do that. I *can't* pretend I don't have a weight problem. I do." Or "I *can't* make my depressed sister disappear. She's not going to go away." Or "My job (or my recovery, or my personal growth) is important to me. I *don't want to* give it up." Perhaps similar thoughts have crossed your mind. Well, I'm not telling you to ignore your problems or deny your fears. I'm not suggesting that you cut troublesome people out of your life completely or abandon the ideals and endeavors that are meaningful to you.

What I *am* saying is that you have to stop letting those things keep you from doing what it takes to have a long-term, committed relationship. Put them in perspective. Think about what you really want, what is truly important and valuable to you. A fulfilling, long-term, committed relationship with a man may or may not fit that description. As I've said, the sort of relationship I'm talking about isn't for every woman. It's only for women who really want it, who want it to be successful and who take it seriously. If you do, you will change the aspects of your life-style that are standing between you and success. You will master the discipline and make the necessary sacrifices. As Hilary did to become more physically fit, you will choose your path, commit yourself to it, and stick to it until you turn your vision into a reality.

WHAT WORKS WITH MEN

To solve 95 percent of your relationship problems (and cope with the rest):

Do not attempt to get into something as serious and risky as a long-term relationship with a man *unless quitting is not an option.*

If You Won't Do What It Takes

I cannot stress strongly enough that the information I will be giving you in the rest of this book is part of a discipline. If you are not willing or able to do what it takes to be successful and productive in your relationship with a man and if you are not prepared to commit yourself to doing that over the long haul, you probably are not ready for a long-term, committed relationship. You're better off not attempting to have that sort of relationship right now. You'll mess it up. You'll get hurt. And you'll want to blame that on my advice, when the truth will be that you resolved to make things better in your relationship or improve the way you deal with men but then slipped back into your old habits after a week or two. I'm not offering tricks, quick fixes or techniques that you can experiment with and then abandon when the going gets tough or you get a little scared. It's probably better to muddle along the way you have been than to do what works for a short period of time only to switch back into your old way of doing things.

But please, take the time to assimilate what you read in the rest of this book and let it sink in before deciding what you will do. You may even find that you are willing to master a discipline and change your life-style in the area of dealing with men and relationships once you tackle the problem I'll be discussing in the next chapter: low self-esteem.

FOUR

There Is No Success
Without Self-acceptance

Carrie

As she stood in front of me nibbling on her lower lip and twirling a strand of hair around her index finger, Carrie, who ran a consumer advocacy agency and was singlehandedly raising three children, resembled a child herself. A nervous one. "What I want . . . a big part of what I want is to be at home to take care of my family, to nurture my family," she said, warily glancing around the room. She was, I assumed, looking for signs of disapproval from the women around her, most of whom had made their careers their number-one priority—as she had herself for the past few years.

"I want to really be there and get to know my kids again and have another child . . . at least one more child. I want to get married again and I want my husband to provide for us. Let him be the provider and I'll be the nurturer, because I've done both. I'm doing both and it's too hard. It's not what I want. I want to be a stay-at-home wife and mother, part of a real family unit, part of a team—not the whole team all by myself."

Some women in the room shared her sentiments. Others did not. But with or without her peers' approval, Carrie wanted a long-term, committed relationship that would enable her to stay at home and take care of her family. A husband who was willing and able to provide for her and her children was an essential element of her vision of a successful, productive and fulfilling relationship. And if that was what she wanted, I told her, then that was what she should have. So, why didn't she?

"Well, I guess you could say I'm a little gun-shy," she replied. "My track record with men has been pretty dismal. I have a real knack for getting involved with guys who turn out to be all wrong for me."

It had been that way from the very start, Carrie claimed. "At fifteen," she recalled, "I was disgustingly average, dull, nondescript, a nobody, completely indistinguishable from dozens of other slightly overweight teenagers with mousey hair parted down the middle and braces on their teeth." But David changed all that, Carrie explained, referring to the "shy, gawky, new kid in town" she began dating soon after he moved into her neighborhood during the summer before her sophomore year in high school.

"I really just wanted a boyfriend," Carrie admitted almost twenty years later. "Any boyfriend." But when David turned out to be an extraordinary basketball player who led their school team to its first state championship in a decade, Carrie ended up with an unexpected bonus. "Suddenly I was accepted by all the popular kids who hadn't known I was alive before," she said. "Even teachers started to treat me better. Being David's girlfriend made me somebody. But it made me sort of nervous too. I always felt that at any moment David might dump me for one of the cuter, more popular girls who were constantly falling all over him."

Rarely did more than a few weeks go by without Carrie jealously accusing David of dating other girls behind her back or tearfully offering to "give him his freedom," because she had convinced herself that he was only staying with her out of a sense of obligation. "I knew that was stupid, but I couldn't stop doing it," she sighed. "I couldn't believe he was actually interested in me. I kept thinking he would get bored with me; and once I started thinking like that, it just snowballed until I wound up creating some sort of scene." After a year, David got tired of Carrie's "scenes" and did exactly what she feared he would do: he dumped her.

The next man in Carrie's life was Ron, an intense college student who seemed so taken with her that Carrie was fairly certain his eye would never wander to other women. As added insurance, she made herself indispensable to him, typing his term papers, tidying his dorm room, bringing him "care" packages and making sure he ate properly—which he tended to be too wrapped up in his studies to remember to do. "Ron was always sort of scatterbrained," Carrie recalled. "He was brilliant, especially in math and science, but forgetful. When you let him loose in a lab, he was either going to discover something incredible or blow the place up."

Carrie and Ron got married three weeks after her high school graduation. Carrie was four months pregnant at the time. "Ron swore he would have married me anyway," she said, but a doubt always lingered in the back of her mind. "There were plenty of times when I wondered if I only married *him* because I was pregnant. I mean, did I just want to be married or did I want to be married to Ron? I wanted security, stability, our child to have two parents—the perfect little *Ladies Home Journal* life. Those *seemed* like good enough reasons to spend the rest of my life with someone." But Carrie was never absolutely certain that she had done the right thing. As it became more and more apparent that her real life bore no resemblance to anything she had read about in the *Ladies Home Journal,* Carrie's uncertainty grew. Still taking care of Ron and all the day-to-day details he seemed oblivious to, once the baby arrived, Carrie says, "I felt as if I was raising *two* kids and I was only a kid myself. I can't tell you how many nights I cried myself to sleep wondering what I had gotten myself into."

Somehow Carrie weathered the storm, and her life settled into a more comfortable routine after Ron completed school and took a high-paying job with an oil company. They had two more children together, bought a home and, in fact, embodied in almost every imaginable way the fantasy Carrie had had on her wedding day. "But I felt empty inside," Carrie sighed.

"Is this it?" Carrie wondered. "Is this all there is for me and all there will ever be?" Encouraged by articles she read and women she met through her involvement in various volunteer activities, Carrie decided to expand her horizons. "I needed a life of my own," she said, and she went after it with gusto, enrolling in college and becoming increasingly active in numerous social causes. Acutely aware of the "inequities on the home front," Carrie began demanding that Ron do his fair share—and then some. "After all I had done for him, he owed me some support. It was my turn to go out and make my mark on the world and his turn to keep the home fires burning." But Ron had always been notoriously inept in that area and he had not changed. Disregarding that reality, Carrie was convinced that "Ron screwed things up on purpose. We fought constantly. I felt that he was letting me down." Ultimately, she concluded that she had simply "outgrown" him. After ten years of marriage, Carrie walked out and, with her children in tow, moved in with "the man who could give me the sort of life I really wanted."

Bill was an "incredibly enthusiastic, important, dedicated" human rights activist whom Carrie had met and fallen in love with while doing volunteer work for the Friends Service Committee. "For a while, our life together was unbelievably exciting," Carrie explained. "Our house was like Grand Central Station with people I'd always read about or watched on the TV news stopping over for dinner, political discussions going on late into the night, people camping out on the living room floor. We took trips to Washington with the kids and trips to Central and South America without them. You can't imagine how thrilling it all was—even if we did have to skimp on things that other families take for granted." Carrie worried about that sometimes, and even more so after her children let her know that they were not as thrilled with their alternative life-style as she was. She began "lobbying" Bill to show more fatherly interest in her kids.

" 'But I'm not their father,' he said, and I can't tell you how much that hurt me. If he couldn't accept my kids, how could he really accept me and what sort of future did we have?" Suddenly, it dawned on her that Bill might not be "all that committed" to their relationship; and with that thought nagging at her, she started "hinting around" about getting married and having a child together. Bill came right out and told Carrie that he liked things the way they were, had no intention of getting married, and was so adamant about not bringing children into the world that he had had a vasectomy years before.

Carrie was stunned, shattered. Since she had always planned to have more children and was sure Bill knew that, she felt deceived and betrayed and thoroughly disillusioned. "It was as if a veil was lifted from my eyes," she said. "Bill wasn't the man I wanted to spend the rest of my life with after all."

Leaving Bill and moving to a nearby suburb, Carrie worked full time and tried to be a full-time mom *and* dad for her kids as well. After four years, she was exhausted. She didn't have the time or energy to date. She was "gun-shy" and doubtful about her ability to attract a man who would be interested in her and her children. "But I know that I'm just not cut out for going it alone," she said. "I want stability and security and a two-parent family for my kids." Carrie had come full circle— again—and it didn't surprise me in the least.

Feathers in the Wind

Like that of most of the women I've counseled over the past decade, Carrie's vision of a successful, productive, fulfilling, long-term, committed relationship with a man was as variable as the weather. She was a feather in the wind, never trusting what she had, constantly questioning her own choices, always looking for something outside herself to silence her self-doubt and compensate finally and decisively for her sense that she was "dull, nondescript, disgustingly average. A nobody."

Time and again, Carrie had turned to relationships with men to supply her with something she believed she lacked: popularity, stability, security, legitimacy, excitement, normalcy and, most recently, relief from the stresses and strains of single parenthood. Yet, soon after she got what she wanted and managed to fill an empty space inside herself, she invariably found another empty space to fill, something else that was missing, something else about herself or her life to doubt, question, feel bad about and try to fix. And regrettably, each time Carrie's opinion of herself changed, so did her opinion of her relationship and her expectations for the men in her life. She began messing around with what she had, altering her vision of the relationship she wanted and attempting to change her man so that he would live up to her revised expectations.

That is NOT the path to success and productivity in a long-term, committed relationship. It is a prescription for disaster. It is also, I'm sorry to say, standard operating procedure for many women today. They are unable to trust or accept the men in their lives, unable to trust or accept their vision of a successful relationship and unable to trust and follow through on their decision to do what it takes to have that sort of relationship because they do not trust or accept themselves.

Like Carrie, countless women today relentlessly search for something to "complete" them. Constantly trying to improve themselves, they are always on the lookout for problems in themselves, their lives and their relationships. More often than not, they find them. They have forgotten or never learned or only glimpsed what it is to accept themselves as women: unconditionally, no matter what, regardless of their role or circumstances, to say to themselves and believe, "This is it. This is who I am and that is good enough for me." Instead, they are plagued by self-doubt and low self-esteem: a pervasive sense that they do not measure up, that in one or many areas— including relationships—they are not adequate or as acceptable as they think they should be.

Women and Self-esteem

Why do women have low self-esteem? I've posed that question to countless women over the years. Here is a small sampling of their answers:

I have low self-esteem because:

- I'm not perfect.
- I'm overweight.

- I'm clumsy.
- I don't have a successful relationship.
- I don't have a successful career.
- I can't control my temper.
- I never have anything interesting to say.
- I was adopted.
- I never went to college.
- My parents constantly pushed me to achieve and I could never please them.
- My parents didn't care enough to push me to achieve.

Such statements and literally hundreds of others along the same lines regularly and repeatedly confirm my suspicion that some women with self-esteem problems are just looking for an issue to relate to. The sources of their self-doubt or self-loathing, the barriers to self-acceptance that they encounter, are infinite in number, limitless in scope, self-generated and self-perpetuating. Low self-esteem is a real problem in the sense that it prevents you from being all you can be or feeling satisfied with who you are. But it is also an artificial problem, created by comparisons and obstacles of your own making.

You set impossible goals for yourself, fail to reach them and then feel bad about yourself for having failed. You let *Cosmopolitan* and *Women's Wear Daily*, "The Cosby Show" and "Lifestyles of the Rich and Famous," your neighbors, friends, relatives and business associates dictate your standards and priorities for you. Whatever is fashionable—whatever other people tell you or seem to think is acceptable at any given moment—becomes the yardstick you use to measure your own worth. When a fashion changes, you feel compelled to change with it. If you did not, other people would think you were weird. They would not approve of you. They would not want to be with you; and to be rejected in that way, to be alone without the support you thrive on would be a fate worse than death. You have been conditioned to think that way: to believe that living up to other people's expectations is the only reliable way to obtain love and acceptance. Unfortunately, your never-ending effort to be acceptable more often than not prevents you from accepting yourself.

You listen to your ego instead of your natural self uninhibited by contemporary influences and pressures. Your ego is the part of your personality that demands to be superior, unique, noticed, apart, alone and self-absorbed. It is the part of you that wants to be right, to be number one, to win by beating out all competitors. As such, it can be used in positive ways. It can be the force that drives you to achieve in business or athletics or other competitive settings. In those settings, your ego is a useful tool. However, like any tool, it can be used incorrectly. It can become a weapon—one which you may have turned on yourself.

Your ego tells you that you *should* be superior, unique, noticed and so on. It generates fantasies and expectations which may have little or nothing to do with who you really are, what you really want and what would make you truly happy. Although you are not your ego, you frequently act as if you are. You buy into those fantasies. You relentlessly strive to live up to your ego's expectations, and in the process, you lose sight of who you really are as a woman. In fact, you act as if the last person in the world that you'd want to be is yourself.

According to a survey of 300 female executives conducted in 1982 by Korn/Ferry International and the UCLA Graduate School of Business Management, the greatest obstacle to professional success those women said they faced was "being a woman." Along the same lines, my own research has shown that hundreds of women from all walks of life identify *men* as their primary role models. Those women based their identities on the attitudes and actions they witnessed in their fathers and brothers as well as male friends, colleagues and "mentors" in their chosen professions, and they rejected the lessons they learned from their mothers, grandmothers and other "feminine" role models. "I knew I didn't want to be like her," is the way they summed up their attitudes toward those women. They described women's best qualities as healing, nurturing, intuition, instinct and access to their emotions. Yet, they viewed those very same traits as potential weaknesses: obstacles to "success in a man's world," traps that kept them in a "one down" position in countless areas of their lives. Clearly, after three decades devoted to trying to prove that they were equal to, as good as and as equipped for success as men, these women seemed more convinced than ever that being a woman isn't as good as being a man, that being a woman isn't good enough to assure success in business or in leading a productive, fully satisfying life.

Losing the Battle, Winning the War

These women have won the battle but lost the war. They have sacrificed their innermost feminine qualities to prove that they were equal to men. They are left with a hollow victory. A woman must always know what her long-term objective is and choose which battle to win and which to lose. Winning and losing in the short term are merely tools to achieve your ultimate objective. For example, Meg's grandmother, Claire, mentioned in Chapter Three, lost at the game of canasta to win depth and quality in her relationship. She had to have enough vision and self-esteem to lose for the moment and gain in the long term. To be successful, you cannot allow your fears of winning or losing to control you.

Women Are Slaves to Low Self-esteem

As a woman, you have been conditioned to win by losing. You have learned to do that. You have watched other women do it. You have listened to them discuss their problems or inadequacies and be comforted, advised and sympathized with by other women. You have seen how women who appear to be secure, self-confident and successful are so often subjected to the scorn, skepticism, mistrust and disdain of their peers. And you have reacted to *your* peers in that manner since grade school. Having low self-esteem—and talking about what you can't do or are afraid to do—has enabled you to feel supported by and connected to other women throughout your life. That is one reason why self-doubt and low self-esteem are so pervasive among women, and self-acceptance so rare.

In addition, to win by succeeding—by accepting, feeling good about and trusting the inherent wisdom of your natural self— is more difficult and more frightening than feeling unsure of and dissatisfied with yourself. Low self-esteem is the easy way out. It gives you an excuse not to be all the woman you can be. It gives you an excuse not to explore the possibilities and assume the responsibilities of being a woman today. You do not have to do the work involved in discovering who you really are. You do not have to put yourself on the line. When you have low self-esteem, no one knows what you are capable of and no one asks you for more than you want to give. When you don't trust your own choices, when you allow other people's opinions and the latest fashion to dictate the path you will take, you get out of making commitments and being disciplined. As soon as the going gets tough, you change your mind. You turn off your path, telling yourself: "I guess I don't have what it takes to get what I want. I guess I'm not strong or secure or otherwise good enough to go the distance."

If you have low self-esteem, your self-doubts, insecurities and sense of your own inadequacy nag at you from the moment you get out of bed each morning until you fall asleep each night. Countless times during any given day, you dissect and analyze and try to fix or conceal those presumably fatal flaws which loom larger than life in your mind's eye. You are a slave to your self-esteem problem. It controls you. Every move you make is dictated by it, so much so that the lion's share of your time and energy goes into molding, shaping and berating yourself into being the woman you think you should be—whether or not that is the woman you are or honestly want to be.

There Can Be No Success Without Self-acceptance

As long as you continue to be a slave to low self-esteem and continue to blame your problems on low self-esteem, you will continue to have failed relationships. There is a direct correlation between how successful your relationship with a man will be and how self-accepting you are. For one thing, you will only allow a man to accept you to the extent that you accept yourself. As Carrie did when she created scenes based on her assumption that David would "dump" her for someone better and ultimately got herself "dumped," you will—for the most part unwittingly and certainly unintentionally—arrange things so that the men in your life treat you in a way that is consistent with your beliefs about yourself. You will select men who reinforce your doubts about yourself, pointing out the very flaws you see in yourself, criticizing the very things that you dislike about yourself or, conversely, doing things for you that you have always thought you should be able to do for yourself (and would if you weren't so darn inadequate). You will get involved in relationships guaranteed to maintain your low self-esteem: relationships with married men, with addicts or alcoholics, with men who abuse you or cheat on you or don't want the same things out of life that you do. And you will get trapped in those relationships because low self-esteem convinces you that they are still better than being alone.

Secondly, when you are not self-accepting and don't trust yourself to make decisions that are in your own best interest, anything can get you off track. One insensitive remark or oversight on the part of the man in your life, one disapproving comment from a friend, a dubious score on an intimacy self-test in your favorite women's magazine or any unexpected turn of events and you begin to doubt yourself. In no time flat, you are questioning everything about your life thus far, feeling uncertain and, more often than not, dissatisfied with everything you've done up until now—including getting involved with a particular man or committing yourself to your present relationship. You start a chain reaction that can ultimately lead to the demise of a potentially successful intimate relationship with a man.

Finally, without self-acceptance, you will fall into the trap of looking for a man or a relationship to complete you, to supply you with whatever you think is missing from your life. But that nebulous "empty space" is transitory. The needs you are trying to fulfill will change. Something else will come along to make you feel good about yourself in that area. Or something else will crop up to make you feel miserable. When that happens, you won't need the same things from your relationship. Or you will want something different from it. Or you will expect the man in your life to change with you. You will try to make him change and that will cause problems.

WHAT WORKS WITH MEN

To solve 95 percent of your relationship problems (and cope with the rest):

STOP believing the fantasies your ego, other people and the prevailing winds of contemporary influences generate about the woman you *should* be and START believing in the reality of the woman you are.

Learn to Accept Yourself

You cannot find yourself or learn to accept yourself through either engaging in or avoiding relationships with men. Protecting yourself from intimacy and refusing to make commitments will not teach you to trust yourself. A job, a career, having children, going on a diet, getting a divorce, finding a worthy cause to support or anything else outside yourself cannot make you feel good about yourself on the inside. The only way to overcome low self-esteem and develop self-acceptance is to get rid of the comparisons and obstacles you have created. Stop building barriers. Stop wanting to be who you are not. Stop selecting situations that guarantee low self-esteem. Forget about the woman you think you should or shouldn't be and discover who you really are.

- *Let yourself off the hook.* Stop reviewing and ruminating about your past mistakes, calling yourself a failure and using that arbitrary label as an excuse not to take new risks. Having failed does not make you a failure. Failing is what you do on the way to success. It is how you learn what works and what doesn't. It is a process that enables you to eliminate paths that lead nowhere until you find the path that will take you where you want to go.

- *Find an outlet for expressing your emotions* so that they do not paralyze you. Unexpressed anger, resentment, sorrow, sadness and loss are hazardous to women's health. Fearing that they will overwhelm you, you bottle up those "negative" emotions and, in the process, stifle your positive feelings and most of your true self. You can express those emotions to other women. Not just any woman, of course, but women who are trustworthy, honest, concerned about your well-being and unlikely to use against you what you tell them. Such women will understand your feelings. They can receive them from you. Your feelings will not hurt other women, but locked inside, they are killing you.

- *Regain your innocence.* Relocate the part of you that is unworldly, unsophisticated, not bogged down by guilt and shame. Take every available opportunity to look at the world from an innocent, unjaded perspective.

- *Rediscover the traits which make you who you are:* your own abilities, priorities and attitudes. Little by little, begin drawing upon them, using them to help you reach various goals. It will dawn on you that you *can* succeed without adopting male priorities and behaviors or doing only what you think other people expect you to do.

- *Dare to be vulnerable,* to leave yourself open to criticism or rejection, exposing your flaws and insecurities even though they could be used to hurt you. Have supportive women in your life to heal you if you do get hurt. And recognize that you might not. Women who are vulnerable actually get hurt less (and learn a great deal more about themselves and their capabilities) than women who control and manipulate and keep their guard up in hopes of protecting themselves from pain.

- *Stop confusing your true self with your ego.* By constantly chasing the expectations created by this competitive, demanding, fantasy-generating part of yourself, you are killing off many things that are important to you. You are denigrating and undermining your real self, drowning out the inner voice that speaks to you in a feminine tone. Stop catering to your ego so that you can hear, listen to and respect that voice— which is the true source of your power as a woman.

Discovering the Source of Your Power as a Woman

Think of a nearly perfect experience: anything that you've been part of at some time during your adult life which was or came very, very close to being ideal in every imaginable way. It might be a nearly perfect sexual experience, a nearly perfect parenting experience, a nearly perfect run along the beach or lazy Sunday afternoon or handling of a challenge at work. Whether it lasted a few minutes or a few hours or for days on end, for as long as it lasted, everything seemed to be "in sync," flowing naturally, almost effortlessly. Visualize that experience as if you had recorded it on videotape. Picture the events leading up to that experience. Envision yourself, the other people involved, your surroundings, all the sights and sounds and smells, in vivid detail. Run through the entire experience in your mind. Then run through it again, only this time stop the videotape at the moment you realized you were having a nearly perfect experience, that everything was somehow unfolding exactly as it was meant to unfold and happening in precisely the way you wanted it to happen. How were you feeling at that moment?

"Powerful . . . light . . . beautiful . . . lovable . . . attractive . . . peaceful . . . feminine"—those are the words thousands of women, women just like you, have used. In the midst of their nearly perfect experience, they felt "adventurous . . . courageous . . . playful . . . desirable . . . irresistible . . . open."

Caught up in a moment that was ideal in almost every imaginable way, they were not looking for anyone else's approval. They were not questioning their own motives, doubting their own virtues, worrying about their deficiencies. They were not fretting over past mistakes or anticipating future problems. They were not trying to control the experience or afraid of losing control as a result of it and they felt "receptive . . . vulnerable . . . ready for anything . . . innocent . . . confident . . . electric."

Coming from the source of their power as women, following an inner voice which spoke in a feminine tone, they felt "trusting . . . passionate . . . magnetic . . . swept away . . . free."

You have felt that way too. Like all women, you have experienced such self-acceptance. You can remember moments when you trusted yourself implicitly and totally, no matter how fleeting those moments may have been. At those moments, the positive energy you emitted virtually guaranteed that positive energy came back to you. At those moments, your natural self, free of contemporary influences and pressures, was in charge. And it is your natural self, your positive energy, your self-acceptance and those feelings of peace, power, passion and much more which you must bring to your relationship, rather than looking to your relationship to find those things.

WHAT WORKS WITH MEN

To solve 95 percent of your relationship problems (and cope with the rest):

Never be in a relationship to make you happy—only to make you *happier*. If you bring your happiness *to* your relationship, then it will make you happier.

Accepting yourself as a woman and bringing your real self to your relationship is absolutely essential for having a successful relationship with a man. So is understanding and accepting the way *men* behave in relationships. You see, even though being a woman *is* good enough, even though being a woman is not only *as good as* being a man, but in many ways is *better,* it is never the same as being a man. Men and women are different. As I will explain in the next chapter, they're exact opposites. Especially in a relationship.

FIVE

Men and Women Are Different

Cheryl

Tony, a forty-year-old architect, and Cheryl, a thirty-eight-year-old mother of two and part-time children's dance instructor, had been married for less than a year when Cheryl began to notice that they were, as she put it, "drifting apart." There wasn't a specific problem, she explained, "just this feeling that we weren't as close as we used to be. We seemed to be caught up in our daily routines, doing our individual things and not really saying anything to each other—not anything important anyway." She could still remember the first time she tried to discuss this matter with Tony. It was a Saturday afternoon and Tony, who had just returned from the local electronics emporium, was attempting to unpack and install the state-of-the-art stereo system he had purchased. According to Cheryl their conversation went something like this:

CHERYL: Honey, we have to talk.
TONY: We do? About what?

CHERYL: Us. Our relationship. How you feel about it.

TONY: I feel fine. Is something wrong?

CHERYL: I don't know. Maybe not. I just . . . well, I feel
           shut out, like we don't really connect anymore,
           like there's this invisible wall between us.

TONY: You're still angry about the fishing trip I took
           last weekend, aren't you? I wish you had told
           me you didn't want me to go.

CHERYL: No. That's not it at all. What I'm trying to
           say is that people who love each other share
           things, they . . .

TONY: But you hate fishing.

CHERYL: Damn it, you're not listening to me. I'm not
           talking about fishing. I'm talking about us.
           We're drifting apart. We're not . . . you know
           . . . together the way we used to be.

Once again, Tony missed Cheryl's point. "He told me I was
being ridiculous," she recalled. "Then he began reminding me
of all the things we *did* together." But Cheryl wanted to know
how he *felt*. "I wanted him to tell me he still cared."

When several more stabs at getting Tony to express his innermost feelings netted Cheryl no more than an invitation to help
him install the stereo, she gave up in exasperation. Undoubtedly
as relieved as Cheryl was frustrated, Tony went back to what
he was doing. Cheryl went off to ponder the state of their
relationship and to worry that a "lack of communication" would
lead to its demise. Wanting to feel closer to Tony and believing
that "talking about us" would bring them closer together, Cheryl
broached the subject again at the next available opportunity
and got roughly the same results.

"It went on like that for years," she claimed. Ten years to be
exact. During those years, Tony remained faithful to Cheryl.
They continued to have a satisfying sex life. They had children
and Tony worked hard to ensure that neither they nor Cheryl
went without anything they needed or wanted. He even took
on freelance design and drafting jobs so that he could build a
nest egg for their future together.

"But I never know how he feels," Cheryl complained. "He
won't communicate. We never talk about the things that matter

to him, and he doesn't want to hear about the things that matter to me. If I bring up something that's bothering me, he doesn't care about my feelings. Right off the bat, he says, 'So, why don't you just do this thing or that thing to solve the problem.' " Cheryl wasn't looking for advice, she explained. "I want his support . . . and I never get it. Even when there's a problem that involves both of us, he just says, 'Well, what do you want me to do about it?' and when I say I want to talk about it, he looks at me like I'm nuts. Then he asks, 'What good will that do?' I swear I have deeper conversations with the woman who does my nails than I do with Tony."

Worst of all, Cheryl declared, was the way Tony "shuts down" when something was troubling him. "There have been shake-ups at work, problems with his parents, even a real scare about him possibly having cancer a few years back. I knew those things had to be tearing him up inside, but he wouldn't let me help. He just shut me out and the more I tried to get him to open up and let me in, the more he withdrew from me."

What sort of relationship was that, Cheryl asked me when I first met her. How were two people supposed to share their lives when one of them wouldn't share his thoughts and feelings? How do you have a successful relationship with a man who won't communicate with you? You don't. However, the problem Cheryl described, which happens to be the same problem that has been presented to me by most of the women I have counseled over the years, was not that Tony didn't communicate with her at all. Their marriage would not have lasted ten days, much less ten years, if there were truly no communication between them. The real problem, the actual source of Cheryl's discontent and the threat to her relationship, was that Tony didn't communicate *the way Cheryl expected him to*. Although Tony had, in fact, demonstrated that he cared and was committed to the relationship in numerous ways, Cheryl wanted him to communicate his thoughts and feelings about their relationship the way she did—in words. She had been stopped dead in her tracks by the most common (and tenacious) obstacle to having a successful relationship with a man: assuming that, in a relationship, men and women are the same; that they think alike, interpret events in similar ways and have the same priorities. They most definitely do not.

Men Are Like Aliens from Another Planet

Men share themselves and give of themselves on their own terms, and those terms are rarely the same as yours. Men do not intentionally or maliciously or even knowingly think and act and express themselves differently than you think they should. It's just that things which are easy for you can be exceedingly difficult for men. Not only communication, but many, many other aspects of relating to others which come naturally to you are unnatural for men. Your "take" on the world baffles them. Simple modes of thought for you—tuning into your own and other people's feelings, for instance, or considering the way events will affect other people—are completely foreign to them. When it is obvious to you that someone is upset or that the tension in the air is thick enough to cut with a knife, most men won't even realize anything is wrong. They don't notice those things. They miss those cues. They miss your point and, from where they stand, it looks as though you are missing theirs or making mountains out of molehills or stirring up trouble when life would be so much easier if you left well enough alone.

These disparities and countless others, which result from the simple fact that men and women are inherently different and have different natural tendencies, explain why men and women in all innocence manage to hurt each other deeply. They disappoint and frustrate and bewilder one another constantly. In fact, the way men and women view life, the way they live life and the things that are important to them are so different that the safest way for you as a woman to approach men is as if they came from another world entirely.

WHAT WORKS WITH MEN

To solve 95 percent of your relationship problems (and cope with the rest):

Rather than expecting your man to be like you, think of him as an alien from another planet.

Yeah, but . . .

Many women are offended by this advice. "Yeah, but men aren't from another world," they protest. "They live in the same world we do. They have a whole lot more in common with us than they would with an alien from another planet. They are members of the same species, members of the human race with the same needs and feelings all human beings have." If you feel that way, I'm not about to argue with you. However, I can assure you that it is not useful to think of men that way. You'll expect too much of them. You'll expect them to act like human beings, and your ideas about how human beings should behave are a reflection of your point of view—a woman's point of view, which is different from a man's.

If, on the other hand, you think of men not as human beings, but as aliens from another planet who have been raised in a culture entirely different from your own and, as a result, have no knowledge of or experience with your customs and no basis for understanding your perspective, your expectations will be much closer to reality than they are now. You will no longer waste so much time and energy feeling disappointed or resentful or waiting around for men to tell you things, to *say* they care and are committed to a relationship, to express verbally their likes, dislikes and innermost feelings, to put their fears and wishes, hopes and expectations into words. Women express themselves that way. Many men do not. Think of men as aliens from another planet and you'll stop expecting them to talk to you

the way a woman would. You'll start observing men's behavior, and you'll realize that they are telling you things all of the time.

Men Communicate Through Their Actions

Men communicate. They are constantly communicating their ideas, attitudes, expectations and emotions. But women have trouble comprehending or accepting or feeling satisfied with such communication because, in a relationship, men don't use words to convey their needs and feelings.

It's not that they don't want to talk about such things. It's just extremely difficult for them. You have no idea how difficult it is because communicating with words is easy for you. Women have a natural ability to connect their emotions with their verbal apparatus. Men do not. Men cannot talk that way. Oh, you can train them. You can show them how to do it, but when the going gets tough, they'll forget. They'll shut down verbally and you'll think that they are shutting you out. If you could just appreciate how difficult it is for men to express themselves in words, you wouldn't feel hurt and rejected when they don't say the things you want to hear. You would stop wasting your energy trying to make them *tell* you how they feel, because they definitely *show* you. Men communicate through actions, as a German shepherd does.

Although an alien from another planet has never landed in your back yard, you probably have a dog or had one in the past or can relate to the idea of having one. So, think about that dog. Did that dog speak English or French or German or any other recognizable language? Of course not. But you knew what to expect of your dog and how to fulfill its needs, didn't you? Sure you did. You knew when your dog wanted to go out. You knew when your dog was hungry, when he wanted to be scratched behind the ears, when he wanted his belly rubbed. You knew when he wanted to play and you knew when to leave him alone. You knew all that and much more about your dog—even though he never spoke a single word of English or any other recognizable language. You and your dog communicated because you took the time to learn his method of communication:

to recognize and comprehend the signals your dog sent you *nonverbally.*

Because dogs can't speak with words, nonverbal communication is all you can rely on to understand your dog. It is all you should rely on to understand a man. Men will tell you anything you need to know nonverbally and there will be no hidden meanings, no reason to wonder what your man really wants from you or how he really feels about you. A man's behavior conveys the truth about him. Just watch him.

WHAT WORKS WITH MEN

To solve 95 percent of your relationship problems (and cope with the rest):

Learn, respect and accept the nonverbal "language" men use to communicate their true feelings.

"But my man isn't a dog," you say? "He's more intelligent than a dog. His needs are more complex than a dog's and he talks. In English. Besides I'm not looking for a relationship like the one I have with my dog." That's too bad because you probably have a successful, satisfying and peaceful relationship with your dog. You provide your dog with something and he provides you with something. You don't expect more of him than his basic nature allows and he doesn't expect more of you than you've already shown him you'll provide. Once you find a dog you like and get to know what he's like and decide that you can live with a dog like that, you will live with him until he dies without ever having your self-esteem threatened. When he barks at you, you don't get offended. If he pees on your carpet, you don't hold it against him for the next twenty years. If he chews on your furniture, you don't go around telling people that your dog hates you because he chews your furniture. You say, "He's a dog and dogs sometimes chew furniture."

You accept the way dogs are and you don't expect them to be like you. Unfortunately, you do expect that of men—and it doesn't do you a bit of good. So, you have a choice here. You can continue to expect men to be like you and continue to be disappointed by men and dissatisfied with your relationships. Or you can change your expectations and pave the way for success and satisfaction in a long-term, committed relationship with a man. Your chances of turning your romantic vision of a relationship into a reality improve dramatically once you come to recognize and accept that, in a relationship, men are as different from you as they can possibly be.

Men Are Evolutionary Aberrations

If you go back through the history of human development you will see that for many millions of years a division of labor has existed between men and women. Men were relegated to the dangerous and highly competitive role of the hunter/warrior/protector and women had the role of child rearing/gathering/community building.

Over the course of time the qualities that made each gender more successful in its tasks were amplified and passed on through the generations. Men and women became increasingly more suited to their roles.

The instincts required by hunters and warriors were not conducive to relationships. Hunters and warriors had to be competitive. They had to be driven to win, to beat out the other guy, to kill. They had to believe that when the time came, they could get the job done, no matter how grueling or dangerous that job might be. They had to rely on their egos and the fantasies created by their egos in order to survive. There was no room in their psyches for compassion, sensitivity or anything else that makes relationships work. When they were facing an enemy, they couldn't afford to think, "Gee, that guy with the poison dart gun can't be all bad. Maybe he's just scared and insecure." Or, "Maybe I shouldn't kill him. Maybe I should get to know him and have a relationship with him." Allowing such thoughts into their consciousness weakened their resolve and distracted them. While they were entertaining such friendly notions, their enemies were going to kill them. Some woolly mammoth was going to pulverize them. And so, men, out of the always prevailing need to survive, did not develop the attitudes or skills necessary for relating. They developed enormous egos, competitive drives and killer instincts instead.

Meanwhile, back in their communities, women, who had taken on the job of fostering growth, passing along the customs and values of their culture and maintaining peace and harmony within those communities, were inventing more and more intricate and effective modes of communication. They were developing more and more complex and socially conscious thought patterns. They were having relationships with one another that were more emotionally expressive, fulfilling and mutually supportive than their relationships with men would ever be. As a result of their relationships with other women and their function as community-builders, women continued to evolve. They grew and developed and evolved into intricately complex, multifaceted, multidimensional beings.

Men did not. Because of their priorities—hunting, fighting, conquering, killing and competition—they got sidetracked. They got stuck in their groove. They were hunters and warriors. Competing and killing was what they knew. And by the time there were no more woolly mammoths to slay and no more barbarians to keep from stealing their women or pillaging their villages, it was too late to learn what women knew. They could not catch up with women. Even if they tried, those ever-changing, constantly evolving women would have stayed miles ahead of them. And the truth was, men were not inclined to try.

Men's instincts and thought patterns, inbred by millennia of hunting and fighting, were so deeply rooted that when they were no longer necessary for survival, men simply channeled their competitive natures, their win/lose mentality, their kill-or-be-killed perspective into different activities—sports, politics, business; you name it. Men are evolutionary aberrations. Modern times and circumstances did not change them. They did not evolve in the same ways women did. And even though they may not look or act or sound like cavemen anymore, deep down inside they still think and react the same way they did centuries ago. It could take centuries to re-educate them about relationships, to reorient them and bring them up to the level where women are now.

Who Am I Trying to Kid?

Right now, you are probably feeling outraged by what appears to be blatant sex-role stereotyping on my part. You may be wondering how, in this day and age, I have the nerve to pigeonhole men and women this way. It's archaic. It's demeaning. It's precisely the sort of "biology is destiny" line of thought that has kept women oppressed for centuries.

"Men *could* be the way we are," you protest. "They *could* learn. If they were just willing to try . . ." They have tried. You have tried to teach them the things that come so easily to you. At the same time that you were becoming more like men in business and other competitive settings, you tried to make men more like women, to tame that unpredictable, strong-willed, exciting object of your original romantic visions. And if you honestly appraise your efforts, you will see that you have, at best, created a bunch of amateur women: men who can go through the motions of being sensitive, supportive and nurturing but who invariably revert back to type when their backs are against the wall or men who have become quite adept at being like women, but who don't "turn you on." You don't really succeed in "feminizing" your man, or you do, but then you don't want him anymore. He doesn't excite you. It's a no-win situation, an uphill battle with ever-diminishing returns. You can go on fighting it forever and have nothing to show for your efforts except battle fatigue because you are bucking the inertia of thousands upon thousands of years of cultural heritage and deeply ingrained attitudes, beliefs, behavior patterns and priorities.

Both before and after the advent of nonsexist child-rearing practices, experts in the field of human growth and development have repeatedly documented boys' tendencies to play aggressive, competitive, even violent games. Girls, on the other hand, tended to act out social and emotional situations in their games. Without any encouragement from their parents or other caretakers, boys were fascinated by explosions, weapons, demolition and destruction while girls immersed themselves in relationship and people problems. Preferring harmony and peacefulness, girls were apt to worry about the potential for playmates to hurt themselves and tried to arrange things so that did not happen. Their male counterparts simply rushed headlong into the fray, seeking thrills and adventure regardless of the possible costs to life or limb.

Research has also shown that those apparently natural tendencies, divided as they are along gender lines and which we as a society have yet to alter in any significant way, stay with men and women throughout their lives. Even when men learn to act as women do and women learn to act as if they were men, their basic natures and natural tendencies continue to serve as the foundation for the fundamental attitudes and beliefs they bring to their relationships. And like the preferences of young boys and girls at play, those attitudes, beliefs and the meanings men and women attribute to everything that occurs in their relationships are totally different. In fact, when it comes to relationships, men and women are not just different. They are exact opposites.

Men and Women Are as Different as Night and Day

The fundamental differences between men and women stem from the difference in their priorities, specifically, their top priorities. Your top priority, your number-one priority, is the aspect of your life that takes precedence, that shapes your life, that determines your other priorities and has an impact on your goals, aspirations, preferences and perceptions. That number-one priority, that powerfully influencing force which you carry with you to every area of your life, is part of your heritage, part of your basic nature and a reflection of your natural tendencies which are different than a man's.

As I've said, women's number-one priority is Relationship: any series of growth-fostering interactions that is built on trust, empathy and emotion. As a woman, you place above all else your desire, your drive to have meaningful exchanges with other people. You experience and understand life through your exchanges and interactions and relationships. You feel more vital, more powerful, more alive because of them. And you are very, very astute and skillful in this area.

A man's number-one priority is the exact opposite: competition. Men love the thrill of the chase, the exhilaration of battle. They are driven to dominate, to conquer, to come out ahead. Although men prefer to win, competing is even more important than winning. If they won at everything all of the time, life would not be as challenging or exciting as they like it to be. Men are expert competitors. They thrive on and know everything there is to know about competing—and none of that considerable skill and determination is conducive to the emotional exchanges or growth-fostering interactions that go into a relationship.

Women are intricately complex, multifaceted, multidimensional, ever-changing and constantly evolving. Men are elegantly simple. What you see is what you get—and get and get. Once men find their groove—something that rewards them in a way which is meaningful to them—they can stay in it forever.

Women are socially aware. Tuned in to interactions and processes, they are curious about the effect events have on people and interested in the way people respond internally to whatever is going on around them. Men are task-centered. They are interested in tools, toys, tinkering and ball-handling: activities with tangible outcomes and which can, in one way or another, bring them recognition or even glory.

Women are problem-oriented. Constantly on the lookout for potential conflicts, sensitive to the slightest sign of impending disasters, they probe and analyze in hopes of warding off future problems. They are inclined to expend more time and energy talking about, reading about and trying to gain insight into any troublesome aspect of their lives than they devote to actually resolving the matter. And as was certainly the case for Cheryl, in their relationships, most women have difficulty letting anything pass or simply letting things be. They believe that a relationship will last and flourish if, and only if, they talk about the state of that relationship on a regular basis.

Men are solution-oriented. If something is broken, they want to fix it as expeditiously as possible. They do not necessarily want to know why it broke. They do not want to analyze all the events that led up to the breakdown or their feelings about it or the long-term repercussions of it. That is why, like Tony, your man gives you advice long before you're finished talking about how you feel. He wants to solve the problem and get on with his life, to have things return to "normal" as quickly and painlessly as possible. In addition, even if something *could* break at any moment, if it is not broken now, men believe it should be left alone. Unless there is a readily identifiable, fixable problem, most men see absolutely no point, absolutely no value, in discussing the state of their relationships.

Men do what works, whatever gets results with the least amount of effort. They are energy-efficient. If something works, if it makes life easier for them and enables them to get what they want, that is what men will do. And while they are wondering, "Will this work or won't it?" you'll be worrying about what's right or wrong.

Women want to be right, to be accepted, to be fashionable. They will actually do things that don't work or refuse to do things that would because behaving otherwise doesn't seem right. If it isn't what other women would do—if it isn't what they, based on current fashions and trends, think they should do—they won't do it, even if it would bring them success.

That natural and decidedly feminine tendency is undoubtedly rearing its head at this very moment because I'm quite certain that most of what you've just read doesn't seem right to you at all.

"I Don't Buy That!"

I'm pretty sure you haven't bought a word I've said. Even though an inner voice is whispering, "Yes, I know that's true. I've seen plenty of proof in my own life," you refuse to believe it.

You believe in equality. You believe that, given the opportunity, women are capable of being as competitive, practical, active and results-oriented as men, and men are capable of being as insightful, sensitive, socially aware and nurturing as women. Well, you are entitled to your beliefs.

What you believe may be right. What you believe may be good. It may be better than what I believe and it may reflect the way things *should* be and would be in the best of all possible worlds. But it isn't practical. It doesn't work. The way you want things to be is not the way things are in the real world, in real relationships; and you have to decide if you want to be right or successful, if you'd rather prove your point or be productive and satisfied in a lasting relationship with a man.

You don't have to believe me. I can't stop you from behaving as if men were capable of viewing relationships and behaving in relationships and experiencing relationships the same way you do. However, I can guarantee that expecting men to be that way will get you into trouble. Thinking of men as your equals in a relationship will prevent you from having a successful, productive, fulfilling, long-term, committed relationship with a man. In that sort of relationship—not a fashionable relationship, but a successful and productive relationship that can last a lifetime—you are NOT equal to men. You are far superior to them. You are by nature socially conscious, compassionate, emotionally expressive and able to manage complex interpersonal situations. Men are not. Men are the opposite. And deep down inside, you know that.

You can wait for men to change. But there is no guarantee that they ever will. You can devote yourself to changing men and teaching them to be the way you naturally are in relationships. However, you have a lifetime of very, very hard work cut out for you. Or you can choose *not* to work so hard and work wisely instead. You can learn to have a successful, satisfying, intimate relationship *with an evolutionary aberration.*

The Law of Electrodynamics

Women are always dismayed and disheartened to learn the things I have been telling you in this chapter. They seem to think that the differences between men and women—the fact that when it comes to relationships, men and women are exact opposites—makes it more difficult to have a relationship with a man. Nothing could be further from the truth. It is women's reluctance or outright refusal to accept those differences and work with those differences that prevents them from being successful and productive in their relationships with men. The differences themselves are not the problem. In fact, the differences between men and women are what make them interesting and attractive to each other.

Opposites attract, come together to create energy which is in turn used to produce results: that is the physical Law of Electrodynamics, and a vital, vibrant, exciting, long-term, committed relationship conforms to the Law of Electrodynamics. The more opposite two entities are, the more they attract and the more energy they produce. The same principle applies to people, to male and female energy. You have intuitively known that since you were a child. The relationship of your romantic vision was not a relationship between you and someone who was just like you. The object of your romantic fantasies was not intricately complex, socially aware, problem-oriented, fashionable and inclined to express his thoughts and feelings with words. He was your opposite: simple, task-centered, solution-oriented, competitive, a man whose actions spoke louder than words. You were attracted to his masculine energy. He was attracted to your feminine energy. Being opposites was what ignited the spark between you and brought you together.

When I talk about the attraction of opposites, please understand that I am *not* talking about opposite values or opposite interests or the sort of love–hate relationship in which you and your man constantly argue, make up and fall into bed to have wild, passionate sex. I am referring to the fact that a successful relationship is the natural, inevitable outcome of being all the woman you can be and allowing, indeed encouraging, your mate to be all the man he can be. Only a very forward-looking,

confident, committed, disciplined, self-accepting woman can do that. And you can only do that if you fully grasp and come to respect, embrace and accept the way men are in relationships— which is the subject of the next chapter.

As you read that chapter and those that follow it, however, please note that to use what I tell you about men and about what works in an intimate, committed relationship, certain conditions apply.

You must be in the right relationship with the right man: a man you trust and whose basic nature, natural inclinations, attitudes and expectations are compatible with yours. My advice won't work with every man you meet and can't work when you are involved with a man who wants things you can't give him or can't give you what you want.

You must be serious about and truly committed to your relationship. The suggestions in the next few chapters are applicable only to long-term, committed relationships. They are not useful and even can get you hurt when you are just dating a man or have not yet learned enough about him to trust him fully.

You must really want your relationship to be successful, productive and fulfilling and to last a lifetime. Every technique that can be used to manage your relationship effectively can also be misused if you are determined to maintain the upper hand, prove a point or find an excuse to end your relationship.

SIX

How Men Behave in Relationships

Cheryl Again

For millions of men, the five most dreaded words in the English language are "Honey, we have to talk." Why? Because men have watched you in action and know what they are in for when you, for reasons they cannot fathom, decide to "work on" your relationship. Tony was no exception. When Cheryl used those words to initiate the conversation I described in the last chapter, he knew that he was in trouble. He knew that the conversation would take him into alien territory, that his wife, in her intricate complexity, had something complicated to convey to him and that she would not only expect him to understand her but also to respond in kind. She would expect him to talk about his feelings and that was extremely difficult for him to do. It was easy for her and Tony knew that too. He knew that Cheryl had him at a disadvantage. If their conversation proceeded the way she wanted it to, he was going to lose; and, being competitive by nature, he did not like to lose.

Being also task-oriented by nature, Tony was not thrilled

with Cheryl's timing, either. Couldn't she see that he was busy installing their new stereo? She knew that he had been looking forward to buying the stereo for weeks. He had driven all the way to the mall and back thinking about putting it together. He wanted to have it set up in time to show it off to his buddies when they stopped by later that afternoon. He wished Cheryl had waited until he wasn't doing anything important before starting the "dumb" discussion they were about to have.

Wanting to get back to the task at hand and realizing that he was going to lose no matter what he did, before Cheryl got halfway through her second sentence, Tony had decided to do whatever it took to get the conversation over with as quickly and painlessly as possible. Because he was simple and solution-oriented by nature and would never think of talking about his relationship unless there were a specific problem that needed to be fixed, he assumed that he must have done something to upset Cheryl which she now wanted him to make up for in some way. He concluded that the most energy-efficient way to get Cheryl off his back and return to the truly important business of installing the stereo was to figure out what she thought he had done wrong, apologize and either promise not to do it again or make some sort of peace offering. That was what Tony was trying to do when he brought up his fishing trip, listed the activities they participated in as a couple and invited Cheryl to help him install the stereo. Of course, he totally missed Cheryl's point. His agenda had been different from Cheryl's from the start.

Had she understood the way men are in a relationship, Cheryl might have avoided that utterly frustrating conversation altogether. Even if she had only recognized and accepted the four facts I've given you thus far—that men communicate through their actions; that their number-one priority is competition; that men are simple, task-centered and solution-oriented; and that they are energy-efficient and geared to get whatever they are after as quickly and painlessly as possible—she would have known that the conversation was going to get her absolutely nowhere. And she could have found a better way to feel closer to her husband. More important, rather than wasting ten years worrying about the state of her relationship and resenting Tony for "not communicating" with her, she could have spent that time enjoying her relationship and feeling good about the many ways Tony showed her that he did care. Instead of working hard for the next ten years, she could have worked smart and had a successful, productive, fulfilling, lasting relationship with her man.

That is what I want you to be able to do and why I am putting so much emphasis on how men behave in relationships and how different they are from you. What I have to say may not be fair. It may not seem right. It certainly is not fashionable. But it does work.

Men are not your enemies. They are simply different from you. In a relationship, they are your opposite. If you keep that in mind, you will never again have to work so hard to understand men or get along with them. If you allow yourself to accept the differences between men and women, if you can learn to recognize and respect and work with those differences, you will automatically relate to men more realistically, more productively and more successfully. Indeed, you will find that by understanding and accepting and adjusting to the way men are in relationships, you can be remarkably happy in a long-term, committed relationship with your alien from another planet, your evolutionary aberration.

Men Do Not Look at Relationships the Same Way Women Do

Because their number-one priority, the priority that shapes their lives, is different from yours, men do not experience relationships the same way you do, and relationships don't mean the same things to them as they mean to you. The agenda men bring to a relationship is different from yours: They do not want the same things from a relationship that you do.

Men don't mind being in relationships. They even like being in them. Relationships are nice to have. But the cold, hard truth is that men don't really care about relationships per se. Relationships themselves do not fulfill men. They are not their top priority. They usually aren't their second or third or fourth priorities either. In fact, on most men's priority lists, relationships rank somewhere below tools, toys, tinkering and ball-handling. If you don't believe me, just try relating to your man or talking about your relationship during the Super Bowl or when he's tinkering with his car or, as Cheryl did, while he's attempting to install your stereo.

With competition as their number-one priority and centuries of programming as hunters, warriors and breadwinners, men naturally tend to see life in very black-and-white terms. You win or you lose, kill or get killed, live or die. In a successful, productive relationship, everyone wins. You grow. You change. You pass on a few customs, instill a few values. You compromise and harmonize and peacefully coexist. That does not make sense to men. It does not compute. There's no logical reward in it for a man—unless the relationship somehow enhances his ability to compete, unless it pumps up his ego.

Men have relationships for ego gratification. That is their agenda. That is what they want from a relationship. A relationship is valuable to a man if it boosts his ego.

Most Men Are Slaves to Their Egos

Men want to be superior, unique, apart, alone, king of the hill, the center of the universe—all the things their egos tell them they must be—and men always listen to their egos. They can't help it. They are slaves to their egos. They need their egos. Without the fantasies generated by that part of their personalities, men wouldn't be able to get out of bed in the morning to face another day of competition. They wouldn't believe they could win. They wouldn't have the will to fight. They would be miserable, ineffective, unsuccessful and not even close to all they could be.

Men live up to their potential by taking orders from their egos, and their egos are very demanding. They insist upon instant and constant gratification. They need to be pumped up, stroked and recharged on a regular basis. Most, if not all, of men's behavior is motivated by their need to gratify their egos. And the good news is that, in this day and age with its limited opportunities to hunt, fight, pillage or conquer, one of the most readily available sources of ego gratification is pleasing a woman. Men love to please women. It is an easy way to pump up their egos.

Let me run that by you again. Men, who take orders from their egos and are slaves to their egos, get their egos stroked by making you happy. They get to be all the man they can be—which happens to be pretty darn close to the man of your romantic vision—by pleasing *you*. How can you screw up a deal like that?

I'll give you a detailed answer to that question in the next few chapters, but for now it will suffice to say that you do screw up that deal because you hate the idea that men are being good to you for their ego's sake. You want men to do things for more altruistic reasons: because they care; because something is the good, kind, compassionate thing to do; because it is right, acceptable, fashionable. In other words, you want men to have the same motives you do. And I'm not saying that they don't. Men care. They will do the right thing occasionally, even more than occasionally. They know how to behave kindly and compassionately. However, their primary motivation and the main reason they get involved in a relationship and want to please you is to gratify their egos. That's just the way men are and you could have everything you ever dreamed of in a relationship if you would simply let them be that way.

But you want them to make you happy, to please you and have a relationship with you *on your terms*. And I'm telling you that they won't. They won't because there's no ego-gratification in being a good boy and doing things your way. And they won't because your terms are too complicated. Your terms are too complex and too costly and too subject to change for men to figure them out, much less adhere to them.

Men Are Simple

Remember Carrie, the single parent and consumer advocacy agency director I described in Chapter Four? When she got involved with her ex-husband Ron, he was an intense, intelli-

gent, but decidedly absent-minded science student. He could calculate complex algebraic formulas, but his bank account was constantly overdrawn because he forgot to make deposits or didn't bother to balance his checkbook. He kept countless facts and figures in his head but couldn't remember where he left his car keys or when he ate his last meal. From the outset, Carrie assumed responsibility for the countless everyday details that Ron was too "hopelessly scatterbrained" to attend to. Since she seemed happy to do it and it made it easier for him to engage in such ego-gratifying activities as excelling in school and later making groundbreaking discoveries at work, Ron was more than happy to let Carrie take care of him that way. Ten years later, he was still happy with the arrangement. As you may recall, Carrie was not. Ready to go out and make her mark on the world, Carrie resented the fact that Ron did not assume more responsibility on the home front. She was convinced that his inept efforts to help out with chores or cooking or child care were intentional acts of sabotage, Ron's way of keeping her from achieving her full potential. But that was not the case. Ron was just doing what he had always done and being the same intense, intelligent but absent-minded man he had always been.

Similarly, Meredith, a thirty-two-year-old special education teacher, met Mike, a thirty-three-year-old psychologist, during a particularly difficult time in her life. "My boyfriend had dumped me," she explained. "My mother had had a massive stroke and we were in the process of getting her into a nursing home, and I had just learned that I was being laid off because of budget cuts in my school district. Needless to say I was a real mess, and Mike was there to pick up the pieces. He listened to me bitch and moan for weeks on end. He took wonderful care of me." And Meredith loved him for it. She let Mike know how much she appreciated every kindness he showed her, how much she needed him, how important he was to her. He got his ego stroked for being the caretaker to her "wounded bird."

But eventually the "wounded bird" healed. Meredith got her life back on track. She felt secure and self-confident again. Her relationship with Mike continued, but she didn't need his caretaking anymore. In fact, she found it stifling. From where she stood now, he no longer seemed kind and caring and help-ful, but instead intrusive, domineering and controlling. Yet, his behavior was actually the same as it had been when Meredith had been a "real mess." Mike was doing what he had always done to make Meredith happy.

I could tell you dozens of similar stories. "My relationship no longer meets my needs," "My husband and I have grown apart," "The man in my life is holding me back, stunting my growth": These are some of the most prevalent complaints I hear from women, and upon closer inspection, I invariably find that they and the terms for their relationships have changed, but their men have not.

Women are intricately complex, multifaceted, multidimensional and ever-changing. They are constantly discovering new avenues for satisfaction and self-expression. That's the way women are, but that's not the way men are. Men are the opposite. Like Ron and Mike, your man will be doing the same thing, treating you the same way ten years from now, as he did on the day you let him into your heart. But as you grow and change, you'll feel differently about your man. You'll interpret his actions differently. You'll want to blame him for all of the problems in your relationship, but he will not have changed.

Men are elegantly simple. They know how to do a handful of things well—mostly competitive, practical, tangible things— and they stick with what they know. As long as there is a reward to be had, as long as a behavior pattern leads to ego-gratification (or they think it will), men will continue to engage in that behavior. That is how simple men are. Once they find their niche, they are comfortable staying in it forever.

That does not mean that the man in your life won't ever change or that he is incapable of treating you differently. Your man wants to make you happy. Making you happy gratifies his ego. He will do anything to please you if you show him that it's worth his while and if he won't have to sell himself out in the process. Men don't look for ways to change as women do. But they will change if changing will enhance their ability to compete. Men view everything including change as a tool. If a tool is useful, if it will pump up their egos and make them better competitors, they will use that tool. They will change whenever changing will insure their success and whenever the tangible rewards outweigh the cost of changing.

Of course, the methods women typically use to try and per-

suade men to treat them differently don't fit that description—
and they don't work. Discussing and analyzing the state of your
relationship, trying to make a man understand how you feel
and hoping that once he understands how you feel, he will do
things your way, just doesn't work. It's too complicated. Telling
a man what he is doing wrong, telling him what you think he
should do, acting dissatisfied and expecting a man to figure out
what is bothering you are tactics that don't produce the results
you are after either. You are making it too difficult and unrewarding for him to try and please you. You are deflating, threatening your man's ego and preventing him from being all the
man he can be.

When you do that, men are going to dig in, resist you and
fight you every step of the way because that is what men do
when they sense that they are losing or that you are trying to
control them. You are going to have to work very, very hard if
you approach men that way—and it isn't really necessary to
work that hard.

Men Are Low-maintenance Items

A woman is like a Ferrari, and Ferraris are very delicate, highly
sensitive and sophisticated machines. You have to tune them
up almost every time you take them out on the road. You have
to tinker with them and take care of them and always be very
conscious of any little rattle or ping. They are high-maintenance
items.

Fortunately for you, men are *not* like Ferraris. Men are more
like Mack trucks. Just put in oil once in a while, fill the gas tank,
crank them up and they'll go forever. If they break down,
they're easy to fix. You don't need special tools or expensive,
hard-to-find, custom-made parts. Men are low-maintenance
items. They are dirt-simple. Their needs are dirt-simple and
very easy to fulfill: Just give them what they want when they
want it.

Before you jump down my throat for suggesting such a thing,
let me assure you that because men are so simple, giving them
what they want when they want it isn't that big a deal. Men don't

want much from you. They want your trust, acceptance and loyalty, a little bit of attention now and then, to be left alone from time to time and to have their egos stroked periodically so that they are primed to do what they do best. Giving men what they want when they want it doesn't take more than forty-five minutes a day.

Yeah, but . . .

You can have anything you want from a man and everything you want from a long-term, committed relationship by spending *no more than* forty-five minutes a day making that man feel superior, unique, special, and as if he is the center of your universe. But the mere thought of doing that sets off all sorts of alarms and sirens in your head. "That's bull. That's outrageous," you think. "I won't do it. Why should I?" You should because it works, because it's a smart, energy-efficient, practical way to be successful in a long-term relationship with a man.

If you don't want to give a man what he wants when he wants it, find out *why* you don't. Is it simply a matter of thinking that it's a crazy, demeaning, male chauvinistic idea; that it isn't acceptable, that no self-respecting "modern" woman would be caught dead catering to a man's ego (not even for forty-five minutes a day)? If so, you need to reassess your priorities. You need to decide what is more important to you: being successful and productive or being fashionable and proving your point?

On the other hand—and this is very important—you may be unwilling to give your man what he wants because you're involved with a man who wants things you can't give him, who is asking you to compromise your values or make sacrifices which are truly unreasonable. If giving a man what he wants when he wants it requires you to be someone you are not, prevents you from accepting yourself or makes you miserable, then he's not the right man for you. He's not worth your investment.

That is why the selection process, the process of dating and really getting to know and coming to trust a man, is so important. Giving a man what he wants when he wants it is not something you can take lightly or should go about frivolously. It is not something you do while you are casually or even seriously dating a man. It is a tool for success and productivity in long-term, committed relationships. Before you can use that tool, before you can say that you can give a man what he wants when he wants it or commit yourself to doing that or even know if you are capable of doing it, you have to find out what that man expects. If you don't, you are going to get hurt.

WHAT WORKS WITH MEN

To solve 95 percent of your relationship problems (and cope with the rest):

Before you get seriously involved with a man,
find out if you can give him what he wants
when he wants it without violating your own
values and standards.

Let Men Show You Who They Are

"Love at first sight" is a phenomenon that works better on paper and celluloid than in real life. It sells novels and theater tickets, but it is foolhardy to believe that being swept off your feet will lead to a happily-ever-after ending the way it does in steamy fiction or on the silver screen. While I would not begrudge anyone that heady, intoxicated feeling of infatuation, I would warn you that "being madly in love" is just what it sounds like: a form of madness, a state of temporary insanity and not a state that is conducive to deciding whether or not the man who thrills and excites you is a man with whom you can have a long-term, committed relationship. Ariel, the model-turned-image consultant you read about in Chapter One, learned that lesson at age nineteen.

"My modeling career was at its peak," she recalled. "I was on top of the world and Paolo was the icing on the cake." Wealthy, handsome, and charming, Paolo waltzed into Ariel's life and swept her right off her feet. "He was worldly, sexy, a little mysterious, a little moody, always in control. He was everything I ever wanted in a man, and I fell madly in love with him."

On the night they met, Ariel went home with Paolo and did not leave until three days later. She didn't need a change of clothes: they rarely left his bed. Within a matter of weeks, they were spending every free moment together. "There were candlelight dinners," she recalled, "romantic walks along the beach, spur-of-the-moment trips to Aspen and Paris and Rome, which was where he was from. It was like a fairy tale." For six months, Ariel was blissfully happy. She was making plans for the future, a future she believed she would be sharing with Paolo and which he, according to Ariel, "talked about constantly. He'd point to a house and say, 'We'll live in a house like that someday.' He'd tell me about places he had been and how he wanted to take me there and show me all the wonderful things he had seen. He talked about how beautiful our children would be. Even picked out their names. It certainly *sounded* like he was planning for us to spend the rest of our lives together."

Unfortunately, what looked like a romantic vision come true proved to be an illusion when Paolo disappeared from Ariel's life as abruptly and dramatically as he had entered it, calling from his parents' home in Italy to tell her "something had come up" and not to fly in to meet him as originally planned. "That was the last time I actually talked to him," Ariel explained. "Oh, I tried to contact him. I called. I wrote. I showed up at his apartment, but his doorman wouldn't let me in." After a month had passed, Ariel received a pair of expensive diamond earrings and a note thanking her for the memories.

As it turned out, Ariel was not the first and probably would not be the last woman Paolo courted and then cut off completely. Paolo didn't want a relationship, one of his friends informed her. He didn't want to settle down. He wanted a beautiful girl on his arm—and a different one every few months. Clearly, he knew just how to get that.

"The wining and dining and romancing, talking about our future. It was all a scam and I fell for it," Ariel said, the bitter-

ness still apparent in her voice even though nearly two decades had passed. She had been betrayed, tricked, wounded. And she felt like a fool. "I was so sure," she said. "Why couldn't I see how he really was? How could I have been so wrong?" Because she had rushed headlong into the relationship, operating on blind faith instead of taking the time to figure out if Paolo were someone she could trust. If nothing else I say gets through to you, I hope this will: *Don't get seriously involved with a man until you have figured out if you can trust him.*

As I have said before and will say several times more before the final page of this book, selecting a lifetime mate is a serious matter. Barring decisions about life-threatening illness or emergencies, it is the most important choice a woman will ever make. You will be more likely to make the best possible choice (and solve 95 percent of your relationship problems in advance) if you learn everything you possibly can about a man and his expectations *before* you decide to be in a long-term, committed relationship with him.

How do you learn those things? By observing his behavior. Just watch the way that man acts over a period of time, in different settings, under a variety of circumstances, with you and others. The behavior patterns you observe will tell you what you need to know about him, his feelings, his expectations, his trustworthiness and the agenda he will bring to your relationship. Men communicate through their actions. That is their "language."

Of course, men also speak your language. But they do not necessarily convey the truth about themselves with words. In a relationship, they rarely if ever express their innermost thoughts and feelings verbally, and you must give up the notion that they can or do. If you persist in thinking that men communicate that way, you are going to listen to what they say. You are going to believe them, you are going to make choices based on what you hear and you are going to get hurt. Men can and will "con" you with their words. While they are courting you, if they feel cornered or threatened by you and when they think it will get them what they want, men are apt to tell you whatever they think you want to hear. In fact, men will say anything to win and they will not necessarily mean a word they say.

Men will lie to you in your language, but they cannot lie

to you in theirs. Deceiving you through their actions is too complicated. It is too complex. Men are too simple not to communicate honestly through their actions. They can keep up a charade for a short period of time the way Paolo did with Ariel, but they cannot "con" you with their behavior for very long. It is too difficult. There are too many things to remember, too much to keep in order. Inconsistencies and contradictions start to slip through and you will see them—if you are paying attention.

For instance, in retrospect Ariel realized that everything Paolo did was carefully calculated, meticulously planned. "Nothing that happened between us was spontaneous," she said. "Every moment was scripted. It all seemed like a chapter from a gothic novel because that's how Paolo orchestrated it. Sometimes he even fed me my lines. 'Aren't you going to say such and such?' he'd say or 'Now you must tell me so and so.' He'd fly into a rage or pout like mad if something happened to interfere with his plans. And we only went places where we would be seen by people he wanted to impress. We always had to make an entrance. On more than one occasion, we waited outside a club or party because some celebrity was making *his* entrance and Paolo didn't want to share the spotlight. I noticed those things at the time, but I didn't think anything of them. If I had, maybe I would have known I was just an actor in his little drama and not the love of his life that I thought I was."

In later chapters, I will tell you more about understanding the things men convey to you in their language, but for now it suffices to say that you must "listen" carefully to men's actions because men are constantly communicating with you on that channel. Through their actions, they communicate their true thoughts, feelings, fears and expectations. What you see is what you get. And because men are simple, because they are slaves to their egos and neither as self-aware nor as inclined to change as you are, because men are the way they are, what you see is also what you will continue to get for years to come. Consequently, if you don't like what you see, if you are unable to accept a man's natural tendencies and cannot picture yourself doing what you can see he expects of you, don't get involved in a long-term, committed relationship with that man.

If you bought a mean, vicious dog or a dog that acted as if

he wanted you to pet him but barked or bit you each time you came near him or a dog that couldn't be housebroken, you wouldn't keep that dog. You would give him back or give him away and get another dog. You wouldn't keep him and spend the next ten years resenting him and complaining about him and trying to break him of his natural tendencies. Well then, don't do that with a man.

Men Have "Killer" Instincts

Although most men will not run the sort of scam Paolo did, their number-one priority *is* competition and, as a result, they have learned to cheat, lie, steal and do whatever else it takes to come out ahead. When they feel it is necessary, men will do *anything* to get what they want. Never, ever forget that.

No matter how mild-mannered, sensitive and willing to accommodate you they appear to be on the surface, underneath it all men are wired to win at all costs. Once they are challenged and accept the challenge, they will use any available means to win and as soon as they sense they are losing, there's no telling what they will do. They can be vicious, vulgar and vindictive. They can hurt you. They can be dangerous and unpredictable and you don't have to take my word for that. According to national statistics on violent crime, every eighteen seconds a man batters a woman, and 33 percent of female homicide victims were killed by their spouses.

At any moment, at any time, a man can be a "killer" or a "hero." He will do what works. He will do what it takes to win. If you stroke his ego, if you provide him with tangible rewards and treat him like a hero, you will bring out the hero in him. He will work hard to please you and to continue to be viewed as a hero in your eyes. But if you back a man into a corner, if you threaten his ego, he will fight back and he will hurt you.

_____ WHAT WORKS WITH MEN _____

To solve 95 percent of your relationship problems (and cope with the rest):

NEVER FORGET that men can be violent or valiant—and you can bring out either side of them at will.

It is up to you to bring out the hero in your man, to allow and encourage him to be the most and the best he can be so that *you* can be successful and productive in your long-term, committed relationship. That is how relationships work. As you will learn in the next chapter, *your* happiness and *your* success are the direct result of *your* ability to manage your relationship effectively and make being in a relationship with you a rewarding proposition for your man.

SEVEN

Labor and Management: *You're* in Charge of Where and How Your Relationship Is Going

Diane

"What if you're not just drifting apart or expecting your man to think like a woman," Diane, a weekly newspaper editor in her early forties, wanted to know. "What if you have a *real* problem, like a husband who's a workaholic and spends almost no time with you?" That problem was a recent development, Diane insisted. "If I had the slightest idea that things would turn out this way, I never would have married Rick," she said. Her husband, an environmentalist with his own flourishing consulting firm, had not been "obsessed with work" when she met him.

"Oh, he was ambitious," she acknowledged. "He had big plans for the future and no doubt in his mind that he would eventually accomplish everything he set out to do. He was very sure of himself that way. He always seemed to know exactly where he was going." That was one of the things that attracted Diane. "I was sort of floundering at the time," she admitted. "I wasn't really sure of what I wanted to do with my life." And so, she bought into Rick's dreams.

"He was going to earn master's degrees in business and environmental sciences, get a job with a company that worked on environmental problems and then start his own business, a sort of trouble-shooting company that helped other companies do business without polluting the environment. He wanted to be his own boss AND make a difference." It sounded great on paper, Diane recalled, and she backed him every step of the way.

Diane worked her "tail off" to help put Rick through school, holding down two jobs while he went to classes and studied. She continued working long hours after her husband was out of school. "I had worked my way up into a very exciting job," she explained. "It was very challenging and time-consuming; but Rick was just as busy with his new job and trying to get the state legislature to pass a recycling bill, so it wasn't really a problem." It wasn't really a problem when Rick took a position that required him to travel extensively either. "I was wrapped up with our kids by then and doing some freelance writing," Diane said. "Besides Rick was making tons of money and getting all sorts of experience that would help him start his own business sooner." That goal was always in the back of their minds and for twelve years, Diane and Rick, in their separate ways, worked toward it. The more Diane talked, the more apparent it became that they had never spent much time together.

"But it wasn't supposed to be that way forever!" she protested. "After Rick got his business off the ground, I thought things would change. Now it's been eight years since he started his company. It's solvent and successful and runs like a charm, even when he isn't there. But he always has to be there anyway. He's hardly ever home and even when he is, he isn't really there. His mind is on that damn business. The way he acts, you'd think his marriage and family meant nothing to him!"

Diane was furious with Rick and had been ever since the relationship she had always expected to have, once Rick achieved his goal, did not materialize on schedule. Suddenly she resented everything she had given and given up over the years. It had all been for nothing, she thought, and she was determined to get a return on her investment. "I've tried every trick in the book to get Rick to pay more attention to me and the kids and our relationship," Diane said.

She had talked about the problem and not talked about it, giving Rick "the cold shoulder" until he "finally got the message"—at which point she brought their problem up for discussion again. She had offered to quit her job and come to work for him. "But that was when he was just starting out and we still needed my salary to make ends meet," Diane explained. "Still, I told him it was an open-ended offer, that I was willing to come into the business at any time. But he never asked." Concluding that Rick didn't want her involved in his business at all, Diane "saw no point in cheering about all of Rick's victories and building him up after every little defeat." Indeed, she had long ago stopped showing any interest in or enthusiasm about Rick's work.

Diane had tried seduction as a means of attracting Rick's attention, "but nine times out of ten, he was too tired or too preoccupied to make love. Of course, he still expected me to be ready and willing whenever he was." Naturally, Diane resented that. She began turning down more and more of Rick's sexual overtures. When they did have sex or on any other of the increasingly rare occasions when they spent time together and enjoyed each other's company, Diane would take the opportunity to remind Rick that there were never enough of those good times. "Look at how good we are together when we are together," she'd say. "So, why don't you want to be together more?"

Had any of Diane's ploys worked? Did they bring her closer to Rick, get him to spend more time with her, or give him any reason to *want* to be with her? Far from it. In fact, they had the opposite effect. "If anything, things have become worse in the last few years," Diane admitted.

Convinced that her marriage would not improve unless Rick started spending more time with her and showed her that he wanted to be with her, Diane was none too pleased when I told her I didn't think Rick would do that. There wasn't anything for him to gain from being with her, I pointed out. Her husband wasn't getting any benefits from their marriage at all.

Day in and day out and in every imaginable way, Diane conveyed the same message to Rick: "I am unhappy. Our marriage isn't meeting my needs. And you have failed as a husband by not making me happy or meeting my needs." Bombarding him with that information had not yet motivated Rick to do what Diane wanted—and it was not going to. It deflated his ego. It made his relationship with Diane so unpleasant and unrewarding that he put as much distance as possible between them. He was so busy getting his ego boosted elsewhere and defending his ego against Diane's constant reminders of his failure to make her happy that he ended up spending less time with Diane instead of more. That wasn't going to change and Rick wasn't going to change until *Diane* started doing things differently, until *she* started managing the relationship more effectively.

Who's Doing What to Whom?

Although she did not realize it, Diane had been mismanaging her relationship for years. She had not tended to it or nurtured it in a way that would lead to success, productivity or satisfaction. In fact, she had "abused" her relationship. Each time she beat Rick over the head with her unhappiness or complained about the time and energy he devoted to his work, she landed another blow to the relationship. Each time she failed to appreciate what Rick did give her and instead criticized him for not giving her those things more often, she bruised and lacerated her relationship. And each time she vented her anger and resentment by refusing to give Rick what he needed from her (whether sympathy, sex or strokes to his ego), she came closer and closer to destroying whatever trust, intimacy and love was left between her and Rick.

Many, many women today treat their relationships that way; but there are no "relationship abuse" hotlines, no officers of the court to protect relationships from "abuse" and no treatment programs or self-help groups for "relationship abusers." Consequently, some women will go on "abusing" their relationships until they have beaten them to death. Then, as Diane did, they will turn around and blame the whole mess on their men.

They say: "He's a workaholic. He won't make a commitment. He lied to me or won't communicate or doesn't even try to understand how I feel. He's always putting me down or trying to control me. He refuses to go to counseling. He's impotent or

possessive or lacks ambition or wants a mother, not a wife."
There are a million ways for women to blame men for the
problems in their relationships. There are a million ways to hold
men accountable for their dissatisfaction and lack of fulfillment.
And there's no question that men do and say plenty of things
that are ignorant, insensitive, even downright abusive. But men,
no matter how despicable their behavior may be at times, are
not the architects of a relationship. They do not have a romantic
vision of the relationship, and so they cannot mold and shape
a relationship to fit that vision or be responsible for making a
long-term, committed relationship into a successful, productive
or fulfilling one. Only a woman can do that. Women have the
vision and the skills to manage a relationship and they are 100
percent responsible for the success of their relationships.

I know that's bad news. That news is even worse than the
news in the last two chapters. But it probably isn't as awful as
you think it is. Experience has taught me that women flagrantly
misinterpret me when I say they are 100 percent responsible
for the success of their relationships. They think I am telling
them that they have to absolve men of all responsibility for
their individual actions or do 100 percent of the work in their
relationships or devote 100 percent of their time and attention
to them. But that is NOT what I mean, and you would be doing
yourself a great disservice if you jumped to those conclusions
and dismissed what I have to say in this chapter without fully
understanding it. I want you to understand what 100 percent
of the responsibility entails and why you should assume it, which
is why I'm going to explain it by putting it in a different context—one that modern women seem to have no trouble grasp-
ing.

Labor and Management

Let's say that you pick up the telephone and a voice on the other
end of the line says, "Hi. I'm Lee Iacocca. You know, the head
of Chrysler Corporation, and I'd like to give you a job." Now,
let's say, that after you get over the shock and go in for an
interview, Mr. Iacocca says, "I want to put you in charge of the

Dodge Ram Truck division. I want you to develop a new product line, a new image and a new marketing strategy. I'll pay you $400,000 to do that. You'll have 24,000 workers to manage. You'll head up that division. You'll be in charge of it and you'll be 100 percent responsible for its success." Would you understand what he meant?

Sure you would. You would know that because of your superior talent and skill, Mr. Iacocca had chosen you to manage a very complex, very challenging, but potentially very rewarding project. You would also know that he did not expect you to pull off the project single-handedly. You would need workers to build trucks and inspect parts, conduct the advertising campaign, type correspondence, order supplies and so on. They would be responsible for those things, those *tasks,* and you would be responsible for managing those workers so that they produced. In this business context, you would not give your workers management responsibility. It's not their job. Even if they express an interest in assuming management responsibility, you cannot trust them with it. They are not committed to it. When the going gets tough, they are going to remember that they were not hired to manage, and are not getting paid to manage, and they will leave the mess for you to clean up.

If you wanted to be successful and were committed to the success of your division, you would not fall into that trap. Instead you would let your workers do their jobs and you would do yours. And if you were a good manager, your workers would *want* to produce for you. They would do what you needed them to do in order for you to be successful yourself—not because they liked you or got some sort of intrinsic pleasure from welding metal or adding figures all day and not because they were nice, altruistic people who wanted you to be happy and successful. No, they would produce for you because you would make sure they were getting rewards themselves. You would not only sign their paychecks, but also see to it that they felt accepted and appreciated and that they knew you were behind them all the way. You would reward them for doing their jobs and they would feel good about working for you. The rewards are what they work for. They will keep producing and making it possible for you to succeed so long as you make working for you a rewarding proposition.

Finally, when Lee Iacocca said that you were 100 percent responsible for the success of the Dodge Ram Truck division, you would understand that at the end of each quarter, he would check on your results and expect to see progress, profits and other signs indicating that you were guiding the Dodge Ram Truck division in a positive direction. If he saw those things, you would get the accolades (and the opportunity to keep your job for another quarter). If he didn't see those things, but instead noticed that your division was unproductive and over budget, Mr. Iacocca would call *you* (and nobody but you) on the carpet. He would ask you to explain the situation and you wouldn't blame your workers. You wouldn't say, "Gee, Mr. Iacocca, I feel rotten about the poor showing this quarter, but it couldn't be helped. The workers didn't perform." If you said that, all you would be telling Mr. Iacocca was that *you* hadn't managed your workers effectively, and you'd get fired. Lee Iacocca isn't going to let you blame the workers for the mess you're in. He's going to hold you accountable for those problems—because *you* were 100 percent responsible for the success of your division.

Well, you assume the same responsibility when you decide to get involved in a serious, long-term, committed relationship with a man. That relationship is based on *your* romantic vision. It is *your* artistic expression. You can make it succeed or you can make it fail because you shape it. You always have. Because of your superior talent and skill in the area of relationships, when it comes to intimacy, love and closeness, you have always been in charge. You are always in charge of how your relationship is going and where it is going. Men don't have a clue about such things. What's more, they aren't judged a success or failure based on the status of their relationships. You are.

You may not like that fact, but it isn't exactly news to you. If you are a single woman, you have undoubtedly noticed that no matter how far up the career ladder you have climbed or how many remarkable things you have achieved over the years, your friends and relatives still act as if they feel sorry for you. You tell them about your latest professional accomplishment, and they ask about your love life. They give you all sorts of advice on where and how to meet men. They want you to be happy and they think that you will not be happy until you are in a long-term, committed relationship with a man. It may not be fair and it may not be right; but people don't think that about men, and they don't buy it when you blame men for the demise of your relationship.

When you tell your mother, your best friend, your next door neighbor or anyone else that your marriage or most recent relationship didn't work out because your man lied, cheated, used drugs, worked too much or beat you, your confidante will sympathize with you. But that person will also wonder why you got involved with such a "jerk" in the first place, why you put up with his shenanigans for so long, why you didn't see certain problems coming and do something to prevent them. We, as a society, simply are not democratic when it comes to holding someone accountable for the success or failure of a relationship. Regardless of the circumstances, when a relationship fails, the consensus is that it was your fault. When it succeeds, you get the accolades and the ultimate reward—the relationship you always wanted. If you look at it that way, if you recognize that in a relationship, it is your success and your happiness on the line, it only makes sense to assume 100 percent of the responsibility for that relationship's success.

But Is It Worth All That Responsibility?

In my earlier analogy, Lee Iacocca was giving you $400,000 for assuming 100 percent responsibility for the success of the Dodge Ram Truck division. He probably threw in a title, an office with a view, a company car and a few other perks as well. He was making it worth your while to be in charge of the Dodge Ram Truck division and if he had only offered you $100,000, you might not have been interested in the job. You might have decided that you could make $100,000 in a job that required less of you, that $100,000 wasn't adequate remuneration for doing everything Mr. Iacocca was asking of you. In other words, you would not have accepted 100 percent of the responsibility for the success of the Dodge Ram Truck division unless it were worth it, unless you were getting a sufficient return on your investment.

Well, the same holds true when you are deciding whether or not to do what it takes to be successful and productive in a long-term, committed relationship with a man. You must ask yourself if having that relationship with that man is worth the amount of responsibility you must assume. If it is, if that relationship is important to you, then you will want it to be successful; you will want to manage the relationship in a way that leads to success, and you will assume 100 percent of the responsibility for its success. You would NOT turn any of the responsibility over to someone who didn't care about your relationship's success the same way that you do and men don't. Relationship is not their number-one priority.

In a relationship, men should never initiate actions. They should respond to your actions. They take their cues from you in the same way those 24,000 workers in the Dodge Ram Truck division would, and, like those workers, men will "do their jobs," make you happy and make it possible for you to be successful and satisfied in the relationship, if you make that a rewarding proposition for them.

WHAT WORKS WITH MEN

To solve 95 percent of your relationship problems (and cope with the rest):

Recognize that in a relationship, women are the managers and men are the workers.

Yeah, but My Relationship Isn't the Dodge Ram Truck Division

Most of the women I have counseled or encountered at Sterling Women's Weekends have no difficulty understanding that their

workers will produce and the Dodge Ram Truck division will succeed if and only if they assume 100 percent responsibility for the success of that division and manage it effectively. They are rarely convinced that the same principle applies to their relationships with men, however. "I believe that a relationship should be an equal partnership," they say. "I believe that my partner and I should have an equal say in what goes on in our relationship and that we should both be responsible for making the relationship work."

Well, that may work in an equal partnership. Sharing—splitting everything fifty-fifty right down the line—is what equal partnerships are all about. You and your partner each have an equal say in everything, a vote. You bargain. You compromise. It's a fifty-fifty relationship. You always know where you stand because you constantly keep score. You keep track of who has given what to whom; and if one partner appears to be giving or getting too much, you hold a conference so that you can bargain and compromise some more. Equal partnerships are nice, fair, easy and very fashionable. They offer career-oriented women a way to have something that resembles a relationship without committing themselves to the discipline or making the sacrifices the relationship of their romantic vision requires.

A man who is your partner acts like a woman. He talks about his feelings. He tries to understand yours. He expects the same things from the partnership that you do. He's predictable and less threatening than a man who behaves like the romantic hero he could be if he kept his masculine edge. But a man without his masculine edge is also less exciting. Equal partnerships are safe, but they tend to get boring. There's no "vroom." No pizazz. No attraction of opposites to produce the energy that keeps relationships vital and electric and alive. After a while, there isn't even enough energy to make all that negotiating, compromising and scorekeeping worth the effort. That's why equal partnerships so often die of neglect. Because they don't fulfill women and are not particularly ego-gratifying for men, both partners end up looking elsewhere for what they need.

Of course, an equal partnership really may be what you want. It may be all you can handle right now. But this book is not about equal partnerships. The things I am telling you do not necessarily apply to equal partnerships. They *do* apply to relationships that conform to the Law of Electrodynamics and express your original romantic vision of a relationship and come as close as humanly possible to being the relationship you always dreamed of having. As I said in Chapter Five, that sort of relationship results from the attraction of opposites. It requires you to be all the woman you can be and to allow your mate to be all the man he can be. A man who is allowed to do that is exciting, unpredictable, competitive and a bit dangerous. He can make you happy. He wants to please you, but he is not like a woman. He may make a terrific mate, but he's a terrible partner, and he cannot be given responsibility for the success of your relationship because he simply does not have the skill, know-how, instincts or natural tendencies that managing a relationship requires.

Men Managing Relationships Are Like Gorillas Doing Brain Surgery

Remember that men are like aliens from another planet. If an alien from another planet landed in your back yard, you wouldn't say to him, "Okay. I like you. I'll let you stay and I'll help you find your way around this planet of which you have no knowledge whatsoever, but you have to assume 50 percent of the responsibility for making the arrangement work." You wouldn't expect him to direct you to places he's never been. You wouldn't expect him to consider your feelings or the long-range effects his immediate actions could have on your ability to explore the planet together. He would never have thought about such things before, and it would not even occur to him to think about them now. That alien from another planet simply cannot handle his half of the responsibility. He doesn't know how. You'll have to remind him and correct him, argue with him and complain to him, and still he'll frustrate and disappoint you at every turn. That is precisely what happens when you expect the responsibility for the success of your relationship to be split fifty-fifty between you and your man. His 50 percent will fail. Even if you do your best with your 50 percent, his 50 percent will still fail; and, more often than not, so will your relationship.

A fifty-fifty relationship is fair, but it doesn't work. Indeed, in my opinion, the fifty-fifty syndrome is the most prevalent reason for relationships *not* working. Divorce rates have soared since women began striving for fifty-fifty marriages; and even if you manage to hold yours together, the best you'll get is 50 percent of what you want, and you'll have to work twice as hard to get it.

WHAT WORKS WITH MEN

To solve 95 percent of your relationship problems (and cope with the rest):

Never forget that any part of the relationship that you deem to be the man's responsibility will be the part of the relationship that will fail.

Men simply cannot be trusted with something as delicate, valuable, vital and in need of nurturing as a long-term, committed relationship. They don't know how to manage a relationship. They are limited in that area. Because of their number-one priority and their deeply rooted instincts and programming as hunters and warriors, they have limitations that prevent them from doing the things that come naturally to you. You can show them how things should be done, but there is only so much they are capable of learning; and putting them in charge of anything beyond their capabilities is dangerous. It's like having a gorilla on a team of brain surgeons.

Think about it. You have this highly skilled, highly trained surgical team: a neurosurgeon, an anesthesiologist, a scrub nurse . . . and a gorilla. You can teach that gorilla how to scrub, where to stand and how to distinguish a clamp from a scalpel, but if you put the scalpel in his hand, he won't know how to use it. Whatever he touches with it is going to be damaged; and if that surgical team actually allows the gorilla to operate, the portion of the brain he works on is going to die. There is absolutely no doubt about it; his part of the operation is going to fail. It doesn't matter if he is willing, if he is agreeable, you can't give him the scalpel and still expect the surgery to succeed. The same holds true in a long-term, committed relationship with a man. The percentage of responsibility for that relationship's success which you abdicate to your man is the same percentage of the relationship that will fail. Anything in the way of intimacy, closeness and so on which you expect a man to manage will die.

Even if your man says he wants to assume some responsibility for the success of your relationship, don't give it to him. It's nice that he asked. You have a superior gorilla on your team. He knows what a scalpel is. But that doesn't mean he can perform brain surgery with it—and it may not mean he actually wants the scalpel. Nine times out of ten, he is asking because he thinks that's what you want to hear. He knows you'll give him a banana—a whole bushel of bananas—for asking. If you believe him and offer him the scalpel, he'll take it (*and* the bananas) and still screw up the operation.

The gorilla can't help it. He's not equipped to perform brain surgery, and a man is not equipped to manage your relationship. Management skills do not come naturally to him and if you teach him those skills, he must give up things that do come naturally to him, including the masculine energy and masculine point of view and masculine unpredictability he brings to a relationship and which make being in a relationship with him exciting and fulfilling.

Men Are Looking for a Good Deal

Not only are men not equipped to manage relationships, they aren't motivated to manage them either. They're not committed to the success of your relationship in the same way you are. For the most part, they just want the bananas. As a rule, men get into relationships for the rewards they can get out of them.

While you are trying to get to know men and get close to them and figure out if you can trust them, men are doing a cost/benefit analysis. "What am I going to get out of this?" they want to know. "And is what I can get going to be worth what I'll have to put into the relationship?" Men want their relationships to be good investments. To have a successful, long-term, committed relationship with a man, you must be a good deal. You have to manage your relationship in a way that allows a man to get a return on his investment and ensures that your relationship gives a man more than it costs him.

Now some of you are going to read that and think that I'm saying you have to give more than you get. I'm not. If you are a good deal, if you manage your relationship effectively and make sure that being in a relationship with you is a rewarding proposition, you will always get more than you give. There is more in a relationship for you to get than there is for a man. A nickel in his currency is worth a dollar in yours. It's seed money. It's the raw material you can use to build a relationship that is 100 times more valuable to you than the dime you're going to give him for investing his nickel. So, stop keeping score. Stop thinking, "It's not fair. Why should he get double his money back? I'm not going to give him one penny more than he puts into this relationship." That's faulty reasoning. It doesn't work to your benefit. If you give your man a return on his investment, *you'll* get an even larger return on *your* investment: your man will do just about anything to please you if you're a good deal.

Show a man a good deal and he'll have no choice but to make sure the deal is provided for—but not because he is naturally generous, benevolent or philanthropic. He just knows a good deal when he sees one. That is something he wants. That is something he'll hold onto because he needs the rewards it offers him. He has to go out into the world and compete. He has no choice in the matter. Competition is his number-one priority. It is what his ego tells him he must do and he is a slave to his ego. But some of the time, maybe even most of the time, he's going to get battered around and frustrated and beaten. When that happens, the first thing he's going to think about is his woman.

"Where's my woman?" he thinks. "I need my woman." He'll come running home to you, not to share his feelings, communicate, talk about the stress he's under or work on your relationship, but rather to have his ego boosted, his battery recharged. He wants to know you are happy to see him, to hear that you've been thinking about him or to receive whatever else he finds personally rewarding and ego-gratifying. Your man will let you know what that is and he'll pay anything to get it. He'll do anything for you—take out the garbage, do the laundry, work two jobs, tolerate his in-laws—*if* you are a good deal. He'll make you happy. He wants to please you. That's his job. That's how he earns his paycheck, how he gets his ego boosted. What you need to remember is that, like any sensible worker, he's not going to do his job unless he's being paid.

Diane proved that. She married Rick—an ambitious man who was sure of himself and seemed to know exactly where he was going—because she wanted a path to follow, a direction for her life and a dream she could do her part to turn into a reality. Rick married her to give her that. He wanted to give her what she wanted. *He* wanted to do what Diane led him to believe would make her happy, and he literally did not know what hit him when she stopped being happy with what he was doing.

When Diane stopped letting Rick know that he was succeeding at his mission and started demanding different things of him and endlessly conveying her unhappiness to him, she cut off his flow of rewards. She withheld the one thing that makes being in a relationship valuable to a man—getting his ego boosted by making his woman happy. Diane changed the terms of the deal, so Rick stopped giving Diane what she wanted. Consequently, their marriage had nowhere to go but downhill. Since nothing Rick offered Diane seemed to satisfy her, Rick stopped trying to please her; and the shame of it was that things need not have turned out that way, if Diane had assumed 100 percent of the responsibility for the success of her relationship and managed it effectively instead of trying to control it and her man.

You Can Control or You Can Relate, but You Can't Do Both

Even though no one can change his desires and emotions on demand, Diane demanded just that of Rick. She wanted Rick to want to be with her, and she complained about the time and attention Rick devoted to his work because she thought that would *compel* him to give her what she wanted. She constantly conveyed her unhappiness to Rick because she thought that would *force* him to be a better husband. She nagged and sulked and withheld the rewards Rick sought from her because she thought she could *coerce* him into spending more time with her. With her unhappiness, Diane was trying to *control* her husband and dictate the direction their relationship was going. But all her ploys, all her attempts to get what she wanted from Rick when and how she wanted it, failed or backfired. She failed to have the relationship she'd always wanted because she tried to control her man and the way he related to her. If you use her methods, you too will fail.

To have a successful relationship with a man, you must manage that relationship without controlling, without intimidating, without dominating, demanding or manipulating. A manipulator gets other people to fulfill her needs with little concern for theirs. She uses threats, punishments, anger, silence, criticism and various forms of emotional blackmail to coerce people into giving her what *she* wants whenever and however she wants it— regardless of what *they* want or need or got involved with her to receive.

Whether in a relationship or a multimillion-dollar business, when you manage by controlling, your workers do what you want because you have forced their hands and not because doing it your way fulfills their needs or rewards them in any way. While that may get you what you want in the short run, since they're working for the rewards and you aren't providing them, they'll eventually lose their motivation to perform. They'll develop morale problems and workers with morale problems are unproductive. They don't produce, and as a consequence, you don't succeed.

In addition, because conflict is the inevitable outcome of having to meet someone else's needs at the expense of your own, when you try to control your man or your relationship, you produce conflict, lots of conflict, constant conflict. You and your man are constantly fighting and whether those arguments are about money, sex, how much time you spend together or who takes out the garbage, what you are really struggling over is control. Your relationship is the "innocent" victim of that struggle. As Diane almost did, you can destroy a potentially successful, long-term, committed relationship by trying to control it.

Unfortunately, like so many women today, you may be more interested in control than intimacy. Intimacy is frightening, risky. In a truly intimate relationship, you have to let your man be who *he* is and that can be a problem for you. It makes you feel vulnerable, exposed, at his mercy. He may not do what you want. He might hurt, reject, disappoint or try to control you instead. In a truly intimate relationship, *you* must be who you really are as well, and you may be afraid that your real self isn't good enough to sustain the relationship. When you're in control you don't feel so vulnerable. If you control your man, you think you'll reduce the risk of being hurt by him. There will be fewer surprises and fewer chances for that man to push you around or control you or limit you in any way. You'll feel safe. But you won't be able to foster growth, have emotional exchanges or do anything else it takes to keep a relationship alive. You simply cannot relate when you control. In fact, to manage a relationship in a way that leads to success and satisfaction, you must constantly, continually let go of control.

Although the mere thought of doing that may scare the living daylights out of you, it can be done. In the remainder of this book I'll show you how to do it and how to develop a relationship management style that will bring both you and your man the maximum return on your investments.

EIGHT

The MBA Degree in Relationship Management: A Successful Relationship Requires Management Skills

Rita

A petite redhead stood in front of me, her face flushed, her eyes flashing fire. Her name was Rita and she was a thirty-three-year-old interior decorator married for three years to Fred, a thirty-one-year-old accountant. "Fred refuses to deal with anything seriously—including me," she complained. "Sometimes he's so condescending I could scream. If I'm angry, it's 'Now, calm down, honey, and try to think rationally.' If I'm sad, it's 'Oh poor baby. Let me give you a hug and you'll feel better.' And if I'm worried about something, I get some ridiculous platitude like 'Don't borrow trouble,' or 'Every cloud has a silver lining.' Even when I'm reacting to something serious, something major, he treats me like a child with a boo-boo on her knee.

"He 'yesses' me to death," Rita continued. "To my face, Fred will agree to anything. He'll apologize before I even finish telling him what's bothering me. He'll promise to do anything I ask him to do, but he doesn't mean a word he says. He's just trying to shut me up and when I tell him I know that's what

108

he's doing, he *does the same thing!* He apologizes and swears he was only trying to make me feel better. But I don't want him to make me feel better. I want him to listen to me and deal with me like a grown-up, not bribe me with little gifts or try to distract me by making goofy faces or turning the things I say into jokes or seducing me. I want him to take me seriously, damn it."

In an effort to get what she wanted from Fred, Rita had given him specific instructions on how to please her. "I've explained things to him until I'm blue in the face," she said. "I've told him at least a thousand times to hear me out and to let me know what he really thinks and feels about what I'm saying. I've literally begged him not to brush things under the carpet or bury his head in the sand." But Fred refused to do as he was told. "He just won't face anything head on," Rita groaned. "If I won't drop a subject, he'll tune me out. He'll walk out right in the middle of an argument, leave for work, go for a drive, hang up on me if we're talking on the phone. Then he'll come home with some stupid peace offering or be all lovey-dovey or pull some silly stunt like wearing a football helmet, holding a garbage can lid like a shield and asking if the coast is clear. That just infuriates me." And Rita would lose her temper or turn cold as ice, giving Fred the silent treatment to let him know that his behavior didn't "wash" with her, that she wasn't going to let him off the hook so easily. Still, Fred's behavior didn't change.

"I'm starting to think that Fred acts the way he does just to get my goat," Rita said, "just to make me lose it so he can feel superior because he's still calm, cool and collected." In the heat of battle, she had accused Fred of doing that. She had threatened to find someone else to meet her needs if he wouldn't. But even that ultimatum had not compelled Fred to relate to Rita exactly as she thought he should. "I'm just about out of patience," Rita said with a sigh. "I'm tired of hitting the same brick wall."

Then, maybe she should stop running right at it, I suggested. Since Fred wouldn't give her the response she wanted when she wanted it, maybe she should stop expecting and demanding that response.

"But I don't think being taken seriously by someone you're sharing your life with is too much to ask," Rita protested. "Two people who love each other are supposed to deal with things together and be open with each other and work through their problems, not run away from them."

Yes, I replied, I understood that those were *her* terms for being in an intimate relationship and *her* assumptions about the way people were supposed to behave in a long-term, committed relationship. It was obvious from the tale she'd just told me that she expected Fred to relate to her on those terms. Indeed, she seemed bound and determined to make him play by her rules no matter what it cost her—and even though the very first thing she had told me about Fred was that he didn't deal with *anything* seriously.

Fred wanted a relationship that was calm, tranquil and pre-dictable. He expected the woman in his life to let him cheer her up and make her feel better without having to delve too far below the surface, without shaking things up or putting him in a position where he had to think about things he preferred to ignore. Those were Fred's terms for being in a long-term, committed relationship, his expectations for *any* woman with whom he would have such a relationship—and Rita knew that before she married him. She admitted that she fell in love with Fred because he made her laugh. His lighthearted, easygoing nature seemed to be a perfect balance for her more serious, driven and somewhat pessimistic perspective on life. She ac-knowledged that nothing Fred had done before they were mar-ried had led her to believe that he would take her concerns seriously or sit still while she expressed her feelings after they were married. He simply did not operate that way—not just because he was a man, but also because he had grown up in a home with an abusive, alcoholic father who could fly into a rage or go on a drinking binge at the slightest provocation.

Taking his cues from his mother and older siblings, Fred had learned to do whatever it took not to provoke his father. He learned how to distract his dad and calm him down whenever he seemed about to blow his stack. "Yessing" people, placating them, brushing problems under the carpet and lightening things up whenever he noticed tension in the air were survival skills Fred had used throughout his life and he wasn't about to abandon those behaviors. His desire to avoid facing unpleasant realities, his aversion to strong expressions of emotion, his need to take the heat off himself as quickly as possible (even if he had to lie or leave the scene to do that) were deeply ingrained attitudes that reflected his upbringing and his personality. They were part of his basic nature, his overall makeup, and as such, it was futile to fool around with them. But Rita did.

Once Rita was firmly situated in the relationship, she began expecting and demanding things from Fred that she knew he couldn't or wouldn't give her, getting angry at him for being who he was and insisting that he be in their relationship on *her* terms. As you could see, that didn't work. It never does.

Although Rita wanted to blame her unhappiness on her husband and his seemingly stubborn refusal to take her seriously, it was actually her expectation and insistence that Fred give her what she wanted when and how she wanted it regardless of his natural inclinations and preferences that was creating conflict in her relationship. By trying to have her relationship on her terms even though Fred couldn't live up to them without changing his basic nature, Rita was virtually guaranteeing that the relationship would be anything but rewarding for Fred and anything but successful or satisfying for her. Relationships are alien territory for men, and no competitive, ego-driven man, no natural-born hunter and warrior will enter or stay in or work to please his woman in alien territory on anything but *his* terms.

Relationships Are Alien Territory for Men

Relationships are your natural habitat. They are the place where your natural instincts and tendencies, your inherent skills and talents give you a decided advantage over men; and men, programmed to compete and fight and preferably win, are not keen on being in a one-down position. They aren't going to give you an additional advantage by agreeing to do things your way. Having a relationship on your terms—talking about feelings, being sensitive to each other's needs, analyzing and discussing the state of your relationship, considering the relationship before taking any action that might affect it and doing anything else that does not come easily or naturally to a particular man— is like going into battle with bows and arrows when his opponents have machine guns.

On your turf on your terms, a man is going to suffer some sort of defeat and he knows it. If he plays by your rules, acquiesces to your demands, tries to change his basic nature to meet your expectations, he will be so badly outmatched that he might as well surrender before the battle begins—and he isn't going to do that. His ego won't let him. Instead, he will simply stay out of *your* territory if the only way he can enter it is on *your* terms. Or a man will enter a relationship on your terms to take whatever he can get—sex, money, offspring, a pretty woman to show off to his friends—and then leave. Or he will remain in the relationship but withdraw from you emotionally, become uncooperative, testy and argumentative or seem hell-bent on doing things he knows are irritating or offensive to you.

Don't be lulled into a false sense of security if, early in your relationship or when your man wants something from you, everything seems to be happening on your terms, proceeding according to your plan and living up to most, maybe even all of your expectations. A man will play by your rules occasionally. He is capable of doing things your way, but the only reason he will is to prove that he can. Once he has what he came for or gets tired of showing you what a nice, cooperative, tame version of himself he can be, he's out the door—literally ending the relationship or engaging you in a psychological battle over the terms for your relationship. You'll get used to the sensitive, attentive, thoroughly agreeable, unbelievably cooperative man in your life, and then "bam!" everything will fall apart. You won't know what hit you. You won't understand what happened. And you'll do everything you can think of to get your man back on track and to make him relate to you on your terms again. But you won't succeed. A man just won't allow you to cage his spirit indefinitely. He won't stay in alien territory on your terms for any length of time.

In addition, for many men relationships are not only seen as foreign and unfamiliar territory, but as hostile, enemy territory as well. Consequently, from the moment a man steps onto your turf, he is apt to be on the defensive, expecting you to want things from him that he is unwilling or unable to give you, anticipating threats and challenges to his ego and waiting for you to start pushing him around or trying to change and control him. Poised and prepared to defend himself, when you actually

he is failing to please you. Instead of feeling like
feels like a failure; and if the source of your
something your man can't do anything about,
t is contrary to his basic nature, he feels impotent
Vhy should he try to please someone who makes
way?

try to control a man and compel him to be in a
on your terms, you are putting him in a position
ween doing what you want and being who he is,
his self-respect and gratifying his ego. If he "sells
s things your way even though there is no reward
, his ego is deflated. His spirit is broken. He loses
e energy that attracted you to him in the first place.
s his ego and his self-respect, in order to defend
et it boosted elsewhere, he will pull away from you,
ou, resist you every step of the way and ultimately
from being successful or satisfied in your relation-
way, you lose.

u withhold the rewards your man hopes to obtain
elationship, his interest in you and efforts to please
minish. Or he'll continue trying to please you at the
his masculine identity, undermining the Law of
amics—the attraction of opposites—that keeps a re-
vital, exciting and alive. You'll be in control, but you'll
have a man who wants to make you happy and you
ve a successful, satisfying relationship with your man.
nt that sort of relationship, if you are ready for and
out and interested in being in a fulfilling, long-lasting
elationship with a man, then you must develop a new
ent style.

-*term vision oriented*. Use what you know about men in
nd your man in particular to manage your relation-
urture it and care for it in a way that will enable you
ccessful, productive and satisfied over the long haul.
sometimes mean *not* getting exactly what you want at
ise moment you want it. As the relationship manager,
t be willing to sacrifice short-term rewards for the sake
term results.

sistible. Stop giving your man reasons to resist you. Stop
him in a position to compete with you. If, like Rita, you

behave in those ways, your man will immediately pounce on or withdraw from you. He may even interpret relatively innocent gestures on your part as cause to resist or rebuff or refuse to accommodate you. That is why it is so crucial for you to manage your relationship in a way that does not prompt your man to deepen his defenses or give him reasons to use his considerable arsenal of hunter and warrior weaponry against you.

As you've undoubtedly realized by now, the foregoing adds up to more bad news. It means that in a serious, long-term, committed relationship with a man you must not only be 100 percent responsible for the success of that relationship—you must also *have your relationship on your man's terms*.

Most of the women I've advised over the years can't even imagine doing that. "How am I supposed to manage the relationship, be in charge of where it's going, be 100 percent responsible for it AND have that relationship on a man's terms?" they ask incredulously. "If the relationship is on his terms, then he's making the rules," they inform me indignantly. "He's dictating what I can and can't do and determining *how* I manage the relationship." They're appalled by the idea of being in a relationship on a man's terms because they think it means being ordered around and controlled by a man, acquiescing to all of his demands (no matter how unreasonable they may be) and having to sacrifice themselves and their needs in order to fulfill his. But it isn't as bad as all that.

An Effective Manager Works with the Resources She Has

Going back to the interview with Lee Iacocca I used as an example in Chapter Seven, let's say things have progressed to the point where Mr. Iacocca is sure that he wants you to run the Dodge Ram Truck division and you're almost sure you want the job. Then he says, "Oh by the way, if you take this position, you'll have to work within this budget and follow this timetable. You'll have to make do with whatever equipment is already on the assembly lines and, of course, you'll be expected to follow all of the policies and procedures that were established before you got here." Those are his terms, his expectations for *anyone* he would hire to run the Dodge Ram Truck division, and he isn't going to hire someone who won't accept his terms. He isn't going to change his terms to suit you either. He'll simply find someone else for the job: someone who will do things his way.

In a business setting, that wouldn't confuse or surprise or offend you. You wouldn't expect Lee Iacocca to turn over something as mammoth and important as the Dodge Ram Truck division to you and allow you to spend as much money as you want, to follow any timetable you feel like following or do whatever you wanted regardless of what he wanted. And the fact that he had certain expectations of you and certain terms and conditions for you to fulfill would not prevent you from assuming 100 percent of the responsibility for the success of the Dodge Ram Truck division. You would simply manage the division within the parameters he had established and with the resources he said were available to you.

Well, if you are smart and if you want to be successful and productive in a long-term, committed relationship with a man, then what you would do for Lee Iacocca, you also will do for your relationship. Know your man and his terms—what he expects and what you can reasonably expect from him—*before* you get seriously involved with him. A man's terms define who he is. Then, once you are involved with him, accept those "givens" and shape your relationship around them. When it comes to the *terms* for your relationship—the raw material you have to work with, the parameters for what you can and can't do or reasonably expect from your man and your relationship—let him be the boss. But you be in charge.

Be realistic. Work with what you have instead of pining over the things you lack or trying to change your man into someone he is not. Stop:

- wanting things your man can't give you;
- giving your man instructions on how to please you;
- constantly criticizing or otherwise conveying your dissatisfaction about the things he does for you;
- unfavorably comparing him to other men;
- letting him know that something is wrong by sulking or mak-

ing cryptic commen[...] he asks;
- hammering away at [...]
- threatening him with [...] an affair, etc.) for no [...] want.

No matter how much y[...] to manage your relation[...] ways, that man will not fee[...] being *unconditionally* accep[...] hoops to jump through i[...] acceptance. He feels loved [...] if and only if you allow him [...] he has to offer you.

Clashing Agendas

A man enters a serious, long-[...] a simple, straightforward ag[...] happy. He wants to perform i[...] wants to be appreciated for hi[...] has pleased you, and being [...] doing that, gratifies his ego. Wl[...] happy with what he has offere[...] about it), it feeds the fantasies [...] makes him feel special, unique, [...] any challenge he faces. He feels [...] is the reward he hopes to obtai[...] relationship.

But when *your* agenda is to get [...] it regardless of your man's terms [...] make it impossible for him to ge[...] cepting your man as he is or accep[...] what he has to offer, you try to cha[...] use his agenda against him as did l[...] introduced in the last chapter. You [...] tunity to tell your man how unhapp[...]

he knows that [...]
a winner, he [...]
discontent is [...]
something tha[...]
and useless. [...]
him feel that [...]

When you [...]
relationship [...]
to choose be[...]
maintaining [...]
out" and do[...]
in it for him[...]
the masculi[...]
If he choos[...]
his ego or g[...]
fight with y[...]
prevent you[...]
ship. Eithe[...]

When yo[...]
from the r[...]
you will di[...]
expense o[...]
Electrody[...]
lationship [...]
no longer [...]
will not ha[...]
If you wa[...]
serious ab[...]
intimate [...]
managen[...]

Be long[...]
general [...]
ship, to [...]
to be su[...]
That wil[...]
the prec[...]
you mus[...]
of long-[...]

Be irr[...]
putting[...]

are tired of hitting the same brick wall, stop running at it. Stop expecting or demanding from your man things that he is at best unwilling and perhaps unable to give you. And if you are sick of fighting with your man, give him what he wants. There is no hope for compromise until a man has what he wants, until he no longer senses a threat to his ego. So long as you are challenging his ego by arguing with him or trying to change him or withholding rewards from him, he will feel that by compromising in the relationship he is compromising himself. However, if you give him what he wants—if you stroke his ego, make sure he knows you love and accept him—most of the time he'll be very open and amenable to compromise. He'll know he can do that without losing his dignity, and you'll win the ultimate prize—a satisfying, successful, lasting, intimate relationship with your man.

Guard against the "victim" mentality that prompts you to think, "He did this or that to me, so I had no choice but to respond the way I did." Remember, in a long-term, committed relationship, a man doesn't initiate the action. He responds to the actions you initiate. And he responds in one of only two ways: to protect himself or his ego or to get a reward for himself or his ego. If he is protecting himself, he will do something that hurts you or pushes you away or prevents you from getting what you are after. If he is looking for a reward, he will do something for you, something that pleases you. You will be the recipient of a positive action. If unprovoked, a man will always respond in a way that *rewards* his ego—and that is how you can tell if you are managing your relationship effectively. If he is responding positively, you are on track. If he is not, it's time to take a look at the way you are handling your management responsibility.

Yeah, but . . .

To many women, the things I've recommended thus far sound like a prescription for martyrdom. They think I'm instructing them to cater to a man's every whim, no matter what it is and even if that means giving up their identity, their autonomy and the fulfillment of their own needs. Well, some men do expect that. And the bad news is that if your man does and you knew he expected that when you decided to have a long-term, committed relationship with him and you want to stay with him anyway, then you are stuck with those terms. You aren't going to change them. You'll have to accept them, work with what you've got and find ways to be autonomous and fulfill your needs when your man isn't around demanding your attention.

However, if you are *not* yet in a committed relationship with a man who seems to expect you to wait on him hand and foot and you don't want to do that, turn tail and run. You don't have to accept *any* terms *any* man offers you no matter what they are. Be selective. Figure out what a man's terms and expectations are before you get seriously involved with him and *only get seriously involved with a man whose terms and expectations are compatible with yours and fit your vision of a relationship.*

Pay More Attention to What Your Man Does and Less to What He Says

When Rita realized she wasn't going to change Fred on her own, she hammered away at him until he agreed to go to a marriage counselor with her. "But that was an exercise in futility," she reported. "At the first session, he painted this ridiculously rosy picture of his childhood and our marriage. At the second, he sat there grinning and agreeing with whatever the therapist or I said. He supposedly forgot the third appointment, couldn't make the fourth because of some supposed crisis at work and said his car broke down on the way to the fifth session. Finally, I confronted him and he admitted he had no intention of going back." Again Rita "lost it." She couldn't understand why Fred had "played games" with her. "Why didn't he just come right out and tell me he didn't want to continue therapy?" she wanted to know.

But Fred *had* told her that—through his actions. He didn't say he thought counseling was a waste of time or that he did not want to be in therapy. However, from the moment he walked into the therapist's office straight through to the moare tired of hitting the same brick wall, stop running at it. Stop expecting or demanding from your man things that he is at best unwilling and perhaps unable to give you. And if you are sick of fighting with your man, give him what he wants. There is no hope for compromise until a man has what he wants, until he no longer senses a threat to his ego. So long as you are challenging his ego by arguing with him or trying to change him or withholding rewards from him, he will feel that by compromising in the relationship he is compromising himself. However, if you give him what he wants—if you stroke his ego, make sure he knows you love and accept him—most of the time he'll be very open and amenable to compromise. He'll know he can do that without losing his dignity, and you'll win the ultimate prize—a satisfying, successful, lasting, intimate relationship with your man.

Guard against the "victim" mentality that prompts you to think, "He did this or that to me, so I had no choice but to respond the way I did." Remember, in a long-term, committed relationship, a man doesn't initiate the action. He responds to the actions you initiate. And he responds in one of only two ways: to protect himself or his ego or to get a reward for himself or his ego. If he is protecting himself, he will do something that hurts you or pushes you away or prevents you from getting what you are after. If he is looking for a reward, he will do something for you, something that pleases you. You will be the recipient of a positive action. If unprovoked, a man will always respond in a way that *rewards* his ego—and that is how you can tell if you are managing your relationship effectively. If he is responding positively, you are on track. If he is not, it's time to take a look at the way you are handling your management responsibility.

Yeah, but . . .

To many women, the things I've recommended thus far sound like a prescription for martyrdom. They think I'm instructing them to cater to a man's every whim, no matter what it is and even if that means giving up their identity, their autonomy and the fulfillment of their own needs. Well, some men do expect that. And the bad news is that if your man does and you knew he expected that when you decided to have a long-term, committed relationship with him and you want to stay with him anyway, then you are stuck with those terms. You aren't going to change them. You'll have to accept them, work with what you've got and find ways to be autonomous and fulfill your needs when your man isn't around demanding your attention.

However, if you are *not* yet in a committed relationship with a man who seems to expect you to wait on him hand and foot and you don't want to do that, turn tail and run. You don't have to accept *any* terms *any* man offers you no matter what they are. Be selective. Figure out what a man's terms and expectations are before you get seriously involved with him and *only get seriously involved with a man whose terms and expectations are compatible with yours and fit your vision of a relationship.*

Pay More Attention to What Your Man Does and Less to What He Says

When Rita realized she wasn't going to change Fred on her own, she hammered away at him until he agreed to go to a marriage counselor with her. "But that was an exercise in futility," she reported. "At the first session, he painted this ridiculously rosy picture of his childhood and our marriage. At the second, he sat there grinning and agreeing with whatever the therapist or I said. He supposedly forgot the third appointment, couldn't make the fourth because of some supposed crisis at work and said his car broke down on the way to the fifth session. Finally, I confronted him and he admitted he had no intention of going back." Again Rita "lost it." She couldn't understand why Fred had "played games" with her. "Why didn't he just come right out and tell me he didn't want to continue therapy?" she wanted to know.

But Fred *had* told her that—through his actions. He didn't say he thought counseling was a waste of time or that he did not want to be in therapy. However, from the moment he walked into the therapist's office straight through to the mo-

behave in those ways, your man will immediately pounce on or withdraw from you. He may even interpret relatively innocent gestures on your part as cause to resist or rebuff or refuse to accommodate you. That is why it is so crucial for you to manage your relationship in a way that does not prompt your man to deepen his defenses or give him reasons to use his considerable arsenal of hunter and warrior weaponry against you.

As you've undoubtedly realized by now, the foregoing adds up to more bad news. It means that in a serious, long-term, committed relationship with a man you must not only be 100 percent responsible for the success of that relationship—you must also *have your relationship on your man's terms.*

Most of the women I've advised over the years can't even imagine doing that. "How am I supposed to manage the relationship, be in charge of where it's going, be 100 percent responsible for it AND have that relationship on a man's terms?" they ask incredulously. "If the relationship is on his terms, then he's making the rules," they inform me indignantly. "He's dictating what I can and can't do and determining *how* I manage the relationship." They're appalled by the idea of being in a relationship on a man's terms because they think it means being ordered around and controlled by a man, acquiescing to all of his demands (no matter how unreasonable they may be) and having to sacrifice themselves and their needs in order to fulfill his. But it isn't as bad as all that.

An Effective Manager Works with the Resources She Has

Going back to the interview with Lee Iacocca I used as an example in Chapter Seven, let's say things have progressed to the point where Mr. Iacocca is sure that he wants you to run the Dodge Ram Truck division and you're almost sure you want the job. Then he says, "Oh by the way, if you take this position, you'll have to work within this budget and follow this timetable. You'll have to make do with whatever equipment is already on the assembly lines and, of course, you'll be expected to follow all of the policies and procedures that were established before you got here." Those are his terms, his expectations for *anyone* he would hire to run the Dodge Ram Truck division, and he isn't going to hire someone who won't accept his terms. He isn't going to change his terms to suit you either. He'll simply find someone else for the job: someone who will do things his way.

In a business setting, that wouldn't confuse or surprise or offend you. You wouldn't expect Lee Iacocca to turn over something as mammoth and important as the Dodge Ram Truck division to you and allow you to spend as much money as you want, to follow any timetable you feel like following or do whatever you wanted regardless of what he wanted. And the fact that he had certain expectations of you and certain terms and conditions for you to fulfill would not prevent you from assuming 100 percent of the responsibility for the success of the Dodge Ram Truck division. You would simply manage the division within the parameters he had established and with the resources he said were available to you.

Well, if you are smart and if you want to be successful and productive in a long-term, committed relationship with a man, then what you would do for Lee Iacocca, you also will do for your relationship. Know your man and his terms—what he expects and what you can reasonably expect from him—*before* you get seriously involved with him. A man's terms define who he is. Then, once you are involved with him, accept those "givens" and shape your relationship around them. When it comes to the *terms* for your relationship—the raw material you have to work with, the parameters for what you can and can't do or reasonably expect from your man and your relationship—let him be the boss. But you be in charge.

Be realistic. Work with what you have instead of pining over the things you lack or trying to change your man into someone he is not. Stop:

- wanting things your man can't give you;
- giving your man instructions on how to please you;
- constantly criticizing or otherwise conveying your dissatisfaction about the things he does for you;
- unfavorably comparing him to other men;
- letting him know that something is wrong by sulking or mak-

ing cryptic comments, but denying that you are upset when
he asks;

- hammering away at him until he promises to change;
- threatening him with dire consequences (leaving him, having
an affair, etc.) for not shaping up and giving you what you
want.

No matter how much you love a man, if, in a misguided effort
to manage your relationship, you treat him in the foregoing
ways, that man will not feel loved. For a man, being loved means
being *unconditionally* accepted—with no strings attached and no
hoops to jump through in order to maintain your love and
acceptance. He feels loved and can find his way clear to love *you*
if and only if you allow him to be who he is and appreciate what
he has to offer you.

Clashing Agendas

A man enters a serious, long-term, committed relationship with
a simple, straightforward agenda. He expects to make you
happy. He wants to perform in a way that pleases you. And he
wants to be appreciated for his performance. Knowing that he
has pleased you, and being recognized and appreciated for
doing that, gratifies his ego. When he hears or sees that you are
happy with what he has offered you (or at least not unhappy
about it), it feeds the fantasies his ego generates about him. It
makes him feel special, unique, heroic and prepared to take on
any challenge he faces. He feels like a winner and that feeling
is the reward he hopes to obtain when he enters an intimate
relationship.

But when *your* agenda is to get what you want when you want
it regardless of your man's terms and natural inclinations, you
make it impossible for him to get his rewards. Instead of accepting your man as he is or accepting and being pleased with
what he has to offer, you try to change him as Rita did. Or you
use his agenda against him as did Diane, the newspaper editor
introduced in the last chapter. You take every available opportunity to tell your man how unhappy you are and to make sure

he knows that he is failing to please you. Instead of feeling like a winner, he feels like a failure; and if the source of your discontent is something your man can't do anything about, something that is contrary to his basic nature, he feels impotent and useless. Why should he try to please someone who makes him feel that way?

When you try to control a man and compel him to be in a relationship on your terms, you are putting him in a position to choose between doing what you want and being who he is, maintaining his self-respect and gratifying his ego. If he "sells out" and does things your way even though there is no reward in it for him, his ego is deflated. His spirit is broken. He loses the masculine energy that attracted you to him in the first place. If he chooses his ego and his self-respect, in order to defend his ego or get it boosted elsewhere, he will pull away from you, fight with you, resist you every step of the way and ultimately prevent you from being successful or satisfied in your relationship. Either way, you lose.

When you withhold the rewards your man hopes to obtain from the relationship, his interest in you and efforts to please you will diminish. Or he'll continue trying to please you at the expense of his masculine identity, undermining the Law of Electrodynamics—the attraction of opposites—that keeps a relationship vital, exciting and alive. You'll be in control, but you'll no longer have a man who wants to make you happy and you will not have a successful, satisfying relationship with your man. If you want that sort of relationship, if you are ready for and serious about and interested in being in a fulfilling, long-lasting intimate relationship with a man, then you must develop a new management style.

Be long-term vision oriented. Use what you know about men in general and your man in particular to manage your relationship, to nurture it and care for it in a way that will enable you to be successful, productive and satisfied over the long haul. That will sometimes mean *not* getting exactly what you want at the precise moment you want it. As the relationship manager, you must be willing to sacrifice short-term rewards for the sake of long-term results.

Be irresistible. Stop giving your man reasons to resist you. Stop putting him in a position to compete with you. If, like Rita, you

ment Rita confronted him, Fred's behavior left little doubt about where he stood.

When it comes to your relationship, unless you are paying cold hard cash for a man to tell you about that relationship or your man says, "Leave me alone," *you can't always believe what a man says. But you must never disbelieve his actions.* Women mismanage their relationships and women get hurt by doing the exact opposite.

In a relationship, men will *say* anything to win, get what they want or defend their egos. Fred proved that. He would agree to, apologize for and promise to do *anything* just to get Rita off his case. Sometimes he meant what he said. Most of the time, he didn't. He wanted to ward off her attack, keep the peace or avoid the latest unpleasant reality she had brought to his attention; and if he had to lie to get what he wanted, he did. He had no qualms about fabricating excuses for missing therapy sessions. They served his purpose at the time. He didn't consider himself a liar for telling those lies. He was just using the quickest, easiest, most effective method for getting himself out of a bind. That's what men do. That's how men think. In alien territory—on your turf, communicating about your relationship on your terms (in words)—there is always a fifty-fifty chance that whatever a man is saying to you is baloney. You can't always trust what a man says in your language. So don't rely on it to manage your relationship.

Men do communicate honestly through their actions, however. Their behavior provides you with vital information. So, never disbelieve their actions. Don't ignore the nonverbal signals your man sends you. Pay attention and take your cues from what your man does. Men don't lie in man language.

If you are paying a man to tell you about your relationship (the way you paid me by purchasing this book or might pay a male therapist), then you should believe what he says. And if you don't, stop paying him. You should also believe your man if he says, "Leave me alone. Get out of my face. Stop bugging me." When men say that, they are telling the truth. They are telling you that you have already missed their nonverbal cues and pushed them to their limit. You've backed them into a corner and they're prepared to decimate you on the way out. Believe them.

Under any circumstances other than these two exceptions, you can safely assume that a man's words are *not* a true or accurate reflection of his actual thoughts and feelings about you and your relationship. You don't have to believe them. In fact, if you have not observed behaviors to back them up or if you have observed actions that contradict them, you shouldn't believe them, *at least not when it comes to your relationship.*

I've stressed that phrase with good reason. I don't want you to think I'm telling you that you can't believe a word any man says about anything. I don't want you to stop listening to men altogether or stop paying attention to your man when he is conversing with you. I just want you to save yourself an enormous amount of frustration and heartache by remembering that men don't necessarily convey their true thoughts and feelings about a relationship or the person with whom they are having that relationship the same way you do. When the issue at hand involves intimacy, closeness, emotional experiences or any other facet of a relationship, they tell you more by continuing to come around or physically avoiding you, making love to you or being unable to, bringing you flowers, taking out the garbage, breaking into a slapstick comedy routine when you are discussing an emotionally charged topic or slamming doors and stamping their feet than they will reveal to you in words. In a relationship, they say what is most convenient, whatever is most likely to bring them a reward, to gratify their egos or protect them. And if you keep that in mind, you can stop taking the things men say so personally. You don't have to take anything a man says personally unless it makes you feel good to do that. If it doesn't, let their words roll off your back.

Every day, dozens of times every day, your man will say something that will hurt you if you believe it. If you bought into all the potentially hurtful things men say without meaning a word of it, you wouldn't have time to do anything but lick your wounds. You would be too wounded to manage your relationship effectively. Let it go. Stop being offended by the things men say; stop using their words as an excuse to distance yourself from them or try to control them. Figure out why you are reacting that way so that your reaction does not interfere with your ability to manage the relationship. Then let the insensitive remark or offensive comment go. Don't believe it. Where a long-term, intimate relationship is concerned, believe what you see, what you sense, what the inner voice which speaks to you from your feminine self tells you is happening in your relationship—and not what a man says.

Let Your Man Do What He Does Best

Fred quite literally wanted to make Rita happy. He was good at making her laugh, at getting her to lighten up when she was taking things too seriously, at providing creature comforts from hugs to jelly doughnuts. He couldn't tolerate emotionally charged discussions, but he would fix things that needed fixing. He gladly would have repaired Rita's car, balanced her checkbook or run errands for her so that there would be less pressure on her. He couldn't sit still while Rita talked seriously about her concerns, but he was more than willing to massage her shoulders, cook her a gourmet meal or perform some hilarious slapstick routine to reduce the tension she was feeling. There were dozens and dozens of things that Fred was capable of doing to please Rita. But Rita made it impossible for Fred to do that. She demanded things he could not give her and refused to reward him and even punished him for giving her what he could.

To solve 95 percent of your relationship problems (and cope with the rest), do exactly the opposite of what Rita did. Look to supportive, trustworthy women, to a therapist or within yourself for the things that your man is constitutionally incapable of giving you and let your man do what he does best. Allow yourself to appreciate what he has to offer you. Reward him with your love, affection, respect and loyalty. And *don't* try to make him do things he never displayed any ability or interest in doing.

In a business setting, an effective manager hires workers who are qualified for and who have the skills to do the job for which they are hired. Then, having determined what they do well, she lets them do that. She supplies the rewards they expect to receive for doing their jobs; and, with a minimum of interference or unsolicited advice, she gives them plenty of opportunities to do what they do well—because that is rewarding for her workers too. When she runs her business that way, the manager's workers not only produce (and make it possible for her to succeed), but they also are naturally motivated to develop new skills and to do more for her because they know she will reward them for their efforts. Well, the same principle applies to managing a long-term, committed relationship with a man.

Start out with the right resources by selecting a mate who is naturally inclined and equipped to give you what you know you must have to feel successful and satisfied in an intimate relationship. Then let him do what he can do and perform the *tasks* he has shown you he does well. Let him be in charge of those tasks. You be in charge of making sure he feels gratified and rewarded when he performs them.

Men love tasks. Tasks are tangible, concrete, simple. There is ego-gratification in completing a task. They can say to their egos (and anyone in earshot), "Look at me. I did this. I'm great because I got this task done." That's why men tinker. That's why they do the same things over and over again. Whether it's taking out the garbage or getting theater tickets, making love to you or making you laugh, if you respond favorably to a task your man performs for you, he will continue to do that task. He will do it forever—if it's rewarding. And if you make being in a relationship with you rewarding in general, if you spend no more than forty-five minutes a day giving your man what *he* wants and showing him that you love, accept and appreciate him, he'll spend much more time than that looking for new, creative, exciting ways to please you.

How many times since you began reading this chapter have you thought, "But that's not fair! I shouldn't have to do all the bending, adjusting and accepting"? A dozen times? Two dozen? Or are you beginning to see how being 100 percent responsible for the success of your relationship, having the relationship on a man's terms and using the management techniques I've described *could* work? It is actually easier on you than trying to make a man give you something that it is not in his basic nature to give you. When you try to make him make you happy on *your* terms regardless of his personality and preferences, you end up frustrated, disappointed and exhausted. On the other hand, when you allow a man to be who he is and work with what he has to offer, you know what to expect, you get what you expect and you are happy with what that man gives you.

Although that premise probably makes sense to you intellectually, I'll bet that the prospect of actually putting my suggestions into practice prompts an insistent voice within you to shout, "I WON'T, I WON'T, I WON'T!!!" As I'll explain in the next chapter, that's your ego talking, and it will destroy your relationship if you let it. To successfully manage a relationship, you must get your ego out of your way—and get your man's ego on your side.

NINE

More Relationship Management: Don't Let Your Ego Destroy Your Relationship

Helen

Helen, a forty-year-old art director, and Roger, a forty-two-year-old magazine managing editor, had been living together for less than eight months when Helen started having "serious doubts" about their relationship. "I'd already been through a rotten marriage to a stubborn, controlling man," she noted. "And I didn't want to make the same mistake again." But she began to suspect she had after "a simple scheduling conflict turned into a full-scale war."

Helen's best friend was getting married, and Helen had assumed that Roger would attend the wedding with her. She was "stunned" when she found out that he planned to "go on some stupid hunting trip with his buddies instead," and, by her own admission, "went nuts" when she realized Roger had no intention of changing his plans.

"He could go hunting anytime," she pointed out with what I assumed was the same outrage she'd felt at the time. "A wedding is a once-in-a-lifetime event." Roger disagreed. For the past ten years he had gone away with the same friends on the first weekend of deer-hunting season and he wasn't about to break that tradition. "We fought about it off and on for weeks," Helen reported. "But he wouldn't bend an inch. He wouldn't compromise"—not even when Helen told him that if he wouldn't come home a half day early to attend the wedding with her, he shouldn't bother coming home at all. In fact, after she laid that ultimatum on him, Roger hardly spoke to Helen and left for his hunting trip without saying goodbye or taping a "cute little cartoon" on the bathroom mirror as he usually did when he was going to be away for a few days. Helen was "crushed" by this omission. "Things were so rotten between us when he left that I wasn't sure there would even be a relation- ship when he got back," she said, and she spent most of the weekend (and nearly every moment of her friend's wedding) worrying about that and reviewing her entire history with Roger.

"He used to be so reasonable," Helen said—referring to the time prior to their romantic involvement when she and Roger had worked for the same publication. "We made a great team. We could talk about anything, work out any differences we had; you know, give a little to get a little and do what was best for the project we were working on." That was what Helen remembered when, a year after Roger changed jobs and soon after her divorce was final, she ran into him at a charity ball and they began dating. Although she had noticed Roger's "stubborn streak" early on and had countless "knock down, drag out" fights with him both before and after they moved in together, she felt "shocked and furious" each and every time Roger put his foot down and flatly refused to see things from her point of view or negotiate a "fair settlement" to some disagreement. Thus far, they had always managed to patch things up, Helen explained, but she didn't know how much longer she could "hang in there" with Roger if he kept trying to "call all the shots and always have the last word" just as her ex-husband had. She wanted the old "give a little to get a little" Roger back so they could be "a great team" once again.

"How can I get Roger to treat me the way he did when we were working together?" Helen wanted to know. "There must be something I can do to make him respect my opinion, admit

when he's wrong and just work things out fairly and equally the
way he used to do before we were lovers."

But they *were* lovers, I reminded Helen. They were involved
in a personal relationship, not a professional one. In a long-
term, committed, intimate relationship with a man, you don't
hammer out deals and demand equal airtime and compete with
him over who gets the last word or who has the most reasonable
position. Living with and loving a man isn't the same as working
with him. It requires a different approach.

"I'd Rather Fight than Switch"

Folding her arms across her chest and setting her jaw defiantly,
Helen declared, "But I don't *believe* that." I knew she didn't. And
I knew she would try to convince me she was right and keep
arguing her position until I either said I agreed with her or put
an end to our conversation. That was what she had done with
Roger. She fought with him for weeks on end, stating her case
repeatedly and even threatening Roger with dire consequences,
because she believed a once-in-a-lifetime event was more important than a ten-year tradition. But what did she gain by
trying to prove that point and be right and force Roger to give
her what she wanted regardless of what he wanted? Absolutely
nothing of value. Helen suffered through weeks of continuous
conflict, put her relationship in jeopardy and still did not convince Roger to attend her friend's wedding—which *she* did not
enjoy because she was too worried about her relationship.

What could she have done differently? Well, for starters, she
could have put the needs of her *relationship* first and asked
herself whether having Roger attend a wedding was worth the
irritation and potential damage to her relationship that bad-
gering and arguing with him would cause. If she had realized
that it was not worthwhile, she could have chosen not to start
an argument at all. Or, instead of continuing and escalating the
conflict, Helen could have stopped arguing with Roger once
she recognized how important the hunting trip was to him and
noticed that "stubborn streak" of his emerging. He was digging
in for a prolonged battle and Helen had never won one of

those. She could have gone one step farther, swallowed her pride, told Roger that she understood and accepted *his* position, and never brought the topic up for discussion again. Or she could have asked Roger to think about coming home early enough to attend the wedding and then made being in a relationship with her as rewarding as possible while he was considering that alternative.

Although Roger probably was not going to give up the entire trip under any circumstances, had Helen handled matters in any of the ways I just described, he might have compromised. And even if he hadn't, Helen's relationship would have been on solid ground when Roger returned. Even though she would not have all of what she wanted, Helen would have netted far better results than the approach she did use produced. But she didn't see it that way.

"Going to that wedding with me *was* important," she protested. "Why should I give up what I want to keep the peace? You wouldn't tell *him* to do that. It's okay for him to be stubborn and unreasonable, but I'm supposed to give in to him even when I know I'm right. That's not fair and I don't care what you or anyone else says about making a man happy so he'll make me happy. I won't let any man win or walk all over me just so he can gratify his ego." She wouldn't because *her* ego— the part of her personality that demanded to be superior, separate, unique, noticed and self-centered—wouldn't let her.

Helen's ego told her that she was right and that being right justified actions that were all wrong for her relationship. Her ego told her that the principle involved took precedence over such practicalities as wasting time and energy trying to force a man she knew "wouldn't bend an inch" to change his mind completely. Her ego even convinced her that getting her way in the short run was more important than doing what it took to have what she *really* wanted in the long run: a successful, lasting, intimate relationship with Roger.

Your ego tells you things like that too. It would rather fight to be right than switch to be successful. It doesn't care whether your relationship succeeds. It wants to prove something. Your ego doesn't know the first thing about Relationship. All it knows how to do is compete. That's what your ego is good for. It is a valuable, viable tool for competition. But a serious, long-term, committed relationship with a man is not a competitive arena and whenever you bring your ego and your competitive skills or outlook into it, they will get in your way. They will prevent you from being successful, productive or satisfied in your relationship.

Women's Egos

Your ego is the side of you that keeps score and gets even and goes after short-term rewards regardless of the long-term consequences. Your ego is the insistent, bullying, sometimes critical, often unreasonable and inflexible inner voice that tells you who you should be and how you must act and what you are entitled to. It speaks in a masculine tone. In fact, your ego sounds just like the men you can't tolerate. You know it's running the show whenever you catch yourself thinking or saying out loud:

- "To hell with them."
- "Why should I?"
- "What's in it for me?"
- "That's not fair."
- "I'll show him."
- "They don't know anything."
- "I'm entitled to my opinion."
- "Oh, really?!"
- "I'll do it myself."
- "You don't understand."
- "Who do you think you're talking to?"
- "Who are you trying to kid?"
- "I can do anything a man can do just as well as he can."
- "You want me to do what?!"
- "How dare you . . ."
- "I have my rights."
- "You've got one hell of a nerve."
- "Nobody's going to tell me how to live my life."

And, of course, "Yeah, but . . ." That's right, your ego is the part of your personality that has been making it so difficult for you to trust or believe or seriously consider using the advice I've been giving you. When my ideas don't fit the fantasies your ego generates about the woman you're supposed to be; when my suggestions don't jibe with the things your ego tells you to do (assert yourself, act like a winner, never back away from a fight or let anyone get the upper hand, go for the gold today and worry about tomorrow when it comes), your ego chimes in with some advice of its own: "You don't have to let this guy push you around. He has some nerve telling *you* what to do. What does he know? He doesn't have to be in a relationship with a man and he certainly doesn't know what it's like to be a woman today." Egged on by the voice of your ego, you mentally argue with me or twist my words around or find exceptions that contradict anything I have to say. You set up a competition between us, one that you'll win by proving me wrong or refusing to accept my ideas. Competing is what egos do. It's all they know how to do.

Big egos are a relatively new development for women. Your ego grew as your independence and interest in having success-ful careers did. It was necessary and useful in the work world. It gave you the competitive edge you needed to get ahead. In what had previously been men's territory, listening to your ego helped you. But, you took it too seriously. You began to believe your ego in situations where it was not useful and to listen to it instead of the voice of the woman you really are.

The voice of your ego makes you feel powerful, unafraid, invulnerable. But in a relationship, the true source of your power lies elsewhere. Unfortunately, you can't tap into those resources or draw upon your natural talent and skill for Relat-ing when your ego is leading you around by the nose. You can't manage a serious, committed, intimate relationship with a man while taking orders from your ego the way men do.

Men's Egos

For a man, ego is the driving force in life. It motivates him to get up, get out and do what he has to do. It gives him the courage and will to compete. Since his number-one priority is competition, he needs the motivation his ego provides. A man is lost without his ego egging him on and telling him, "You're the greatest. You can do it. No one can stop you. Don't let anything slow you down." With his ego generating fantasies and convincing him to make them into realities, a man can do amazing things. He can win triathlons and build skyscrapers, invent marvelous, time-saving machines and spend hour after hour, day after day looking for and eventually finding the cure to some dreaded disease. Thanks to his ego, a man can do incredibly stupid things too, like waging wars or getting himself beaten to a pulp in a bar fight or polluting the environment while trying to beat out his competitors in the petrochemical industry. He can build or destroy, be valiant or violent, and the same principle applies to men (and their egos) in an intimate relationship with a woman.

Men can be "killers" or heroes. If you make being in a relationship with you a rewarding proposition for your man and a gratifying experience for his ego, he will be your hero. He will do amazing things for you. But if you, at your ego's insistence, challenge or threaten your man's ego, you'll see him turn on you in no time flat. He doesn't want to hurt you, but he will because he can't choose not to fight. If you give him an opportunity to compete with you and beat you on his turf, he has to seize it. If he doesn't, he loses face and feels like a fool. And once he has accepted your challenge and started competing with you, he won't give a second thought to the long-term consequences of his actions or the damage he might be doing to you or your relationship. In fact, if he senses that you are getting the better of him, he'll pull out all the stops. He'll use every trick in his considerable repertoire in order to win or avoid losing.

Even though you win a round now and then, if you choose to go head-to-head with a man's ego, when you lose, you'll lose big. You'll be decimated. You are only trying to prove a point or to get something you think you are entitled to at that particular moment. But your man is defending and protecting the thing that makes him tick. He has more at stake and his ego is more powerful than yours. If you don't believe me, just think of all the times you have argued with a man who "hit below the belt," making cruel, vulgar or vindictive remarks, bringing up sensitive subjects that you thought were off limits, going straight for the jugular and attacking you in the area where you were most vulnerable or getting back at you days or even weeks after you thought the conflict had been resolved. Men do that, and you are "crushed" when they do. Your ego picks a fight, but when your man's ego beats the living daylights out of yours, *you* take it personally. You pay for the folly your ego got you into. You must stop letting your ego do that to you.

Two Egos Add Up to No Relationship

When you bring your ego into your relationship, you create adversarial situations—competitions from which only one person can emerge the "winner." Wanting to be right, you try to prove your man wrong the way Helen did. Determined to get what you want when and how you want it, you angrily hammer away at him as Rita did or you nag, complain and try to control him with your unhappiness as Diane did. Taking orders from your ego, you insist upon doing things your way—even when you have ample evidence that your way isn't working. You refuse to give your man what *he* wants when he wants it or to have your relationship on his terms. "If you do, he'll get cocky and arrogant and try to control you," your ego says, and you believe it. You don't even try to find out whether he would really react as predicted or if it would really be the travesty you imagine. Your ego won't let you.

If your man says or does anything you dislike or disagree with—no matter how insignificant in the overall scheme of things it might be—your ego won't permit you to let it pass. Your ego says, "You can't let him get away with that. If you give him an inch, he's going to take a mile. He's going to walk all over you, so you'd better set him straight right this minute. You have to make him pay for what he did." You listen. You follow your ego's instructions and everything you do at your ego's bidding challenges, threatens or makes it impossible for your man to gratify *his* ego. That's when your relationship problems begin. A man can't find a way to love you and, more often than not, ends up hurting you when you put him in a position that requires him to defend his ego.

Men are slaves to their egos. They do whatever is necessary to gratify or protect their egos. Whether you like it or not, whether you want to believe it or not, that's the way men are. That is how they are programmed and conditioned to operate. Although they do not behave egotistically, argumentatively or in an obviously self-centered manner 100 percent of the time, they can never ignore their egos or truly get them out of their way.

You can. You have other aspects of your personality to draw from, other more reliable inner voices to listen to and a vast array of relationship skills that make doing your ego's bidding in your relationship unnecessary. If you choose not to use those skills, if you use your competitive skills and bring your ego into your relationship instead, you *always* get yourself into trouble.

Because men are slaves to their egos and can't go anywhere without them, allowing your own ego to enter the picture puts two egos in your relationship, and two egos in a relationship are like two pit bulls in a pen. They will fight until one of them is dead. In fact, two egos in a relationship add up to *no* relationship because all egos know how to do is compete. And when you compete with a man in a serious, long-term, committed relationship, you *always* lose. Even when you win, you lose because your relationship suffers. Competition kills intimate relationships.

So here's the bad news: In a serious, long-term, committed relationship with a man, there is absolutely no room for *your* ego. Get it stroked elsewhere. Use it to go after instant gratification and short-term rewards in other arenas. Your relationship offers you other, more satisfying and longer-lasting rewards. To get them and to solve 95 percent of your relationship problems (and cope with the rest), keep your ego out of your relationship and use your considerable skill and talent for Relating to keep your man's ego from destroying you or your relationship.

Yeah but, Yeah but, Yeah but . . .

The concept of being egoless in a relationship is one of the most difficult ideas for women who attend Sterling Women's

Weekends to accept. Time and again, they challenge me and try to debate with me and bombard me with vehement protests—most of them aimed at what they *think* I meant and not what I actually said. Just in case you are getting hot under the collar and feeling ready to explode in anger or righteous indignation, let me set the record straight before I go any further.

When I said you had to keep your ego out of your relationship, I was not telling you to give in to your man at every turn, to give up everything you believe in and let a man walk all over you or take advantage of you. Getting your ego out of your way does *not* mean being a doormat, settling for whatever crumbs your man happens to toss in your direction and never getting what you truly want or need from your relationship. I want you to have what you want, but you can't get that by doing things your ego's way. A man won't give you what you want when you challenge or attack or refuse to gratify his ego—and that is what *your* ego convinces you to do.

Even if you successfully stifle, deflate or win out over a man's ego, you end up with less than you originally wanted. You domesticate your man. You tame him and break his spirit. You take him down a peg or two and take away his ego—even though you wanted a man with an ego in the first place. You wanted a lifetime mate who was successful, ambitious, self-confident, stable, secure and so on. A man like that needs his ego. His ego makes him who he is, who you love—so why would you want to take it away from him, to kill it? Because men with strong egos think of themselves first and want to make themselves happy first? Because they always want to win? What difference does that make? They'll still make you happy if you let them. And *you* want to be happy. All your ego wants is to win, and if you listen to it, you'll end up losing what you really wanted in the long run.

Getting your ego out of your way does *not* mean ignoring your feelings, going against your values or losing your integrity. Your ego is none of those things. Those aspects of your personality don't say the things your ego says. They don't tell you to be superior, special, unique, noticed, separate and self-centered or urge you to compete with a man in order to prove that you are. Learn to recognize the difference so you can stop listening

to your ego and start benefiting from your other internal resources.

Being egoless in your relationship does *not* mean being selfless
either. Your ego is *not* your identity. It is *not* who you are. It
speaks in a masculine tone, not a feminine one. It sees things
from a perspective different from your true self, the woman
you really are. In fact, it doesn't know the real you. It thinks it's
better than you are and comes up with all sorts of expectations
you try to live up to, and when you cannot, you suffer from low
self-esteem. When you listen to your ego, you are not being true
to yourself—as so many women seem to believe. You are being
true to your ego and you're so busy trying to prove yourself to
your ego that you kill off the very things that are truly important
and valuable to you as a woman.

Get Your Ego Out of Your Way

The moment you let your ego take over, you lose your ability
to manage a relationship effectively. You can't do what's best
for your relationship because your ego tells you to be self-
centered, to put your immediate needs and desires above all
else. You can't be long-term vision oriented and think about
what you want from your relationship over the course of a
lifetime because your ego demands instant gratification—at any
cost. It doesn't want you to wait. It convinces you that you are
entitled to those short-term rewards and urges you to grab them
right away. And because getting what you want when you want
it *is* gratifying, listening to your ego has an addictive quality to
it. You are reluctant to give it up. It feels good. You feel powerful and sure you can accomplish anything you want by asserting
yourself or arguing your case, using a few dirty tricks or attempting to control other people. If you want to, you can still
do those things and get the thrill of victory or any other positive
results you are after—in any area of your life *except* your long-
term, committed, intimate relationship with a man. Gratify your
ego at work, through athletic competition, by chairing a committee or leaving your mark on your community. But be ego-free
in your relationship. That's absolutely essential for its success.

Train yourself to recognize when your ego has entered the picture. Learn its vocabulary so you will know when it, rather than your real self, is doing the talking. Some of the more subtle signs include telling your man how to please you, testing to see if he really loves you, complaining that he does not make you happy or criticizing the things he does for you. He's in the relationship to make you happy. Making you happy gratifies his ego and your man will give you what you want *if you let him* but not if you tell him how to do his job. Doing your bidding, following your instructions about what makes you happy makes him no more than an errand boy—and there's no ego-gratification in that. If your man doesn't make you happy without your asking him to or telling him how, either he's the wrong man for you or you've been mismanaging your relationship.

Whenever you notice the voice of your ego clamoring to be heard, stop. Think about the things you really want, the things that are truly important to you as a woman. Ask yourself what's best for the success and survival of your relationship over the long haul. Then act accordingly. Doing that won't always be easy. It won't always feel good. But it will work. As I've said, Relationship is a discipline. It requires certain sacrifices and instant gratification is one of the things you'll have to sacrifice from time to time. However, putting the needs of your relationship first and doing what's best for your relationship does not necessarily mean giving in and going without. In fact, you'll find that you get more of what you want and more satisfaction overall once you *surrender*—accepting, respecting and yielding to the greater power of your man's ego and no longer engaging it in open warfare.

There are plenty of alternatives to going head-to-head with a man's ego. Way back in Chapter Three, Claire, who was celebrating her fiftieth anniversary, mentioned a number of them when she said to her granddaughter Meg, "I let him win at canasta. Canasta and everything else. Your grandfather's only five-foot-six, but I make sure he feels ten feet tall . . . He wants to think he's the world's best businessman, the world's greatest husband. I make sure he does. Every chance I get, I tell him it's true." Claire spent less than forty-five minutes a day making her husband "feel like a king" because that made him happy. *"When your grandpa's happy, he makes me happy,"* she said and *that* is the key to success in a serious, long-term, committed relationship with a man. You find it and become willing to use it when you stop keeping score and getting even, when you stop worrying about being stepped on or taken advantage of, when you stop doing things your ego's way and start doing what you as a woman do best—Relating.

Get His Ego on Your Side

A man's ego is like a junkyard dog primed to attack anyone who invades his territory, anyone who appears to pose a threat to him in any way. But that junkyard dog won't bite the hand that feeds it and, in fact, will fight to protect the person who fulfills its needs. Keeping that metaphor in mind, become an asset to your man's ego. Remember that it's a formidable enemy, respect it, tend to it and avoid interfering with it so that it won't decimate you or destroy your relationship. Keep your man's warrior spirit alive, but manage things so that your warrior fights for you and your relationship instead of against you. As I mentioned in an earlier chapter, you do that by finding out what your man wants and giving it to him. *When* he wants it. *How* he wants it.

If you are involved in a long-term, committed relationship already, you know what your man wants. I know you know, because that is what you're *not* giving him. Those are the rewards you withhold from him. Those are the things you keep arguing about. He wants to stay in his robe until noon on Sundays, but you nag him to get dressed or invite guests over for brunch so he has to get dressed. He doesn't like it when you complain. In fact, he clams up and sulks around the house whenever you do. So what do you do then? Complain about his silence and sulking. He hates it when you tell embarrassing stories about him at parties. You even say, "Joe hates when I do this," and then you do it anyway. Or you know that your man needs at least an hour to unwind after work, but you start pouring out your troubles to him as soon as he walks through the door. Then you feel hurt and rejected because he doesn't seem interested and won't be supportive when the truth is that he would have been if *you* had just given him that hour to unwind.

You find out what your man wants and then you don't give that to him or you give him exactly the opposite—to pay him back for not giving you something you wanted or to keep him from getting too cocky and being too sure of himself. It's a silly system. You don't get anything from it but the illusion that you are in control. Giving a man what you want to give him the way you want to give it and not giving him the rewards he entered a long-term, committed relationship to obtain creates conflict. It starts arguments. It prompts men to look elsewhere for ego-gratification. It is your ego's way of doing things, and it doesn't work.

Giving your man what he wants won't hurt you. His needs are very simple, very basic, and if you are with the right man, you won't have to violate your standards or sacrifice your real needs to fulfill his.

If you give your man what he wants when he wants it, he will stop wanting things when it is inconvenient or impossible for you to accommodate him. That's one of the ways men try to regain some semblance of control and it's unnecessary if you are not being controlling in the first place.

Give your man what he wants when he wants it and he'll make you happy—because that's his job and because you're a good deal. A good deal is what men are looking for and what they want from a long-term, committed relationship with a woman. If you make being in a relationship easy for him and rewarding for him, he'll know he has a good deal and he'll fight to keep it. If you pump up his ego and avoid doing things to threaten or deflate it, you'll be his ego's best asset and he'll do anything for you. He'll even look for things he can do to please you. That's the way men are. And when your ego says, "Why should I do that for him? Why should I make life convenient for him?" just tell it you should because the more convenient you make things for your man, the more time he will have to make you happy.

What Works: Eight Egoless Ways to Manage a Relationship

1. A long-term, committed, intimate relationship has zero tolerance for competition. Don't bring it in ever. You're playing with fire and will get burned. A man doesn't want competition and conflict in his relationship. He gets enough of it in other areas of his life. If you do challenge him, however, he will rise to that challenge and do whatever it takes to come out the winner. Your best bet is not to start—not to point out the things you know that he does not know or remind him of the things you've accomplished that he has not or to gush over how well your career is going when his is temporarily at a standstill. There's no valid reason for saying "I told you so" when your man screws up and no value in being right about some premise or principle if it means making your man wrong. And if *he* starts it, if he initiates a competition or conflict between you, then *you* initiate something that gets him off track.

2. Make sure he wins any arguments you do have. If you are arguing with your man, you have already mismanaged the situation. You have already unleashed or attacked his ego, so why compound the problem and escalate the conflict by trying to best him? Despite your ego's protests to the contrary, letting him win will not cost you anything and it could save your relationship. Instead of continuing the battle and ending up with nothing more than battle fatigue, lose the battle in order to win the war. Stop fighting. Tell your man that he has a point, that you can accept his position, even that he may be right. Then reassess the situation to determine whether or not what you were fighting for is truly important to you. If it is, find a different way to get it, one that does not challenge or threaten your man's ego. If it isn't essential, let it go. Losing arguments works. It may not prove a point. But it does work.

3. Have your relationship with your man's ego. Find out what gratifies it and what threatens it. Tend to it. Massage your man's ego whenever an opportunity to do so arises. In addition, figure out what provokes your man's ego and *stop* doing those things.

If you cut out the middleman and spend as little as fifteen minutes and no more than forty-five minutes a day relating to your man's ego, your man will make you happy and your relationship will succeed.

4. Don't help your man unless he asks you to and even then don't help too much. Taking care of a man and taking care of things for him should make life more convenient for him, but that is not always the case. When you step in too quickly to make your man feel better or do too much (especially if your man is perfectly capable of doing those things himself), chances are that you don't trust him to handle the situation effectively or cope with it at all. Under such circumstances, you are helping yourself to feel useful and in control and your man to feel impotent and inadequate. Rather than boosting his ego, you're deflating it. When your ego feels good about what you're doing or you're thinking "Isn't this nice of me? I'm putting my needs on the back burner to meet his. I sure hope he appreciates it," you'll know that you're helping too much or helping for the wrong reasons.

5. Stop keeping score. It's a waste of energy. When you are committed to your relationship and willing to do what it takes to succeed in your relationship, you don't need to tally up the things you do for your man and the things he does for you and then compare those totals to make sure you aren't giving more than you're getting. Your relationship isn't a contest. If you do your job and let your man do his, you'll get what you want. You'll have the relationship of your romantic vision.

6. Never give a man an ultimatum. He'll get even.

7. Allow and encourage your man to be alone with other men. Let him have his clubs, his poker games, his hunting trips or whatever else he likes to do with other men. Although it bothers many modern women when men go off by themselves, men get their batteries recharged and their egos boosted by "hanging out" together and doing "man things" together—and that makes your job easier in the long run.

8. Remember why you fell in love and why you selected your man as your lifetime mate. After all, he didn't force you to get involved in a relationship with him. You picked him and you need to recall why you did. You need to rediscover the things you knew about him when you picked him and the things he has shown you about himself over the years so that you can figure out what you need to do or learn in order to be successful, productive and satisfied in the relationship you have. If you are with the right man—and regardless of the problems in your relationship right now, many of you are—you can get your relationship back on track by remembering why you fell in love and letting the things you love about your man be more important than the things that tick you off. Although it is primarily directed at women who are not involved in long-term, committed relationships yet, the next chapter may refresh your memory.

The Path to Success Starts with the Selection Process

Everything I've suggested thus far works. It will lead to a successful, lasting, intimate relationship with a man—but not just any man. In fact, most of the advice I've given you won't do you much good at all if you select the wrong man to have your relationship with in the first place. That is why, before you get into a serious, committed relationship, you must ask yourself:

- "Who is this man?"
- "What does he need, want, and expect from a woman and a relationship?"
- "Given this man's basic nature and way of looking at things, can I be in a long-term, committed relationship with him on his terms, without violating my standards or giving up what I want and need?"

In the next chapter I will show you the most effective way to go about answering those questions and tell you what to look for in a lifetime mate.

TEN

How to Select a Lifetime Mate

Debra

When I met Debra, a twenty-seven-year-old physical therapist, she and Ben, a thirty-year-old partner in his family's restaurant supply business, had been together for almost a year. Their first encounter occurred at the fitness center where they both worked out regularly. "There I was, huffing and puffing away in my baggy sweat suit, when this unbelievably gorgeous man gets on the treadmill next to mine and strikes up a conversation with me," Debra recalled. She was delighted to discover that Ben had more than his good looks going for him. "He was probably the wittiest, most charming and articulate man I'd ever met," she said.

After several more not so coincidental meetings at the gym, they began dating, and with Ben romancing her in much the same way that Paolo courted Ariel, Debra felt herself falling in love. Everything about Ben—from his Eastern European accent to his tales of arriving in the United States at age fifteen and getting acclimated to life in America—fascinated Debra. "He's sophisticated and down to earth at the same time, serious about certain things without taking himself too seriously," she explained and then, breaking into a mischievous grin, added, "And sexy as hell. He has this way of making me feel like I'm the most exciting, desirable woman in the world. It's almost mesmerizing." But not quite. As Debra, the veteran of several "almost" long-term, committed relationships, put it, "From the start, I really *wanted* Ben to be the man I could spend the rest of my life with. But I knew better than to be completely blinded by my infatuation."

As Debra and Ben grew closer and spent more time together, Debra, unlike Ariel, made a concerted effort to keep her "eyes open and both feet firmly planted on the ground." From her relatively realistic vantage point, Debra saw "lots and lots" of things she loved about Ben, but a few "little problems" as well. The way the women in his family were treated was one of them.

"The first time Ben took me to meet his family, he warned me that they were very Old World and old-fashioned," Debra explained. "And he wasn't kidding. The women were friendly and talkative when they were by themselves, but as soon as the men came around, they hardly said a word. When I tried to join in the dinner table conversation, the men ignored me and glared at Ben, as if they were disgusted with him for not controlling his woman. After that, Ben would bump my knee or elbow me whenever I went to open my mouth." Naturally, Debra wasn't thrilled about that, but she concluded that Ben's family had been the way they were for years and never entertained the notion of trying to change the situation. "It wasn't going to kill me to be seen and not heard for a couple of hours now and then," she said. But then she began to notice that Ben sometimes treated her like a "nonentity" too.

"If he runs into a guy he knows I've never met, he doesn't introduce me," Debra observed. "He'll have a whole conversation while I just stand there." According to Debra, she had no choice but to "just stand there" because Ben ignored her attempts to get his attention and got angry at her if she walked away. "It doesn't really bother me," Debra claimed. "I figure *some* of the male chauvinism in his family had to rub off on him and I try not to let it get to me." When they were window shopping or in a museum and Ben was ready to move on, he grunted or tapped Debra on the shoulder and expected her to follow him immediately. When he was driving and they got lost, she had to remain absolutely silent while Ben figured out how to get them back on the right road—without stopping to ask for directions or consulting a map. "Of course, when I get us lost, you can't shut him up," Debra said. But she didn't let those "little quirks" get to her either. And she had "learned her lesson" when it came to making even completely innocent references to other men.

"I made the mistake of mentioning that one of the doctors at work was a real flirt," Debra explained. "And Ben hasn't let it rest yet. If I say I had a good day at work, he asks, 'Did that doctor flirt with you again? Is that why you had such a good day?' Since it's really pretty silly, I usually chalk it up to his insecurity and try not to take it too seriously."

The longer Debra went on describing her relationship with Ben, the more "little" problems she uncovered, and it began to dawn on her that, taken one by one, she had been able to laugh off Ben's quirks and habits or explain them away; but when she put them all together, they added up to a major philosophical difference. Ben, like the other men in his family, expected women to be subservient to men: to fade into the woodwork in mixed company, to defer to man's supposed superiority in certain situations and put up with whatever macho posturing he happened to indulge in. He would expect that of *any* woman with whom he had a relationship, but Debra had not been raised to do such things. That didn't mean she couldn't do them. The time had come, however, for her to decide whether or not she would.

Debra needed to do some serious soul searching and to ask herself if she could accept Ben's point of view. If he were to think of and treat her as "less than" men for the rest of their lives, could she put up with that? Would she be able to live with Ben's attitude and adjust to his expectations for the duration of their relationship or raise children in a household where she would be subservient to Ben? She needed to be totally, brutally honest with herself because the future of her relationship depended on those things. If she could not allow Ben to be who he was and if she could not accept his terms for being in a relationship without expecting to change him at a later date, she was not going to be successful, productive and satisfied in that relationship over the long haul. It was better for Debra to face that now than to be hit in the face with it two or five or ten years down the line.

A Good Manager Hires People She Can Work With

Whether in business or in a relationship, it is a whole lot easier for a manager to be successful if she has the right workers in the right jobs. That is why managers in business settings thoroughly and carefully interview candidates for crucial positions in their departments. They prevent future problems by hiring people who are willing and able to give them what they need to be successful themselves (and by not hiring people who can't or won't provide what they need). Well, you can eliminate a lifetime of struggling, straining and fighting to turn the wrong man into the right material for your relationship by doing that too. Make sure you're in the right relationship in the first place—by picking the right man.

Start with a clear vision of the relationship you want: a long-range vision that includes the elements I described in Chapter Two. A long-term, committed relationship with a man is your artistic expression, your masterpiece. You need a blueprint for it, a plan and a design in order to know what to look for in a lifetime mate. Without that blueprint, you're taking a big risk. There's a good chance that you'll use a "buy now, pay later" approach and go all out to get a man, only to spend the rest of your life working on your relationship.

I want you to work smart instead: Keeping your long-term vision of a relationship in mind and developing a "job description" of sorts, identify the qualities you want your lifetime mate to possess. Then look for a man who has those qualities. Find a man who wants the things you do, a man who already has what it is going to take to please you, a man whose basic nature, natural tendencies, expectations and habits are compatible with your needs and standards and your vision of a relationship.

Be choosy. You can't settle for less than you need. If you are passionate about something (your career, your political activities, running marathons), you shouldn't have to give that up. The man you get seriously involved with need not be as passionate about that thing as you are. He doesn't have to be interested in it at all. But one of the first things you need to figure out is whether or not he will try to stop you from pursuing your passion or make it difficult for you to do that. If that's the case, the wisdom of allowing the relationship to develop into a serious, long-term, committed relationship is questionable. It will require you to sacrifice something that means a great deal to you and you must decide whether or not you can do that without resenting it and making your man pay for it somewhere down the line. If you can't, let him go.

Be realistic. Think about who you are and what you have to offer a man. You have to face the fact that you can't buy a Rolls-Royce on a Ford budget. If you are a thirty-five-year-old woman with two children, you are not going to be able to compete with a twenty-two-year-old woman with a multi-million-dollar trust fund. If you live in rural Pennsylvania, your chances of meeting a man who comes anywhere close to resembling a Texas oil baron or the Prince of Wales are slim. That doesn't mean you can't have or won't find a terrific man who is the best possible man for you and who can give you everything you want from a relationship. You just have to be realistic about the pool of men from which you can choose, and develop your "job description" accordingly.

Be picky, but not too picky. There are lots of great men out there; more than enough men who would be the right material for your artistic expression if you let them. But there are no perfect men. You can't set your standards so high that no man on earth could live up to them. That's what you do to avoid intimacy. You get out of taking risks, mastering a discipline, making sacrifices or committing yourself to your relationship by establishing impossibly detailed criteria for selecting your lifetime mate and then saying, "But there are no decent men out there." Even though many of the qualities you think a man should possess have little or nothing to do with what it takes to have a successful, long-term relationship, you claim that the man who could fit your romantic vision of a relationship doesn't exist. Well, I'm telling you he does. He's out there. You're just afraid to find him. Or you're not looking for him in the right places.

The man who could be your lifetime mate isn't going to come knocking on your door. Your boss isn't going to hire him and assign him the desk next to yours. To find the man you want you have to go out and look for him. You have to meet men. You have to date men. You may have to date lots of men before you find one who might be a likely candidate for your long-term, committed relationship. It's like screening job applicants over the telephone before setting up a formal interview. You can tell that certain people aren't qualified for the position, and you don't waste your time or theirs by having them come in to talk to you anyway. If you have the time and you're having fun, you can casually date a man you know isn't long-term, committed relationship material for as long as you want. But most of you are busy women and you don't have time to waste on men you realize, after one or two or five dates, are not right for you. Let them go and keep looking.

Be serious about selecting a lifetime mate. That doesn't mean you can't have fun while you're looking or that the process of getting to know a man isn't enjoyable. You just need to remember that you're preparing to make an important decision, one of the most important decisions you'll ever face. You can't make that decision by going out and playing the field and haphazardly dating men, thinking you'll somehow stumble upon your lifetime mate. You need to be more purposeful and disciplined about it. When you do find a man you think might be the right material for your relationship, learn who he is, what he is, what he wants and what he needs from a woman and a relationship. *Before* you get seriously involved with him, find out as much as you can about his basic nature, natural tendencies and deeply ingrained attitudes or expectations and figure out if you can accept that man as he is, love him for who he is and give him what he wants when he wants it without violating your own standards or thinking that there are things you'll change about him once you get him where you want him. That is how you establish a strong, healthy foundation for success, productivity and satisfaction in a long-term, committed relationship with a man.

WHAT WORKS WITH MEN

To solve 95 percent of your relationship problems (and cope with the rest):

Before you get seriously involved with a man, make sure his terms and expectations do not violate the elements that you consider absolute essentials in a relationship.

"Interviewing" Candidates for the Position of Lifetime Mate

When it comes to relationships, an interview is not a conference. It is not a discussion. It is not like the conversation with Lee Iacocca where he tells you what he expects from you and you ask him to clear up any points you didn't understand and maybe describe some of your expectations to find out if they are acceptable to him. You can't sit down with a man and say, "Okay, since it seems like we're pretty compatible and it looks like this relationship might be going somewhere, let's talk about our expectations. What are your terms for being in a relationship?" A man isn't going to tell you what his terms are verbally. He doesn't convey his innermost thoughts and feelings in words, and when it comes to your relationship, you can't rely on the things a man says (unless you're paying him or he says "leave me alone"). You have to observe and interpret his behavior, as Debra did.

Although she did not realize it at the time, Debra had been "interviewing" Ben from the moment she met him. She noticed the customs and behavior patterns in Ben's family and rightly assumed that some of their attitudes and habits had been passed down to Ben. She watched Ben in action, observing the things he did and how he treated her under a wide variety of circumstances. She made mental notes about his reactions to her behavior, "red flagging" the things she did which seemed to disturb or bring out the worst in him. Because she kept her eyes open and both feet on the ground and took her cues from Ben's behavior, Debra was able to recognize the things he did and the attitudes he conveyed to her consistently and often enough to indicate that they were part of his general makeup. She was able to piece together an accurate picture of Ben's overall expectations and his terms for being in a long-term, committed relationship with a woman. She did a good job during the interviewing process. Follow her example and you will too.

Take as long as you need to discover whether or not a man can fit into your romantic vision of a relationship without changing his basic nature. And at the same time you are observing and learning about him, seriously ask yourself if you can be successful and satisfied in a long-term, committed relationship with that man, given his terms and conditions for being in such a relationship and what he expects from a woman. If you *can't* live with a man's terms, if you can't accept them and shape your relationship around them without violating your own standards or going against your own basic nature, then *don't get involved in a serious, long-term, committed relationship with that man.* There is no point in pursuing a relationship with a man who expects things you can't give him and can't give you what you want. Somewhere down the line the habits, attitudes and expectations you find unacceptable will catch up with you and you will end up resenting your man for being the way he is. You will end up rejecting your man for who he is not. You will try to make him live up to your expectations and find yourself in the same mess as Rita and Fred or Diane and Rick or most of the other couples I've described thus far.

On the other hand, if you find a man whose attitudes, expectations and habits *are* acceptable and compatible with what you want and need, then you have a likely candidate for the "position" of lifetime mate. That man is someone with whom you *could* have a successful, productive, fulfilling, long-term, committed relationship. On an intellectual, rational level, you know that you can get along with that man, that he can offer you what you want from a relationship, that you can accept him as he is and that you are capable of managing your relationship with his terms and expectations in mind.

But is he really the right man for you? Some of you will intuitively know the answer to that question. On a spiritual level where things are trusted and not tested, where you instinctively know rather than intellectually believe, you will see that certain intangible aspects of a man's unique personality and true nature fit yours like an interlocking puzzle piece. You will feel a connection that is more powerful than your doubts or your fears and recognize that the man you like, respect and have grown to love is also the man you want to spend the rest of your life with.

Unfortunately, if you have lost touch with the part of yourself that knows a spiritual connection when it sees one (and many women today have), you will choose a man and get involved in a long-term, committed relationship with him for other reasons. That's okay. Just make sure they're not the wrong reasons.

How Not to Select a Lifetime Mate

Do not choose a lifetime mate because he needs you. A man who needs you makes you feel powerful and in control. You can take care of him or make yourself indispensable to him as Carrie did with her "scatterbrained" ex-husband Ron. You don't have to worry about losing him because he cannot live without you. But a man is not marriage material until he is fully self-reliant, and you will end up resenting him and feeling overburdened by the role you assumed when you married him. A time will come when you, like Carrie, will decide that it's your turn to be taken care of. But your dependent man won't deliver and you'll hate him for it.

Do not choose a lifetime mate only because he fulfills your immediate needs. A man who fulfills your needs is a seasonal mate because your needs will change and when they do, that man will no longer be useful to you. You'll change and grow and decide that you've outgrown that man or blame him for not meeting needs you did not have when he married you.

Do not choose a lifetime mate because he completes you, supplying you with whatever you believe you lack. When you get seriously involved with a take-charge guy because you're wishy-washy or a brainy guy because you think you're dumb or a fun-loving man with a devil-may-care attitude because you think you're dull and lack spontaneity, you are letting low self-esteem dictate your choices. Nine times out of ten, you will be getting yourself into a situation that does further damage to your self-esteem. That man is going to treat you as you think you deserve to be treated; and since you have low self-esteem, that isn't very well. Your chances of ever feeling successful, productive or satisfied in your relationship are minimal.

Do not choose a lifetime mate because of the short-term rewards and instant gratification a man can offer you. Status, prestige, sexual chemistry, good looks, world travel, rubbing elbows with the rich and famous or access to anything money can buy feels great while you've got it, but you can't decide to get involved in a long-term, committed relationship with a man because of such things. They may not last. Your man could lose his prestigious job tomorrow or squander his fortune on bad real estate investments. That devastatingly handsome guy may have a receding hairline and a protruding belly five or ten years down the line. Are you going to love him and accept him and do what it takes to succeed in your relationship then? Not if you based your decision to get seriously involved with him on his surface qualities or how you happened to feel about him at one moment in time. Feelings are a response to the immediate. Because they change constantly, you can't rely on feelings alone while making what may very well be the most important decision of your life.

Do not choose a lifetime mate because he'll have you. Some women never worry about liking or accepting a man. They are too busy worrying about whether or not he likes them. Their self-esteem is so low and their desperation to find a man is so great that they consider any man who seems interested in them a likely candidate for their lifetime mate. "If he'll accept me, I'll take him," they think, and then they get stuck with a man who isn't even close to the object of their romantic fantasies and keeps them in a constant state of anxiety. They never stop worrying that the man who accepted them will change his mind and reject them.

Do not choose a lifetime mate until you are ready for a long-term relationship. You are ready when a long-term relationship is what you want and not what you think you need or must have to accept yourself or be accepted by others. When you need a relationship, you tend to play down or forgive negative habits and tendencies that shouldn't be minimized or forgiven. You tend to settle for less than is sufficient to satisfy you. And you tend to expect your man and your relationship to bring you self-acceptance and happiness. They cannot. You have to be in the right frame of mind before you even begin the selection process and that means having an accepting attitude toward yourself and confidence in your ability to live *without* a relationship until you have the right relationship.

If you select your lifetime mate based on any of the foregoing criteria, I guarantee that the qualities you chose him for will be the very characteristics you will berate him for when anything goes wrong. What's more, because you got involved in a long-term, committed relationship for the wrong reasons, you'll spend so much time and energy trying to correct or compensate for your mistake that you'll never get around to enjoying or feeling successful, productive and satisfied in that relationship.

So, How Do You Select a Lifetime Mate?

Once a man makes it through your interview process, you'll be able to tell if he is the right man by considering his acceptability as breeding stock. That's right, breeding stock: a man who has qualities you want to pass on to your children and none that you don't. Use that criterion even if you don't want to have children because it will force you to look beyond yourself and your immediate needs or other short-term rewards. You have to have a long-term vision to select a lifetime mate and not just a playmate or a seasonal mate or a partner who you'll stick with only until the going gets tough. To make the right choice, the smart choice, you have to think about the future—the future of your family and your community and all the other long-range issues that women throughout history have considered before embarking upon something as important and serious as a long-term, committed relationship with a man.

You keep the future in sight when you ask yourself: "Does this man have qualities I want my children to inherit, observe or emulate?" and "Is this man free of traits or habits that I would have to protect my children from or compensate for or cover up?" Consider those questions and all those hard-working, sensible, stable men who don't look like Adonis or have bank statements like the late Malcolm Forbes will start looking better to you. All those alcoholics and abusers, wounded birds and nitpickers won't wind up in your life. You won't let them. If you fearlessly appraise a man and come up with yes answers to the foregoing questions, you'll know you're on the right track.

The second foolproof criterion for selecting a lifetime mate is whether you trust him enough to let him control you. Please note that *trust* is the operative word here. I am not telling you to let a man control you or suggesting that you should. I *am* pointing out that if you trusted a man so completely that if he did try to control you it would be okay, then you would know beyond a shadow of a doubt that you had found the right man. What's more, control would cease to be a source of conflict or an excuse not to be intimate.

Fear of being controlled is the major obstacle to intimacy for women. It is the major barrier to opening their hearts to a man and being who they really are in their relationships. It is the major reason women won't allow their men to be who they are. They won't do what it takes to be successful in their relationships and rationalize that decision by saying, "I don't want to just hand my life over to a man and lose control over it and be at that man's mercy. I can't give him what he wants when he wants it or allow him to win this argument or let that insensitive remark pass without commenting on it. If I did that, he'd have the upper hand. He'd be controlling me."

Well, I'm telling you that you don't have to feel that way. When you trust a man enough to let him control you, then you don't have to live in fear that he might. You eliminate your fear by not allowing a serious relationship to develop until that trust exists. Again, I'm not saying that you should actually let your man control you or that he will even try to. But if you do not trust him enough to allow him to do it or trust him to treat you the way you want to be treated in general, then you are with the wrong man.

You Can Accept Whatever You Choose to Accept

Choosing a lifetime mate is one of the most important decisions you'll ever make. You are not just picking a man. You are establishing the foundation for your entire relationship. So please, take it seriously and base your decision on your knowledge of yourself and NOT on other people's opinions, the latest fashion or some dime store novel/Hollywood fantasy version of how a man and a relationship should be. Trust that inner voice which speaks to you from your feminine self. Use as a guide what that inner voice tells you about yourself and what is right for you—because what you accept is entirely up to you.

If you could live with a man like Fred who expects to brush reality under the carpet and can't tolerate the expression of negative emotions, fine. If it is not going to bother you to be involved with a man like Rick, who is dedicated to his work and expects his family to take a back seat to his career, then go for it. If you could be happy spending the rest of your life with a man who is scatterbrained and needs someone to handle the details of daily living for him, as Carrie's ex-husband Ron did, or a man who is dead set against having children as her lover Bill was, then don't let anyone talk you out of it. Who are other people to judge what you accept? Only you know enough about yourself to recognize what is right for you.

You can accept whatever you want to accept. What you *can't* do is accept a man as he is for the moment and expect to change him at a later date or act as if you accept his terms and then, after you get him where you want him, ignore his expectations and do what you darn well please. As those of you who have been looking back over your existing relationship may have already realized, even when you select the right man for the right reasons, you tend to make two lists during the courtship phase of your relationship: a "wonderful" list and a "not so wonderful" list. The second list—the list of things that are wrong with your man—gives you something to blame if your relationship fails. When things begin to go wrong in your relationship, you haul out that "not so wonderful" list and start bringing up items on it. You start fighting about and trying to change the aspects of your man's personality and basic nature—including the qualities you knew about all along and implicitly agreed not to mess around with when you got seriously involved with him. As a result, you end up mismanaging and damaging what could have been a successful relationship.

You have to stop doing that. After all, you would not listen to Lee Iacocca's terms and think, "Okay, I know what Mr. Iacocca expects of me; I know he means business because I've watched him operate; I've seen what happens to people who cross the lines he's drawn. I also know I can't live with those terms, but I really want this job and the $400,000 and all the other perks I'll get. I'm going to accept the position; and once I'm in it, once my contract is signed and I'm settled in the position, I'll just do whatever I think is best. I won't do what Lee wants. I'll do what I want."

There is only one reason you would do something like that: to prove a point, to prove that nobody—not even Lee Iacocca—can tell *you* what to do. You're not going to gain anything by following that scenario. It's a big mistake. You're not going to win. You're not going to convince Lee Iacocca that your way is better than his. Instead you'll lose your job. You'll get fired for not operating within the parameters you knew existed and led Mr. Iacocca to believe you accepted before you took the job.

Well, if you do that in a long-term, committed relationship with a man, you're going to lose too. At any point in your relationship, at every turn in the road that could lead you to the relationship of your romantic vision, you have the option of accepting your man for what he is or rejecting him for what he isn't. At any given moment, during any of the countless interactions you'll have during the course of your relationship, you can remember why you fell in love with your man or focus on the things that are wrong with him, trust the choice you made when you selected him as your lifetime mate or doubt it, do what needs to be done or what you want to do to feel good or powerful or in control at that moment. As I will explain in the next chapter, you make the right choices when you put the needs of your *relationship* first: when you are truly committed to your relationship and honor that commitment by doing what is best for your relationship in the long run.

ELEVEN

From Casual Dating to Commitment: How to Get and Keep Your Relationship on Track

Meredith

As you may recall from my reference to her in Chapter Six, Meredith, a thirty-two-year-old special education teacher, met Mike, a thirty-three-year-old psychologist, when she was on the rebound from a failed relationship, in the midst of a family crisis and in danger of losing her job. "I was also drinking heavily," Meredith admitted. "I was so out of control by the time Mike came along that I'm not exaggerating when I say he saved my life." She would always love him for that, Meredith explained, "but I think I may have made a mistake by marrying him."

Three months before her wedding, feeling stifled and boxed in by Mike—whose caretaking had begun to look like control to Meredith—she had an affair with a young man who was, according to Meredith, as exciting, fun-loving and uninhibited as Mike was stable, sensible and predictable. "I just had to cut loose," she said. She owed herself that much, Meredith claimed. "If I didn't have that experience, I would have always wondered what it would be like. I would have felt like I was missing something." Telling herself that she had wiped the need for adventure out of her system, Meredith ended the affair soon after it began and went ahead with her plans to marry Mike.

Less than a year later, she began to feel "suffocated and unfulfilled" again. "I knew there had to be more to life than the dull routine we had drifted into. Mike seemed perfectly happy to go to work, putter around the house, see the same friends and talk about the same mundane topics. But I wasn't. I was bored to death." This time Meredith decided to explore her spiritual side and spent her ten-week summer vacation living in an ashram, without Mike. "I don't regret it," she said. "It opened me up. It made me more receptive and self-aware. I honestly believe I'm a better person because of it." And, she insisted, she was more willing to do what it took to make her marriage work than she ever had been before.

Unfortunately, a year later, Meredith had changed her tune again. Mike was trying to run her life, she claimed, and she felt that being married to him was stunting her growth. Although she initially said that she came to a Sterling Women's Weekend in hopes of saving her marriage, Meredith summed up her "real dilemma" this way: "I've met this man, this incredibly sensitive, creative man who completely understands the artist in me. He brings out the intuitive, expressive part of me that I've never had a chance to explore before. We haven't slept together yet. He wants to and I want to, but I'm really torn right now. On the one hand, I love Mike and promised myself that I wouldn't be unfaithful to him again. But on the other hand, there has always been something missing from our marriage."

There was something missing from Meredith's marriage all right: *a committed relationship*. She was no more than a guest in her own marriage, coming and going whenever she pleased. She stayed until staying stopped feeling good and then flitted off in search of excitement, spirituality, creativity or some other source of personal fulfillment. Meredith was committed to doing whatever she felt like doing at any moment in time and *not* to doing what it took to be productive and feel fulfilled in her relationship. She should not have been in a serious relationship with Mike or anyone else for that matter because long-term, intimate relationships with men are too risky and too fragile to be involved in unless you *are* commited to them.

"To give in trust, entrust or surrender for safe-keeping": that is the definition of the word "commit." When applied to a long-term relationship with a man, it means having faith in the decision you made when you selected your lifetime mate, believing with all your heart that you did the right thing when you got seriously involved with him and never questioning that choice again. When you are truly committed to your relationship, you stop looking for escape hatches, reasons to change your mind and excuses for not doing what you know is best for your relationship over the long haul. When you notice your relationship getting off track, you simply honor your commitment and do what works for your relationship. You eliminate quitting as an option and look for other options—for ways to manage the relationship you have so that it brings you the success and satisfaction you want.

Of course, that is far more easily said than done. Although Meredith may be flightier and more self-absorbed than most women, her predicament is hardly unique. In fact, in recent years women have been so reluctant to commit themselves to their relationships or honor commitments that might stunt their personal growth, distract them from their professional aspirations or otherwise prevent them from doing whatever they want whenever they want to do it that it actually took a plague—the AIDS epidemic—to make committed relationships fashionable again.

In this day and age, in this culture, women have more options than women in previous generations have had or women from more conservative cultures have, and they want to keep their options open. They don't want to put all of their eggs in one basket or possibly miss out on an opportunity for personal fulfillment that might present itself farther down the line. Some are afraid of losing their autonomy and independence. Others have low self-esteem and, doubting their ability to make decisions effectively, constantly question the choices they do make.

Most don't want to be held captive in their relationships or to get stuck with them if they look like they're going to fail. Assuming that their relationships *will* fail, they won't get involved in them unless there's a back door to escape through if things start to go wrong.

Those are just some of the reasons why commitment is a problem for many women today and why most modern women don't have truly committed relationships with men. Instead, they have negotiated "agreements between two consenting adults usually involving sexual exclusivity." They unilaterally renegotiate those agreements whenever the going gets tough or being in the relationship stops feeling good or doing what it takes for their relationship becomes inconvenient or uncomfortable for them.

"But It's Not Us. It's Them."

At this juncture in any Sterling Women's Weekend, someone invariably tries to set me straight. In no uncertain terms, I am told, *"Men* are the ones who won't commit. They're the ones who want to keep their options open. We're ready to have committed relationships with them, but they act like we're asking them to jump off a cliff when we even mention the 'C' word."

There is certainly an abundant body of literature to support that contention. In the self-help/psychology sections of any bookstore, you'll find dozens of books about men with cold feet and men's fear of intimacy and men who dance away from relationships. Well, I'm going to let you in on a little secret: the majority of men are ready to commit long before you are and *you* are more afraid of intimacy than they are.

Intimacy is much more dangerous for you than for men. You are more sensitive. If you get hurt, you'll hurt more. Because you are judged by the success or failure of your relationships, you have more on the line in a relationship. And because your already shaky sense of self-worth can so easily sustain further damage, you have more to lose by letting a man get close to you. That is why you knowingly or unknowingly, willingly or unwillingly create obstacles to intimacy. You put off truly committing yourself to your relationship for as long as you possibly can. And many of you get involved with men who won't commit because it is easy to be committed to a man who won't commit himself to you. You never have to find out whether or not you would honor *your* commitment. You just get yourself a reluctant partner and avoid facing your fears about intimacy or admitting that you have no idea what truly committing yourself to a relationship means.

Although men tend not to get married until being married is convenient for them and doesn't interfere with other pursuits, they *do* understand commitments. They take them seriously. For centuries, they have committed themselves to defending their countries and literally have laid down their lives to honor those commitments. In their book, a deal's a deal, and they make deals all of the time. Their handshake is enough to cement a contract. But they won't shake someone's hand if they can't keep up their end of the bargain or if they suspect that the other person will go back on his word or welch on the deal. That's what men think you'll do. That's why most of the men I encounter at Sterling Men's Weekends and while lecturing throughout the United States and Canada tell *me* that they want to be in long-term, committed relationships with women—but they won't tell *you* that. They won't because you can't be trusted.

You'll *say* that you want to be there for your man, that you love him, unconditionally support him, are ready to make a commitment and will stand by him through thick and thin. But you don't *act* as if you mean it. You turn around and put a price tag on your love and loyalty. You establish conditions, lots of conditions, constantly changing conditions for men to meet in order to earn your support and affection. Everywhere they look there is another hoop they must jump through and another test they must pass in order to prove that they really love you.

Although men test too, their tests are few in number; and once women "pass," men will rarely test them again. Most women, on the other hand, constantly test their men. They administer daily tests and hourly quizzes. They are always keeping score. Every insensitive remark, every missed cue, every failure to provide what they want when and how they want it—whether intentional or coincidental—is a potential source of conflict, a reason for women to doubt their original decision, an excuse to question the viability of continuing the relationship and evidence that they were not truly committed to the relationship in the first place.

Making a Commitment

Commitment dissolves problems. When you are *not* committed to your relationship and things start to go wrong, you haul out that old "not so wonderful" list and begin blaming your man for your unhappiness. You attempt to control your relationship instead of managing it. You try to force your man to give you what you want when you want it instead of making it worth his while to please you. In the process, you create new problems and new conflicts that take you farther and farther away from success, productivity and satisfaction.

When you are *not* committed to your relationship, you constantly get bogged down and sidetracked by such questions as: Did I do the right thing? Is this really the right relationship for me? Is this problem a sign of even bigger problems yet to come? Does he really love me? Do I really love him? Was I a fool to trust him? Is there someone or something out there that could make me happier than I am now? The more you search for definitive answers to those largely nonsensical questions, the more you doubt. And the more you doubt, the more likely you are to perpetuate your problems instead of solving them.

In contrast, when you *are* committed to your relationship, all you have to ask yourself is: "How can I do what's best for my relationship?" Instead of looking for someone to blame or a way out and an excuse to quit, you put the needs of your relationship first. You give its success and survival precedence over getting or hanging onto a man, bowing to the pressure of other people's opinions, the latest trends, saving face or catering to your own ego.

Naturally, some problems cannot be solved no matter how committed you are. Some situations are too dangerous or demoralizing to withstand. Some relationships have already been abused and damaged beyond repair. But such circumstances

tend to be the exception rather than the rule. Far more often, once you make a commitment and honor it by doing what works and what you know in your heart is best for your relationship, you will be able to keep your relationship on track. In fact, you will finally be able to relax, enjoy and thrive in that relationship.

Of course, you can't expect to reach the level of commitment I've been talking about overnight. You get there through a gradual process of getting to know and learning to trust yourself and your man.

WHAT WORKS WITH MEN

To solve 95 percent of your relationship problems (and cope with the rest):

Never let a man you don't trust
get close to you.

You Can't Hurry Intimacy

Trust—the firm belief and confidence in the honesty, integrity, reliability and justice of another person or thing—is the cornerstone of any long-term, committed relationship. Without it, there *is* no relationship, only hopes and illusions that can be shattered in an instant. Never, ever marry or otherwise commit yourself to a long-term relationship with a man unless you trust him. If trust is not there, you are going to spend the rest of your life trying to control, change and compensate for the things you do not trust your man to do or be—and you'll destroy your relationship in the process.

To have a successful, satisfying, intimate relationship with a man you must have enough faith in yourself to be yourself in your relationship and feel confident about your ability to manage your relationship. And you must have a firm belief and confidence in your man's honesty, integrity and reliability *before* you get seriously involved with him. When you let a man you don't trust get close to you, you run the risk of having information you share used against you, having vulnerabilities you reveal exploited or being hurt in other ways. Even if a man does not actually do such things, if you don't trust him, you will waste enormous amounts of time and energy worrying that he will hurt you and interpreting his words or actions so that you become convinced that he has somehow betrayed you.

On the other hand, with trust as the cornerstone of your relationship, you'll be less inclined to protect yourself. You'll be more accepting, more forgiving and more willing to do what it takes to succeed. When you trust and have faith in your man and your relationship, you don't have to watch for and try to prevent things from going wrong. There is a margin for error. Mistakes can be made without sending you into a tailspin, causing you to question your entire relationship or inciting you to take drastic, usually controlling measures to prevent similar mistakes from being made in the future.

Trust is the foundation on which you build your relationship. It is the most important part of the structure and it is not easily or quickly established. You must *learn* to trust a man and you must give yourself time to do that. You are creating the framework for your artistic creation, your masterpiece, your relationship with a man, and you want that framework to be sturdy and stable enough to support you as you move through the remaining phases of developing intimacy. They are:

- CLOSENESS: a matter of familiarity, proximity and the sharing of thoughts and feelings that are close to the surface. Closeness is skin-to-skin intimacy, limited by the realities of the physical plane. It is most powerful when two people are together and less so when they are apart.
- LOVE: a deep and tender feeling of affection, attachment and devotion that transcends the physical plane. It is there whether or not you are with the person you love. It is possible only if you are absolutely certain of the other person's trustworthiness.
- EMPATHY: the ability to understand, be aware of, be sensi-

tive to and vicariously experience another person's feelings even though he has not explicitly communicated his thoughts, emotions or experiences to you. On a purely emotional level, you can be as one with another person, feeling and thinking *with* him.

- INTIMACY: a spiritual bond, a tie of great intensity with an intangible quality that breathes life into your relationship. When it exists between two people, they are able to exchange thoughts or feelings of a very private or personal nature and reveal the very essence of who they are.

Moving through those phases, experiencing and coming to trust those emotions takes as long as it takes. You cannot speed up the process or force any aspect of it without paying at a later date for the corners you cut early on. Although making a commitment to your relationship ultimately requires a leap of faith, if you leap too soon, if you meet a man, fall madly in love and marry just weeks or months later, you are taking a big risk. Loving a man and being in love with him are not reasons enough to marry him. The sort of passionate, romantic love that draws you to a man is a form of temporary insanity. You are too intoxicated to think clearly. In fact, making a commitment when you are in love is equivalent to deciding to invest your entire life savings in a business venture while you are falling down drunk.

Although marriages that start out that way have been known to last, they are much more difficult to manage because you don't know what you're getting into or what it will take to be successful. You have to learn as you go. It is much safer and more beneficial in the long run to make those discoveries when there is less at stake and to let your relationship gradually unfold through casual, serious casual and finally serious dating.

Casual Dating

Dating, as I define it, encompasses everything that leads up to actually committing yourself to be in and do what it takes to succeed in a long-term, intimate relationship with a man. As

I've mentioned more than once, most of the advice in this book applies only to that sort of relationship. It does not lead to success and can even work against you while you are dating, especially casually dating.

Casual dating involves spending time with a man you don't know well and doing things together for fun. It is a recreational activity and a preliminary screening process. It provides you with an opportunity to find out what you *don't* want in a lifetime mate. Make casual dating a project and don't expect anything from the men you casually date. In fact, expect to date a lot of losers.

You cannot give a man what he wants when he wants it while casually dating. You don't know him well enough to do that. You have not had enough time or contact with him to be able to trust him, and you'll get hurt. In addition, casual dating should not involve sex, unless sex is all you're after, and even then you're playing with fire. You are not only putting your physical health in jeopardy but your emotional well-being as well. A great deal of the sexual anxiety and sexual insecurity women feel and which often becomes a source of conflict in their long-term relationships can be traced back to having sex with men they didn't know well enough to trust. Believing that sex is a prelude to intimacy, many women feel hurt, betrayed or bitterly disappointed when that proves not to be the case. They feel used and devalued, as if they could have been any available body rather than a unique individual with needs and feelings. They wonder whether they would not have been hurt or dumped if they had been better sexual partners, and the general mistrust and sense of inadequacy that stem from such experiences remain with most women for years to come. In addition, many women's feelings and expectations change after they have sex with men they've been dating. Even if they did not want more from the man or the relationship beforehand, they often do afterward and frequently start to think and act as if that man has more potential to be a lifetime mate than he really has.

Serious Casual Dating

Casual dating becomes serious casual dating when you recognize that a man might actually fit your romantic vision of a relationship and decide that you want to get closer to him. You begin to conduct more in-depth research, figuring out what his terms, expectations and habits are and determining whether or not those largely unchangeable aspects of his personality are compatible with what you want or need from and are willing to give to a long-term relationship. Through serious casual dating you learn to trust a man. You also begin to show him that being in a long-term, committed relationship with you could be a rewarding proposition for him.

How do you do that? By offering him things he can't get anywhere else. That might be consolation when he's suffered a setback or defeat, encouragement to pursue his dreams or an appreciative audience for his corny jokes and blow-by-blow descriptions of victorious tennis matches or "brilliant" business strategies. You might reassure him when he is doubting himself; express loyalty, acceptance, admiration; show pleasure in having things done for you or anything else your man thrives on and cannot purchase, obtain by competing for it or find on any street corner. You get a mate by attracting him in that manner. The only reason a man will enter the alien, "enemy" territory of a long-term, committed relationship is if you offer him something he wants that he cannot get by himself in his territory.

Sex does not fit that description. Although you are certainly free to have sex with a man you trust at the serious casual dating stage, if you think that will help you "catch" him or keep you from losing him, you're fooling yourself. Men can obtain sexual gratification anywhere. They can get it all by themselves. Consequently, sex is not enough of an incentive to persuade a man to enter or stay in alien territory; and if you have sex with a man for that reason, you are setting yourself up to be hurt and disappointed. Again, that does not mean you should not have sex at all, but merely that you should not have sex for the purpose of attracting a mate. Besides, a good relationship will be more rewarding than sex—if you make it that way. Even insistent men who pressure you to have sex before you are ready will take "no" for an answer if you reward them in other ways.

Although you *do* want to attract your mate by offering him things he can't get elsewhere, you do *not* want to do so too quickly or in a cavalier manner. Where serious casual dating is concerned, it is important neither to expect nor to give too much too soon. You need time to establish trust and to learn what gratifies a man's ego, what deflates it and what you can expect him to do when his ego is threatened. In other words, you must get to know your man's ego, and you can't do that if you surrender what it wants too quickly. Show your man what you have to offer him a little bit at a time, and keep finding out what you need to know about him until you can say with few if any reservations that he is the man you want for your lifetime mate.

Serious Dating

Serious casual dating becomes serious dating when you are ready to make the leap and are merely ironing out certain details, such as sexual compatibility, financial matters, religious differences and other practicalities. Up to this point, you and a man—even a man who meets all of your criteria for a lifetime mate—were merely interacting. You were drawn together and then you drifted apart. You had wonderful interactions and felt as if you could be blissfully happy with that man for the rest of your life. Then you had a few horrible interactions and felt as if you'd be just as happy if you never saw or spoke to him again. Serious dating starts when that roller coaster ride ends. You have an intimate relationship, and all that is left for you to do is to remove any remaining obstacles to committing yourself to it.

Getting Married

In recent years, both men and women have come to view marriage as a mere formality. "I know that I'm committed to my relationship," they say. "I don't need a piece of paper to prove that." But marriage is much more than a piece of paper. It is a public affirmation of your commitment. In front of people who are important to you (friends, family and the community), you promise to honor your commitment for as long as you and your mate shall live. When you are truly committed to your relationship, you are willing to make that promise. You *want* the world to know that you are in a successful relationship, that you are serious about your relationship and plan to have it last a lifetime. You are ready to enter into a legally binding contract which will make it much more difficult and complicated to back out of your commitment because you are not looking for ways out anymore. You already know that you have made the right choice, that you trust that choice and won't be changing your mind. If you don't feel that way, don't get married. Don't waste your time living together either.

If you feel strongly enough about your relationship and trust your man enough to want to live with him, why not marry him? Because you want to test things out, to take a trial run and find out if a marriage would work? If you're testing your relationship that way, you're not committed to it. You're still keeping your options open. You're actually trying to find out if your relationship will *fail* so you can get out without losing as much as you would if you got married. And in all likelihood your trial marriage will fail—because you are not commited to it. If you were, you wouldn't need to test it, and living together would be pointless. Why bother unless some external circumstance—the lease on your apartment ending several months prior to your wedding date, for instance—makes living together practical? Either keep dating until you can fully commit yourself to your relationship or face the fact that you're in the wrong relationship and do both yourself and your man a favor by ending it.

Do *not* get married until you can walk down the aisle *without* thinking, "If this doesn't work out, I can always get divorced." You reach that point, that absolute certainty and faith in your man and your relationship, by going through the conscious selection process I described in the last chapter, by learning to trust and by allowing closeness, love, empathy and intimacy to develop naturally and gradually. Then:

1. You and your man should each make a list of things you want from each other, this relationship and your marriage.

2. Read each other's list. Without changing the list or conducting negotiations, ask yourself if you can honestly agree to fulfill the needs and expectations on his list. If you cannot, don't marry that man. But if you can agree to his terms and he is willing and able to fulfill the wants and wishes on your list, you can feel secure in the knowledge that you are in the right relationship with the right man.

3. Exchange lists and include them in your wedding vows. Then, do what it takes to live up to your vows. Take them seriously. Rely on them. Let them guide you and help you steer your relationship in the right direction. Remind yourself of your commitment whenever you are in doubt and you will be able comfortably to assume 100 percent of the responsibility for the success of your relationship and know just what you must do to manage it effectively.

If you follow the guidelines I've presented in the last four chapters, you'll solve 95 percent of the average, run-of-the-mill problems in your relationship before they snowball into major, ongoing conflicts with your mate. You will also have the right attitude and the right tools for getting yourself and your relationship out of trouble should more serious problems arise. In the next chapter, I discuss one of those "big" problem areas: sex.

TWELVE

Sex in a Serious, Long-term, Committed Relationship

Kate

The easiest way to derail and even destroy a potentially successful long-term, committed relationship with a man is through
sex. Just ask Kate, a thirty-one-year-old buyer for a national
department store chain, who has been married to Pat, a forty-
year-old real estate broker, for seven years. "Our sex life was
never anything to write home about," she said. "But it's become
progressively worse. We fight about sex more than we have it.
In fact, we hardly ever make love anymore, and when we do, I
don't really enjoy it. I know Pat knows that and I know it bothers
him, but he isn't willing to do anything about it." Kate knew
that because she had been trying to "get Pat to be a better lover"
for years.

"Even though he's almost ten years older than I am, I'm more
sexually experienced and definitely more comfortable with my
sexuality than Pat is," Kate claimed, and went on to explain how
she had been pretty "wild and adventurous" during her late
teens and early twenties while Pat, on the other hand, had

married his high school sweetheart—the only woman he'd ever slept with—and never cheated on her. "When his wife left him," Kate continued, "Pat was so depressed, he didn't even go out on a date for almost a year." According to Kate, once Pat did start dating, he had "mostly unpleasant experiences." Pat told her that the women he'd been involved with before her were so aggressive and seemed to expect so much from him sexually that he had never really felt comfortable with them.

Kate wanted Pat to be comfortable with her. "I knew in my heart that he was the right man for me," she said. "So I was willing to take things slow and easy. We were together for close to six months before we slept together." Even so, their first time "wasn't exactly an earthmoving experience," Kate recalled. "Pat was very sweet and gentle and I felt closer to him than ever, but I'd be lying if I said his insecurities and inexperience didn't show." Patiently Kate waited for Pat to "loosen up and relax" and as soon as he did, she began "sort of subtly showing him" what she liked. Pat usually did the things Kate showed him and their sex life did improve. "It still wasn't great," Kate admitted. "But I figured it would keep getting better." It never occurred to her to consider how she would feel about Pat and their relationship if it did not.

Once they were married, Kate felt freer to ask Pat for what she wanted sexually and to even "run the whole show" from time to time. Everything she read in women's magazines and heard on TV talk shows encouraged her to do that. "Experts were always saying women should be the aggressor sometimes, that men liked that and that they didn't want to always be in charge of what went on during sex." Kate was more than happy to take that advice. "Sex was always better for me when I initiated it and sort of directed how we did it. Pat just wasn't particularly daring or innovative in the bedroom." And he became less so over time. In fact, after several years of marriage, he seemed "completely unenthusiastic" about sex.

To compensate for Pat's lack of enthusiasm, Kate put herself in charge of keeping their sex life from "withering away to nothing" and tried to "inject some excitement" into their love-making in any way she could. Unfortunately, her efforts—which ran the gamut from renting erotic video tapes to reading

sex manuals and trying out the suggestions she found in them—created tension instead of excitement. And that tension began to spill over into other aspects of her relationship with Pat. "It's become so bad that there's hardly anything I can say to Pat without him snapping at me or accusing me of trying to order him around and run his life. He even picks fights for absolutely no good reason. Right out of the blue, he'll start harping on me about some ridiculous thing I said or did hours or even days earlier."

Pat usually started those skirmishes right before bedtime, dampening Kate's interest in lovemaking considerably. "Maybe that's what he wants to do," Kate said with a sigh. "I don't know. All I know is that our sex problems are ruining things between us. They're tearing us apart. They're tearing *me* apart because I want to be with Pat for the rest of my life, but I'm not sure I'm willing to go the rest of my life without a better sex life than the one we have."

"Bad" Sex Is a Big Problem — but It May Not Be the Real Problem

Kate's dilemma is hardly unique. Over the years I have heard hundreds of stories like hers. I have heard hundreds of women complain that the men in their lives make love too quickly or too slowly, too cautiously or too roughly, too little, too much or too early in the morning. I have listened to them tell me of their valiant efforts to remedy or cope with their own lack of interest or responsiveness or their mates' inhibited desire, overactive libido, impotence, clumsiness, bad timing, insufficient foreplay or refusal to engage in sexual behaviors they enjoy. I have seen the pained and puzzled expressions on their faces as they acknowledged that their sexual problems were causing so much conflict and tension between them and their mates that their relationships were coming apart at the seams. Dozens of formal and informal surveys of married and cohabiting couples back up their accounts. Research has repeatedly revealed that with the possible exception of money, sex is the most common cause of arguments and the most frequently mentioned source of dissatisfaction in intimate relationships.

That's why I decided to devote an entire chapter to helping you solve 95 percent of your sex problems—when sex *is* the problem. But I must point out that it usually isn't.

For countless couples today, the bedroom has become the stage on which they act out the deeper, more personal and more intangible problems in their relationship. Bad sex is what they blame for the demise of relationships that they did not have faith in and were not truly committed to or that may have been wrong for them in the first place. Their sexual problems are actually a symptom of more fundamental problems having to do with trust, intimacy, vulnerability, self-esteem or control.

Without a solid relationship built on a strong foundation of trust, sex almost always becomes just one more way to abuse, neglect or control your relationship—and if that is the case in your relationship, there's a good chance that you'll use the advice I'm about to give you to do more of the same. That won't help you. It may make matters worse. So please, as you read this chapter, bear in mind that I am not proposing solutions for trust problems or fears about intimacy or ongoing power struggles that are being played out in your bedroom. The information you find in this chapter may reveal problems of that nature which you were not aware of before, making it possible for you to use suggestions found elsewhere in this book to begin resolving them. However, the suggestions contained in the pages that follow only work on sexual problems.

Again, Men and Women Are Different

As in other areas of long-term, committed relationships, when it comes to sex in an intimate relationship, men and women are as different as night and day. That shouldn't surprise you. When I say that men and women view sex differently and experience sex differently, I'm not telling you anything you haven't heard before or learned through firsthand experience. However, to be successful and satisfied in the sexual aspects of your relationship, you must not only recognize that those differences exist, but also respect them, embrace them and take them into account when dealing with any sexual problems that occur in your relationship.

The most notable difference between men and women in the area of sexuality is found in the agendas they bring to lovemaking—the meanings they attribute to sex and the reasons they have sex. For women, sex has many different meanings. In their mind's eye, sex is a package deal that involves more than just sexual activity. They associate sex with romance, love, affection, tenderness, fidelity. They have sex for a zillion different reasons: to feel close to a man; to be cuddled, comforted or reassured; for physical pleasure and emotional nourishment; to prove that their relationship is working; to keep it exciting or to bolster their self-esteem by proving to themselves that they are still attractive and still have the power to seduce and excite their mate.

There is nothing wrong with attributing so many meanings to sex or having sex for a variety of reasons. That's just the way women are. However, it is vitally important for you to recognize that looking at sex the way you do means that when you are not getting enough romance, tenderness, cuddling, reassurance, emotional nourishment or anything else you want that really is not sexual in nature, you will be disappointed and dissatisfied with sex. And in order to fulfill the needs you bring to sex which have nothing to do with sex per se, you will try to improve your sex life. More often than not, you will do that by trying to change the way your man makes love to you. However, you are judging sex from a feminine perspective. And even though you have a right to do that and to a certain extent cannot help but do that, the fact that sex is not all you hoped it would be does not necessarily mean that your man is doing something wrong.

For men sex is sex. That's it. That's all. They have sex with a woman for only one reason—and it's not physical pleasure. Most women believe men have sex with them for the physical sensations lovemaking provides, but they don't. For that, they can do it better themselves. Men have sex with women for their egos—to score points and feel superior, separate, unique, pleased with themselves or like a real winner because they performed splendidly and were noticed and appreciated for their performance. Because being a good sex partner is good for their egos, men are highly motivated to perform well sexually. They want to do a good job and they are, in fact, good at their jobs. Although every man you meet won't have the sexual style you prefer, all men are *naturally* good sex partners.

Now, before you get all huffy and start thinking about the men you've slept with who were no good at all and tell yourself that I can't possibly know what I'm talking about, notice that I stressed the word "naturally." As they exist in nature, innately and when their inherent tendencies are not impeded or interfered with in any way, men cannot help but be good sex partners. They naturally know *how* to have sex. It is practically an instinct for them. If they were allowed to and encouraged to do what came naturally to them and rewarded for doing that, the only sexual problems they'd ever have would be those resulting from illness, medication side effects or other medical matters. But, as you no doubt know, that is not the case.

With the advent of the sexual revolution, the proliferation of expert opinions on how to have good sex and modern women's determination to assert themselves in the bedroom as well as the boardroom, men's natural tendencies *have* been impeded and interfered with. Their sexual performances have been analyzed and criticized to death. Their attempts to do what comes naturally have been frustrated at every turn, undermining their instincts and preventing them from doing a good job or wanting to. Having lost their enthusiasm for sex, they wind up in some sex therapist's office where they are informed that they have performance anxiety. But it isn't performance anxiety that prevents today's men from being the good sex partners they instinctively know how to be. It's a lack of appreciation.

An Unappreciated Performer Won't Perform for You

When it comes to making love to a woman, men want to do a good job—but not because they want to give you something special or feel closer to you or for any of the other reasons *you* have for making love. Men are motivated to be good sex partners because they want to show you how good they are and have you confirm that fact. They want to be noticed and appreciated and treated like conquering heroes. Being good in bed is one of the few opportunities modern men get to feel the way they did when they were hunters and warriors. Unfortunately, because of your sexual agenda, you may not make your man feel that way.

When you are not receiving something which your man does not naturally associate with sex, you start tinkering with his technique or asking him to change his style or suggesting things that he is not naturally inclined to do. Since men don't look at sex the way you do, your man won't understand what you're hoping to accomplish. All he'll know is that in one way or another, you are trying to tell him how to do his job and criticizing the job he's doing and preventing him from scoring points for his ego. He's having sex for his ego, but instead of rewarding his ego, you complain about his technique or hand him a sex manual or tell him what you think would make him a better lover, and then you wonder why you fight about sex and why he's not interested in having sex with you and why your sex life is getting worse instead of better.

When your man makes love to you, he's on stage. He's like a stage performer who loves to perform and knows his routine and comes out on stage every night to do that routine, expecting applause and favorable reviews. If a stage performer puts his heart into every routine, works hard, sweats, gives his audience everything he has to give and no one applauds, he doesn't feel good about his performance. And if night after night he does his routine and waits for applause that never comes or worse yet, performs for a roomful of critics who come backstage after every show to tell him what he did wrong and how he could improve his performance, he loses his enthusiasm for performing. He doesn't *want* to perform for an audience that doesn't appreciate his work.

Well, without applause, your man won't perform for you either. When you critique and analyze and try to control or correct the way your man makes love to you, having sex with you stops being fun or rewarding for him. He loses his motivation for doing a good job and your sex life suffers.

In a long-term, committed, intimate relationship, you can't tell a man *how* to make love to you. You can't even suggest new and unusual techniques for him to try. Whenever you try to decide or control *how* you and your mate have sex, you threaten his ego or prevent him from gratifying his ego. He won't give you what you want when you conduct yourself that way. In fact, as Pat did by starting arguments with Kate right before bedtime, your man will find a way to make you pay for your unapprecia- tive, critical or controlling behavior. I guarantee it.

Good Sex in an Intimate, Committed Relationship

Kate said that sex with Pat "had never been anything to write home about." Their lovemaking had never been as "wild and adventurous" as many of her earlier sexual experiences had been and she had never been as "turned on" by Pat as she had been by other, more confident and innovative lovers. But did that mean Pat was a lousy lover? Was having sex with him unpleasant, repulsive or completely unsatisfying?

"No, of course not," was Kate's reply. "Sex was always okay. It was sort of nice in a quiet, low-key way."

Okay then, had she ever actually disliked anything Pat did during sex, been disgusted by his lovemaking or felt it was abusive in any way? "No," Kate murmured. That had not been the case either. So why had she tried to change how he did it? Because their sex life was not as fun, energetic, exciting, or- gasmic or full of surprises as she expected it to be.

Now, Kate's expectations were not necessarily unreasonable. There was nothing really wrong with wanting what she wanted. However, given Pat's sexual style and preferences (which Kate knew about before she married him), it *was* unrealistic to expect him to transform himself into the daring, innovative sexual partner she thought she wanted. As Rita, the interior decorator I introduced in Chapter Eight, did when she tried to make Fred take her seriously even though he was not naturally inclined to take anything seriously, Kate was trying to control her sex life.

Paying little or no attention to what Pat wanted or expected, she was trying to have sex in an intimate relationship on *her* terms. And it didn't work.

Earlier in her relationship with Pat, Kate had a choice to make; to accept or not accept him as he was sexually. She could choose to marry him knowing that he had a "quiet, low-key" sexual style which could be enhanced but not altered dramatically. Or she could decide not to marry him because she was sure she couldn't be happy without a "daring and innovative" sex life. Instead, she married Pat expecting to change his sexual style and preferences once she had him where she wanted him. But that approach—which doesn't work in any other area of a long-term, committed relationship with a man—won't lead to a successful, satisfying sex life either.

Before you commit yourself to being in and doing what it takes to succeed in a long-term relationship, you must figure out what you want sexually and how important the sexual aspect of your relationship is to you. Clearly define what good sex means to you. Decide which criteria are absolutely essential and which you could sacrifice without feeling dissatisfied or cheated. Know all of that before you get seriously involved with a man. Look for a man whose sexual expectations and general approach to lovemaking are compatible with your own and you'll solve 95 percent of your sexual problems in advance.

No matter how many sex manuals you consult or experts you listen to, only you know when sex is good for you and when it isn't. So, don't let other people set your sexual standards for you. Don't compare your sex life to the latest statistics on the number of times per week the average couple has sex or the number of orgasms the average woman tells some research scientist she has. And try not to make a mistake that Kate made—thinking that good sex in a long-term, committed relationship is supposed to be the same as good casual sex.

Good casual sex is fun and exciting. Fun and excitement is what people who have casual sex are after, and all that fun and excitement is the product of lust, not love or intimacy. There is usually a powerful physical attraction between casual sex partners and little or no emotional attachment. In addition, what a woman can ask a man to do or tell him to do or show him how to do in a casual sexual situation is limited only by her imagination and her partner's willingness to experiment along with her. Most men are perfectly willing to experiment during casual sex. They'll tie you up or dress up or stand on their heads if you ask them to, just to show you that they can. They'll perform for you and take direction from you and when they get tired of doing that, they'll move on. You can demand anything you want from a casual sex partner. He doesn't care. If you start to demand too much, he'll just dump you and find a new, less demanding partner. Likewise, when you don't like what a casual sex partner does, you don't have to do it with him anymore. Your immediate needs and desires are the only things at stake and if they're not being fulfilled, there's no reason to have sex with that man any longer.

Very little of the above holds true in a long-term relationship with a man. Although sex can still be fun and exciting, in an intimate, committed relationship, lovemaking is equally and sometimes more satisfying when it leaves you feeling peaceful, fulfilled, pleased with and accepting of yourself and your mate. Good sex with your lifetime mate does not rely heavily on "chemistry," lust or physical attraction. In fact, it must go beyond physical attraction, because your physical attributes and the nature of your attraction to each other will change over the course of a lifetime. Because you are close to and emotionally attached to your mate, there is also much more on the line during lovemaking than there is during casual sex. You have more to gain if your sex life is satisfying and more to lose if it is not. There is more at stake than your immediate needs and desires. Making demands, giving instructions or "running the show" in your bedroom with little or no regard to your mate's preferences (or his ego), is as potentially damaging to your relationship over the long haul as it is to try to compel a man to spend more time with you, communicate the same way you do or take things seriously when it is not in his basic nature to do so.

The same principles that apply to other aspects of a long-term, committed relationship with a man also apply to sex in an intimate relationship. You can't always have exactly what you want whenever and however you decide you want it. But does that mean you never can get what you want sexually and that you have to put up with how your man makes love even when you don't like it? Absolutely not.

If You Like How He Does It, He's Doing It Right

Sex in an intimate relationship always occurs within the context of the relationship. It influences and is influenced by whatever is happening in other areas of your relationship. That is why I strongly recommend waiting as long as you can before having your first sexual encounter with a man you think has the potential to be your lifetime mate. Your relationship will never be the same; and if you have not yet come to trust that man, you increase your chances of being hurt by him. All too often, you will also be sleeping with him for the wrong reasons: to get him where you want him, to prevent him from leaving you, to prove you are attractive to him, to manipulate him into doing something for you or because you are afraid he'll lose interest in you if you don't. You're setting a dangerous precedent. Chances are that for the duration of your relationship, you'll continue to have sex or withhold it for those very same reasons and not only your sex life, but your entire relationship will suffer.

There *is* one positive reason to have sex with a man before marriage: to find out if you like how he does it. If you don't— if having sex with him turns you off, if he abuses you or expects you to engage in activities you find offensive or repulsive—don't pursue the relationship any further. Things are only going to get worse. Sex is going to become a source of stress and conflict that will eventually destroy your relationship anyway, so don't allow a long-term, committed relationship to develop unless a man can give you what you are sure you must have and you can give him what he wants without violating your own standards.

If you don't believe in having sex before marriage under any circumstances, you are going to have to be very intuitive about choosing your lifetime mate. Take extra time to learn to really trust him and to appreciate his positive qualities. And realize that if you love that man and are committed to your relationship and he winds up having a sexual style you don't like, you're going to have to live with it and not allow it to drive a wedge between you. Fortunately, a man's attitude about life generally reveals his attitude about sex, and his attitude about sex is a pretty accurate clue to his lovemaking style. Consequently, you don't really *have* to have sex before marriage to figure out what you need to know.

Remembering that good sex in a long-term, intimate relationship means feeling pleased, fulfilled, peaceful and accepting and not necessarily experiencing a multi-orgasmic, mind-blowing roller coaster ride each and every time you have sex, if you do have sex before marriage and if you do like the way your man does it, then he's doing it right. Never allow yourself to think or say he isn't. If, at some point later in your relationship, you find that you are not enjoying sex, assume that something other than your man's style or technique is getting in your way, find out what that obstacle is and get it out of your way.

How to Solve 95 Percent of Your Sexual Problems — When Sex Is the Problem

In a long-term, committed relationship, all sex problems that are *not* medical in nature, the result of basic sexual incompatibility or symptoms of trouble in other areas of your relationship fall into two categories: conflicts over *how* to have sex and conflicts over *when* to have sex. You can solve both problems through a simple division of labor. You decide when. He decides how.

That premise will no doubt set off the usual alarms and stir up the usual protests, but if you give the idea some serious thought, you'll see that it makes perfect sense. First of all, there's no way for you to control how men make love without provoking their egos and creating the sort of power struggles that destroy potentially successful intimate relationships. Putting yourself in charge of *how* can only get you into trouble. What's more, men understand how to have sex. They want to perform for you and show you how good they are. Since they are interested in doing a good job, why not give them the job they want and let them be in charge of how they do it? If you do that and reward them for doing their jobs, they'll work hard to make you happy.

Secondly, the vast majority of needs that sex satisfies for you, as a woman, are a matter of *when*. You become interested in sex when you feel romantic or affectionate or playful. You are ready for lovemaking when you need comfort or cuddling or reassurance. And when you're not ready—when you feel pressured, irritable, exhausted or unattractive—no matter how good your man is, sex isn't good. You simply are not going to like how your man does it or enjoy lovemaking unless you're physically and psychologically, emotionally and spiritually ready to have sex—and that is why deciding when should be your job.

To do your job, you need a set of nonverbal signals that will let your man know when you are interested in lovemaking. Those signals include "when conduct"—leaving a trail of clothing from the front door to your bedroom, dimming the lights and playing soft music, seductive touches, sensual movements and so on. You might want to put together a "when wardrobe"—lingerie, leather and lace, even elaborate fantasy costumes that are a turn-on for your man and make you feel sexy as well. Use your "when conduct," wear your "when wardrobe" and your man will get your message and respond to it. If he doesn't, you'll know that there's a nonsexual problem getting in your way.

For instance, Kate couldn't rush home from the Sterling Women's Weekend she attended, send out a few signals and expect Pat to come running. After years of having his sexual performance controlled, criticized and corrected, he would assume that there was more ego-bashing in store for him; and he wouldn't take Kate's bait, no matter how enticing it might be. Before she could employ the system I'm recommending, Kate had to back off for a while and do some relationship repair, building up Pat's battered ego and showing him that he could trust her again.

Similarly, a woman who is actually interested in getting her own way, controlling a man or punishing him for some earlier transgression will haul out her "when wardrobe" and "when conduct" at inopportune moments. She sends her signals when her man is absorbed in some task, frantically trying to finish work he brought home from the office, obviously exhausted or clearly conveying that he wants to be left alone. Under those circumstances, he won't respond; and, even though she knew her timing was off, she'll feel resentful, hurt or angry and justified in starting a fight.

Without trust, closeness, empathy or other elements of an intimate relationship in place and working effectively, the system I'm describing will become abusive, controlling and self-serving. Don't even try it. You'll get hurt.

Once your man receives your signal and responds favorably to it, he's in charge. He decides how to make love to you. You don't try to control what he does. You don't criticize, correct, make "little" suggestions or evaluate his performance after the fact, telling him how sex could have been better if he had done this, that or the other thing. You *can* influence him during sex, however—by showing him that it is worth his while to do what you like.

Learn to moan. He'll sacrifice his agenda if you moan. Moaning and any other nonverbal means of expressing pleasure have the same effect on your man that applause has on a stage performer. When he intentionally or inadvertently does something you like or anything even close to what you like, moan. He'll know you appreciate what he's done and he'll do it again or he'll do more of it—because he knows more applause will be forthcoming.

Sex is a dance of give and take which cannot begin or be successful until you decide who will lead and who will follow. Once you have agreed upon that, there is no limit to the beauty, grace, spontaneity and creativity of your dance. Prior to love-making, you lead. During lovemaking, he does; and your primary responsibility is to follow his lead, enjoy his performance and let him know that you enjoy it. Moan, moan, moan!

If you can't do that, if you still don't like how he does it, then you weren't really ready. You only sent out your "when" signals because you felt obligated to, because you were afraid your man would get bored with or reject you if you didn't have sex with him soon or because you wanted to prove that this system wouldn't work—that sex would be lousy even if you decided

when to have it. You have to figure out why you did that and what unresolved issue prompted you to do it so that you can get that obstacle out of your way.

If you follow the advice found in this chapter and your sex life does not improve, if you try the when/how system I've suggested and it's not fun, then you'll know that the problem isn't sex. It's trust, love, intimacy, control or some other "glitch" in the system you are using to manage your ongoing relationship. You need to look for solutions to that problem—and not just to improve your sex life. As I'll explain in the next chapter, continuing conscientiously to care for and nurture your relationship is absolutely essential for its success and survival.

THIRTEEN

Raising a Healthy Relationship: Because You Never *Really* Get Divorced

Valerie

After sixteen years of marriage Valerie, a thirty-eight-year-old emergency room nurse, and her husband Richie, a thirty-nine-year-old building contractor, had separated. "Our relationship just wasn't working anymore," Valerie stated matter-of-factly. She was convinced that it had been "dying a slow death" ever since she stopped being "helpless little Valerie who always did as she was told and didn't have a mind of her own."

According to Valerie, "For the first ten years we were married, I worshipped the ground Richie walked on. Anything he said, I agreed with. Anything he wanted, I gave him. As far as I was concerned, he could do no wrong." In retrospect, Valerie saw herself as a "real doormat." Yet, she acknowledged that Richie hadn't treated her like one. He never took advantage of her adoration and willingness to defer to him, Valerie claimed. "He was very good to me and, to tell you the truth, I was pretty happy back then. I liked taking care of him and our kids and

our home and being this earth mother type woman who baked bread and had half the neighborhood kids in my yard after school every day." But somewhere along the line, Valerie began to question that arrangement.

"I was completely dependent on Richie financially and emotionally, and that didn't seem right," she said. "It didn't seem healthy to put him on a pedestal the way I did and let him make all my decisions for me. What if something happened to him? What would I do? Would I be able to manage without him?" Needing to know that she could survive on her own, Valerie, with Richie's support and encouragement, took a nursing refresher course and went back to work part-time.

Their troubles started soon afterward, Valerie recalled. "I was feeling more confident and competent in general and more capable of handling things that I'd always left up to Richie," she explained. One of those "things" was money. "Since I was contributing to our family finances, I thought I was entitled to more of a say about how we spent our money," Valerie said. "But Richie and I never did see eye to eye on that subject." He wanted to put Valerie's earnings into a savings account earmarked for emergencies and future expenses, while Valerie thought she and their children deserved a few of the "little luxuries" that Richie had always insisted they couldn't afford on his salary alone. "We've probably had that same basic disagreement a thousand times over the past five years," Valerie said. And that conflict led to countless others. "I just wasn't the same passive, dependent, obedient Valerie anymore, and Richie couldn't handle that. I didn't need him to make all the decisions anymore, and he couldn't accept that. There were things I wanted to do or needed to do that weren't necessarily the things he wanted me to do and he definitely didn't like that." In fact, he seemed determined *not* to adjust to or accept the "new" Valerie and their once peaceful, productive relationship turned into a war zone.

"Richie and I constantly sniped at each other," Valerie continued. "Instead of really duking it out and having loud, vicious arguments, we made each other miserable in small doses. I'd complain about something he did. He'd criticize something I did. I'd get sarcastic. He'd put me down in front of the kids or our friends. I'd do something I knew he hated. He'd sulk. It could go on like that for days." And with the exception of occasional cease-fires, it went on like that for years.

Whenever Valerie couldn't take anymore "sniping," she would turn to Richie and say, "Look, this isn't working. I'm unhappy. You're unhappy. Maybe we can't make each other happy anymore. Maybe we don't belong together anymore." Richie would invariably agree. "Maybe you're right. Maybe it *is* over between us," he'd mutter. But for one reason or another, he never got around to leaving and Valerie never got around to insisting that he go—until the day, eight months prior to the Sterling Women's Weekend Valerie attended, when Richie responded to one of Valerie's all-too-familiar declarations of unhappiness by saying, "Okay, I'll move out."

A week later he had his own place and the couple's lawyer was drawing up a separation agreement. "It was all very reasonable," Valerie said. "Richie is a very *reasonable* man."

I couldn't help but notice that she made it sound as if being reasonable was equivalent to having leprosy. "Well, *that's* the problem," Valerie groaned. "Richie's *too* logical and sensible and reasonable. He isn't passionate. He isn't spontaneous. He's always level-headed and practical and, yes, that *is* what I wanted when I married him. But I got fed up with only doing what made sense to *him*. He wouldn't try anything new unless you gave him at least ten rational reasons for trying it, and I was sick and tired of having to come up with logical, airtight arguments for everything I wanted to do. I was bored with the same old routines: dinner on the table at 6:30 sharp, the same meal on the same day every week; sex on Wednesday and Saturday like clockwork; brunch at the same restaurant after church every Sunday. You could set your watch by Richie. That's how predictable he is. He could be happy repeating the same exact patterns for the rest of his life. But I couldn't. I was dying inside. I was shriveling up and dying. I needed some variety, some excitement, *something* in our life together that was a little frivolous and fun and different."

Valerie also wanted to be more than an extension of her husband. "I wanted to stand on my own two feet, make my own decisions, be a person in my own right," she explained. And she got a chance to do that once Richie moved out. "I had to," she continued. "For our kids' sake. They were upset and confused about the separation so I couldn't exactly mope around the house. I got my act together. I handled whatever little problems or crises came up. I learned that I *could* be strong and decisive and independent."

But did she really have to break up a sixteen-year marriage to learn that? I asked. Did it make sense to throw away an entire relationship because she was bored with certain routines, because she was restless and determined to prove she could make her own decisions?

"I thought so at the time," Valerie replied. But after eight months on her own, she was not so sure. "I keep telling people that Richie and I had irreconcilable differences, but more and more lately, I've been thinking that we didn't really try to resolve those differences. We just gave up."

Is Quitting the Answer?

"I'd be lying if I told you I'm any happier now than I was before we separated," Valerie continued. "Going it alone is tough. And it's lonely. Finding someone else was never an issue for me; but if we do get divorced, I guess I'll end up doing that, and the prospect doesn't appeal to me one bit."

Richie seemed to be having second thoughts as well, Valerie reported. "He's been calling a lot and when he drops off the kids after a visit, he finds excuses to hang around and talk. Or he'll spot something that needs to be fixed and stop by on Saturday with his tool kit. I'm pretty sure he'd agree to try again if I suggested it, but I just don't know if I should. The kids would be thrilled. But would I be happy? Would Richie expect things to be the way they used to be before I became more confident and assertive? I know I don't want that. But I don't want anyone else or to go it alone for the rest of my life either. It's all so confusing. It's a difficult decision to make and I'm really agonizing over it right now."

Good, I said. I was glad to hear it, I told her. Discarding a sixteen-year marriage, especially when children were involved, was something she *should* agonize over. She should examine it

from every angle, question her motives, try to figure out where
and why things went wrong. She should think about the long-
term repercussions of making her trial separation permanent
and seriously consider every other option available to her because getting divorced, pulling the plug on a long-term, committed relationship, is a drastic measure. It is a measure of last
resort. If she was going to take it, she had better make sure she
did so for the right reasons and *not* because she thought getting
out of her marriage would make her happy or end her unhappiness. It wouldn't.

Happiness, inner peace, the strength to stand on your own
two feet and a zillion other things you may think your man
prevents you from having can be found *without* dissolving a five-
or ten- or twenty-year marriage. Why mess up or give up on a
pretty good relationship, a relationship that still has the potential to be successful, productive and fulfilling, because you are
stuck? If you want to be happy, get happy. Look for peace
within yourself. Go out and be assertive where it will do you
and others some good. Learn how to be strong and independent
and married. With few exceptions, you are more likely to find
happiness by tending to and staying in the long-term, committed relationship you have than by getting rid of it and trying to
start over with someone new.

You Never Really Get Divorced

Divorce is a legal maneuver that gets you out of an uncomfortable situation. It eliminates the stress and inconvenience of being in a relationship that isn't working out as you hoped it
would. Divorce frees you and your spouse from your obligation
to one another, making your marriage contract null and void.
Legally speaking, you are no longer joined together. However,
a legal maneuver doesn't actually undo your marriage. It does
not sever the powerful emotional and spiritual bond that
prompted you to get married in the first place. That intense
connection almost always remains long after the divorce papers
are signed.

By getting divorced, you correct the error you made when

you selected your lifetime mate. But you do not really get rid of him. His ghost, his memory, bits of not quite finished business from your marriage reappear at inopportune moments to disrupt and influence and interfere with any new relationships you develop. Sometimes you feel as if scenes from your first marriage are being replayed word for word in your second. Or you may be so worried about repeating your past mistakes and getting hurt again that you can't really allow yourself to trust the new man in your life. You don't let your guard down when you are with him. You compare him to your ex-husband. You overreact to certain situations. You hold something back, and that is often the very thing you need to give freely for your new relationship to succeed.

Your new mate has an invisible relative to contend with—a husband-in-law—and if you get seriously involved with a man who has been married before, you inherit a wife-in-law who pays frequent, unexpected and unwelcome "visits." You're in the kitchen or in the bathroom applying your makeup or in bed with her ex-husband and there she is, taunting you with reminders of all the ways she was better than you. She lurks around every corner, warning you to watch your step, making sure you never forget that you could end up being your mate's ex-wife too. Whether they are yours or his, those "ex"-in-laws and your emotional and spiritual ties to them make second marriages crowded, perilous and even more likely to end in divorce than first marriages.

Divorce almost always creates more problems than it solves, especially when there are children involved. To young children in particular, the trauma of divorce is second only to having a parent die. They don't understand divorce. They blame themselves for it. They feel as if they are betraying one parent by loving the other, yet they can't stop loving either one without feeling riddled with guilt. They are plagued by their divided loyalties even when the split is relatively amicable. And they are tortured by them when they are placed in the middle of bitter divorces and brutal custody battles. Thanks to the ease with which divorces are granted and our nonchalant attitude toward them, we are raising a whole generation of quitters. When faced with a problem, the first solution children of divorce consider is quitting. In every area of their lives, they would rather give up than weather a storm. And as you might expect, they have little faith in their ability to have lasting, intimate relationships. Children of divorce have a 70 percent chance of getting divorced themselves. Clearly, the effect of divorce—which may very well be today's most prevalent form of child abuse—can last a lifetime.

Yeah, but . . .

Am I telling you these things because I support the notion of staying in even a loveless, volatile, destructive marriage for your children's sake? Am I saying that you shouldn't get divorced under any circumstances? Of course not. Every situation is different. Some of the "diseases" that debilitate relationships can be cured. Others cannot. Some dying marriages can be resuscitated. Others are damaged beyond repair. Divorce can be a viable, even life-saving option when staying married endangers your health or welfare, when your husband abuses you or repeatedly betrays your trust or when he is so hopelessly addicted to drugs, alcohol or gambling that he can't meet his family's needs. I am *not* suggesting that you sacrifice your sanity or survival to save your relationship. However, because of the problems it leaves in its wake, I want you to think of divorce not as an easy out but as a last resort. And if you take care of your relationship properly, you may never have to use it.

The Care and Feeding of Long-term, Committed Relationships

Over the years I've met an astounding number of women who claim that the demise of their relationships took them by surprise. Suddenly, with "absolutely no warning," after five, ten, even twenty-five years of marriage, their husbands informed them that the marriage was over, that they had found someone else, didn't love them anymore or just didn't want to be married.

"I didn't know what hit me," those stunned women say. "I had no idea he was unhappy," they swear. And that never ceases to amaze me. How can a woman live with a man for that many years without knowing when he is unhappy—unless she isn't paying attention to her relationship or nurturing it along at all?

A serious, intimate relationship is a living thing. It has substance and power. It grows and develops over time. It's like a child, and managing your relationship is like raising a child. You have to nurture it, protect it from harm, gently guide it down a positive path. You have to tend to your relationship as you would tend to a growing child, with an eye on its future as well as close attention to whatever is happening in the present. You have to think about what's best for your relationship in the long run and what you can give to it now that will help it be alive and well ten or twenty years from now.

For better or worse, in sickness and in health—the future of your relationship is in your hands. For the most part, men don't want to leave their long-term, committed relationships. They don't like to welch on a deal and they don't want to change. They're used to you and comfortable with you. They've made an investment in your relationship and they would rather stick with it and see it pay off than cash in their chips and invest in a new relationship. If they had their choice, they wouldn't start over with someone new.

Knowing that, when you realize that your relationship is ailing and in danger of dying, *you* have to decide whether you are going to pull the plug and let it die or allow it to stay alive and nurse it back to health. Unless your relationship is already dead and your man has walked out with absolutely no intention of returning, *you* hold the future of your relationship in your hands. *You* can kill it or you can save it. And you *cannot* under any circumstances expect your mate to save it for you.

You can't think, "If he wants this relationship, he has to work for it. It's his turn to make it work." You can't say, "I've done enough. It's up to him now because I'm not going to take all the responsibility anymore." If you feel that way, you might as well forget about saving your relationship. Go find a good divorce lawyer. Get a fair settlement because your relationship is as good as dead. If your relationship is in trouble, you can't turn it over to someone who doesn't know the first thing about managing a healthy relationship much less saving a troubled one. That's like handing a scalpel to a gorilla and saying, "Here, you perform this delicate, life-or-death operation. I'm tired of operating. I don't want to be responsible for this patient any-more. You handle it." Well, you might as well call the morgue. Your man can't save your relationship. He doesn't know how. It isn't his job. He isn't equipped to do it. You are. Anything he does will only cause more problems.

You have to roll up your sleeves and get in there and do your job. Manage your relationship. Nurse it back to health. Get it back on track. If you don't want to do that, if you don't want to be bothered, then don't expect your relationship to improve. It's going to die and when it does you're going to say, "I tried. I hung in there as long as I could." Well, hanging in isn't re-building or repairing or managing your relationship. It's just better than being alone and easier than starting over with some-one new. Hanging in is what you do when you've already de-cided not to save your relationship. You're just killing time while you wait for your relationship to die or prepare yourself to ask (or be asked) for a divorce.

Remember that you are 100 percent responsible for the success of your relationship and 95 percent of your relationship problems can be traced to the way you've been handling that responsibility. Frequently, you'll discover that you really haven't been manag-ing your relationship at all. You've been sitting back and letting it run itself, only springing into action when a crisis occurs. You put the ship on autopilot until a storm hits and then you grab the wheel and fight to keep it from capsizing. When you manage your relationship that way, when you limit your responsibility to taking care of emergencies and bandaging flesh wounds without looking for internal injuries or concerning yourself with the general health of your relationship, that relationship won't stay healthy. There will be more and more emergencies and you'll end up running yourself ragged trying to keep up with them.

Instead, keep your finger on the pulse of your relationship and try to be aware of your mate's moods, his needs and his emotional state. Although you don't have to watch him like a hawk or cater to his every whim, you do have to pay enough attention to him and to your relationship to know when he is unhappy and to recognize when your relationship is starting to get off track. Then you can make minor adjustments in the way you are managing your relationship. You can get it back on course before minor trouble mushrooms into a major problem. If you let things go and especially if you wait for your mate to tell you in words that he is unhappy, it may be too late to save your relationship.

Remember that relationship is a discipline. To be successful in a long-term, committed relationship with a man, honor the discipline, make the necessary sacrifices and do what it takes to succeed—even when you don't feel like it. And as you no doubt know, there will be plenty of times when you won't feel like it. You'll get tired of managing and tending to your relationship. You'll have a bad day or hear about some wonderful thing a friend's husband did for her or read about relationships that seem ten times more exciting than yours, and you'll try to improvise, to fiddle around with a pretty good relationship because some outside source of information has convinced you it should be better. Or something inside you will shift and you'll stir up trouble in your relationship because you feel antsy or stifled or unhappy or bored. Don't do it. To raise a healthy relationship, you have to do what works and what needs to be done—and not just what you want to do whenever and however you want to do it.

Have a vision and a plan for success. Look ahead, look at the big picture and don't try to hold your relationship together based on your immediate needs and feelings. If you do that, you'll get lost. Your needs change periodically and your feelings, which are merely responses to whatever is happening at a given moment, change constantly. If you follow them, you'll change course at the drop of a hat. You'll never get where you want to go.

Trust your feelings and figure out what they are trying to tell you about yourself or your situation. But do not rely on them to manage your relationship. The only feelings that can help you do that are the ones you had when you selected your lifetime mate and walked down the aisle with him and exchanged wedding vows. When the going gets rough, remember why you married that man and put your faith in the feelings you had when you committed yourself to your relationship. Let your original commitment be your guide—no matter how you or your circumstances may change.

Realize that you'll expect your man to change and he'll expect you to stay the same. Those expectations have led to the demise of many a potentially successful, productive and fulfilling, long-term, committed relationship—including Valerie and Richie's.

After a decade of deferring to her husband, Valerie went out into the world and proved that she was capable of earning a living, garnering the respect of her colleagues and making life-or-death decisions. Her success outside her marriage changed her, and those changes felt good. "I loved my work and the people I worked with and just knowing I was doing something worthwhile and getting paid for it," she said. And her ego loved it when she asserted herself and stood up for herself and expressed her opinions. Naturally, her ego wanted more of those rewards and Valerie began to look for them in her relationship. She began to change the way she related to Richie and expected him to accept that, to change with her.

However, for more than a decade Richie had been the decision-maker, the provider, the "head honcho" in his household and the center of Valerie's universe. *His* ego had been lavishly rewarded for that. But when Valerie changed, he lost his familiar, reliable source of ego-gratification. The things he had always done to please Valerie no longer satisfied her. She tried to take over his tasks. She complained. She did things she knew he hated to get back at him for being who he was. Although she did not realize it or intend to, Valerie had changed in ways that made being in a relationship with her unrewarding for Richie; and, as a result, instead of changing with her, he tried to get her to change back into the same woman she had been when he married her.

Men will do that. That's the way men are. Men are elegantly simple and unless there's a reward to be received, unless they can clearly see that changing themselves or their circumstances is worth their while, they prefer to stay the same. Women, on the other hand, are intricately complex. They are constantly evolving, changing and adding new dimensions to their multi-layered, multifaceted personalities. That is one of the inherent differences between the sexes, and it will cause problems in your relationship unless you use what you know about men in general and your man in particular to make sure your relationship survives your natural tendency to re-create yourself.

If, during the course of your relationship, you have changed and are now struggling to change your mate, give up the idea of *compelling* him to change. Stop pushing, prodding, threatening and backing him into corners. It won't work. Instead, learn to accept him again. Reacquaint yourself with the needs he married you to fulfill and the rewards he has stayed with you to obtain. Then give him what he wants when he wants it. Instead of taking away his rewards because they aren't compatible with the new you, find ways to reward him that *do* fit the person you've become. As long as you tend to your relationship (and your man's ego) and make sure that your changes don't cost him more than he's willing or able to pay, you can change in any way you want. As long as you care for and nourish your relationship, you can be whoever you want to be and still have a successful, productive, intimate relationship with your man.

First, foremost and above all else, there must be trust. You keep a long-term, committed relationship vital and alive by letting go, by accepting your man as he is and resisting the urge to control him or the direction your relationship is heading. If you want your relationship to succeed and to last, you can't control it, pushing and shoving it to meet your needs and fulfill your expectations. You have to trust it, allowing yourself to be guided by your firm belief and confidence in the honesty, integrity, reliability and justice of your mate, your relationship and your own instincts.

- Don't turn off your trust valve and replace it with a bookkeeping system—comparing what your mate does for you with what you do for him, maintaining a mental record of his transgressions, building a case against him and then confronting him with the evidence you've gathered.
- Don't keep your guard up and look for signs that your man might hurt or reject you and when you spot them, withdraw or strike first in hopes of minimizing the pain.
- Don't repeatedly question the decision you made when you selected your lifetime mate and wonder if you did the right thing by marrying him.

- Don't allow isolated incidents or your mate's occasional unexpected and unwelcome actions to stir up skepticism about
your entire relationship, seeming to negate all of the positive
aspects of your relationship and convincing you that its potential for success is limited at best.

If you do any of those things, then you have a trust problem
and it is apt to be creating problems in your relationship. You
may not trust yourself or accept yourself or believe that you are
capable of making healthy, positive choices for yourself. Your
self-doubt makes anything your man says or does feel like criticism, rejection, character assassination or a threat to your self-
esteem. To salvage your relationship, you may have to go back
to basics, discover the woman you really are and learn to listen
to and have faith in your natural self.

Until you do that, you'll be easily frightened, hurt or offended
and whenever you feel that way, you'll run for cover or try to
protect yourself by controlling your man and testing his love or
loyalty. You'll want your mate to prove that he is trustworthy,
but no amount of proof will ever be enough to satisfy you. As
soon as that man says or does something that can in any way be
construed as hurtful, you feel betrayed and you stop trusting
him. "He lied to me," you say. "He knew how I felt and he did
thus and such anyway. He didn't care enough about me to do
this or that or the other thing. So I can't trust him. He's going
to have to earn back my trust. He's going to have to show me
that he deserves to be trusted. I'm going to put him to the test
and keep my eye on him until I know beyond a shadow of a
doubt that he'll never hurt me again." But you'll never know
that. There's nothing a man can do to conclusively prove that to
you. Trust isn't based on cold, hard facts and tangible evidence
alone.

Certainly if your man betrays your trust over and over
again—if he regularly conceals the truth from you, repeatedly
cheats on you, consistently inflicts physical or emotional pain—
then you would be foolish to trust him and you probably
shouldn't be married to him. However, if your man doesn't do
such things and if he is generally honest, just and reliable, then
put your faith in him. Believe in him. Trust him—even when
it doesn't seem like he deserves it and even when it looks like

he's about to screw up in some way. You just can't expect your relationship to succeed if, year after year, you tell your man you trust him and then when he needs you to, you don't.

Realize that your mate is going to mess up now and then. He'll make mistakes. He'll do or say something that is truly unacceptable to you and you'll feel hurt, betrayed, frightened. Deal with those feelings. Talk them over with someone. Get them out of your system. But don't let them control you and prompt you to lose faith in your man or look for additional reasons not to trust him. If he's been paying his premiums for years, don't cancel his insurance policy because of conduct that is not typical for him. He isn't going to stick around if you do that. He isn't going to stay with you if he thinks you'll stop trusting him and renege on your commitment every time he makes a mistake. One of the most important qualities a man looks for in a woman is loyalty. If you're loyal to him, he'll be loyal to you.

Crisis Management

Like Valerie, many of the women who attend Sterling Women's Weekends are already involved in long-term, committed relationships—but not successful, productive or fulfilling ones. "I'm here to save my marriage," they say. "I need to know if my marriage *can* be saved," they explain. "My relationship isn't working right now but I think maybe it could," they comment. "I've made mistakes in the past," they admit. "But I'd like to try again."

Okay, that's a start, I tell them. Then I ask them what they plan to do to get their relationships back on track. "Well, I don't really know," they reply—and that's why they're in trouble. No one's in charge. No one's steering the ship.

In a relationship, men don't initiate the action—they respond to it. They don't manage your relationship. They follow the management policies you make—or they rebel against them. If your relationship is in trouble, *you* have to find out what the problem is and look for solutions to that problem. And *you* have to take charge. You have to know where you want your relationship to go and come up with an emergency management system that will get you there.

You can't "freak out" and fall to pieces when you realize your relationship is in trouble. If you do, who's going to manage the relationship? You can't afford the luxury of going into therapy to work on yourself and understand yourself and take care of yourself. Although there is nothing wrong with that in general, the time to seek self-awareness and personal fulfillment and insight into the tendencies you developed during childhood is not when your relationship is crumbling around you. Learning to assert yourself or "heal your inner child" or resolve the conflicts left over from your Oedipal stage won't save your relationship. In fact, if your primary concern is taking care of yourself when your marriage is dying, then you aren't really interested in saving your relationship. You're interested in saving yourself. You want to be prepared to deal with things when your relationship dies. And it will—unless you make it your top priority for as long as it takes to get it back on track. If you feel a need to work on yourself, by all means do so—*after* you do some damage control.

To save the life of your relationship:

- examine it and find out what went wrong, when that happened and why;
- figure out what's needed;
- plan a strategy for getting your relationship back on track and put that plan into action.

Use the advice I've been giving you throughout this book to come up with an effective crisis management plan. Make sure you want the relationship and don't just want to hang onto your man or get him back after he's left you. There's a big difference. Clarify your vision of a successful relationship and figure out if you can have that sort of relationship with your man. If you can't or if you aren't willing to do what it takes to succeed over the long haul, don't waste his time—or yours.

But if you *are* prepared to do what works and are committed to rebuilding your relationship, take steps to attract your man again. Do the sorts of things you did during serious casual dating. Slowly, a little bit at a time, *show* him what a good deal you can be. Offer him the rewards he got involved with you to obtain. Figure out what he wants and give it to him—when he wants it, how he wants it. That will get your relationship back on track—and keep it there.

Take a fearless look at what you have been doing to drive your man away or threaten his ego or stir up conflict in your relationship. Then stop doing those things. Make a commitment to change the way you've been relating to your man. It's not enough to say, "I'm sorry. I won't do that anymore," because it wasn't just your actions that precipitated the problems in your relationship. You need to know what prompted you to act the way you did. Were you catering to your ego or expecting your man to think and act like a woman? Did you want to prove a point or protect yourself from some catastrophe you'd conjured up in your own mind? You need to know what was happening and why it was happening. You need to accept the fact that similar circumstances will arise again and that you have a natural tendency to react to such circumstances in a certain way. Armed with that awareness, you can work around those tendencies instead of letting them get in your way.

If you're unhappy, stop assuming that being in your relationship is making you unhappy or that your man is stopping you from doing the things that would make you happy. "He won't let me" is the excuse many women use to avoid taking risks. It gives them an easy out and a rationale for not taking responsibility for their own unhappiness. Test out your theory before you jump to the conclusion that you'll never be strong, independent or at peace with yourself in your relationship. Take steps to do what you've been saying you want to do. Just make sure that what you do doesn't cost your man too much. Don't withdraw your affection or set up a competition or demand things from your man that you know he can't or won't deliver. You may not get everything you want, but you'll be somewhat independent and relatively happy in a successful, productive and fulfilling relationship instead of tough and self-sufficient but unhappy and alone.

Finally and perhaps most important, discontinue the practice of making your man miserable and setting yourself up for disappointment by expecting him to fulfill needs that he is constitutionally incapable of fulfilling. Once your relationship is moving in a positive direction again, look elsewhere for the things your man can't supply without selling himself out and sacrificing his self-respect. Reserve competition for competitive arenas. And for the sort of deeply felt, emotionally expressive communication you crave, turn to other women. As I will explain in the next and final chapter of this book, strong, supportive relationships with women are a crucial part of the equation for doing what works with men.

FOURTEEN

Staying on Track: With a Little Help from Your Friends

Renee

According to thirty-six-year-old Renee, an organizational consultant and newlywed, she and her three closest friends are "about as different as four women can be." She is the "driven, ambitious, overachieving" one, Renee explained. "I'm always flying off someplace on business and dispensing long-distance advice over the phone from my hotel room." Carol, an X-ray technician who is single, is the "cute, entertaining" one. "We call her the camp counselor because she organizes the things we do together." Married and a children's book illustrator, Lyn is "the princess. She comes from an unbelievably wealthy family and knows things about culture and etiquette that would never even occur to the rest of us." Dina, a divorced mother of two grown daughters, is ten years older than the other three women. "When they made Dina they threw away the mold," Renee chuckled. "She looks like a conservative midwestern Sunday School teacher. But then she opens her mouth and out comes something that could make a truck driver blush. We laugh until our sides hurt when we're with her."

People who have seen them together have a hard time understanding how four such diverse women could be friends, Renee claimed. "But we are. We've been through all kinds of trials and tribulations together, the worst of times and the best." And even though they currently live in four different states and only get together as a group on special occasions, Renee, Carol, Lyn and Dina keep in touch by telephone and meet one-on-one from time to time. "When we do, we catch each other up on whoever isn't there," Renee said. "We probably know everything there is to know about one another. We can talk about anything, and over the years we have."

The four women have been there for each other through thick and thin, Renee explains: when Carol broke up with the Svengali-like man she had lived with for three years; when Lyn panicked after the man who would later become her husband first proposed marriage; when Dina began dating a widower with three teenaged sons and realized that she didn't want to "do the wife and mother trip" again. "And there's no doubt in my mind that without them I'd still be an unattached, obsessed workaholic, finding fatal flaws in every man I went out with," Renee said.

Lyn introduced Renee to her future husband, Scott, a thirty-year-old studio session musician. "I can still hear her saying, 'Look, he isn't your usual type. He's younger and wouldn't know an organizational chart from a blueprint for a jet engine. But promise me you'll give him a chance.'" And because she promised Lyn she would, Renee gave Scott a chance and, according to Renee, "It wasn't too long before we clicked. It wasn't love at first sight by any stretch of the imagination, but the more time we spent together, the more obvious it was that we were made for each other. We fit together just right." Even so, Renee's relationship with Scott had its "fair share of ups and downs."

There was, for instance, the "lost Labor Day weekend" when Scott went to Maine to visit an old girlfriend. "She was a singer and said she wanted him to play on a demo tape she was recording," Renee recalled. "Since I didn't believe that and I wasn't sure Scott was really over her, I was your basic basket case. Thank God Carol drove down to babysit me. We watched stupid movies and ate chocolate and dissected every relationship we'd ever had. I talked about Scott until Carol must have been ready to gag me. I kept saying I couldn't compete with a woman who was younger and had ten times more in common with Scott than I did. But *she* kept saying that if the relationship mattered to me I couldn't give up on it just because I was feeling insecure. 'So you're older. So you can't carry a tune. So what?' she said. 'He fell in love with you. He hasn't wanted to be with anyone but you for the past two years. You must be doing something right; and if you keep doing that and don't look for reasons to screw up a good thing, it will all work out.' " Renee listened to her friend and was glad she did.

After she and Scott had a "monster argument" over their wedding plans, she was glad that she had listened to Dina as well. "We had this huge fight just as I was about to board a plane for Kansas City," Renee said. "And by the time I got there I was ready to call the marriage off." She called Dina instead. "I can still picture the scene," Renee laughed. "Me crouching behind my bed because there was a tornado warning and bab- bling to Dina, who was making me laugh and invoking her infa- mous three-day rule. She made me promise not to make any decisions for the next seventy-two hours, and of course by then Scott had called and everything was okay between us again."

According to Renee, on many other occasions and in many other ways, her friends had saved her—and her relationship. She sincerely believed that without those women in her life she never would have "stuck it out and worked things out" or learned to trust herself enough to have a successful, productive, fulfilling relationship with Scott. And she was right. No matter how willing and determined you may be to follow the path I've been describing in this book, you'll get lost if you travel alone.

Why You Need Relationships with Women to Do What Works with Men

Throughout history, women have turned to each other for guidance. Since the first seeds of civilization were sown, women have comforted and reassured one another in times of crisis and celebrated together at each joyful passage in their lives. They have shared their wisdom with one another, teaching their daughters and granddaughters, sisters and friends the secrets of Relationship which they had learned from other women and from their own life experiences. They developed a bond—a tie of great intensity—that enabled them to grow and evolve and survive. That bond still exists. Women still thrive on their emotional exchanges with other women. They feel better and go farther when they have women to turn to for sympathy, support and an occasional kick in the butt. What women can do for each other and give to each other is of the utmost importance when it comes to intimacy and relationships. Women *shouldn't* be left alone to figure out what works with men.

To find the relationship of your romantic vision, you must first find and accept yourself. Emulating men and using them as your role models won't help you do that. Nor will you be all the woman you can be by competing with men or avoiding them, by defending your ego or protecting yourself from possible pain, failure or disappointment. You will not discover the woman you really are through your career or your accomplishments or your daily meditation. The only way to find yourself and accept yourself and tap into your natural resources as a woman is through your relationships with women.

As Renee did, you'll need Carols and Lyns and Dinas to help you over the rough spots and get you through the tough times so that you can keep your serious, long-term committed relationship on track. Without them, you'll get frightened. Your doubts and insecurities will get the better of you and you'll stop listening to the inner voice which speaks to you in a feminine tone. You'll abandon the discipline Relationship requires and talk yourself out of doing what it takes to turn your romantic vision of a relationship into a reality.

That sort of relationship is risky. It is challenging and scary to open yourself up and really let a man get close to you, to accept him as he is and trust him enough to have your relationship on his terms—especially when you are afraid to love as much as you love, to be yourself and give of yourself and possibly be rejected, abandoned or disappointed by a man. Your fears make you reluctant to allow intimacy into your life and you'll miss out on the relationship you *could* have by trying not to be vulnerable and not to expose yourself to the sort of pain you imagine you'll feel if your relationship should fail.

Doing what I've been telling you it takes to succeed in a long-term, committed relationship with a man feels dangerous and different and difficult—especially when you are angry at men, and you may have plenty of reasons to be. Like every woman, you have stories to tell about a father, brother, colleague, boss or lover who got to do things you couldn't because he was a man, who belittled you, abused or molested you, patronized, betrayed or humiliated you. Whether they intended to or not, men have hurt you and abandoned you and done unforgivable things to you that you cannot help but resent or be angry about. Even when you don't realize how angry you are, even when you don't feel the anger or have been conditioned not to express it or are afraid to unleash it, your anger is there. It affects you and what you will or will not do in an intimate relationship with a man. It is also the tough outer shell that keeps other, more painful and frightening emotions at bay.

Many of you hang onto your anger so that you don't have to feel your fears or your grief—the intense emotional suffering, acute sorrow and deep sadness caused by loss, disaster or misfortune which none of us truly escapes. Life is full of loss, disaster and misfortune. When the feelings attached to such events are stifled, smothered and otherwise unexpressed, they can be debilitating, and they pose a threat to your physical and emotional health. And when you bury your unsettling, unpleasant emotions you also limit your ability to feel joy, love, caring, happiness and inner peace. You can't open yourself up to a man, accept him, allow him to accept and love you or let intimacy into your life when you are cut off from or have no way to express your anger, fear, grief and sorrow safely.

Until you gain access to your emotions and push past your fears about intimacy, your relationships with men will not be successful, productive or fulfilling. You will wait and wait and wait for ironclad guarantees and irrefutable proof that your man won't hurt you. You'll never truly commit yourself to your relationship and never actually do what it takes to succeed. While your emotional clock (which is a much more serious time-keeper than your biological clock) is ticking away, counting the hours, days and years until you'll allow yourself to trust and get close to a man, your capacity for intimacy diminishes. You become more and more inclined to protect yourself by controlling your interactions with men in general and your man in particular. As you know by now, that approach along with almost any other action you take to make yourself less vulnerable to rejection, disappointment or pain *destroys* intimate relationships, and you end up more hurt than you would have been if you had just taken the plunge.

With women to lean on, depend on, talk to and have as resources in your life, you are more likely to take that plunge. Through your relationships with honest, supportive, caring, trustworthy women you maintain the balance, inner peace and self-acceptance you must bring to your relationship with a man. Because you know there will be someone there to pick up the pieces if you should fail, you are more willing to be vulnerable. You take risks and, more often than not, learn that you *can* have the relationship you want and manage it effectively.

In conversations with your women friends, you can confront the old demons and unfinished business from past experiences with men that prevent you from making smart choices today or trusting the choices you do make. Instead of using the things that happened to you in the past as excuses to be a loser in the present, you can accept and learn from those experiences and even use them to your advantage.

With the support of strong, self-aware women, you can release your anger and resentment. By rekindling your bond with other women and rediscovering the ways women can support and understand each other, you'll find an outlet for your other emotions as well and also have the two-way, deeply felt communication you crave.

Women Can Give You Things That Men Cannot

Over the course of your lifetime, your solid, supportive relationships with women will be the most satisfying relationships you have. You may need only one good relationship with a man, but you need many relationships with women. The more of those you have the better off you will be because women intuitively know how to support one another during times of crisis. They can be there for you when men hurt, baffle or abandon you. They are the ones you should talk to when you have deeply felt emotions to express. Women speak the same language you do. You can communicate with them about things and in ways you will never be able to with your man.

While men have feelings and respond to events emotionally, they don't feel things as intensely or in the same way you do—and they can't really comprehend the intensity of your emotions. Your man may want to understand your feelings. He may try to do that. But he has to translate the information you convey to him and make it fit into a framework that he can grasp. By the time he "gets it," your feeling may be gone.

In addition, when you try to convey your feelings to a man, his natural inclination will be to make you feel better. You'll finish telling him that you're at your wits' end and ready to be locked up in a padded cell somewhere and he'll say, "I'll tell you what. Don't cook tonight. I'll take you out to dinner." Or he'll tell you that you need a vacation and start describing the trip one of his colleagues took. Hoping to stem the flow of your emotions, he'll suggest: "Look, since it's obviously upsetting you, why don't we just drop this subject." His need to get over and get out of an uncomfortable situation as quickly as possible will prevent you from fulfilling your need to express and explore your feelings—and that will frustrate the hell out of you.

Women, on the other hand, have a natural, instinctive ability to understand other women's feelings. They are better equipped to handle your expression of strong, unsettling emotions. They can listen to you cry or complain, babble or shout for as long as you need to do that. They can recall feeling the way you feel and can use experiences from their own lives both to help them empathize with you and to help you gain a clearer understanding of what is happening to you. Not every woman you meet will be the right confidante for you; but if you turn to women who *are* willing and able to be there for you, you won't have to look to your man for something he is constitutionally incapable of giving you and then feel as if he let you down.

Cultivate Relationships with Women

Expanding the circle of women in your life may not be easy for you. There is a good chance that at one time or another women have caused you as much if not more pain than men have. Women have abandoned you and given their pursuit of men precedence over their relationship with you. They have competed with you for men and in recent years for jobs and promotions and recognition. Some have controlled and manipulated and betrayed the confidences you shared with them. They have been traitors to their gender, severing their ties to other women in order to get something they felt was more important to them at the time. And as a result, you may be reluctant to trust women or turn to them for the comfort and communication you need.

With certain women you are completely justified in feeling that way. Naturally, you want to proceed with caution and *not* share personal information with women who are likely to use it against you. Be selective about whom you rely on for support, and realize as well that relating to women can help you even when those women are not supporting you directly.

Whether you would confide in her or not, every woman *is* a potential reflection for you. In other women you can see things, both delightful and despicable things, that you think are not true of you but which actually may be. In fact, the women who seem least like you or whom you least want to be around sometimes have the most to teach you. You can learn about yourself by watching them and listening to them.

Form a Support Group

Whether with women or with a man, relationships are the cornerstone of our society and they are the area where you as a woman can excel and most naturally influence the direction of our future. The principles I have put forth in this book will help you do that. But reading about what really works with men (and what doesn't) is just the beginning for those of you who are serious about finding success, satisfaction and genuine intimacy in a long-term, committed relationship with a man. Putting the advice I've given you into practice and making the attitude and behavioral adjustments necessary for changing the way you relate to men simply cannot be accomplished without the support and encouragement of like-minded women.

That is why I urge you to look around your offices, neighborhoods, families or social circles and locate other women who might be receptive to the ideas I've presented. Encourage them to read this book and then begin to get together on a regular basis to discuss the progress you're making or the troubles you're experiencing in your life and relationships. Together, you can bring the art of Relating back into your lives and help one another solve 95 percent of your relationship problems.

Find women you can trust. Then, open up and receive what they have to offer you—their anger, fears and pain as well as their wisdom and comfort. Let go and share your thoughts and feelings, your doubts and your wishes. Work together instead of against each other and you won't have to carry all your "stuff" around with you anymore. You won't have to figure things out all by yourself anymore. You'll rediscover parts of yourself you thought were forever lost—your tenderness and your passion for living, your innocence and vulnerability and faded dreams. Your relationships with women will lead you back to yourself so that you will finally be able to make those dreams come true.